JAZZ REVOLUTIONARY

JONATHON GRASSE

THE LIFE & MUSIC OF ERIC DOLPHY

JAZZ REVOLUTIONARY
THE LIFE & MUSIC OF ERIC DOLPHY
JONATHON GRASSE

A Jawbone book
First edition 2024
Published in the UK and the USA by
Jawbone Press
Office G1
141 – 157 Acre Lane
London SW2 5UA
England
www.jawbonepress.com

ISBN 978-1-916829-08-4

Printed by Short Run Press, Exeter

1 2 3 4 5 28 27 26 25 24

FOREWORD

BY JEFF SCHWARTZ

You are holding what is likely to be the definitive biography of Eric Dolphy. Jonathon Grasse has assembled a remarkably detailed narrative of Dolphy's life and work and added informed opinions on nearly every released recording.

The title raises a question: *what was revolutionary about Eric Dolphy?* At the end of his introduction, Grasse aligns Dolphy's relentless pursuit of a unique musical voice connected to established Black musical idioms with the Civil Rights, Pan-African, and Black Nationalist movements of his time. It is easy to support this with a playlist of Dolphy collaborations such as Charles Mingus's 'Original Faubus Fables,' John Coltrane's 'Africa,' Max Roach's 'Garvey's Ghost,' and Abbey Lincoln's 'African Lady,' which more-or-less explicitly dedicated musical creativity to Black liberation. There is also Ornette Coleman's *Free Jazz*, a title in which, as Amiri Baraka wrote, 'free' can be read as a verb.

As Grasse recounts, Dolphy regularly performed as part of the third stream movement. Gunther Schuller coined the term in 1957 to describe a synthesis of jazz and contemporary composition. A thorough history of the third stream remains to be written, but the critical consensus has been that, despite notable contributions by Schuller, Mingus, John Lewis, Jimmy Giuffre, George Russell, and Milton Babbitt, this attempt at fusion was frequently less than the sum of its parts.

Grasse notes that Dolphy passed in June 1964, just months before Bill Dixon's October Revolution In Jazz festival and the launch of Bernard Stollman's ESP-Disk label, which presented and documented an emerging second wave of free jazz musicians. Dixon's success with DIY shows inspired the formation of the Jazz Composers Guild, a musicians' cooperative, which in turn inspired the formation of the Association for the Advancement Of Creative Musicians (AACM) in Chicago and the Black Artists Guild (BAG) in St. Louis. The artists in these collectives asserted their right to work in every medium and genre and to have their experimentation taken as seriously as that of white musicians such as John Cage and Karlheinz Stockhausen. Eric Dolphy was part of a small cadre of players who moved comfortably in the spaces between the jazz and classical avant-gardes while also functioning in mainstream jazz and commercial music.

Like Dolphy, the AACM and BAG musicians also claimed those spaces. Many of them, such as Henry Threadgill, Roscoe Mitchell, Anthony Braxton, Julius Hemphill, and Oliver Lake, played alto saxophone with a tone and style related to his, and the organizations encouraged multi-instrumentalism (following Dolphy's use of the bass clarinet and flute) and solo performance (following his 'Tenderly,' 'Love Me,' and 'God Bless The Child').

While most jazz composers, such as Duke Ellington, Thelonious Monk, and Horace Silver, created a single continuous body of work and led a single primary ensemble throughout their careers, Dolphy's writing included several distinct books of music for different projects. The numbers on his Prestige albums, which he also played with pickup groups in Europe in his final months, took catchy melodies in unexpected harmonic directions, such as the blues '245' and 'Serene.' With a medium-sized group on his July 1963 sessions, he revisited the exotic modal sounds of Coltrane's *Africa/Brass*, using brighter timbres and more dissonant harmonies, while the compositions on his final studio album, *Out To Lunch!*, extended the percussive and angular sound of Thelonious Monk songs like 'Evidence' and 'Criss Cross' as a setting for free improvising. The AACM and BAG musicians, and many of their peers, emulated Dolphy in working simultaneously in multiple dialects of their musical language, in structures ranging from fully scored works to free improvisations, and in instrumental configurations from solo to orchestra and beyond.

In 1965, the year after Eric Dolphy died, the Pulitzer Prize board chose not to give a prize for music rather than follow their music committee's recommendation to recognize Duke Ellington. Wynton Marsalis, no fan of the avant-garde, was the first jazz artist to receive a Pulitzer, in 1997; he was followed by Ornette Coleman (2007), Henry Threadgill (2016), Anthony Davis (2020), and Tyshawn Sorey (2024). The ranks of recent MacArthur Fellows and Guggenheim grant winners are similarly populated with AACM and BAG members and their collaborators and students, who are realizing the goals the third stream set over sixty years before. Dolphy is the link between these movements, and artists like Threadgill, Davis, Sorey, Braxton, Wadada Leo Smith, and George Lewis are living the revolution he anticipated and modeled in his short career. Threadgill is a member of the AACM, while Davis and Sorey are close associates of AACM members Lewis and Braxton, and Sorey's piece is dedicated to AACM member Smith.

In the next few hundred pages, Grasse will take you through Dolphy's life and discography, straight ahead and outward bound. You'll want to stop frequently to stream some of the classic, obscure, and archival recordings discussed. I am sure you will be provoked and inspired.

JEFF SCHWARTZ
MAY 2024

Jeff Schwartz is a bassist, improviser, and the author of books on free jazz for Routledge's Music Bibliographies series and SUNY Press's Jazz Styles series. He lives in the Los Angeles area.

INTRODUCTION

BY JONATHON GRASSE

This book chronicles the life of jazz musician Eric Dolphy, recounting the artistic range and creative depth of his work as a multi-instrumentalist, composer, and bandleader. The Los Angeles native and American original collaborated with some of the biggest names of the early 1960s avant-garde. A leader on seven albums released during the last four years of his tragically short life and several more posthumously, his innovative sound also appears on a remarkable number of recordings as a sideman. Dolphy famously worked with the John Coltrane Quintet, Charles Mingus's Workshop and Sextet, and Ornette Coleman on his seminal album *Free Jazz*, recorded in 1960. The stylistic paths of these musical giants led from the hard-bop successes of the 1950s toward a diverse broadening of styles and an expanse of vital cultural references characterizing the early 1960s. Dolphy helped pioneer post-bop's frontier with free jazz, though he regularly plied the tonal waters of standard tunes and brandished a license to play as he liked, in a style all his own, spicing up even ordinary sessions with floridly chromatic, expressive solos. His musical poetry spoke of what was possible.

The only child of Afro-Latin immigrants, Eric came of age in mid-century segregated Los Angeles immersed in adolescent dreams of performing classical music before awakening to swing jazz and 'race music' styles soon relabeled R&B. As a teenager, he consumed bebop, experienced the WWII-era jazz culture of Central Avenue clubs, and embraced a studious life of music. His multi-instrumentalism emerged from artistic curiosity and youthful plans of augmenting a career in modern jazz by becoming a professional musician, perhaps even a studio session player for film, radio, and television, though during a time when non-whites were very rarely considered for such positions. After serving three years stateside in the US Army during the Korean War, he returned to a rapidly changing Los Angeles, Central Avenue's bright lights fading as his early career blossomed. Dolphy participated in rock'n'roll recording sessions, cutting-edge club dates, and innovative after-hours jams of an experimental nature. There he met and played with Mingus, Ornette, and Coltrane, and counted Southern California jazz legends Gerald Wilson and Buddy Collette among his closest friends and musical mentors.

At twenty-nine, Dolphy joined the Chico Hamilton Quintet with its nationwide touring schedule of club dates, festivals, and recording sessions, landing in New York a mature player in late 1959. He emerged on the East Coast from the West Coast's shifting tides of cool jazz and experimentation as a late bloomer, recording his first album as leader, *Outward Bound* (Prestige, 1960). His star shined for the next four and half years, until his death from undiagnosed diabetes barely two months after relocating to Paris to start a new chapter and to marry his fiancé, American dancer Joyce Mordecai. He left the USA for Europe to make a career playing his own music and never came back, a sad and shocking end to a short life full of promise. Accompanying his recordings and compositions, the Dolphy legacy includes a deep and positive impact upon many friends and colleagues who uniformly recall a quiet, giving individual offering support and gratitude; one who smoked and drank socially while avoiding the pitfalls of substance abuse, alcoholism, and heroin addiction that plagued some of his closest friends in the music community. In contrast to his kind, low-key offstage personality, this introspective musician was, onstage and in the recording studio, a fiery preacher, a sublime magician, and a renegade fugitive all rolled into one rebellious artist playing three instruments.

Jazz historian Ted Gioia summarized the 1950s West Coast jazz scene by stating that 'no other place in the jazz world was as open to experimentation, to challenges to the conventional wisdom in improvised music, as was California during the late 1940s and the 1950s,' spotlighting 'The Chico Hamilton Quintet's swinging chamber jazz to Ornette Coleman, and big-band writing as diverse as Roy Porter's bop band, Gerald Wilson's harmonically rich and Latin-influenced charts.'[1] Dolphy was deeply involved with all four of these iconic artists: an essential voice in one of Hamilton's best groups, he jammed with Ornette in 1954–55, was an original member of Porter's 17 Beboppers, and became one of Gerald Wilson's closest friends and musical associates. 'It is the enormous diversity of the music, the ceaseless churning search for the different and new,' Gioia continues. 'It is this characteristic that unites a Stan Kenton and an Ornette Coleman, a Charles Mingus and a Jimmy Giuffre, a Shelly Manne and an Eric Dolphy.'[2] Jazz scholar George E. Lewis also places Dolphy squarely within the late 1950s avant-garde Los Angeles, brimming as it was with radical approaches to improvisation and experimental sensibilities, partly transplanted to New York's expanding vortex of progressive jazz. There, he and his close friend and musical partner John Coltrane influenced each other as they broadened their solos in live performances together beginning in 1961, launching extended journeys of epic durations into the unknown. Dolphy engaged Mingus's embrace of the radically new in his suite-like works, in studio recordings, and in monumental excursions captured live, a major driver in jazz's push forward from cool and hard bop into post-bop and the uncharted territory of free improvisation.

Jazz Revolutionary approaches the artist's recordings as essential cultural artifacts, as primary texts. Beyond live performances, first-issue vinyl albums and reissues in the years and decades following his passing were the principal means by which his music was shared and appreciated. These recordings are here identified chronologically and placed within the context of his development and collaborations, balancing descriptive narrative and accounts of artistic growth with select discographic detail in footnotes. Live performances including bootlegged radio and television broadcasts and illicit club recordings trickled out over the decades, vital live concert recordings of Dolphy's groups, the Coltrane quintet, and outfits led by Mingus offering some of his most stunning solos.

Impulse's 1997 release *Coltrane: The Complete Village Vanguard Recordings* from November 1961 offers revelatory examples of Dolphy's playing, far outshining what listeners originally heard of him from those dates on *Coltrane Live At The Village Vanguard* (1962) and *Impressions* (1963). Over a half-century following its recording, *Musical Prophet: The Expanded 1963 New York Studio Sessions* (Resonance Records, 2018) provided the complete set of FM Record's substantial July 1963 sessions resulting in the albums *Conversations* (1963) and *Iron Man* (Douglas International, 1968). In July 2023, Impulse! released the double-LP album *Evenings At The Village Gate: John Coltrane With Eric Dolphy*, capturing the quintet's first club appearances. Many albums enlist his sideman skills—a job for which he never failed to give his all—and there exists a broad range of such supportive work, from that of a featured guest voice lending a major improvised sound as soloist to that of a background or secondary player reading parts. *Jazz Revolutionary* examines the full scope of this recorded work and focuses on his most important achievements.

Dolphy's musical vocabulary was imbued with the phrasing and contours of human speech, bird calls, animal sounds, and timbral excursions employing extended techniques. Dolphy used microtonal inflections and multiphonics resulting from special fingering and embouchure methods. To his mastery of post-bebop technique he added unconventional yet disciplined sonic worlds, making room for extreme melodic leaps, non-pitch-related phenomena, and unusual sounds. His solos frequently make use of uncommon formal schemes employing unique gestural repetition, groupings of free-ranging melodic figures and multi-directional statements, and sound shapes demanding fresh interpretation. He could wrestle a solo away from a tune's confines, foregrounding compositional notions of improvisational freedom. His reimagining of the solo's role in the jazz tune often avoided routine form, conventional phrasing, and development based solely on harmonic progressions and thematic variations. Yet, while arguably striving to defeat audience expectations, Eric always said that his playing and hearing followed the harmony, speaking of his solos in terms of chordal tones and scale degrees. His music contains sophisticated reflections of Charlie Parker, Thelonious Monk, and Sonny Rollins, as well as the blues, and honking R&B—a playful, sometimes humorous vision at once futuristic and primitive, space-age puzzles draped in an African American–derived spiritual past, championing the human voice, sounds of nature, and modern jazz aesthetics. The octave displacement found in Baroque-era compound melody, and wedge-like alternations of moving lines against reiterated pedal points, are here achieved masterfully on three instruments in the atomic age of Dolphy's shamanistic Iron Man.

Hard-driving numbers such as 'G.W.,' 'Les,' 'Miss Ann,' and other original compositions such as the blues-noir classic '245' and 'Serene,' from his first albums as a leader, remained on his set lists until his passing. He recorded compelling duets with bassists on each of his instruments, creating absorbing, chamber-music-like pieces often transcending jazz. Flutist, composer, and Dolphy scholar James Newton writes, 'Eric was developing multiple styles of music simultaneously. . . . There was this highly chromatic post-bop; then music that combined elements of jazz and contemporary classical; and jazz combined with world music.'[3]

As Eric's virtuosic musical prowess earned praise from progressive jazz audiences eager for the 'new thing', his skills and interests also gained entry into the third stream crossover world combining jazz with contemporary concert music. With composer and conductor Gunther Schuller, his closest supporter and collaborator in this milieu, Dolphy engaged in third stream modernist conflations of jazz and twentieth-century concert music of European descent, broadening his celebration of creative freedom.

Jazz Revolutionary also examines this innovative musician's critical reception, both good and bad, to illustrate his world as seen through the pages of, among other periodicals, *DownBeat* magazine. Championed by a circle of collaborators, connoisseurs, and those with an ear for innovative playing, Dolphy also faced stiff resistance from high-profile music journalists, critics, venue owners, and fellow jazz musicians. Today, some of that negative criticism appears painfully dated, proof of his status as a cultural subversive bridging polarized aesthetic camps within a moving musical landscape. This book balances an understanding of Dolphy's charisma of aesthetic deviance and cultural Blackness with the value and nature of his artistic genius while considering a surrounding world of change. Framed by a clear timeline of events and developments, the ebb and flow of this book stays close to Dolphy's development as an artist, his recording sessions, performances, and collaborations, its pace slowing to reflect on his influences, evolution, and accomplishments, quickening to catch up with that changing world.

Jazz has always been defined by the eloquence and power of collective expression and individual improvisation. In Dolphy's uncompromising solos on alto saxophone, flute, and bass clarinet, and in his dynamic original compositions, audiences heard a revolutionary voice that helped launch a new era of expressive freedom in jazz. He forged a unique style within an emerging climate of post-bop, experimentalism, and free jazz, at a time when African Americans were engaged in intense political struggles for freedom and equality. These vitally important Black Americans were his contemporaries: Martin Luther King Jr., Medgar Evers, and Malcolm X. Dolphy died less than two years before Stokely Carmichael's introduction of the 'Black Power' slogan, yet it is clear to many that his music channels a similar vein of dissent and liberation challenging America's deep stain of inequality. Those political battles for change were only the beginning, and this harrowing era of violence, and protest in the United States historically weaves into the global crossroads of the Cold War and postcolonial liberation within parts of the so-called developing world, including African nations finding their independence. This current of Black pride and Pan-Africanism empowered anew some corners of the jazz world.

Dolphy appeared on the emerging radicalized stage of the Civil Rights Movement's push against the injustices of racism and racial segregation, and his revolutionary voice speaks to a self-awareness perhaps best described by James Newton:

> Eric understood so well that an artist has a responsibility to the past and the future. His studies led him as far back as the timeless beauty of the music of the African Pygmy. (Sometimes I wonder if his constant use of octave displacement didn't come from the register modulations of vocal pygmy music.) In his music one can hear the crying, moaning, and wailing that has characterized the hopes and dreams of the first Afro-Americans who came not through Ellis Island, but through the stench of the bottom of a slave ship. In his music, one can hear a vocal quality that can be traced back to the tonal qualities and nuances of the Western African languages and transferred through the tributaries of gospel music and blues.[4]

Transcending polite jazz entertainment's traditional roles, he moved toward a new musical kingdom of artistic creativity, conflating notions of socio-political justice, independence, and musical individuality.

Freedom obviously encompasses areas vaster than music, and as Albert Ayler said in the context of surviving a harsh, inner-city Cleveland upbringing, 'I've lived more than I can express in bop terms.'[5] These words are no less true for Dolphy, whose life experience and universalist aesthetic that embraced bird song, Indian music, and Stravinsky, comprised a warrior-monk dedication to exploring diverse musical resources beyond what the extant jazz vocabulary provided. His sound proved a catalyst for other musicians, a contemporary voice of both revolution and reconciliation.

JONATHON GRASSE
JANUARY 2024

01 FAMILY ROOTS, COMING OF AGE IN LOS ANGELES

1928–1948

Born in 1903, Eric Allen Dolphy Sr. was a seventh-generation, mixed-race Jamaican whose mother, Sarah Jane Tulloch, had deep family roots in the southern parish of Clarendon and island ancestry dating to the mid-eighteenth century. Part of Britain's Caribbean colonies (West Indies), Jamaica's trade in enslaved Africans was abolished in 1807 and the region's inter-island slave trade ended four years later, leading local plantation owners to purchase enslaved laborers from among themselves during a twenty-three-year period starting in 1811. Full emancipation was proclaimed three years after the island's 1831 Christmas Rebellion uprising of sixty thousand slaves. Sarah's father, the shoemaker John Gregory Tulloch, was born free in nearby Shady Grove in 1845 and had seven children. It was likely in the nearby port of Old Harbour that Sarah met Eric Sr.'s white father, Ernest Gerald Dolphy, one of twelve children of Isaac and Esther Dolphy, a commercial clerk in the family's long-established port business dating to Ernest's maternal great-grandmother Dinah Isaacs, who was born there in 1780.

Less than a year after Eric Sr.'s birth, the United States assumed control of France's moribund Panama Canal project, which had stalled due to financial woes and high rates of worker mortality. Rejuvenated construction sites attracted tens of thousands of workers, with the canal finally opening in 1914, by which time up to fifty thousand mostly West Indian laborers were on the Panama Canal Company payroll. Perhaps as many as two hundred thousand Black immigrant workers from the French and British West Indies entered Panama between 1900 and 1930. In August 1905, Ernest, Sarah, and a two-year-old Eric Sr. relocated to Las Cascadas in the United States' Panama Canal Zone, one of several Calubra Cut villages thrown together for workers toiling on the canal's difficult Calubra portion dig, close to the Gulf Of Panama. Ernest found work there as a construction timekeeper.

Though he was born in Jamaica, Eric Sr. later indicated Las Cascadas as his place of birth, claiming the advantages of US Canal Zone status. On documents, he always answered 'unknown' for the birthplaces of both of his parents. Ernest died of colon cancer when his son was five, and the boy and his mother remained in Panama, where she later remarried. At seventeen, he worked as a waiter while living with two other young men in Ancón, now a suburb of Panama City, a job and location he would leave within the year.

Eric Sr.'s future wife and the mother of his son, Sadie Clemencia Gilling, was born Sydexter (also Cedexter) Clemencia Gilling Plummer on December 12, 1905, in Guácimo, a canton within the Costa Rican province of Limón. The date differs from her previously established birth date of March 19, 1907. Sadie was then typically a nickname for girls named Sarah; Sydexter's parents likely used Sadie for its proximity to Syde, a truncation of her unusual given name. Sadie's parents, Thomás Augustus Gilling and Marie Ann Maud O'Connor, were both from Costa Rica and of Jamaican descent. They were married eight days before her birth. Sadie's grandmothers were Jamaican, both part of the nineteenth-century migration of Black laborers from the West Indies to French construction sites in Central America. Denied citizenship before 1948, *Afro-Costaricans* rarely traveled outside of Limón province, where many West Indian Blacks spoke an English creole language known as *Limonese*. There, the United Fruit Company's union- and strike-busting tactics manipulated sociopolitical divisions among ethnic, racial, and national rivalries, resulting in social destabilization and racial violence aimed at Black immigrants. Due solely to the color of her skin, Sadie was not allowed a path to citizenship in the country of her birth, and as an adolescent she left Costa Rica for Panama with her family to find work in the Canal Zone. Sadie's sister, Luzmilda Thomas, married a pharmacist from Saint Vincent, immigrating to New York City in 1948 with her husband and toddler son, Eric Jr.'s cousin Lorenzo. For the remainder of her life, Sadie reported 'unknown' for her father's birthplace, and 'Panama Canal Zone' for her mother.

In early April 1923, seventeen-year-old Sadie boarded the SS *Aconcagua*, sailing from Colón to New York City and arriving on April 6. It is not known when she then traveled to Los Angeles via passenger train, but she had settled there by 1926 at the downtown address of 1216 1/2 E. 16th Street (since demolished and now a downtown South-Central Avenue onramp to the westbound 10 interstate freeway that replaced Route 66). In the meantime, her future husband left his waiter job for the steam-driven oil tanker SS *Lompoc*, part of the Union Oil Line created by a burgeoning Central California firm that would later become UNOCAL. At eighteen, he shipped out of Panama City's Balboa port complex in mid-April 1921, en route to New Orleans. Over the next two years, he sailed West Coast routes on ships transporting oil from storage tanks dotting the hills around Central California's San Luis Obispo and Avila Bay. He gained knowledge of Los Angeles during extended stopovers and eventually sailed the SS *Lompoc*'s loop back through the Panama Canal to New Orleans, arriving on April 23, 1923—seventeen days after Sadie's arrival in New York. It is of course possible that the two had met in the Canal Zone that April (or earlier), and that they planned to reunite in Los Angeles. Or perhaps they met there, and bonded over their Caribbean, West Indies heritage, and Canal Zone experiences.

Disembarking in New Orleans, Eric Sr. ended his work for Union Oil. He settled in Los Angeles before marrying Sadie in August 1926. The couple became naturalized US citizens at the onset of the nation's involvement in WWII.

CHILDHOOD

Eric Allan Dolphy Jr. was born at 2:45 on the afternoon of June 20, 1928, at the twenty-bed Dunbar Hospital, four years after its construction. The hub of a newly burgeoning African American cultural corridor along Central Avenue, the Dunbar Hotel, completed the year of his birth, was famous for its association with the venerated Club Alabam, one of many local jazz clubs where Eric would later play. The young family's duplex in a mixed-race neighborhood at 466 N. Burlington Avenue sat a five-minute walk from Echo Park Lake (today, the site is a medical building situated directly next to the 101/Hollywood Freeway, the northeast corner of what is now Historic Filipino Town). The Dolphys' radio would be tuned to any number of stations, including the 5,000-watt KFI, owned by Eric Sr.'s future employer. They rented from the building's resident owners, Alphonse Osborne, a caterer from Missouri, and his second-generation Californian wife Madelaine, a forty-something African American couple with a nineteen-year-old son. Their neighbors included whites; a few other Black families; Spanish speakers; immigrants from Mexico, Hawaii, and Hungary; and newcomers from the Midwest and the South. They were butchers, maids, servants, retail clerks, a boxer, warehousemen, and a solicitor, and less than half of them were born in California. Eric Sr. worked as a laborer and a janitor, and at an 'auto laundry,' as the first car washes were called—a position that led to his career as a driver and 'garage man' with influential city booster and multi-millionaire Earle C. Anthony, a businessman who designed and constructed his own automobile prototypes and controlled the West Coast Packard car business. Eric Sr. was later employed at his downtown dealership on Hope Street.

In the 1920s, Los Angeles became home to Jelly Roll Morton, Kid Ory, and the Original Creole Band, representing a major traditionalist base of New Orleans-style jazz culture. The Black-owned Sunshine record label was founded by the Spikes brothers, John and Benjamin 'Reb,' who in their downtown store at 12th and Central Avenue in 1922 pressed and sold ten-inch shellac discs featuring Roberta Dudley and Ruth Lee singing with Kid Ory's Sunshine Orchestra. African American migration to the city from the South brought established strata of the blues and church music. Older styles were soon challenged by swing-era big bands—a division further inflamed by discursive wars over 'old fashioned' and 'modern' definitions of jazz.

Eric was born into a fast-paced city quickly becoming the center of a thriving entertainment industry, spearheaded by Hollywood film studios, radio production, and eventually television. The rhythm, style, and brand of big-band dance hall swing came to define the jazz world throughout the Great Depression and into the WWII era. Dolphy's childhood and adolescence unfolded as these popular music genres were swept along by whirlwinds of change and innovation. When Eric was fourteen, influential R&B artist Louis Jordan moved to Los Angeles to record 'soundies,' as the precursors to music videos were known. A few years later, Charlie Parker and company brought bebop to town. Eric would soak up all of this and more.

Several years after the Panamanian Congress passed anti-West Indies legislation banning the immigration of non-Spanish speaking Blacks, Sadie's mother arrived in New Orleans on the SS *Saramacca* from Cristobal in the Panama Canal Zone, entering the USA in late May 1929. The first rumblings of the Great Depression would emerge a few months later. Soon settled into her daughter's bicultural, bilingual home, Maude met her grandson as he approached his first birthday, learning Spanish and English, revealing a fascination for toy horns and drums, and engaging the world with a curiosity for sound, music, and the flow of the family radio. Though the child liked to sing, aside from the family's later involvement with church choirs, there is no record or evidence of musicianship within the family, or of Eric being introduced to a particular type of music.

Eric's first school was five short blocks away at Rosemont Avenue Elementary, where Ola Ebinger started students on harmonica, graduating them to more elaborate instruments if they showed promise. She enticed Eric with a clarinet that must have captured his attention, since he joined the school orchestra within a few weeks. Thus began nearly a quarter-century of woodwind practice in the Dolphy family home. (In the early 1950s, many years after introducing Eric to formal music training, Ola taught classical clarinet to a young Zan Stewart, who went on to become an accomplished jazz tenor saxophonist and music journalist, winning the ASCAP-Deems Taylor award for his liner notes to the 1996 Prestige box set, *Eric Dolphy: The Complete Prestige Recordings*.)

In 1934, amid the Great Depression, the family moved to a 923 square-foot, two-bedroom, one-bath cottage with a yard at 1593 West 36th Street, in the Jefferson Park district. Eric was almost seven, and West 36th Street Elementary (today Birdielee V. Bright Elementary) was less than two blocks away. Except for his three years in the Army, he would live at this address with his parents until the age of thirty, one of the sources of his well-centered identity and confidence.

The budding clarinetist excelled at West 36th, and after earning a seat in the All-City Orchestra Of Elementary Schools, he began to dream of playing classical music in a professional orchestra. The Dolphys lived three miles west of Central Avenue's culture corridor of live music venues like the Elks Hall ballroom, the Downbeat, Jack's Basket Room, and the Club Alabam. At that time, African Americans in Los Angeles were mandated to live in only a few other areas of the city, such as east of downtown, Boyle Heights, Venice, and Watts (the latter two towns consolidated with the City Of Los Angeles in 1925–26), and in small, flatland neighborhood enclaves west of the University Of Southern California, where the Dolphys now lived.

By the 1930s, this figuratively enclosed area of segregated Los Angeles was home to twenty or more African American churches, including the People's Independent Church, founded in 1915 and located three miles from the Dolphy home. Eric Sr. and Sadie were devoted choir members; the former would recall that their son 'was exposed to the music of our church from a very early age … as soon as he could walk, my wife brought him to all the services.'[1]

Eric joined the choir and attended Sunday school just as the church's influential reverend and community leader, Clayton D. Russell, was beginning his career as a prominent Black community leader, organizing the 1941 Negro Victory Committee and sponsoring protests against African American worker discrimination. The church was a welcoming environment for Eric's ever-expanding musical curiosity; he absorbed hymns, religious anthems, and holiday repertoire such as Handel's *Messiah*—and, perhaps equally importantly, the intensely musical patter and cadences of preachers, the heightened speech and responses of worshippers, and the testimonial intoning of human sounds. When he was not singing, he watched and listened to people expressing wonder, joy, and hope through music. The People's Independent Church was home to one of the city's first gospel choirs, the N.P. Greggs Gospel Choir, and played a role in the rapid expansion of gospel music in the area during the 1930s as it spread from Chicago and the South.

It is not known when the Dolphy family left the People's Independent Church to attend Westminster Presbyterian Church on West Jefferson, five short blocks from their home. There, the Reverend Dr. Hampton Hawes appointed young Eric as assistant to the junior choir director, evidence of his advancing musical skills. Eric was soon to enter Foshay Junior High School, four short blocks south of the family home; Sadie would later share that during her son's junior high years, the reverend gave him a key to the church to practice piano. Hawes was the disapproving father of acclaimed jazz pianist Hampton Hawes, whose mother Gertrude was the church pianist. The young Hampton, whose family lived in Watts, was Dolphy's age. These two children of the Great Depression would come to influence one another in their first jazz forays, hanging out and playing at Eric's house with friends and future bandmates. Hawes also befriended Charles Mingus and began playing jazz professionally while still a student at Los Angeles Polytechnic High School, and at eighteen he played in Howard McGee's local bebop group with Charlie Parker.

THE YOUNG MUSICIAN

Eric engaged in music lessons with seriousness, incessantly practicing scales, fingering, and sightreading, perfecting his tone and embouchure while learning clarinet parts to new ensemble pieces. The bright, talented son of immigrants received early, close-knit family encouragement to embrace music as a possible profession, and a solid public-school music education awaited his every new stage with the growing expectation of a future livelihood. Building on Ola Ebinger's tutelage, he completed the 36th Street School's music curriculum, progressing to Foshay Junior High and music studies with Helen Bicknell. Under her supervision, Eric took up the oboe, his sights still set on becoming a professional orchestra musician and performing classical music. The thirteen-year-old clarinetist earned a certificate of accomplishment in the Seventh Annual Band & Orchestra Festival sponsored by the California School Band & Orchestra Association, Southern District (an organization in which Helen held secretary and treasurer positions during the 1940s). He also participated in audition-based All-City concerts, where he met lifelong friend Elvira 'Vi' Redd (b. 1928), a talented musician and singer, and advanced into the competitive Los Angeles City School Orchestra.

The budding clarinetist earned an audition-based scholarship to the summer program for young musicians at the University Of Southern California, an esteemed private institution less than two miles east of their home. However, school officials rescinded the opportunity after learning of his dark skin. Though Eric was advancing through public-school music programs with recognized, hard-earned skills, he had now been betrayed by one of the West Coast's most influential institutions of higher learning, his world of supportive family and caring music teachers running headlong into the harsh reality of a segregated city and institutional racism. This devastated the Dolphys, who celebrated their son's success, discipline, and character.

Some have remarked that this humiliation brought an end to Eric's connection to classical music and led to him dropping out of school, though neither is remotely the case. Rather, the deep-seated social bigotry clarified that, despite his superior abilities, he would likely never have that orchestra career or find stable employment in Hollywood's lucrative studio system. Racial segregation clearly separated his classical and popular music experiences, and Eric's dream died slowly, surviving only in family lore.* The racist USC rebuke muddled the young man's outlook on a classical music career without destroying his admiration for concert music or a universalist aesthetic embracing both classical and jazz. His enduring sensibility and advanced skills would later open professional doors to early 1960s third stream music performances and recordings.

Though he never turned his back on classical music, Eric's growing passion for

* Luzmilda shared family lore about USC and Eric's scuttled childhood plans for a classical music career in the 1991 film *Eric Dolphy: De Laatste Sessie* (*The Last Date*).

jazz and the notion of popular music being fun and challenging was clarified by the USC fiasco. He moved on from the incident, broadening his music interests by listening to Fats Waller, Duke Ellington, and Coleman Hawkins. It was around that time he attended Ellington's stage show *Sweet And Hot*, likely held at the Avenue's Elk's Hall. He would later note that he watched Jimmy Blanton play bass, meaning Eric would have been around thirteen years of age, as Blanton left Ellington in late 1941.

It was at fifteen that the alto saxophone entered his life. Though it is associated with jazz, the alto sax was also used in classical music, and young Eric learned of its presence in nineteenth- and early twentieth-century works by Bizet, Debussy, Richard Strauss, Ravel, Milhaud, and perhaps even Alban Berg's opera *Lulu* and *Violin Concerto*. Racism would not deprive him of contemporary classical music's pleasures. From the single-reed clarinet and alto saxophone, with their similar fingering, to the double-reed oboe, followed soon by the bass clarinet and non-reed flute, Dolphy tackled the full breadth of woodwind types and ranges. Neither was his dedication to formal learning impacted by bigotry as he eagerly completed high school, later enrolled in Los Angeles City College, attended the College of Puget Sound, and earned a certificate from the US Naval School Of Music in Washington DC.

Also attracting Dolphy's teenage interests was the emergence of R&B, which replaced 'race records' as a *Billboard* charts category in 1949. Local tastes in popular music were measured in part by Art Rupe's wildly successful Specialty Records, founded in 1944, which pumped out 'big city Black music' drawing from boogie-woogie, jump blues, Chicago-style urban blues, country blues, and gospel-tinged precursors to R&B and rock'n'roll. Eric joined several small bands and learned to play Louis Jordan tunes with Hawes, who simultaneously encouraged him to dig deeper into swing jazz. He developed a focused, bright saxophone sound, eventually playing a 1949 Selmer Super Balanced Action alto model. During this time, *Los Angeles Sentinel* newspaper columnist Stanley Robertson played in another Dolphy band with Eric's high-school classmates Bernard 'Ben' Roberts and Roy Johnson. Vladimir Simosko and Barry Tepperman quote at length an anonymous source describing how Roberts began sharing improvisational techniques he learned from their band's leader, an Eastside Black kid named Harry Allen. Though Eric was a good sight reader with a musical ear capable of copying simple solos from records, Bernard and Harry were developing their improvisation skills through lessons with a German teacher, studying with the great Lester Young's father, and lots of woodshedding.

Expressing himself through jazz improvisation soon became Dolphy's primary artistic goal. Aunt Luzmilda later confirmed that Sadie was concerned for peace and quiet—their own and the neighbors'—as Eric practiced in a backyard outbuilding for over six hours each day. In Raymond Horricks's account, Eric Sr. and Sadie talked about a separate practice shed during his high school years, and bandleader Roy Porter remembered visiting that studio during Eric's time with his big band, dating it to at least 1949. The room—used for practice, rehearsal with bandmates, and 'take down' sessions for transcribing recordings—would be described by Eric's friend Lillian Polen as 'the little house Eric's dad built for him.'[2] Researching the Dolphy home, Alan Saul discovered a 1955 invoice detailing improvements made following Eric's discharge from the Army, providing evidence of the shed's later transformation to a more proper space that would eventually house a Wurlitzer electric piano and a reel-to-reel tape recorder. In the film *Last Date*, Buddy Collette is interviewed in the studio, the camera panning the creative environs where, after returning from the Army, Eric hosted professional musicians passing through Los Angeles. It was the site of Harold Land's audition for the Clifford Brown–Max Roach Quintet, just prior to the August 1954 recording of the seminal hard-bop ten-inch album *Clifford Brown & Max Roach* (Capitol). Ornette and Coltrane likely visited and played there too.

DORSEY HIGH SCHOOL AND ELISE MOENNIG

In the context of Dolphy's upbringing in segregated Los Angeles, music and his family's neighborhood offered a comparatively safe center to a childhood and adolescence within what amounted to a small-town network, their own corner of the big city. Music studies absorbed his soul. This early success was not achieved entirely on his own, however, as he benefited from ambitious immigrant parents and their hopes for their only child's future. The many testimonials to his optimistic, kind demeanor and humanitarian ways are not markers of raw innocence or indicators of a naïve life free from racism and hate. Yet despite the obvious challenges, the young man navigated the white-run educational institutions by channeling a dedication to music.

When Dolphy entered Dorsey High School, opportunity prevailed again, thanks in part to music teacher and flutist Elise Baxter Moennig, the first to encourage him to take on that instrument. The addition of flute to his instrumental arsenal did not evolve from jazz but from his experience with the school band and orchestra, with Collette and Jerome Richardson soon guiding him toward true multi-instrumental jazz virtuosity. Elise was the daughter of Harry and Millie Baxter, her father being the co-owner of the Baxter-Northrup music store (which to this day remains California's oldest), then downtown on Olive Street. In the decade before she met Eric, Elise had become an active chamber musician and had married Horst Moennig of the renowned German woodwind instrument-making family. In addition to advanced music lessons and leadership roles in school ensembles, Dolphy gained confidence and knowledge of the larger music world through this trusted proximity to Elise's professional machinations—an empowering perspective encouraging harder work and career focus.

At Dorsey, Eric was one of a few African American music students in his class, and under Elise's tutelage he became a pioneering student director of the school orchestra, joining Vi Redd and bandmates Ben Roberts, Roy 'Froggy' Johnson, and Maurice Simon (later with Roy Porter's big band and the Gerald Wilson Orchestra). In a high-school essay entitled 'Music And People,' Eric shared his thoughts:

> The Negro spiritual [reflects] the negro. The blues is also a reflection of the negro. Jazz is a reflection of our country and its people. In jazz, everyone has the freedom to create . . . but of course within certain bounds. . . . A lot of people don't like the music that is being written, played, or created today, because of dissonance, rhythm, harmonies, and melodic lines. But all this is a reflection of people and times.[3]

Dolphy was always welcomed back to Dorsey, as was the case in March 1949 when he returned to his alma mater with his alto sax, eighteen-year-old drummer Ed Thigpen, and bassist Gilbert Nunn, in a jazz combo invited to play a Friday noon concert.

BIRDSONG

The teenage Eric met new musical challenges with stubborn dedication, as Sadie shared, by rising early and practicing before school in the 'little studio outside,' only to hurry home to get in more playing before evening.[4] Eric Sr. recalled that while in the backyard practicing his growing array of wind instruments, his son 'copied birds singing. He'd copy them by playing his instrument. I guess those birds knew he was copying them because they'd whistle back at him.'[5] Neighborhood friend Margareth Satchell Boswell recalls hanging out there, listening to Charlie Parker records and to Eric explaining the importance of nature's sounds, such as birds, night crickets, and wind blowing through trees.[6]

Birdsong informed Eric's artistic sensibilities, augmenting his technical command and infusing his musical language—not unlike the mystical French composer Olivier Messiaen, who was codifying similar compositional sources during this time. Translated into English in 1944, when Eric was sixteen, Messiaen's *My Musical Language* includes a chapter entitled 'Bird Song' in which he writes, 'Their melodic contours, those of merles especially, surpass the human imagination in fantasy.'[7] The composer presents notated examples of melodic fragments transcribed from the merle, lark, and sparrow. Transcriptions of birdsong and Messiaen's *Le Merle Noir* were among Dolphy's belongings. James Newton has noted that 'Dolphy was into Messiaen before he died in '64. It is possible that Messiaen's music could very well have inspired some of Dolphy's own birdsong explorations.'[8] One must imagine the teenager sharing these ideas in his own way, discovering this natural music and incorporating its subtler elements such as microtonality into his practice and performance. However, a new period of artistic growth soon involved a 'Bird' of a different sort...

DOLPHY'S NEW SCHOOL: CHARLIE PARKER, BEBOP, AND LLOYD REESE

A musical wave of mid-century modernism hit during Eric's junior year in high school that would forever change his artistic outlook, instrumental technique, and aesthetic path: the bebop embodied by alto saxophonist Charlie 'Bird' Parker, followed by the music of pianist/composer Thelonious Monk. The new style's fast, double-time execution of scalar runs, sequences, and arpeggios drew from a freshly expanded harmonic sensibility of extended and altered chords, and a driving post-swing rhythmic sensibility, dissonant fluidity having less to do with increasingly old-fashioned charts, riffs, and blues-based elements enmeshed with swing. As Dolphy himself later stated, 'Bird was it. I went to school with Hampton Hawes, and he was the first to tell me about Bird. I didn't believe him at first. I couldn't believe anybody could be faster than [Coleman] Hawkins, for one thing.'[9] This was virtuosic, combo instrumental playing that looked past the entertainment model of popular dance music.

At the dawn of 1945, the Guild label released some of bebop's first ten-inch shellac 78rpm discs, led by trumpeter Dizzy Gillespie and Parker—just the start of revelatory recordings from which Eric and countless others challenged their musicianship, style, and taste. Then, as if from a Hollywood script, New York's bebop masters quickly showed up on Los Angeles stages. Gillespie's Rebop Six residency at Billy Berg's club kicked off to a packed house on December 10, 1945, their stretch of performances marred by a generally hostile media reception yet etched into the local jazz psyche, sparking a West Coast bebop revolt. Hawes had been one of the first to push Eric toward jazz, and he was now swept up into the cultural explosion, playing with and growing close to Charlie Parker himself, sharing the role of Bird's personal driver with eighteen-year-old saxophonist Sonny Criss. Bebop legend Howard McGhee had already relocated to LA from New York in 1945 and was now gigging and recording in the city regularly, while accomplished saxophonists Wardell Gray and Dexter Gordon both returned to the city the following year as bebop practitioners. A small handful of local radio stations produced bebop shows dedicated to spreading the modern art form. In a few years, Eric's first sustained, professional gig would be in a band led by Roy Porter, one of Central Avenue's top bebop drummers, who played and recorded with Parker and McGhee, among others.

While still attending Dorsey High, Eric took another big step along his artistic path by finding Lloyd Reese, one of the most influential music teachers associated with the African American cultural experience of Los Angeles's Central Avenue jazz scene. Reese was born in the mixed-race Ballona township of Ocean Park City in 1909, a year before the town's name changed to Venice. His parents purchased a home at a time when restrictive covenants and redlining limited Black home ownership, and near to the house was (until the early 1930s) one of the few beach areas where Blacks were allowed to swim in Santa Monica Bay. Reese's father came from New Orleans and worked as a janitor at the Abbot Kinney-designed 'Coney Island of the West' amusement park and canals that opened in 1905. Lloyd took his alto saxophone twenty-five miles due east to study music at Whittier College, broadening his training and taking on the piano and trumpet (the latter becoming his primary instrument). In the early 1930s, he earned his way into Les Hite's Orchestra, playing both alto saxophone and trumpet at venues such as Frank Sebastien's massive Cotton Club near Culver City's MGM studios. The orchestra included Lionel Hampton, frequently broadcasted performances on KHJ radio, and recorded with Louis Armstrong during his prime. Reese also played in after-hours combos at Central Avenue's Turban Room, Lovejoy's, Ivie's Chicken Shack, Shirley's Ritz Club, and Brother's, doubling on trumpet and alto in Cee Pee Johnson's band, and recording with legend Art Tatum. But teaching was his passion, and with his wife, Jeannette, he opened a music school in their home on East Jefferson Boulevard, less than a mile from the Avenue. Jeannette was a classical pianist, and their house featured several piano rooms and a tight schedule of dedicated students enjoying the hangout as much as the lessons.

'With [Reese's] sophisticated attitude toward race and life, he had the sort of polish and élan Ellington projected,' Mingus biographer Gene Santoro writes; his 'well-furnished home' presented 'a kind of cross between a musical salon and a school. Star musicians like Ellington horn men Rex Stewart and Ben Webster dropped by, sometimes to take some notes, sometimes to swap jazz gossip.' Next to the main teaching room was an alcove 'stacked high with copies of *DownBeat* and other jazz magazines.'[10] Dolphy's younger peer Horace Tapscott recalled that Reese 'looked like Duke [Ellington], was a chain smoker, and could party his ass off.'[11]

Some of Reese's young students from those years later helped define jazz: among many others, they included Charles Mingus, Buddy Collette, Dexter Gordon, Hampton Hawes, and bassist Red Callender. His students met for Sunday afternoon ensemble sessions in the Musicians Union's upstairs rehearsal space; they chipped in to buy charts, and the newly arrived Gerald Wilson, already a proven star and arranger with Jimmie Lunceford, gladly offered his arrangements. Reese was vice-president of the Local 767 and—along with Buddy Collette, Marl Young, and Gerald Wilson, among others—spearheaded the desegregation of the white and Black musicians' union locals leading to the legendary amalgamation of Latino Local 47.

Sadie stopped paying for lessons after she and Eric Sr. learned Reese had told their son that success in jazz did not require a college degree. Mingus would recall, 'Eric Dolphy worked his way through Reese's school by cutting the grass and hedges. He used to sit on the steps watching the band rehearsals. He was younger than the others.'[12] Collette recalled him at the Reese house: 'Eric was just learning his craft ... with piano, with clarinet, with saxophone, and with hearing everybody ... He was the clean-up guy and errand guy and everything, doing that [in exchange] for his lessons.'[13] Tapscott recalls, 'Eric cleaned inside the house, and the rest of us would be outside doing it. Eric would tell us, Y'all the field n-----s,

I'm the house n-----. That was Eric. He'd do that shit. He was the oldest [among the five], so he had the edge.'[14]

Central Avenue boasted other music teachers who intersected with Dolphy's musical growth, namely Percy McDavid and Alma Hightower. Alma was Vi Redd's great aunt, and Redd's father Alton was a New Orleans jazz drummer who moved to Los Angeles becoming a Central Avenue fixture as the co-founder of the Clef Club. 'When I had my little band,' Redd recalled, 'Eric would come down and sit in, and we used to always kid him about playing so many choruses. If someone played four choruses, Eric would play eight.'[15] Hightower directed the Melodic Dots big band, which included trombonist Lester Robinson, for whom Dolphy wrote the tune 'Les.'

Tapscott recalls Collette, Mingus, Britt Woodman, Callender, and Dolphy performing in city parks on Sunday afternoons under the direction of Percy McDavid, Lafayette Junior High School's music instructor and founder of the International Symphony Orchestra. Following Eric's Army service from 1950 to 1953, McDavid would hire him for formal concerts.[16] In 1936, Jefferson High hired classically trained musician Samuel Browne, an African American, thereby breaking the color barrier in Los Angeles public high schools; Browne famously developed the school's innovative jazz program, with young cornetist Don Cherry subsequently lying about his address to enroll there. Some of Browne's more successful students populated Eric's musical coming of age, forming a tight yet musically competitive community.

CHARLES MINGUS AND BUDDY COLLETTE

Collette talked a fourteen-year-old Mingus into switching from cello to bass: for a Black cellist in the 1930s, a classical music career path was far less realistic than that of a bassist playing popular music. The two Watts friends later ran into drummer Chico Hamilton at a Million Dollar Theater battle of the bands, after which they briefly became members of the Al Adams Band. To say that each of these jazz legends would prove elemental to Eric's musical career would be a significant understatement. From his earliest years, the iconoclastic Mingus sought an artistic path that included classical music, taking composition lessons with Reese, and developing bass skills as co-founder, with Collette, of the short-lived Stars Of Swing.

An underage Dolphy was already absorbing what he could of Central Avenue's thriving music scene when, on a tip from Reese, he attended a Stars Of Swing gig at the Downbeat club and first saw his older cohorts play outside the confines of music lessons and student ensembles. 'What Love,' a Mingus tune from this time written for Collette and using the chord progression from 'What Is This Thing Called Love,' later became a vehicle for musical 'conversations' between the bassist and Dolphy in Mingus Workshop New York performances starting in 1960. Mingus was just launching his career as a musician and composer, traveling for West Coast gigs and recording under his name, the first such session taking place soon after the drummer on that recording, Roy Porter, arrived in Los Angeles in 1945; Porter described Mingus at that point as being 'so far ahead of his time that people didn't quite know how to cope with him as a person or his playing.'[17]

Legend states that Dolphy's first paying gig was for a Mingus dance band in 1946, by which time Central Avenue had become Eric's real school, bebop the style, and Charlie Parker his figurative teacher. Decades later, Mingus gave conflicting accounts of Dolphy's playing at this stage of his development, in 1960 recalling Dolphy playing 'the style he does now in high school,' and in 1971 remembering that in 1960 he thought Dolphy was 'crazy' because 'he wasn't playing anything like I heard him play before.'[18] Regardless, Dolphy and Mingus both found in music a spiritual comfort and an expression of self—a form of individual identity as well as a type of social equalizer. For Mingus, this came in the form of his own compositional genius, inspired by everything from Ellington to film scores. Unapologetically enamored with late-Romantic and modernist twentieth-century concert music, both Mingus and Dolphy adopted in their respective manner a universalist vision of classical music's potential to conjoin with jazz, and of jazz to transcend its stylistic limitations through classical music. For Eric, this came partly in the form of his involvement in the third stream music spearheaded by Gunther Schuller, John Lewis, and others in the late 1950s.

Lifelong friend Collette was at first a mentor, providing saxophone and flute lessons by 1948 and inviting Dolphy to student jam sessions. He would prove to be a Los Angeles survivor, developing a successful career in television studio work, film music, and scoring sessions. In 1952, he became one of the first Black contract musicians at NBC, playing in Jerry Fielding's band for Groucho Marx's *You Bet Your Life* when it was still a radio show. Eric took his Dorsey High flute lessons with Elise to heart, but he flourished with Collette's way with the instrument, and it was through jazz that he sensed the instrument's potential.

In the 1940s, the flute did not possess the alto sax's historical presence in jazz. By the 1950s, following developments on the instrument's performance by Alberto Socarras, Wayman Carver, and Frank Wess, Dolphy's mentor Jerome Richardson would be the most prominent jazz flutist; when the instrument's popularity grew, *DownBeat* added a new 'best of' poll category in 1956.* Back in post-WWII Los Angeles, Richardson encouraged Dolphy's multi-instrumentalism as the jazz flute category became populated by Sam Most, Yusef Lateef, and Herbie Mann, the latter abandoning the saxophone to become perhaps the first jazz musician dedicated almost solely to flute. Mann sporadically played bass clarinet on recordings in the mid-to-late 1950s, presaging Dolphy's recordings on the instrument.

Chico Hamilton, with whom Dolphy left Los Angeles in 1958, sought out the flute's exoticism for his cool West Coast quintet in hiring a series of flute-playing saxophonists: Collette, Paul Horn, Dolphy, and Charles Lloyd. Jazz flute performers played a significant role as conduits in the incorporation of non-Western wind instrument traditions from India, Asia, Africa, and the Near Eastern sounds of Persian, Turkish, and Arabic music. While Eric and others are on record as having studied traditions from other parts of the world, it was Lateef who perhaps took the first step in jazz of playing a non-Western wind instrument, using the Chinese globular flute known as the *xun* on 1961's 'The Plum Blossom' (*Eastern Sounds*, Prestige). The crystalline tone of the Western flute offered none of the reedy qualities of the saxophone or clarinet but all the bright headroom of a full octave-plus above his saxophone's range.

LOS ANGELES CITY COLLEGE

By the summer of 1946, graduating from Dorsey High meant registering to vote (Democrat) and looking forward to a freshman year majoring in music at Los Angeles City College, less than five miles north of his home. Mingus had attended LACC only a few years before, studying classical music, and claimed to have adopted aspects of his 'workshop' approach from his teacher's rehearsal methods.

* Dolphy was eighteen years old when he met Richardson, who hailed from San Francisco. While playing in a WWII-era US Army band, Richardson met Vernon Alley, Buddy Collette, Marshal and Ernie Royal, and Jackie Kelso. They formed a bond during training in Great Lakes, Illinois, played in a large ensemble directed by Clark Terry, and were then transferred to the San Francisco Bay Area. Ernie Royal referred Richardson to the Lionel Hampton Band, with Charles Mingus on bass.

Though in the mid-1940s jazz was not a degree option, music majors performed in musicals, theater, dance bands, and other popular music productions. Dolphy was a member of the LACC jazz band and orchestra, and, with fellow student Jimmy Knepper on trombone, performed contemporary chamber works such as Stravinsky's demanding *L'histoire du soldat* (*The Soldier's Tale*), with its challenging metric structures and modernistic exploration of rhythm, form, and temporal relationships. Vi Redd was a classmate, working toward a career as a jazz saxophonist and singer, recording albums as a leader in 1962 and 1964.

The subject of Eric's college education and professional career were hot topics at the Dolphy residence as his parents encouraged him to consider the future: as economically struggling immigrants, they wanted their son to fit in as much as possible with establishment institutions and to make friends with serious students. Sadie wanted him to pursue higher academic degrees in hopes that her son would eventually find a teaching position, at least as a side profession.

As the Central Avenue/Buddy Collette/Lloyd Reese axis of Eric's life blossomed, so too did his academic pursuits. At the start of the 1947 fall semester, he attended a late September pledge rush smoker for Black LACC fraternities at the Pueblo Del Rio Clubhouse—a rather strait-laced affair, considering where Dolphy's jazz direction was heading. This period of growth led to a serious turn during his first years at LACC, with his hard-won musical chops, networking among players, and professional demeanor paying off. Not necessarily an event to brag about later in life, the nineteen-year-old's first advertised gig as a bandleader came that December at the Masonic Hall, playing for the Woodlawn Branch of the Young Women's Christian Association's fifth annual semi-formal on New Year's Eve, where the girls expected 'four hundred guests and their company to dance to the splendid music of Eric Dolphy.'[19] At eighteen, he was a professional bandleader starting college, and it was time for his first car. He also had to register for the US military draft, giving May 20 as his birthdate rather than June 20.

MERLE JOHNSTON

When Collette's schedule became too busy for weekly lessons, he encouraged Eric and budding saxophonist Frank Morgan to study with Merle Johnston, a recently relocated New York tenor saxophonist, conductor, and teacher who emphasized technique, tone, and sight reading. Collette also directed Dolphy to take lessons from Naples-born orchestral flutist Soccorso Pirolo, who lived with his wife

Minnie in Arlington Heights, less than two miles from the Dolphys. Johnston found recording and performance success as early as 1925 (on the Columbia label), and the following year New York publisher M. Witmark & Sons printed his sixty-five-page collection *The Artistic Saxophonist*. Johnston was a sharp, old-time swing musician and reeds expert and the founder of several jazz groups active in 1920s and 30s New York.* He now met private students with old-school discipline in a tiny, cramped storefront office at Melrose Avenue and Western Avenue, where he also repaired and sold electronic equipment. Collette suggested Eric study with him for only a year before risking his originality and sense of musical identity, stating that the younger player needed only to improve his sound, intonation, and musicianship: 'He had the right attitude, had a great family. Mr. and Mrs. Dolphy believed in the kid. He had good manners and upbringing. All good qualities.'[20]

In 1948, Johnston assisted Eric in the purchase of his first bass clarinet, an instrument Richardson had also encouraged him to adopt, and another step toward multi-instrumental doubling Collette argued would benefit any career in studio work. The young musician returned from a pawn shop with his new axe, having invited his new teacher along. Johnston was a key player in the development of reed mouthpieces throughout the 1930s as a designer for Selmer's new line of the Johnston–Selmer Mouth Piece, made from a harder, lightweight rubber. This new formula was, as an ad claimed, 'designed to produce a sweeter, more vibrant tone with added volume and carrying power, without forcing. High tones and low tones come easier and clearer, with less reediness, less rasp, and less harshness.' Magazine spots featured Johnston's portrait and his personal offer to 'answer questions.'

The mouthpiece was an improvement for standard instruments, but a liberating one for bass clarinet, as James Newton clarifies: 'Merle had developed a mouthpiece that gave the instrument a presence almost equal to a saxophone. Dolphy developed a facility and extended the range to the point that it was a new instrument with an entirely new set of possibilities.'[21]

In four decades as Duke Ellington's baritone saxophonist, Harry Carney was one of the few jazz musicians dabbling in bass clarinet. Though flutist Herbie Mann recorded solos on the instrument on several Riverside albums of cool jazz

* Merle Johnston recorded on the Columbia label in 1925, and in 1929 his quartet cut 'Do Something' and 'Baby, Oh Where Can You Be?' He founded the Merle Johnston Saxophone Quartet, the Ceco Couriers, and the Merle Johnston Orchestra.

recorded in Los Angeles during 1957, no one in jazz had dared to regularly solo on bass clarinet until Dolphy did so with the Chico Hamilton Quintet. What he did with the instrument remains nearly unparalleled today.

ON HEARING MONK

Thelonious Sphere Monk's first Blue Note singles hit record stores and radio airplay in January 1948, three years after Bird's ascension, and two years after Dolphy started college.* Where Parker offered a galaxy of mind-blowing techniques demanding years of woodshedding, Monk, though capable of pianistic flair and up-tempo chops, offered groundbreaking compositional imagination. The label slowly released a follow-up series in the months to come—truly modern tunes that a twenty-year-old Eric heard on record players and radio broadcasts.

Monk absorbed and emphasized innovative and avant-garde details from Waller, Art Tatum, and Earl Hines, such as complex rhythmic phrasing and metric displacement, dissonant harmonies, and chordal voicings, and manipulated expectations of form, register, and texture. The pianist laid the groundwork for Eric's own creative idiosyncrasies, such as playfully engaging rhythmic patterns, truncated and extended repetition, percussive attacks, unusual metric accents, unexpected phrasal gestures, and most notably wide melodic intervals and striking melodic contours. This stylistic impetus suggested spontaneity itself—an extemporaneous-sounding vocabulary championing unpredictability.

Monk's compositions twisted the framework for improvisers wishing to play along, and what had formerly been the smooth metric flow of swing material over a longer phrase length now had soloists crossing an obstacle course of rhythmic displacement and asymmetry with two, three, and four-measure phrases foregrounding shorter rhythmic groupings. There is also plenty of wry humor in Monk, whose suggestion that his sound 'makes other musicians think' surely resonated with Eric's growing esotericism and intellectual curiosity: modern jazz as the thinking man's music.[22]

Dolphy later doubled down on his own stylistic exaggerations, aggressively promoting a post-bop style in solos and compositions that incorporated bird calls

---

* Monk tunes released in 1948 include 'Round About Midnight' / 'Well, You Needn't,' 'Evonce' / 'Off Minor,' and 'In Walked Bud' / 'Epistrophy.' From the late-fall 1947 recording sessions, two more singles were released in 1949: 'Ruby, My Dear' / 'Evidence' and 'Humph' / 'Misterioso.'

and both animal and human vocal sounds. James Newton argues that 'Dolphy rightfully looked to Monk's far-reaching compositional output as if it were indeed a contributing blueprint for the future of jazz,' explaining further that 'Monk's incredibly advanced timbral knowledge would lead him to use the full range of the piano. As with Ellington, it is not uncommon for a Monk phrase to cover three or four octaves. Each register's color has a strong tie to what is trying to be accomplished rhythmically and emotionally. The same qualities that are often inadequately called 'angular' can be found in Eric's playing.'[23]

During this period of his artistic growth, Eric's Jefferson Park neighborhood was becoming known as 'Little New Orleans' due to a WWII-era influx from the Deep South—a Creole, Caribbean blend of newcomers from Louisiana, Mississippi, Texas, and other parts. Creole restaurants and bakeries were opening, and the cultural inflection likely sparked his parents' now dimming, twenty-year-old memories of West Indian roots and Afro-Caribbean and Central American heritage. Though institutional racism would continue to haunt bank mortgage and property ownership policies for decades to come, the United States Supreme Court in 1948 outlawed the restrictive covenants barring people of color from buying homes. White families south of Jefferson Park slowly began leaving for other parts of Los Angeles, and the Black community expanded beyond formerly redlined borders into the roughly sixteen square miles of what became known as South Central.

As members of the Progressive Musicians Organization during 1948–49, Collette and fellow reeds player William 'Bill' Green rented the Crystal Tea Room at 48th Street and Avalon Boulevard, organizing Sunday jam rehearsals for students and younger players.* Dexter Gordon, Wardell Gray, and a fourteen-year-old Frank Morgan were regulars. There, the older mentors worked more closely with Dolphy and his future musical friends Walter Benton, Sweet Pea Robinson, and Ernest Crawford. Then, at the Chicken Shack restaurant on Vernon near Avalon, two blocks west of Central Avenue, an eager twenty-year-old Eric Dolphy Jr. walked into his future.

---

* In addition to Collette and Bill Green, the PMO included David Bryant, Jewell Grant, Bobby McNeely, and Clarence Thomas.

02 ROY PORTER, THE ARMY, NEW FRIENDS, THE OASIS CLUB

1948–1957

Drummer and bandleader Roy Porter was elemental to bebop's Los Angeles flourishing, gigging and recording with Charlie Parker, and later offering Dolphy his first solid professional gig leading the alto section of his 17 Beboppers big band. Born in 1923, he came of age in Colorado and, following a stint in trumpeter Milton Larkin's touring band, traveled west in 1944, quickly becoming a fixture on Central Avenue's jazz scene. By the end of 1945, he was playing in Howard McGhee's group featuring Parker, Sonny Criss, Teddy Edwards, Bob Kesterson, and Dodo Marmarosa.

McGhee had arrived in March, remaining in town following a residence with Coleman Hawkins at Billy Berg's—the same gig Hawkins's pianist, Thelonious Monk, did not make. Porter played with McGhee through 1946 at the Club Royale, the Final Club (operated for a time by McGhee and his wife), and other venues, recording with the group for the Dial label, including Parker's recording of 'Night In Tunisia,' featuring Miles Davis. Nearly a year later, after Parker's six-month psychiatric stay at the Camarillo State Hospital, the drummer joined McGhee's Quintet at the Hi-De-Ho Club in March 1947 for one of Parker's last gigs before returning to New York. But following months of LAPD harassment and threats of violence (including a failed frame-up on drug charges), McGhee fled Los Angeles with his white wife, the dancer Dorothy Schnell.

That December, Porter recorded four tracks with Dexter Gordon, Red Callender, and pianist Jimmy Rowles, then left Los Angeles with Gordon for a series of Chicago and New York gigs booked for early 1948. Then, tiring of the traveling sideman routine, the drummer returned to Los Angeles and formed his own group, teaming up with others that summer to apply for postwar USO circuit contracts. Porter directed the show, leading a 'sixteen-piece swing crew,' gigging in Seattle and touring 'some of California's smartest nite spots,' but only to see their USO plans fail.[1] *Los Angeles Sentinel* columnist and local radio disc jockey Hunter Hancock noted in an October article that Porter 'organized this band for another fellow who was to take it on tour. That deal fell through, so Roy just decided to keep the band.'[2] Porter then adopted Dizzy Gillespie's modern-jazz big-band format and attracted the likes of Charles Mingus, who briefly rehearsed with them in 1948.

Porter next settled into the large back room of the Chicken Shack restaurant, just up the street from where Dolphy had jammed at the Crystal Tea Room. With a core octet in place, he put out a call to form a big band, the ranks of which would soon include many young players affiliated with Jefferson High School. Chet Baker briefly joined the group. Students on their way home from school were always stopping by the Chicken Shack to hang out, grab a bite, or pick up takeout orders. Then, Porter writes, 'In walks this funny looking dude looking like a junior high-school student, with an alto case in one hand and a flute or clarinet case in the other.... When I first met Eric, he reminded me of a doctor or lawyer or even a Certified Public Accountant.'

The twenty-year-old Dolphy joined Porter's group sometime during 1948, getting to know bandmates including twin brothers recently arrived from Phoenix, trumpeter Art Farmer and bassist Addison Farmer. According to the bandleader, Dolphy was 'very polite and had a nice personality. He was actually rather quiet at this time and seemed a bit shy, especially with the chicks.'[3] Well-rehearsed by fall, they hit the road for three nights of dance shows in the Central Valley city of Bakersfield, playing the weekend of October 14. Porter rented a ballroom, hoping to make expenses and earn extra cash with door receipts from their mostly Black audience: residents of Bakersfield's segregated strip known as the Cottonwood Road community, a dirt road spotted with barbecue restaurants, a motel, and beer joints.

Though the two-hundred-mile-round trip was a financial disaster, the experience bolstered the bandleader's determination to keep and grow the ensemble. Soon after returning to Los Angeles, the group crammed into Billy Berg's club for a big local debut, with the trickle-down economics not really making it to each musician. This was during Southern California's infamous backlash against bebop, when modern jazz faced the ire of conservative journalists, media, and reluctant venue owners; bebop was banned by some regional radio stations, and regular newspaper alerts warned of the music's alleged drug culture and negative social influences.

Though accounts differ over Dolphy's role, Porter clearly recalled that, with 'Eric riding hard as the first alto, our reed section started to come together'— a hint that the young saxophonist played his share of solos along with fellow altoist LeRoy Robinson.[4] Eric's individual sound was emerging, with Collette noticing that, by this time, '[Eric] loved all those strange notes to the point of being out there even when the tune didn't call for it.'[5] Writing in the *California Eagle* on December 16, 1948, Charles E. Lloyd singled out Dolphy during a LACC 'Operations Jazz' concert produced for the World Student Service Fund Drive by fellow student Richard Bock (founder, in 1952, of Pacific Jazz Records, later World Pacific Records):

> Eric Dolphy, City College student, played alto sax for the Porter band. This was no novel experience for Eric. He recently played with Slim Galliard at Billy Berg's and can be found almost any Sunday at one of the several jazz sessions around town. Besides the saxophone, he plays the clarinet, piano, and oboe.[6]

The passage suggests a club sideman with lingering interests in classical music. Multi-instrumentalist, singer, and comedian Galliard had played Billy Berg's at the end of October (an engagement featuring Dolphy), and many clubs, including Berg's, hosted Sunday jam sessions in which Eric would have participated. The college student's Central Avenue jazz life included side gigs during his time with Porter; in addition to Slim Galliard, Jimmy Witherspoon, and Monte's Challengers, he briefly joined trumpeter Nat Meeks's Be-Bop Orchestra, a group directed by Vi Redd's husband. The 'popular young trumpet star is organizing a small Be-Bop combo complete with bongo drums,' the *California Eagle* noted that November. 'Meeks, a local boy who plays terrific trumpet, has Clyde Dunn, Eric Dolphy, Hadley Caliman, [among others] lined up as personnel.'[7] All were affiliated with the 17 Beboppers.

FIRST RECORDINGS

Porter's band outgrew the Chicken Shack, and rehearsals moved to the storied Club Alabam, with many doors opening after he signed a Savoy contract for four sides. The well-oiled group entered Hollywood's Radio Recorders Studio on January 19, 1949, to capture four of the seventeen tunes Eric would ultimately record with the 17 Beboppers, a band name Savoy foisted on Porter for these record releases: 'Pete's Beat,' 'Sippin' With Cisco,' 'This Is You,' and 'Gassin' The Wig.' Though the tracks reveal some subpar playing by young musicians (Savoy would quickly drop the band), one is reminded of the historical importance and youthful energy behind the launch of Dolphy's recorded legacy. On 'Gassin' The Wig,' one clearly hears a nascent Dolphy individuality on his first recorded solo, and he can be easily heard trading phrases with Robinson on 'Sippin' With Cisco.' This exchange between altos reveals significant timbral differences, with Robinson's smooth tone and wholesome, reserved improvisational strategy contrasted by Dolphy's biting, bright palette, confident restlessness, and idiosyncratic explorations of instrumental range. Here, one can hear the earliest version of one of Eric's signature licks, beginning with the aggressive rhythmic gesture of an accented, wide ascending leap to repeated on-beat pitches, followed by a traipsing descent in fragmented figures of unusual turns emphasizing non-chordal pitches and unexpected metric accents.

The *California Eagle* provided news the following week of the fast-climbing band, with Eric billed as 'lead sax,' again suggesting his share of solos. Meanwhile, Dolphy branched out and accepted Monte Easter's invitation to join his Challengers, who shared billing with the 17 Beboppers at the *Eagle*'s 1948 Christmas party at Elk's Hall on Central Avenue.*

One of the many professional Black musicians relocating to Central Avenue after the war, trumpeter and vocalist Easter (Isadore Leonidas Easter), came from Kansas City, establishing himself on four 1946 Aladdin Records singles backing singer Mary DePina and directing Bertram Jackson's dance band. Many years later, Easter outlandishly claimed that he was the first to hire Dolphy after a reference from Eric's friend and future Army buddy, pianist Ernie Crawford, adding that Sadie lectured him, 'I'll let him play, but you gotta make sure he comes back home.'[8] Easter, the 'aggressive young orchestra leader,' then augmented the Challengers for 'a tour now being arranged and scheduled to commence on the West coast soon,' though there is no documentation of Eric recording or touring with the band.†

The 17 Beboppers returned to the studio to record five more tracks on February

* Easter's group gained recognition in 1948 as the house band of the recently opened Watts rhythm & blues club the Barrelhouse, featuring venue founders Johnny Otis on drums, Bardu Ali on guitar, and Chuck Thomas on tenor.

† Monte's Challengers included Dolphy, Chuck Thomas (tenor), Andre Ramos (baritone), Alice Young (piano), Johnnie Parker (bass), Eddie Hall (drums), and vocalist Gloria Shannon.

23: 'Phantom Moon,' 'Howard's Idea,' 'Love Is Laughing At Me,' 'Little Wig,' and 'Minor Mode.'* Their performance at Elk's Hall the following Sunday was prematurely described in the local press as their last before a three-week Southwest tour: 'Eric Dolphy, sax player in the band, checked out of City College to make the trip. Too bad they couldn't wait till school was out.'[9] Porter, however, was still drumming in Los Angeles at the end of March, and with new manager Jerry Sparks moved band rehearsals to the San Pedro Club in preparation for an April tour that was launched in three cars to save money on bus rental. In the meantime, Savoy dropped the group, but Porter quickly reconstituted his players for a third recording session that spring, this time for the Knockout Label, a low-budget R&B outfit with very little distribution. The session was held in a Glendale studio sometime between late March and mid-April and produced 'Hunter's Hunters' (after the disc jockey and columnist who championed the band), 'Blues A La Carte,' 'Sampson's Creep,' and 'Moods At Dusk'—the last presenting a Dolphy solo.

Before touring, the same 17 Beboppers line-up recorded two more numbers for Knockout: 'Frantic Dream,' a poorly recorded busy arrangement with powerful chordal jabs obscuring lighter solo textures; and 'Everything's Cool.' Collector Manfred Scheffner and Dolphy's Dutch acquaintance Paul Karting provided Alan Saul with a dub of this single, dated by them to spring 1949 (though Porter recalls this last Knockout date as occurring in early 1950). The album *Black California* (Arista/Savoy, 1976) presents several of these Porter tracks featuring Dolphy.

Despite the group being dropped by Savoy, those recordings led to many local performances for the 17 Beboppers during Dolphy's tenure, including those at downtown's Avodon Ballroom and Zenda Ballroom, and at Lincoln Theater, Avalon Theater, Club Alabam, the after-hours Jack's Basket Room, the Jungle Room, and the San Pedro Club, among others. (By this time, Eric was also freelancing at the Allegretto Club in support of Jimmy Witherspoon with tenorist/arranger Joe Howard, Art Farmer, pianist James Powell, and drummer Earl Collins.) Some venues offered door money, with no guaranteed minimum for the musicians. As Porter recalls, one night at the Hole in Wall, a small club with sawdust on the floor but no bandstand, LeRoy Robinson and Eric 'got to blowing

---

* Three Porter songs from these two sessions appear on *Central Avenue Sounds: 1921–1956* (Rhino Records, 1999), and five appear on the double LP *Black California* (Savoy, 1976): 'Pete's Beat,' 'This Is You,' 'Phantom Moon,' 'Howard's Idea,' and 'Love Is Laughing At Me.'

and battling for chorus after chorus on "Sippin' With Cisco." . . . This battle of alto saxes must have lasted damn near an hour . . . those kinds of things made it all worth the while even when the money wasn't happening.'[10]

NEW STRUGGLES

The tour barely got underway in late April before crashing to a halt. Following their first club date in Phoenix, Porter, Clyde Dunn, and hometown hero Art Farmer were hospitalized with injuries from a car accident. Dolphy pulled ahead with the rest of the band, attempting to fill as many scheduled appearances as possible. They managed to play Hobbs, New Mexico; Lawton, Oklahoma; El Paso, Texas; and a one-nighter in Wichita Falls on Tuesday, May 3. Instead of achieving Porter's goal of bringing his West Coast bebop big band to Chicago, the group limped back to Los Angeles and struggled to regain a foothold. Dolphy turned twenty-one as the 17 Beboppers reconstituted in various forms throughout 1949, playing their first big post-tour gig at the Elk's Club Halloween concert on October 30, then joining T-Bone Walker and Scatman Crothers for a Jefferson High concert in late December.

Dolphy made his last recording with the group at a 1949 Rex Hollywood label session that produced a ten-inch 78rpm single featuring Roy Porter and Orchestra performing the drummer's B-side composition 'Don't Blame Me,' the A-side featuring Charles Mingus & Orchestra laying down his 'The Story Of Love.' A second single from these sessions features Porter's 'Inspiration' appearing in two parts on sides A and B. Dating this recording is difficult, but with Porter in the line-up following his injuries, the session could have been held as early as that summer.

In a last-gasp effort to promote the group, a mid-March 1950 plug in the *Los Angeles Sentinel* emphasized that 'Moods At Dusk' and 'Little Wig' 'are best sellers.' Dolphy solos on both. But due to a lack of paying dates and fizzled hopes for a new record contract, Porter gradually disbanded the group, gigging as a drummer in Los Angeles as late as May 1950 before temporarily relocating to Oakland with Sonny Criss for gigs at the Wolf Club. There, his plans sadly went awry as the talented musician lost battles with drugs and alcohol, spending much of the 1950s in and out of prison and rehab before returning to Los Angeles at the end of the decade seeking to rebuild his career. His name appears in many Central Avenue testimonials as a drummer and bandleader deserving of more attention, and one who had garnered great respect from his peers.

ARMY LIFE AND CENTRAL AVENUE'S COLLAPSE

During the sixteen years the Dolphys had lived on West 36th Street, the immediate neighborhood changed little, except for the recent arrival of a Japanese American couple from Hawaii (the only non-Blacks on their street), and Jefferson Park's slow but steady influx of Southern-born African Americans from Louisiana, Mississippi, Georgia, Texas, and Tennessee. Less than a third of nearby residents were born in California. Neighbors made their living as gardeners, office workers, maids, industrial laborers, and post-office employees. Eric Sr. worked at the Packard dealership 'checking cars for delivery,' while Sadie seems to have left the job market. A US census team interviewed the family on April 8, 1950, unceremoniously listing Eric as an unemployed musician living with his parents. The Korean War started five days after Eric's twenty-second birthday, and now, having registered for the draft five years earlier, he took advantage of the military's buddy-system agreement with the musician's union to enlist in the US Army with friends Ernie Crawford and Walter Benton. Spared combat duty in Korea, they became members of the 21st Division Band at Fort Lewis, Washington: three square meals per day, lots of instrumental practice, plenty of band rehearsals and performances, and regular checks.

While stationed in Fort Lewis, Eric performed with the Tacoma Symphony and either enrolled in or audited music courses at the College Of Puget Sound, possibly playing in school ensembles. An enlisted musician British by birth, Robin Sinclair, witnessed slices of Dolphy's Fort Lewis life, stating that he played 'a few impromptu things with him. Other times I just listened. He was still "emerging," of course, but even then, I saw and felt he was going to become one of our outstanding modern jazz soloists. … He worked hard, practiced all the time. Sure, he was inspired by Charlie Parker, but already one could hear something very personal.'[11]

Missing their son during his first extended absence from home, Sadie and Eric Sr. joined the local Dilletanti social club, then visited Fort Lewis in August. His first leave found him back in Los Angeles that November. He returned again in mid-March 1952 to visit his parents and sit in at Music Town jam sessions with Hawes, Clark Terry, and Wardell Gray. Later that year, he was accepted to Washington, DC's US Naval School Of Music, from which he earned a certificate of completion in mid-December. Over a three-year period in the Army, Dolphy spent several thousand hours practicing, rehearsing, jamming, and performing in formal concerts.

Following his discharge in 1953, Eric returned to live with his parents. His bedroom and practice shed awaited unchanged; the city he knew, however, had been transformed. The formerly robust cultural strip of Central Avenue faced economic decay, as did greater South Central, with the Watts district particularly hard hit by worsening postwar unemployment, hostile policing, lack of political representation, and the isolation of segregation. Mingus, who had grown up in Watts, had stayed in New York in 1950; hoping to land a television broadcast gig in Red Norvo's group, he was instead replaced by a white player. As Tapscott observed of their hometown while Eric was away, the hardships brought by the Korean War, unemployment, and hard drugs quickly decimated the music scene:

> [But] it had to do with more than narcotics. It had to do with everyday living in the kind of society at that time in the early fifties for Black people, and the Black male in particular. Maybe he had a family. Maybe he couldn't work the way he wanted to. Maybe he was worried about getting drafted and going to the front line, where they were putting all the Black soldiers at the time, and dying.[12]

Heroin was pervasive, as famously illustrated by the story of Charlie Parker, who arrived in Los Angeles at the end of 1945 and turned many jazzers onto the drug. Too young and technically unprepared to make a name in the immediate post-WWII bebop craze, Dolphy opened up to Parker, Monk, and Central Avenue while staying clean; he then spent a highly productive five years of post-Army life in Los Angeles playing professionally at any and every type of gig.

Harsh reactions by authorities in the face of the growing Civil Rights Movement piled like stones onto the Black community. At fifteen, Eric's acquaintance Frank Morgan was offered Johnny Hodges's spot in the Ellington orchestra; at nineteen, Morgan joined Lionel Hampton's orchestra, followed by a series of recordings with top jazz leaders. A heroin addict by 1950, his first arrest in 1955 led to a thirty-year-long string of harsh sentence incarcerations and recovery periods before he re-established his career in 1985.

In tragic tones, Eric's childhood friend Hampton Hawes echoed Horace Tapscott's comments on an urban wasteland ravaged by drugs: 'Everybody I knew, except Wardell [Gray], was using heroin at that time—[but] it was the times and the environment that strung most of us out.... And the casualty list in the

50s—dead, wounded, and mentally deranged—started to look like the Korean War was being fought at the corner of Central and 45th.'[13] Tragically, Gray was found on a desert road outside Las Vegas in 1955, fatally overdosed and with a broken neck. Free that same year from military duty and hassles stemming from his own addiction, Hawes embarked on a series of high-profile Contemporary label albums with *Hampton Hawes Trio*, before his own drug arrest in 1958. In 1963, the brilliant pianist received a presidential pardon from John F. Kennedy, releasing him from a ten-year jail sentence for heroin after he'd spent six years in federal prison.

NEW FRIENDS: ORNETTE

A stable home life coupled with a dedication to music helped form a path through that darkness. Eric possessed rare bootlegs of Charlie Parker's live performances, a testament to a grounding in Bird's style, onto which he layered diverse influences and individual concepts. The sociable and confident twenty-five-year-old began absorbing and transforming the new sounds emerging from various corners of Los Angeles. Upon returning to his hometown, the challenged jazz scene was otherwise reinvigorated by a fortuitous wave of talent including Ornette Coleman, John Coltrane, and Clifford Brown and Max Roach's hard bop quintet. The sadness that tinged Dolphy's memories of a vibrant jazz community was buoyed by new faces, each uniquely impacting his life and artistic path. The margins of the city's jazz scene, including the Dolphy backyard, formed an incubator for innovation and experimentation.

Ornette purchased his plastic alto saxophone in Los Angeles sometime after arriving in town with the Pee Wee Crayton band in 1953, the year of Eric's discharge. Ornette was born and raised in Fort Worth, attending high school and playing music with, among others, multi-wind player William 'Prince' Lasha and drummer Charles Moffett, both of whom later recorded with Eric in New York. This was Coleman's second Crayton tour stop in Los Angeles; this time, he stayed, quitting the tour and moving into the Morris Hotel, exploring his new city in search of jam sessions with rare, like-minded musicians. He worked at various day jobs, including a two-and-a-half-year stint as a Bullock's department store elevator operator and stock person, and would make Los Angeles his home base until he moved to New York in 1959. While in LA, he met and married his first wife, the remarkable Jayne Cortez (born Sallie Jayne Richardson), a writer, sophisticated jazz listener, founder of the Watts Repertory Theater, and mother of their son Denardo Coleman.

Ornette met Eric within a few months of getting off that last Crayton bus, around the same time he reunited with an old acquaintance, fellow former Texan and future collaborator Bobby Bradford, the avant-garde cornetist, trumpeter, and composer. Drummer Ed Blackwell had already come to Los Angeles from New Orleans in 1951, adding great energy and timekeeping innovation to Ornette's sound, and later becoming an important Dolphy collaborator. The drummer's former New Orleans collaborator, the pianist and future jazz family patriarch Ellis Marsalis, occasionally augmented these sessions and later noted that witnessing Blackwell and Ornette just as a duo, without a harmony instrument, brought to light the rhythmic integrity of Ornette's music despite its lack of conventional harmonic implications—an element that it no longer necessarily needed. The 'pulse/no changes' mantra of early free jazz's emphasis on melody and rhythm had its roots in these years.

Native Angelenos Billy Higgins (drums) and Don Cherry (trumpet) played in an edgy group called The Jazz Messiahs with two other Bradford friends, tenor saxophonist James Clay and pianist George Newman. In Ornette's circle by 1956, Higgins and Cherry replaced Bradford and Clay after they were drafted into the Korean War. Most musicians bristled at Ornette's thorny tunes, how he routinely altered and revised his material, his confusing notation system, and his strangely open approach to improvisation. Buddy Collette recalled that they 'had jam sessions every weekend at places like Normandie Hall, with Eric and Ornette Coleman ... we didn't know that they'd get as good as they did and no one else knew.'[14] Bradford remembered this clique also playing at the California Club, the Victory Grill, and the Rose Room, sometimes rehearsing at Walter Benton's garage, candidly recalling the nascent free jazz scene with Ornette, and that Eric 'was not playing any free jazz, nothing even close to it ... there is a lot of people who would argue with that, but I was there.'[15]

Bradford's point is an important one. Dolphy was not yet engaging in the techniques and attitudes of performing music so independently from fellow ensemble members, or leaving behind chordal and harmonic anchors, ignoring tonality, keys, and scalar references. It was a challenge to forego the formal standards guiding musical structure and performative relationships with other players while confidently forging ahead with one's own gestures and lines. Bradford, then a twenty-year-old known to freely adapt Fats Navarro's improvisational style as a basis for his own, would recall that Eric, at the time, was deriving much of his style from Charlie Parker. Thus it remains a myth that Eric entered this circle as a fully formed free jazz guru at the heart of Ornette's revolutionary cell. Rather, he was a twenty-six-year-old proto-virtuoso, a professional musician open-minded enough to recognize the valuable potential of free-jazz principles to which he was being exposed. He had the wherewithal to befriend and admire the likes of Ornette, but he did not abandon the core techniques and approaches to improvisation he'd gleaned from Parker's bebop bible and Monk's eccentricities. The highly trained Dolphy filtered these experiences on the road to a post-bop style of his own design, absorbing what he could of Ornette's unique approach. A learned universalist simultaneously engaging divergent styles, playing techniques, and approaches to the ensemble, he was attracted to the freedom of soloing and to Ornette's often oddly playful compositions, executed so confidently at the head in unison or in twisted, remarkably intuitive counterpoint with Cherry.

This striving, energetic, and groundbreaking music pointed the way toward a new creative world. As Dolphy later shared, 'Ornette was playing that way in 1954. I heard about him and when I heard him play, he asked me if I liked his pieces, and I said I thought they sounded good. When he said that if someone played a chord, he heard another chord on that one, I knew what he was talking about, because I had been thinking the same things.'[16]

It is telling that Ornette's recollection conjures a slightly condescending Dolphy: 'I had known Eric in the fifties, when I shared some music that I had been working on with him. He was very open to the things that I was doing. I think that he thought I was not in his class of perfection because I had just come to California from the South. But it didn't bother me. There was an appreciation from one musician to another.'[17]

One can imagine Eric—a trained musician steeped in bebop and disciplined in traditional notation, instrumental methods, and ensemble playing—initially appearing to Ornette as cocky, perhaps arrogant. As the new guy in town with something to say, Ornette recalled the socially standoffish condescension of a native Angeleno who was likely more dismayed at his odd appearance, idiosyncratic notational method, and loose manner of explaining his own music than with his regional or socioeconomic background. Several players have commented on Ornette's constant reworking of materials and frequent alterations of his pieces.

In terms of a Dolphy/Coleman comparison, it is worth noting Gunther Schuller's recollections of Ornette as a private student of musicianship and theory in the early 60s—and how, in Schuller's view, the saxophonist had clearly misunderstood a variety of basic elements of pitch names, transposition functions, and notation, correlating idiosyncratic concepts with fingering the keys of his instrument. These differences are important when considering Eric, a Naval School Of Music graduate and studious technician who returned to LACC in the spring of 1955, jamming and exchanging ideas, with the innovative, individualistic, and younger Coleman, a kindred spirit who resonated with his growing vocabulary of birdsong, free sounds, outside playing, and human speech inflection. In New York, the two would hook up again in 1960, playing under Schuller's baton and on Coleman's groundbreaking *Free Jazz* album.

THE CLIFFORD BROWN/MAX ROACH QUINTET

Walter Benton was Dolphy's supportive comrade in this proto-free jazz circle, and some of these gatherings were held in the comfortable environs of his family's garage. The two were doubly capable insiders, music partners navigating and collaborating with the separate cutting edges of early free jazz and hard bop. Some of these free jazz pioneers jammed at Dolphy's studio, where Benton participated in another event crucial to Dolphy lore and around the time of the sessions with Ornette: the 1954 Harold Land audition for the Clifford Brown–Max Roach Quintet. Through the decades since, conflicting accounts offer various details regarding those who attended the audition and related jam sessions, their frequency, and who among this list of visitors played together.

Roach came to Los Angeles in 1953 to replace Shelly Manne at the Lighthouse for a six-month residency, at a time when his quintet had already hosted a series of top players, including Sonny Stitt, bassist George Bledsoe, and Carl Perkins. Miles Davis and Charles Mingus also made appearances with them at the club. Teddy Edwards had just declined a tour with the group, thus necessitating the search for a replacement. Twenty-year-old Frank Morgan, Dolphy's wunderkind fellow student in the late 40s, was reportedly passed up by Roach and Brown due to his drug habit. In April 1954, Clifford Brown joined Roach at the Pasadena Civic Auditorium for a Gene Norman–produced headline concert billed as the Clifford Brown–Max Roach Quintet, after which several members quit the band.

Brown's biographer, Nick Catalano, points to the backyard scene at the Dolphy house where Eric hosted jam sessions: 'Dolphy, even then a brilliant eclectic, was experimenting with different sounds and instruments, and his jam sessions had become known far and wide as a must for Black jazzers passing through the city.... Dolphy's home had become a virtual laboratory for new ideas and players. What better place to search for talent when a new group was being formed?'[18] Brown had been mentoring Don Cherry, and the two attended a shed jam session with drummer Larance Marable, who later played trumpet for Dolphy's Oasis Club sextet.[19] It is safe to assume that at various other times, Dolphy hosted Ornette and Coltrane there.

Following his discharge, Dolphy possessed the talent and confidence to attract gifted players to the shed, and a friendly support network mushroomed into musical gatherings with known professionals, even though Eric himself remained unfamiliar outside a local circle. He met jazz musicians passing through Los Angeles and was known to give up his own gigs to those players with families, even offering them rides. In recounting this period with Eric, Harold Land, then twenty-five, recalled, 'He'd come down to San Diego and we'd play together, and when I moved up here, we'd go over to his house and have sessions that would last from morning until night ... one day I was over there playing and Max Roach came by—he'd heard about our all-day sessions. And the next day Max came by with Brownie; they heard me play and asked me if I'd like to be part of their group.'[20]

Land's reference to Dolphy's visits to San Diego likely included gigging at that city's Miss Barron's Black & Tan Club, and perhaps the Palace. 'Eric Dolphy and I were very good friends,' Land later added. 'We'd play all day [in] a little music room in the back of their house, where he would play practically all day. All the musicians who really loved to play, who were very serious about getting into the music, could always go by Eric's and play.'[21] Another source attesting to the quintet's presence in the Dolphy backyard was Eric's friend Lillian Polen: '[Pianist] Richie Powell's girlfriend at that time was a hooker, and badly treated by Richie, but Eric showed her the greatest respect and deference, almost as if to make up for Richie's attitude and abuse. Also, Eric was playful and gentle with children. I remember him with Harold Land's son.'[22]

The illicit seven-track CD *Clifford Brown + Eric Dolphy—Together: Recorded Live At Dolphy's Home, Los Angeles 1954* (RLR Records) appeared in 2005. Eric's alto is present on several tracks. Never meant to be heard by outside ears, the recordings lack documentation. A sextet with Dolphy performs 'Deception' and

'Fine and Dandy' with bassist George Morrow, Roach, Powell (Bud Powell's brother), Brown, and Land; these are obviously audition tunes, since Land is playing with the entire quintet. On 'Deception,' Eric follows Brown with the second solo, lending keen passages that energetically explore standard phrases but also meandering through pat sequences, stalling with awkward silences, and dying out at times. Land holds his own on the double-time changes of 'Fine And Dandy.' Brown plays piano on three tracks with Dolphy and Land: 'Unknown Original Tune' contains a fluid, aggressive Dolphy solo, but one lacking his mature style; 'Crazeology' and 'Old Folks' find Dolphy and Land reading through an arrangement. 'There'll Never Be Another You' and 'Our Love Is Here To Stay' find Brown playing poorly, including a mediocre solo obviously not intended for the public. The track's mystery pianist of intermediate skills may even be Eric.

These are the first known examples of Dolphy's multi-chorus extended soloing with advanced players, and in the company of well-known, consummate professionals on the verge of making jazz history. Land and Morrow were hired, and the quintet quickly recorded the ten-inch album *Clifford Brown & Max Roach*, today considered one of the finest hard-bop recordings of its time, at Capitol Records' Hollywood studio in early August.

Sonny Rollins joined the Brown–Roach Quintet in Chicago in 1956 and later related that during a Los Angeles gig, Dolphy, already twenty-six, stepped up to the stage and asked to sit in. During the two years since the Land audition in his backyard he had woodshedded a great deal, and according to Rollins he did quite well that night. At some point following Clifford Brown's tragic death at twenty-five in an automobile accident less than two years later (along with Richie Powell), a young trumpeter named Booker Little got his break with Roach's group before collaborating with Eric on the *Far Cry* album, the Dolphy–Little Quintet, and other studio projects.

COLTRANE

In early 1954, before joining the Johnny Hodges group in March, tenor saxophonist John Coltrane was freelancing in and around Philadelphia. He had dived into bebop after his discharge from the Navy in 1946, appearing on four Dizzy Gillespie recordings between 1949 and 1952 and four more with other leaders before Hodges. Coltrane, like Dolphy, incessantly practiced his horn, coming of age with the late swing of Coleman Hawkins and Don Byas, and navigating the new trail cut by Charlie Parker. That May, he played Hollywood's Royale Room with Hodges's One Mint Julep Band, the group recording four sides for Norman Granz's Norgran label in August. Very much unlike Eric, though, Coltrane was strung out on heroin all summer, prompting Hodges to fire him and replace him with baritone saxophonist Harry Carney.

It is not known exactly when and where Dolphy first met Coltrane. A year into civilian life and living with his parents, the sociable multi-instrumentalist was reconnecting with old friends and making new ones such as Ornette, Roach, Clifford Brown, and now Coltrane. Though Coltrane was down and out, far from home, and struggling with a bad drug habit, Dolphy helped him out with food and money, as he had done, and would do, for many other musicians. The two connected, played a bit, and exchanged ideas and contact information, with Coltrane becoming lifelong friends with the Dolphy family. Soon after returning to Philadelphia, the tenorist received Miles Davis's invitation to join his first great quintet ahead of the recording of the seven-inch 45rpm EP *The Mastery Of Miles* that November. Perhaps the first Dolphy–Coltrane reunion came at the 1958 Newport Jazz Festival, when Davis's sextet appeared alongside the Chico Hamilton Quintet, with whom Eric had been a member for a little over two months. In less than six years, Dolphy and Coltrane would initiate a groundbreaking collaboration.

Settling into 1955, Eric found his way into Buddy Collette's casual dance group, and that spring he played in Percy McDavid's orchestra with Wardell Gray, Red Callender, Robinson, and other friends in the ninth annual *Los Angeles Sentinel* Easter Promenade. He returned to Los Angeles City College and enrolled in performance ensembles. Composer LaMonte Young claimed to have outplayed him in an audition for the second alto chair in the school's dance band; in the orchestra, Eric was first chair clarinet to Young's second chair. The two became friends after sharing their mutual experiences with Ornette's emerging free jazz circle. Young befriended and gigged with Billy Higgins, Don Cherry, and guitarist Dennis Budimir, a future bandmate in the Chico Hamilton Quintet, inviting those players to dance gigs for which 'we rarely got hired back . . . because we played jazz all night long.' He continued:

> [Eric] was at LA City College at the same time, and his playing was an example of repetition used in yet another inventive way ... Eric Dolphy had

> an incredible set of licks—melodic fragments—that he would repeat in the most various and happy combinations at any frequency transposition that sounded right to him at the time.[23]

When Eric's schedule became too busy he gave gigs to Young, who later studied composition with Karlheinz Stockhausen at Darmstadt and took graduate courses at UC Berkeley. Young became a world-renowned avant-garde composer and pianist specializing in minimalist microtonality and drone-based music, embracing classical Indian vocal techniques and joining the Fluxus movement after moving to New York in 1960, soon after Eric relocated there. However, Dolphy never returned to his college career at LACC following that 1955 spring semester, probably the result of an ugly confrontation involving a bigoted teacher. Ted Gioia claims that Eric 'lost his desire to continue when a racist faculty member told him to leave the college orchestra, saying that he ruined the color scheme.'[24] He would never return to a classroom.

GERALD WILSON AND THE INDUSTRY

Ornette and Coltrane left their marks on Dolphy. The same can be said of another important figure in mid-50s Los Angeles. Gerald Wilson arrived in the city many years earlier, in February 1940, with the Jimmie Lunceford tour. He fell in love with the place, feeling right at home on booming Central Avenue and settling into an ever-expanding career as a composer, big-band arranger, trumpeter, and ensemble director. Within a year, he had met Eric, a Lloyd Reese student ten years his junior, jamming on a Sunday upstairs at the Union Hall. Before the end of the war, and amid bebop's quick rise, a newly minted Gerald Wilson Orchestra emerged, touring for several years before headlining a weekend at Billy Berg's in November of 1948.

Wilson was kept busy as a trumpeter and arranger with some of the biggest names in jazz—including Ella Fitzgerald, Count Basie, Billie Holiday, Duke Ellington, and Dizzy Gillespie, in whose big band he met a young John Coltrane—but by 1950 he had grown tired of the road and the limitations placed on his creative development. He returned to California, living first in San Francisco for several years, where his band included future Dolphy mentor Jerome Richardson, then returning to Los Angeles in 1954. At this time, Wilson also sequestered himself in studies focusing on early modernists such as Stravinsky and Bartók, maintaining progress as a composer, and pushing more modern sounds into big band voicings. The established jazz veteran now approaching his late thirties had started to outlive the once flourishing big band swing era and Central Avenue's formerly vital music scene, which had begun to evaporate:

> By the time I got back [to Los Angeles] in 1954, things had moved. The Oasis was the big thing. It was on Western Avenue... the Blacks had gotten over to Western Avenue... Exposition and Figueroa. And Central Avenue, I guess, just kept declining. The theaters were gone, the Lincoln [Theater] and all of that stuff was kind of just going down, and it was not happening anymore.[25]

Wilson's ten-inch album for the Federal label, *Progressive Sounds*, was recorded and released in 1954, and in July of that year, his seventeen-piece orchestra played the Oasis Club for a week. The clean-living, hardworking, and still up-and-coming Eric Dolphy had returned home from his Army stint and was readjusting to a now bare-bones jazz scene. At South Western Avenue and 38th Street, the Middle Eastern–themed Oasis Club sat a half mile from Eric's home, exemplifying the geographic shift of live entertainment from Central Avenue. The venue's Dixieland bills gave way to the fresher jazz tastes of the owners who took over in 1949, and Lester Young's brother Lee Young's new house band there included Dolphy, Ernie Freeman, and Wilfred Middlebrooks.[26] The Wilson orchestra returned to the Oasis periodically, notably for a long stint in April 1955, supporting a stage show developed by dancer Lou Fontaine. Tapscott recalled hanging out with Eric during Wilson's band rehearsals, and Dolphy was brought into some of their gigs at this time. Buddy Collette, Red Callender, and eventually Eric became Wilson's closest friends in music. Wilson's Oasis engagement completed the connection and sparked Dolphy's future extended engagement there as bandleader.

It was also at this time that Wilson hired singer Peggy Hutcherson, who began dating Eric and introduced her teenage vibraphonist brother, Bobby. Dolphy performed with Bobby Hutcherson at the Sunset Strip coffeehouse Pandora's Box, and they stayed close, hooking up again in New York in 1960. There, over the coming years, Dolphy would hire Hutcherson for club dates and the *Conversations / Iron Man* and *Out To Lunch!* sessions.

By 1956, Wilson was playing in Collette's small group and had proven his value as arranger and trumpeter for Capitol and Mercury, continuing to make a name for himself among musicians, West Coast record labels, the entertainment world, and an aging yet dedicated audience of older school jazz. Through his employment as an orchestrator, conductor, and arranger in the entertainment industry, Wilson hired Eric as a multi-instrumentalist for recording sessions and public stage performances for Mercury and Capitol Records. He never provided specifics regarding the many recording dates for which he hired Eric on flute, clarinet, bass clarinet, and likely tenor saxophone in addition to alto and baritone.* Jazz producer Michael Cuscuna provides more detail from conversations with Wilson in their close work on their Mosaic Records compilation project, sharing that, as a staff arranger for Capitol, 'he used Dolphy on almost all the dates and this includes many known and unknown pop singers,' with Wilson adding that 'there are no Dolphy solos or leads' and that he 'really has no idea how many records there were or what they were.'[27]

BUCK RAM, THE PLATTERS, AND *ROCK ALL NIGHT*

Wilson worked a lot of pop and early rock'n'roll dates, including arranging for The Platters. Formed in Los Angeles in 1952, The Platters were transformed with Buck Ram's guidance and songwriting from their unsuccessful Tin Pan Alley and novelty song act, appearing in the groundbreaking 1956 blockbuster film *Rock Around The Clock* singing 'Only You (And You Alone)' and the no.1 hit song 'The Great Pretender,' both written by Ram. His Mercury contract to produce The Platters and The Penguins led Ram to hire Wilson as trumpeter and arranger. Wilson has called this time his 'commercial period,' which can be partially applied to Dolphy during 1954–58 as he earned his way into a series of Wilson and Ram projects.[28] Though no documented evidence exists, it has been claimed that Ram acted as Eric's agent and that Dolphy toured and recorded regularly with The Platters, possibly appearing on some of their top-selling recordings.

Ram brought Dolphy into The Eddie Beal Combo to back The Platters, while Beal himself joined Wilson's band in 1956. Dolphy performed with Wilson at

* This author was Gerald Wilson's officemate in the ethnomusicology department at UCLA for various school terms between September 1999 and June 2004. Wilson spoke to me of his relationship with Eric, but he never mentioned dates or specific events from a half-century earlier. This was more than thirty years after he declined to give such details to Simosko and Tepperman in 1970.

a big Ram-produced midnight show at Los Angeles's Paramount Downtown Theater on Saturday, December 8, 1956, delivering Ram's line-up of The Platters, The Penguins, The Blockbusters, and Sugar 'N' Spice, plus Wilson's orchestra and disc jockey Hunter Hancock. According to the *Los Angeles Evening Citizen*, Wilson 'and his nine sidemen opened the show with the number "Rock 'N' Roll Freeway," which never quite reached the speed limit.'[29]

During the year-long period following the release of *Rock Around The Clock*, The Platters charted with nine songs, adding a second number-one hit, 'My Prayer,' and were featured in Roger Corman's low-budget spin-off film, *Rock All Night*. Dolphy appears in that film, playing baritone sax with The Eddie Beal Combo backing up The Platters, and can be seen in a still on the original soundtrack album's rear cover.* The Mercury soundtrack album features the group performing 'Pussy Foot,' 'Honey Buggin',' 'Leadfoot,' and Breezin',' all composed by Ram, and each with solidly arranged saxophone charts (likely by Wilson) within which it is impossible to single out Dolphy's playing on any particular instrument. Released as a double feature with *Dragstrip Girl*, the film predictably received a horrible review in the issue of *Variety* dated May 1, 1957: 'Lowgrade stuff attempts to cop a fast-buck ride on music fad,' the article read, highlighting the easy-to-dismiss nature of rock'n'roll in its infancy (maybe even a dig at fast-Buck Ram?). The review spotlighted appearances by The Platters and the white rock'n'roll group The Blockbusters but did not mention The Eddie Beal Combo. On May 13, Eric took his baritone sax into the studio with the group to record 'Toni's Tune,' the B-side to The Blockbusters' 'Fulltime Baby,' a seven-inch 45rpm single on Buck Ram's Antler label.

Dolphy also played with Wilson and Collette in bands led by R&B pianist/arranger Ernie Freeman, with whom Eric had played in Lee Young's Oasis house band in 1949. After Freeman's role as pianist on The Platters' classic 'The Great Pretender,' Cash Records began releasing his so-called 'raunchy' instrumental rock'n'roll records, featuring plenty of saxophone charts. The Ernie Freeman Combo then appeared in *Rock Around The Clock* and soon signed with Imperial Records, releasing twenty-nine singles and seven LP albums by 1963. Gerald likely kept Eric in the studio loop during Freeman's time with Cash and/or Imperial, with Freeman singles from 1956–57, such as 'Puddin'' and 'Dumplin',' featuring

---

* There also exists an undated seven-inch 45rpm Italian pressing of 'Pussy Foot' and 'Honey Buggin'.'

either solo backup baritone or tenor, or horn sections providing simple riff-based rock figures. What is certainly known of Eric's otherwise undocumented session work arranged by Wilson was his 1958 recording on crooner Ed Townsend's songs 'For Your Love,' 'Over And Over Again,' 'What Shall I Do,' and 'Please Never Change'—pop-infused numbers on which Wilson also appears on trumpet. In October of the same year, Eric played on sessions for the Ernie Andrews album *Travelin' Light*, produced by Gene Norman. But though he was mentored, befriended, and employed by Wilson, Dolphy was never invited to be a featured soloist in any of the bandleader's many gigs and recordings during Dolphy's remaining time in Los Angeles, those spots going to Sonny Stitt, Sonny Criss, Stan Getz, Wardell Grey, Zoot Sims, and other Los Angeles–based freelancers.

Dolphy was never one to criticize non-jazz genres the way he did cheap commercialization or musical insincerity. When asked if he believed all music was good, he responded simply, 'Yes, all music has its own message. Music is just like people, places, and things. Everything has a message for someone. And I'm in no position to criticize anything.'[30] Citing the recent release of Bobby Timmons's soul-jazz single 'Moanin',' he continued, 'A lot of people are talking against that kind of music, but these people are playing it different, in a modern way.' He then suggested that only by playing a piece and understanding its structure is one able to criticize it.

Eric never put down the music he played in Los Angeles studios during his 'commercial' period. The pay was good and he was still living at home, where he composed 'G.W.' for Gerald Wilson in 1957—more than a nod to his friend and benefactor—and the ear-catching opening track of his first album as leader, *Outward Bound*. That same year, Wilson inaugurated a large rehearsal ensemble to test out his growing list of recent works. Dolphy sat in with the group, which eventually became the second coming of the Gerald Wilson Orchestra in 1961. The January before Dolphy's death, the group recorded Wilson's composition 'Eric' for his 1964 Pacific Jazz album *Portraits*.

THE OASIS CLUB

Notwithstanding US Army service and his commercial work, Eric rose toward the top of Los Angeles's post–Central Avenue jazz scene. Seven years after gigging in Lee Young's Oasis house band, and interim appearances there with Wilson's ensembles, Dolphy got a break by landing a regular club engagement as bandleader.

Perhaps the earliest notice of what would become an epic gig at Club Oasis is a *California Eagle* advertisement from February 23, 1956, announcing 'West's Most Famous Sepia Cabaret Presents Aland Dixon's new and exciting revue starring Jeanette Williams and vocalist Bill Butler.' The list of supporting acts—'The Three Stepp Sisters, Eric Dolphy's Men Of Jazz, Curvaceous Club Oasis Chorus Cuties'—appears above the large, boxed text, which states, 'Sepia burlesque Monday Nights, dawn show every Sunday Morning at 6:30am, dining and dancing, no cover—no admission.'

The club, at Western and 38th Street, sat two blocks past Eric's junior high school and half a mile from his home. His sextet included Norman Fagion and Larance Marable on trumpet, Wilfred Middlebrook on bass, Arnold Palmer on drums, and Fran Gaddison and Army buddy Ernest Crawford on piano. Dolphy's temporary contract was then extended; Club Oasis ads mentioning his engagement continued to appear through March and April as he transitioned to the leader of what was now a house band. The *Night Owl Pocket Guide* calendar entry for May 31, 1956, lists 'Eric Dolphy and his Men Of Modern Jazz held over at the Oasis Club on Western Avenue for fourteen weeks, sign new contract.' Local newspapers note the extended engagement running into April of 1957, proving Dolphy a regular weekend job less than ten minutes from home by foot and ultimately lasting fourteen months.

The Oasis had a storied presence in the Golden Age of the Los Angeles jazz scene, hosting Louis Armstrong, Sarah Vaughn, Billie Holiday, and a stream of other top acts, and as Gerald Wilson commented on his 1954 return to Los Angeles, it emerged as one of the most important venues as Central Avenue gradually lost its sheen. Locals such as drummer Lee Young gigged there either as opening acts, in house bands, or playing special engagements. Young hired Charles Mingus for a quintet that played the Oasis regularly in the 1940s. Its cabaret fare included comedians such as Slappy White, jazz groups such as Slim Gaillard, lounge acts, floor shows, and crooners. Among the professional dancers who regularly took part in floor shows were Donna Jones, Sylvia Moon, and Frances Neely. It was both dance hall and supper club, where 'the swingsational band of Eric Dolphy will provide the music for your listening and dancing pleasure.'[31] Radio station KGFJ occasionally broadcast a live show from 1–2am on Sunday mornings, while the 6:30am Sunday 'Yawning' show grew in popularity during Eric's tenure. His friend Lillian Polen remembered:

> I would fall by the Oasis and listen to him, and my opinions seemed important to him. The questions from him were almost intense. Did he sound like Bird to me? That seemed all-pervading. He seemed happy at the Oasis—deliriously happy at just being able to play professionally. That he was the leader of the gig did not appear to impress him. He played behind the acts at the Oasis; used the baritone sax for that but played mainly the alto with his group.[32]

Dolphy led more than one group at the club and another on his own clock. Directing an all-purpose house band on baritone, he picked up the alto to explore new directions in hard bop with an edgier Oasis group. Saxophonist Curtis Amy arrived in Los Angeles in 1955 and became a fan of those sets, attending every chance he could and stating that Dolphy 'was playing out then.'[33]

The Club Oasis residency, in allotting Dolphy stage time with a second, progressive group, formed an important strand of avant-garde direction in relation to his discovery of Ornette's work. As Steve Isoardi describes, by early 1958, 'Dolphy was leading another ensemble at the Oasis, which included Lester Robinson and Billy Higgins'—one that had an 'adventurous sound,' organized in part 'to stretch bop's approach to harmony.'[34] Dolphy was allowed to blow at the Oasis, and he brought various players in and out of that second, progressive unit.

On days off, Dolphy jammed with another, freer group. Simosko and Tepperman maintain that his Club Oasis activities remained separate from his ten-piece ensemble featuring Les Robinson, stating that this other band 'may have been a testing ground for Eric's arranging abilities.'[35] Tapscott also attested to Dolphy stretching the tradition through arrangements and solo material with a band separate from the Oasis, noting that 'Eric also had his own group by this time with Lester Robinson and a few other cats… Eric was looking outside even then.'[36]

This is the band Dolphy refers to in the liner notes to his first album, naming the trombonist Robinson as a member of his ten-piece band. Later in his career, he would arrange again for large ensembles, including Coltrane's *Africa/Brass* album, a 1963 University Of Illinois festival concert, plans for a Dutch large ensemble in 1964, and during his final weeks in Paris.

Simosko and Tepperman allude to a traveling combo gleaned from Eric's independent group:

> [There were the] Sunday-afternoon-in-the-park type [gigs], for which the pay was small, but Eric was always happy for every opportunity to play. Occasionally it was necessary to travel as far as New Mexico for work, and on one occasion transportation was by an old car which proved unreliable. Broke and stranded, Eric phoned home and his parents wired him fifty dollars to buy food and to pay for his return home by public transportation. However, instead of returning immediately, he used the money to have the vehicle repaired so that the combo could limp back to Los Angeles together and bought food for the whole band.[37]

However, getting work for his independent groups proved difficult. With no recordings or further descriptions of the progressive music Dolphy was performing at this time, one can only speculate about how it might have related to his future output.

During the third week of February 1957, Dolphy sat in on alto sax for several nights with Dizzy Gillespie's big band at Hollywood's plush Peacock Lane club. He covered for Ernie Henry, recently arrested on drug charges with bandmate Percy Heath and others. However, that brief, last-minute fill-in gig, brokered by former Gillespie band member Wilson, was as close as the twenty-eight-year-old had come to big-time jazz. Central Avenue's glory days were past, as was his Men Of Jazz gig at the Oasis, whose advertisements in the *California Eagle* stopped appearing in April 1957. Dolphy's replacement there was the R&B legend Johnny Otis.

By August, Eric was sitting in with the Jimmy Cowan Trio with Brauz Freeman, including a stint at the Club Intime on South Western Avenue, less than two miles south of his home. Though he was still living with his parents, his professional career barely scraped by the remaining months of 1957. Practicing incessantly though gaining only local recognition, he sensed that a move would be part of his future. Likely subbing for Collette, Dolphy appeared as flutist with Eddie Beal and other musicians at an early December Philharmonic Auditorium event headlined by the 'black panther of the dance.' The Savage Dancers, led by pioneering African American choreographer Archie Savage, were in town to film their appearance in the romantic musical *South Pacific*, the Rogers & Hammerstein vehicle directed by Josua Logan and released the following year.

In early 1958, Dolphy learned that Ornette had signed a contract with Lester

Koenig of Contemporary Records and would be going into the studio in February and March to record *Something Else!!!! The Music Of Ornette Coleman*, released later that year. Dolphy was waiting to stand up and play, and his *Outward Bound* liner notes speak to these struggles as a creative musician during this time:

> A lot of guys have been trying to put forward a new approach and a different sound, something in which they honestly believe. But they've been put down. Nobody wants to listen so the cat goes back to the popular sound, he loses heart and gets discouraged. This is particularly true on the West Coast, a guy doesn't have much of a chance to be heard anyway, the clubs come and go all the time. The sounds the guys play among themselves are a lot further advanced than what is heard in the clubs. The new sounds are there if somebody wants to listen.

03 THE CHICO HAMILTON QUINTET, FIRST MONTHS IN NEW YORK

1958–1960

In April 1958, Buddy Collette recommended to quintet leader Chico Hamilton that Eric replace the exiting Paul Horn. It had been ten long years since the hard-working Dolphy joined Roy Porter's band, and Collette could see that his former student had hit a professional and creative wall and needed to stretch his musical wings beyond Los Angeles. Collette had helped found the quintet in 1955 and was its first wind player at a time when Hamilton was coming off a twenty-year career as a drummer for Duke Ellington, Count Basie, Billie Holiday, Lester Young, Lionel Hampton, T-Bone Walker, Sammy Davis Jr., Nat King Cole, and six years with Lena Horne.

Hamilton's work in Gerry Mulligan's piano-less quartet led the skilled stickman toward what was quickly emerging as a more sparse, even experimental, 'classical' side of West Coast cool jazz, as exemplified in the 1952 ten-inch album *Gerry Mulligan Quartet* (Pacific Jazz) with bassist Bob Whitlock and trumpeter Chet Baker. Hamilton had perfected softer brushwork in helping to develop Mulligan's sound, later propelling the cool sound in his own quintet with more formally structured compositions using unusual colors, detailed instrumental arrangements, and restrained tempi.

Far-Eastern themes of spiritual meditation and an exoticized non-Western world color their 1957 Pacific Jazz album *Zen: The Music Of Fred Katz*; Paul Horn and a small chamber group of flute, oboe, clarinet, bassoon, and trombone joined Chico's group, which included Katz on cello. The following year, their *South Pacific In Hi-Fi* album was released with an exotic cover featuring Paul Gauguin's sensuous and colorful 1892 work *Fatata te miti*, encouraging jazz audiences to listen for artistic mood music and easy sophistication, and to take liberties with the dreamy island references. The quintet had developed a filigree chamber sound, with intimate contrapuntal lines and unisons and doublings among alto sax/flute, guitar, and cello for melodies. The format and style demanded restraint from the ensemble members, and their recordings are sometimes blemished by meandering arrangements.

Some critical listeners found the addition of Eric's unique and independent solo voice jarring and out of place in this sonic environment, his avant-garde leanings framed by a group sound later playfully identified as the 'forerunner to future new age bands.'[1] Suspending the standard notion of a jazz rhythm section in favor of rich, chamber-like textures, the quintet can be heard as a third stream precursor laced with contrasting up-tempo references to swing, modern bebop, and fiery solo work. Dolphy's blend of Parker and Monk, mixed with his own unique vocabulary, found its way in small doses into many of the quintet's recordings and performances; the group's sound brought focused attention to Eric's technique, range of expression, and use of registers on alto sax, flute, and bass clarinet.

Though reined in by Hamilton's cool aesthetic, the soon-to-be thirty-year-old Dolphy had arrived at the first stage of his mature style, on display in the quintet's handful of albums and national tours and via his appearance, at the 1958 Newport Jazz Festival, in the documentary style film *Jazz On A Summer's Day*. He remained with the group until he made New York his home in December 1959. As this career opportunity took flight, over a period of fifteen months Los Angeles witnessed the recording of Ornette's next two albums with Cherry, *Tomorrow Is The Question* (Contemporary, 1959) and *The Shape Of Jazz To Come* (Atlantic, 1959). This last work and the following year's *Change Of The Century*, recorded by Atlantic in New York, launched their breakthrough concert at New York's Village Vanguard, which is where Dolphy would reunite with the burgeoning free jazz crowd.

TOURING AND RECORDING WITH HAMILTON'S QUINTET, THE NEWPORT JAZZ FESTIVAL

Two months before his thirtieth birthday, Eric headed to the East Coast with a newly configured Chico Hamilton Quintet consisting of guitarist John Pisano, bassist Hal Gaylor, and former Cleveland Symphony Orchestra cellist Nate Gershman, playing Chicago's Butterfield Firehouse before landing for Eric's New York debut at Birdland sometime in May. Gigs along the way included Cleveland, the home of Hale and Juanita Smith, close friends of Hamilton and former quintet member and guitarist Jim Hall. After that show, Eric was invited, with Hall, to the Smith residence and became instant friends with the couple.

On May 23, the group played Rochester's East High School, and in mid-June New Jersey's new Palisades Park amphitheater series of free family concerts, held every Monday and Friday, working up to Fourth Of July's Newport Jazz Festival, where on the 4th and 6th they performed 'Chrissie,' 'Nice Day,' 'I'm Gonna Wash That Guy Right Out Of My Hair,' and Collette's 'Blue Sands' in front of an appreciative audience. It was the group's first widely exposed appearance with Eric, who turned in a convincing alto solo on 'Pottsville USA' and blistering flute on 'I'm In Love With A Wonderful Guy.'

Bert Stern's and Aram Avakian's documentary *Jazz On A Summer's Day* captures the quintet's July 6 performance of 'Blue Sands' along with intimate house rehearsals. The film premiered in August 1959 at the Venice Film Festival, with its theatrical release following in 1960. East Coast audiences were getting their first taste of a Parker-esque multi-instrumentalist with a whole new vocabulary of never-before-heard hard-bop chops on bass clarinet. Dolphy knew Ornette, Coltrane, and Mingus, but no one knew Eric, and decades would pass before the Newport recordings were issued.* At the festival, the newcomer reunited briefly with Coltrane and Max Roach, whose post–Clifford Brown group +4 debuted twenty-year-old wunderkind and future Dolphy collaborator Booker Little on trumpet.

Following Newport and a New York sojourn lasting through July, the five musicians recorded the ill-fated *Ellington Suite* in Los Angeles on August 22. The recording was Dolphy's first high-profile jazz session, his brilliant musicianship outshining the session's less-than-stellar arrangements. His flute solo on 'In A Mellow Tone' adds a pleasant edginess to the upbeat swing classic, and he owns 'In A Sentimental Mood,' conquering the opening theme with a warm, romantic alto, his solo ranging from pointy hard bop to a whimsical landscape of leaps and rhythmic iterations. 'I'm Just A Lucky So And So' finds him sitting out the plodding arrangement's opening statement only to jump in with a scored, bluesy swing flute

---

* They were eventually issued as *Chico Hamilton & Eric Dolphy: Complete Studio Recordings* (Phono Records, 2016). Performances of 'Chrissy' and 'Nice Day' were released on the Swedish CD *Mulligan In The Main* (Phontastic, 1992). They were also made available as bonus tracks on *Charles Mingus, Eric Dolphy Quintet/Sextet: The Salle Wagram Concert Complete Edition* (Domino Records, 2015).

line, played with flair. The good-time feel of 'Just A-Sittin' And A-Rockin'' runs the same profile as the previous track: a lackluster arrangement improved by a gutsy alto solo, brimming with blues, idiosyncratic rhythmic gestures, and distinct twists and turns. Flute caps off 'Everything But You,' featuring short improvisations scattered about this scored piece's grooves, with Hamilton building up polymetric escapades against Hal Gaylor's walking bass. On 'Day Dream,' Eric's gracious and milky B-flat clarinet tone renders simple scored lines behind Gershman's cello in a drummer-less chamber quartet, and he returns with the same instrument on 'Azure.' On 'I'm Beginning To See The Light,' Dolphy takes off with signature oddities, pushing a bebop line into an easygoing, fun number on which playful and Monkish weird blues riffs mix with gasps and leaps, while his cocky solo on 'It Don't Mean A Thing' delivers unpredictable electric energy.

Ellington Suite was the first of what might have been a total of six studio albums the combo made with Dolphy; Ron Carter insisted that Warner Bros passed on a 1959 Chico Hamilton Quintet album that the label deemed too 'far out.'[2] This was certainly true of the *Ellington Suite* recordings, which World Pacific Jazz rejected, in part due to Dolphy's adventurous playing. Label founder Richard Bock and producer George Avakian were the likely sources for this decision. However, 'I'm Beginning To See The Light' and a heavily edited 'In A Sentimental Mood' were included on the label's 1966 anthology *Chico Hamilton: Jazz Milestones Series*, and a truncated version of 'In A Mellow Tone' found its way onto a World Pacific Jazz promotional sampler shipped to radio stations. The quintet's former line-up was then hired to record the same *Ellington Suite* material the following January, using as introductions the original transitional bridge material connecting contiguous tracks.

The story of the album's eventual rediscovery is the stuff of legend. The only test pressing of that original recording with Dolphy was placed in an album jacket made for the follow-up session. The original tapes were subsequently lost. That one-of-a-kind, erroneously packaged *Ellington Suite* test pressing found its way into the world. Almost forty years later, the one-off disc somehow landed in a used record shop in England, purchased in near-mint condition in 1995 by jazz collector John Cobley. With the assistance of producer Michael Cuscuna, the 2000 Pacific Jazz CD *Chico Hamilton Quintet With Eric Dolphy / The Original Ellington Suite* was transferred into twenty-four-bit form from that singular test pressing.

Immediately following the *Ellington Suite* session, the group traveled to New York's Randall's Island Jazz Festival, appearing the next day with, among others, Thelonious Monk and Art Blakey's Messengers, the Dave Brubeck Quartet, and the Miles Davis Sextet with Coltrane. Hamilton's September tour took the group to Minneapolis's New Lakeview Club for ten days, and to venues such as Kansas City's Orchid Room. Back in Los Angeles in early October, Eric was called by Gerald Wilson to do sessions for vocalist Ernie Andrews's album *Travelin' Light* (GNP, 1958), on which Wilson plays trumpet and arranged four songs. On this day he played no solos, reading his part for scored arrangements on an unidentified instrument.

The Hamilton Quintet again returned from the road to Los Angeles later that month, entering Hollywood's Radio Recorders studio to record *Chico Hamilton With Strings Attached* (Warner Bros, 1959), for which Fred Katz conducted his string arrangements. Dolphy's short *Strings Attached* solos reveal a mature voice with a new vocabulary of ornaments, leaps, pyrotechnic runs, and individualistic expression. In light of the *Ellington Suite* fiasco, the album would be the first on which he was heard by a broad, worldwide jazz audience. One can only imagine listeners putting this record on their turntable in 1959 and hearing his convincing work: flute solos on Ellington/Strayhorn's 'Something To Live For,' the Hamilton/Howard McGhee collaboration 'Don's Delight,' Benny Golson's 'Fair Weather,' and Hart/Rodgers's 'By Jupiter' and 'Ev'rything I've Got,' plus alto sax solos on 'Pottsville, USA,' 'Modes,' and 'Close Your Eyes.' He is asked to lay almost completely out of 'Andante,' for which he read a simple alto line. It is likely that the group also recorded 'Under Paris Skies' that same day (released on the 1959 Warner Bros compilation/sampler album *Jazz Festival In Stereo: Hear In And Far Out*).

The Weill/Nash classic 'Speak Low' showcases Dolphy's first recorded bass clarinet performance, a whirlwind solo obeying none of the instrument's traditional registral limitations and partially obscured by the muddy guitar and cello arrangement. Where typical parts for bass clarinet avoid the uppermost *clarino* register, let alone the highest octave, Dolphy had already developed various solo contexts for virtuosic, wide-interval leaps to many of those high pitches, and sustained, post-bop runs throughout the instrument's full range, despite the challenges of tone production and timbral variety; and he routinely mined the instrument's characteristic middle *clarino* down to lower extremes of the harmonically rich *chalumeau* register. From his liberating 'Speak Low' essay emerged a new vocabulary of reedy attacks and articulations—a sound world augmented by joyous squawks, squeaks, smacks, micro-tonal inflections, cries, and noises. No one had ever recorded the bass clarinet in this manner.

RAVI SHANKAR AND CREATIVE IMPROVISATION

A mindful 'East meets West' dynamic was important to Dolphy, as witnessed in his pursuit of classical Indian techniques and non-Western music as sources for melodic and rhythmic invention. Similar concerns were common threads with Yusef Lateef and Coltrane, the latter eventually taking sporadic lessons with Indian sitarist Ravi Shankar and naming his son after the musician. In 1955, violinist Yehudi Menuhin invited Shankar to demonstrate Indian classical music through performances in New York City. The thirty-six-year-old virtuoso toured the United Kingdom, Germany, and the USA the following year. Some of his performances included lectures and demonstrations on classical Indian music principles, and that year he released his first album, *Music Of India: Three Classical Ragas* (His Master's Voice).

Hindustani classical music, as with many other global music traditions, made little or no use of harmony, placing extra focus and energy on an enormous variety of scalar resources for thematic development, variation, and melodic improvisation, coupled with compelling rhythms and metric concepts. Dolphy's LACC schoolmate Richard Bock, the founder of World Pacific Records, embraced Shankar's potential and signed him as a recording artist after seeing him perform during that first American tour. In Los Angeles, Bock recorded and released Shankar's classic 1959 album *India's Master Musician*, featuring Chatur Lal on tablas and N.C. Mullick on the tambura drone instrument, its tracks clocking in at eleven, twelve, and thirteen minutes—luxurious durations compared to standard recordings of Western popular music.

Dolphy's meeting with Shankar, referenced several times by the jazz musician, likely occurred when the two crossed paths while recording for World Pacific in 1958, when, between August and December, the Hamilton Quintet made three albums. Though World Pacific did not run its own studio until the early 1960s, Shankar's *India's Master Musician* was recorded by the label during the same period, and it is worth imagining the two being introduced, shaking hands, exchanging compliments, and discussing music. Eric would later state that they spoke about the melodic/scalar system of Indian music known as raga, adding, 'I see how we can incorporate their ideas . . . Indian music sounds to us like one minor chord; they call it a Raga or scale and they'll play on one for twenty minutes.' By *we*, he meant jazz musicians searching for new directions in music. Pointing toward a characteristic of his later soloing efforts and those of Coltrane's, he added, 'It's a challenge to play a long time on just one or two chords.'[3] During his first year in New York, Dolphy will study with a dancer/musician familiar with classical Indian music and make a practice tape focusing on rhythmic and metric principles.

Though they could have met at another time and place, Shankar did not tour the USA again until 1961. He played New York's Town Hall that year on Monday, October 2, when Dolphy was with Coltrane in Los Angeles; by the time Shankar's tour came to Los Angeles that November, the Coltrane Quintet was touring Europe.

THE TIMEX CONCERT, *GONGS EAST, THREE FACES, THAT HAMILTON MAN*

There probably could not be a starker contrast to the heady Dolphy/Shankar meeting than the nationally televised disaster that was the *Timex All-Star Jazz Show*. Dolphy and the Chico Hamilton Quintet were on prominent display and paid well, but the reviews were awful. 'Jazz for the masses is an incongruous grouping in itself,' barked *Tampa Tribune* staff writer Art Smith in describing the November 10 broadcast from the Americana Hotel, Miami Beach. 'And what CBS tried to do the other night,' he continued, 'proved such music might not be quite right for television consumption.'[4]

Syndicated UPI columnist William Ewald's storyline was 'Timex Jazz Show Was Death On Jazz.' Writing the day following the broadcast, he concluded, 'I can't think of anything more likely to kill off this nation's growing interest in jazz than TV's all-star jazz shows.'[5] He and other journalists wrote in defense of jazz as a unique art form requiring more intimate, respectful, and authentic environs. Instead, viewers listened to a 'terrible shallow and muddy' show 'beamed from the pretentious hollow of a Miami Beach hotel, surroundings more suited to quarter-finals of a Cha-Cha contest.'

Tampa Bay columnist Art Smith offered the best line: 'Satchmo [headliner Louis Armstrong] was completely perplexed . . . ill at ease in the vast chromium wilderness of the resort hotel.' Two nights later, the group played in the more faithful jazz environs of Birdland, where they appeared often, occasionally alternating with Miles Davis's band featuring Coltrane.

Hamilton's outfit revisited Los Angeles's Radio Recorders studio for the *Gongs East* album, recorded on December 29 and 30, wrapping up four numbers in each session and finishing off two of the tracks in January. Considered one of the strongest of the quintet's works from the 1950s, its original, unattributed liner notes mention Eric's youth, versatility, and welcome array of tone colors from four instruments. The commentary veers toward his extroverted wailing and 'the vital jazz element so happily evident in his alto sax and flute solos,' noting, 'when Eric enters on a free jazz line, That, as Chico Hamilton puts it, is where the soul comes in!'[6]

The album appears conservative in light of Dolphy's later musical ventures, and his work here is often straitjacketed by time limitations. Awkward arrangements on three tunes submerge his unimaginatively scored B-flat clarinet. Otherwise, he does not hold back. Opening the album, the bebop-ish, up-tempo 'Beyond The Blue Horizon' showcases an utterly fluid flute solo. Gerald Wilson's 'Where I Live' is a contemplative chamber piece teasing out a ballad defined by cello, bowed bass, and scored flute part from which is launched a swinging accompaniment for feel-good solos from flute and Dennis Budimir's guitar. The title track, colored by its low-end, retro-swing riff, reveals a bass clarinetist wearing two hats: a technician with total command over scored arrangements, and an exuberant soloist capable of Parker-esque agility and defining new paths of instrumental jazz. 'I Gave My Love A Cherry' is another moody chamber-like piece, one that finds Eric switching from B-flat clarinet to flute for straight part reading.

The bland start to side two's 'Long Ago (And Far Away)' includes Eric's problematic B-flat clarinet intonation and was the kind of number that might easily have chased away progressive listeners. But they would have missed two of Dolphy's most impressive alto solos from his Hamilton days. Gerald Wilson's other piece on the album, 'Tuesday At Two,' features a strong alto solo pointing toward future adventures, while 'Nature By Emerson' is Katz's graceful ballad vehicle, and after Dolphy lays on the charm over a sparse and restrained arrangement, his precise solo develops special legs. Swing pianist Nat Pierce's 'Far East' is a flute showcase, though its easy-listening qualities and some indecisiveness on Eric's solo hold back the track's promise. Billy Strayhorn's 'Passion Flower' is marred by an odd arrangement that leaves the exposed support lines of Dolphy's altissimo register in unfriendly stratum. (He would learn to avoid such unattractive mistakes in his own work.)

Abandoning Southern California's clement winter, the group kickstarted 1959 with two freezing January weeks playing Freddie's in Minneapolis, only to return to the studio for their fourth album project in five months. *Three Faces Of Chico Hamilton* would baffle Dolphy fans, frustrating them with what could have been. The label promotes the album as the 'talented sides to Chico Hamilton: his vocals, his solo percussion, his quintet.' Singing on this aesthetically unbalanced record, Hamilton delivers four numbers in a breathy, cool *sotto voce*, adding in his liner notes that while the set may prove a surprise to some, 'it even may annoy others'—an understatement for this author. The augmented reed section reuniting Paul Horn (alto), Buddy Collette (tenor), and William Green (baritone)—'to bring back the old Jimmie Lunceford sound'—oozes lush, four-part arrangements, but only on these vocal tracks. Hamilton fought for the addition of three unaccompanied drum/percussion tracks, including 'No Speak No English, Man,' a tour de force that poses the question of how much better the quintet would have been if Hamilton had cut loose on his instrument more often, rather than restrain the group through comparatively tired arrangements.

Eric's own twirling composition, 'Miss Movement,' opens side A, welcoming listeners to a sneak preview of his energetic writing to come. It was his recorded debut as a composer, and there is a certain irony that it appears on such a disjointed release, perhaps explaining how easily it would be lost on Dolphy's fan base. Gershman keeps up on cello, sawing away at the driving, chromatically curious head, doubled by Eric's alto sax (a prequel to his work with Ron Carter on *Out There*). With its repeated twelve-bar theme, the fast tune takes us quickly into Eric's blistering yet short solo, complete with a variation of his favorite signature phrases: after several measures of exploring low-to-middle registers with conjunct, snaking sixteenth-note runs, he leaps to a high-register downbeat attack, repeating the heavily accented note four times, then leaving that plateau with dotted rhythmic sequences falling to the lower register. This Dolphyism, often a near-jocular jolt that breaks the flow, is typically inserted unpredictably into legato passages of fast, stepwise scalar runs.

Another solid number for Eric's alto is Kenny Dorham's 'Newport News,' which has a truncated version of his signature riff embedded in a hard-swinging, bluesy line. He briefly takes it up a notch into a held vocalization, reattacking the sustained, lip-controlled pitch bend, microtonally scooping and conversing with the audience in human-cry-like intervals and timbral modifications of the kind that he would develop so richly in later recordings. In a significant passage, an astute Hamilton responds to Eric's increasingly expressionistic material, but it is all too brief: this solo, like the one on 'Miss Movement,' suffers from brevity.

While Eric was back in Los Angeles, Gerald Wilson tapped him for the Capitol Records recording of *New In Town* by crooner Ed Townsend, who later helped pen Marvin Gaye's 1973 hit 'Let's Get It On.' Dolphy played on four tunes arranged by Wilson—'For Your Love,' 'Over And Over Again,' 'What Shall I Do,' and 'Please Never Change'—but this brief taste of his old home was cut short by the Hamilton quintet's return to the road during the spring of 1959. Chicago-based promoter Ed Sarkisian's Jazz For Moderns tour had the group playing Midwest clubs, festivals, and residencies, such as their gig at Cincinnati's Emery Club on Sunday, April 27, where Eric was a guest of the Cincinnati Jazz Club.

They were back in a Los Angeles studio for the recording of *That Hamilton Man* on May 19 and 20. Though the group was still to release records with Pacific Jazz and Warner Bros, this session was a promotional effort undertaken by SESAC Recordings, and the material did not bode well for free-flowing jazz solos, or for quality music.* SESAC briefly specialized in promoting jazz and country artists through transcriptions for radio airplay, including Duke Ellington, Count Basie, Woody Herman, Coleman Hawkins, and Chet Atkins. *That Hamilton Man* was a limited-release promotional effort with track durations ranging from 1:21 to 3:20 and six tracks per album side.

Though some tracks reveal valuable yet brief solo work by Eric and others, overall the disc is the worst of two worlds. Only haphazardly marketed as a commercial release after the fact, the music was an array of mediocre mood pieces and a bid at mildly raunchy rock'n'roll, in what amounts to a sales pitch promoting the quintet's most 'accessible' (and thus most bland) sound, clarifying Simosko and Tepperman's rightful concerns over the album's tape editing, truncated arrangements, and solos 'sandwiched between the opening and closing ensembles,' the result of 'sacrificing quality for quantity.'[7] Nonetheless, a small collection of nice Dolphy solos brighten this otherwise forgettable attempt at commercial accessibility. The opening track, 'Fat Mouth,' is a pointillistic blues with a punchy, short alto solo—a good-timey rockin' type much like the same

* Founded in 1930, the Society Of European Stage Authors & Composers (SESAC) is the second-oldest performance-rights organization in the United States.

disc's 'Cawn Pawn.' These two numbers echo Eric's rock'n'roll session work with Ernie Freeman a few years earlier. 'Lady E,' a cutesy tune with a flat arrangement, is saved only by the middle section's moderate tempo walking bass supporting Eric's bluesy but painfully short flute solo. 'Truth' is a darker blues featuring alto, and Eric whines and whimpers with the best of them here. He creeps out of 'Lost In The Night' with suddenly cheery musicianship, and turns in a quick and dirty solo on 'Frou Frou.' 'Opening' finds him at his athletic best on this disc, running circles around the beat, and Budimir rips a nice solo as well.

Sessions for *That Hamilton Man* were sandwiched between a residency at Los Angeles's Seville club, where the quintet shared billing with the Sonny Rollins Quartet from May 13 to 26. Rollins recalled Dolphy playing flute, clarinet, and baritone and tenor sax, without mentioning alto sax or bass clarinet.[8] The tenor virtuoso later noted that, while he was in town, he introduced his trumpeter, Freddie Hubbard, to Ornette and Don Cherry, the three of them jamming at the Watkins Hotel, to Hubbard's delight. This was likely Eric's first encounter with Hubbard, who became his close friend, musical collaborator, and Brooklyn roommate.

The very poorly attended Seville engagement gave way to the road in early June, the two groups next appearing together at Sacramento's Senator Hotel. Though he was drawing good pay and gaining wide exposure, Eric must have been uneasy with *That Hamilton Man's* step toward mainstream jazz and easy listening. By contrast, Ornette had released the groundbreaking *The Shape Of Jazz To Come* that May; Coltrane and Wilbur Harden co-led two albums which appeared later in 1958, *Jazz Way Out* and *Tanganyika*. Hamilton's sometimes questionable charts stood in stark contrast to what listeners would eventually hear from Eric's unfettered aesthetic vision and capabilities as composer, soloist, and leader on his own albums. But his time with Hamilton was far from over, and at some point during the summer, bassist Ron Carter joined the group. The two became quick friends.

This was a hard-working ensemble: on July 27, they played New York City's Village Gate (perhaps with Carter), then Indiana's French Lick Jazz Festival on July 31, followed by a week at Baker's Keyboard Lounge in Detroit in early August, Birdland again in mid-August, Randall's Island Jazz Festival on August 22, and jazz in the round at the Westbury Music Fair, as it was billed until 2005. On September 21, they were the house band for jam night at the Village Gate.

While on the road, Dolphy kept adding to his first tastes of press coverage; most local newspaper reviews that mention him note his multi-instrumentalism and originality.*

In 1964, noted critic Nat Hentoff recalled what many New York jazz insiders experienced when this new face and challenging sound suddenly emerged on their scene. 'I heard about Eric Dolphy before I actually heard him ... several musicians told me around 1958 to be sure to listen to Chico Hamilton's combo when he next came through New York.' He remembered being told that Hamilton had 'a guy who plays alto and other reeds, and he's set that group on fire.' His first impression was that 'Eric was on fire. He was able to project a sweeping, searing intensity when he played. There was also in his work an element of explosive unpredictability. You never quite knew what was going to happen because Eric was never of a temperament to settle into any comfortably safe groove.'[9]

The fast-paced pro circuit had the quintet back in Los Angeles in October for a break before their last Sarkisian Music For Moderns tour back and forth across the country. In November, the musicians found themselves with their busiest tour schedule yet, playing El Paso's Pass Of The North Jazz Festival on the first, and later, due to overbooking, flying over Texas and skipping out on three dates there as they rushed from Philadelphia back to Los Angeles. Visiting his parents before relocating to New York City, Eric would gradually, excitedly stop thinking of Los Angeles as his home. The quintet was tight yet fraught with road-induced friction, run ragged yet well paid. Hamilton was done for now; after playing this quintet's last date, he disbanded the group and took a rest before starting over again in the spring with new faces. Dolphy was first replaced with reeds player Carrington Visor, and then, before the end of 1960, with a twenty-two-year-old Charles Lloyd.

THE MOVE TO NEW YORK

Though specifics of his departure from Hamilton will never be crystal clear, Eric had been champing at the bit for months, and he may have already negotiated a contract with Prestige. The 1950s were now history, Los Angeles already becoming a memory. His hometown had devolved into something that even a prodigal son

---

* For example, *Indiana News* staff writer Fremont Power wrote in his review, 'Leg-Slappin' Jazz Rocks French Lick,' that 'Eric Dolphy, whose fine talents range from alto sax, clarinet, and bass clarinet to flute.'

could curtly dismiss in the liner notes of his first 'New York' album. 'Things are so bad on the coast,' he wrote, meaning there was no place in Los Angeles for independent, avant-garde jazz musicians.

Eric's first real exposure in the jazz press, a Martin Williams interview earning mention on the cover of the June 1960 issue of *The Jazz Review*, came with some mystery and the undertow of this cultural collapse: 'Dolphy was for many years a part of that Los Angeles jazz underground about which a great deal more should be known; that city is full of talented musicians only a few of whom make the recording studios or are able to earn their livings by playing their horns.'[10] There was the sad ring of a much larger truth, as hard blows kept hitting Dolphy's former musical community. Compounding South Central's tightening vise of inequality and social disparity, legendary music educator Lloyd Reese died that year, and jazz education pioneer Samuel Browne transferred out of Jefferson High about the same time, bitterly noting the collapse of community and student interest in serious jazz studies at the school.

For too many, only Eric's relocation to New York City marked the start of his mature period. It must have seemed to the East Coast jazz establishment that this thirty-one-year-old had magically emerged fully formed from the mists of the Hamilton caravan of cool chamber jazz, rolling into town from California. For these jazz listeners and critics, the newcomer's past was irrelevant, including the advanced ideas revealed in the challenging solos he had already thrown down in clubs, on festival stages, and on Hamilton Quintet recordings. He appeared to them as the fresh, new player who had to prove himself to New York. Criticisms suggesting he had yet to develop his own voice can be grounded in the challenges facing a true multi-instrumentalist seeking a standout sound on each of his axes, an interpretation proffered by James Newton: 'Maybe his early development took a little longer. Part of that was dealing with three instruments, and half-good was not good enough for Eric Dolphy. A lot of people double, and there's nothing wrong with that, but they tend to play the same language on each instrument, the same ideas in different timbres. But Dolphy wanted each one to have its own personality. And he got inside the language of each instrument in a way no one else had.'[11]

Though he was now hearing his name spoken by people he had never met and jamming with a whole new crowd, Dolphy was still a working musician, which included playing charts for commercial sessions, as he had done with Gerald

Wilson. Yet as a soon-to-be leader and sideman under contract with Prestige, Dolphy would record three of his own albums in 1960, and watch his name receive increasingly larger print on the album covers of other leaders. He had a little over four years to live, a time during which he would amaze, entertain, and perplex—and, in doing so, challenge, redefine, and become himself.

Dolphy attended the December 30 Town Hall concert featuring Ornette, Coltrane, Monk, and Cecil Taylor, among other big names, as he sought out reunions with Los Angeles connections. The first was Mingus, who at the end of 1959 started a ten-month club residency at Greenwich Village's new Showplace. Dolphy was already a member of the Mingus Workshop when he contracted the highly contagious mumps virus, which would have laid him out for up to two weeks. He later shared some of his first New York experiences with his friend Hale Smith:

> Dear Brother . . . I am looking for you any moment now that I am in New York . . . I am still working on the flute things you did. Wish you would write something for clarinet. Since I have been here, have worked with Mingus (lost it when I got sick, the mumps) and now at Minton's working with George Tucker.*

Bassist George Tucker had studied with Mingus and was working with Eric's Los Angeles mentor Jerome Richardson, playing most recently on *Roamin' With Richardson* (Prestige/New Jazz, 1959). He would go on to play on Eric's first album, *Outward Bound.* Smith earned a master's degree in classical music composition at the Cleveland Institute Of Music in 1952, embracing modernist academic music techniques such as serialism yet remaining connected to jazz as a pianist, arranger, and composer combining both worlds. 'Although Mr. Smith, an adviser for the Center For Black Music Research in Chicago, was routinely listed among the leading Black composers of his day, he bristled at the designation,' wrote William Grimes of the *New York Times*, adding that 'he wanted his work, and that of his Black peers, to appear on programs with that of Beethoven, Mozart, and Copland.'[12]

* From an undated letter from Eric Dolphy to Hale Smith. George Tucker died suddenly and tragically while playing onstage in October 1965.

Echoing some of Dolphy's and Mingus's concerns for a universal stream of art music connecting jazz with classical, Hale wrote in 1971, 'We don't even have to be called Black. . . . When we stand for our bows, that fact will become clear when it should after the music has made its own impact.' Soon after meeting Eric, the Smiths moved to New York, where the horn player became 'an assertive participant' in the 'seminar-like sessions' the Smiths held at their Flanders Hotel residence in Harlem, and later at their home on Long Island.[13] Eric developed an informal course of study with Smith in which the academic instructed the jazz virtuoso in advanced theory, twentieth-century compositional methods, and counterpoint.[14]

Like his own vibrant solos, Eric struck up several directions at once, joining Minton's Playhouse house band, channeling Monk's spirit at the legend's former Harlem roost, breathing in relief as he let loose his horn. Reedman and future collaborator Ken McIntyre would recall a warm welcome from Dolphy and Freddie Hubbard at Minton's, including an invitation to step onstage and play alto and flute with the group. That evening, McIntyre added, Dolphy 'played like there was no tomorrow.'[15] Though there is no hard evidence of gigs, Eric apparently formed a working combo at this time with his Los Angeles friend vibraphonist Bobby Hutcherson, bassist Eddie Khan, and drummer Joe Chambers—a group that intermittently included trumpeters Freddie Hubbard and Blue Mitchell. Always in need of work, Eric welcomed a studio gig augmenting the Count Basie Orchestra (without Basie) for Sammy Davis Jr.'s album *I Gotta Right To Swing* (Decca), joining a January 7 session on four tunes arranged and conducted by Sy Oliver: 'There Is No Greater Love,' 'This Little Girl Of Mine,' 'Gee Baby, Ain't I Good To You,' and 'Mess Around.' Though he was given no solos, he was reunited there with Central Avenue brothers Ernie and Marshall Royal.

COLTRANE AND ORNETTE

Eric Sr. and Sadie drove cross country to deliver their son's Volkswagen Beetle, meeting the Smiths and visiting Aunt Luzmilda's family. Another reunion came when Eric moved into Slide Hampton's home at 245 Carlton Avenue in Central Brooklyn's Fort Greene neighborhood, joining housemates Hubbard and artist Richard Jennings, a frequent visitor who painted the original works used for Eric's *Outward Bound* and *Out There* album covers. The house formed a significant hotbed among serious jazz insiders: Coltrane's cousin Mary, who hosted Friday-night jam sessions at a loft frequented by these and other associates, lived there with trombonist Charles Greenlee (Harnifan Majid), whose tune 'Miss Toni' is found on *Outward Bound*. Wes Montgomery and bassist Larry Ridley rounded out Hubbard's Indianapolis contingent.

Coltrane played the November Town Hall concert with Ornette on the bill, then toured Europe with Miles, whose group he left following their last show in Stuttgart, Germany, on April 10, 1960. Upon returning to New York to front his own group, Coltrane began visiting the Carlton house regularly. He was entering an exciting new phase of his artistic journey and would join Dolphy often in Brooklyn that spring and summer, practicing and jamming, with Hubbard later recalling that time by stating simply that Coltrane loved Eric. Coltrane's career was taking off. His playing on Davis's *Kind Of Blue*, released the previous August, saw him hailed as a cornerstone voice of the timeless classic (today the biggest-selling jazz album of all time), and the February release of his own wholly original *Giant Steps* showcased harmonically complex compositions and hard-bop soloing. His interest in Ornette led him to pay for lessons—certainly not to lift Coleman's playing style but rather to understand his concepts of music so far from the tradition. That summer, he recorded several Ornette pieces with Don Cherry, Charlie Haden, Percy Heath, and drummer Ed Blackwell. The new thing partially provided Coltrane with an impetus to move beyond the harmonic intensity of *Giant Steps* toward music that was less determined by chordal frameworks.

In another sign of artistic change and growth, Coltrane, who had been playing a soprano sax lent to him by Davis, purchased his own from the Selmer factory that spring. He had, of course, already played the instrument, but a new focus led to its use on the massively popular *My Favorite Things* later that year. He was now at work forming his own quartet with Billy Higgins, bassist Steve Davis, and pianist Steve Kuhn—a transitional unit predating the Elvin Jones/Reggie Workman/McCoy Tyner juggernaut that Eric would help make a quintet in the summer of 1961. It was Coltrane's heightened success with these musicians and albums that empowered him to call the shots, leading to Dolphy's hiring in 1961, creating a quintet that would turn jazz on its head.

Back in mid-November 1959, the Ornette Coleman Quartet with Cherry, Haden, and Higgins had opened at the Bowery's Five Spot—a historic event generating so much response that the group stayed for ten weeks into late January.

The venue took its name from its street address, 5 Cooper Square, and had opened its doors to the world three years earlier with a month-long residency by Cecil Taylor's uncompromising jazz trio featuring bassist Buell Neidlinger and drummer Dennis Charles, later joined by soprano saxman Steve Lackritz (soon known as Steve Lacy). Thelonious Monk had also held down a famous six-month engagement there in 1957, with Coltrane among the band members.

The buzz around the Coleman quartet's club appearance, recordings, and reviews led to a second installment at the Five Spot starting April 5. The venue had become a touchstone for the jazz avant-garde, and Dolphy was watching closely as Ornette received at least partial vindication for his risky revolution: he took Ornette's success to heart during his New York transition, and elements of free jazz gained in his approach to music making. Coleman and company had done the initial heavy lifting for others like Dolphy, whose sound was just starting to get across to a wider audience.

Though it was a breakthrough career opportunity and the pinnacle of Dolphy's financial success, the Chico Hamilton Quintet was not part of the aesthetic landscape on which Eric wished to plant his flag. A handful of talented players were struggling to create a new aesthetic space, positioning themselves within a distinctive niche, distanced from the past, from tired traditions that were now increasingly challenged and dated. Instead, it was his renewed friendships with Coltrane, Ornette, and Mingus, progressive jazz masters representing a revolutionary framework of genius, that would go a long way in defining the rest of Eric's life work—a primordial soup from which diverging paths of progressive jazz emerged. At the end of the year, he would play an integral role in the zeitgeist's most evocative document, Ornette's *Free Jazz.*

MINGUS

Eric's move to New York brought about a life-changing opportunity when he took all three of his instruments to the Showplace alongside Charles Mingus's Workshop. Some of his most powerful work was recorded in studio and live performances with the restless bassist. Mingus biographer Brian Priestly summarized this important node of early 1960s jazz history by stating that 'one further event which partially obscured the significance of the Dolphy/Mingus collaboration, was the simultaneous arrival also from Los Angeles of Ornette Coleman.'

Trumpeter Ted Curson shared this colorful recollection of getting called up for the Workshop:

> That night, the phone rang . . . 'Can you start now?' Curson ran into Dolphy on the stairway; he too had gotten the call. They walked to the club. When Mingus saw them, he gestured at the band onstage and said, 'Ladies and gentlemen, I have an announcement to make. These cats are fired!' Dannie Richmond alone stayed onstage, and the new cats joined him.[16]

The reality was far less dramatic: Mingus fired his entire group by having an assistant send each a formal, typewritten letter. He then rebuilt a piano-less core quintet player by player, first rehiring drummer Dannie Richmond, then calling Eric, Curson, and finally Yusef Lateef, the latter a recent arrival from Detroit who played with the Workshop for three months. At the Showcase, Eric joined Curson, Richmond, and a flux of musicians such as another Los Angeles friend, trombonist Britt Woodman; alto sax player Charles McPherson; and saxophonist Booker Ervin. 'The group was constantly changing,' Curson later recalled. 'I expected change every night. I could say every set. The drummer, Dannie Richmond, was the only person I expected to see,' he added, though other participants remember healthier attendance.[17]

Eric grew to cherish duets with bassists on each of his instruments and gratefully accepted the challenges of playing with Mingus: the demanding arrangements, the welcomed expectations of adventurous soloing, and the confrontational leader's dramatic club antics and infamous temper. Though Dolphy's fulfilling 1960 Workshop gigs at the Showcase and elsewhere artistically eclipsed his Chico Hamilton experience, the pay did not. Even so, the New York buzz around this new face and his smorgasbord of sound—perhaps the first true multi-instrumentalist in jazz history—grew steadily with Workshop exposure.

Though a newcomer, Dolphy fit in as an equal thanks to his complex relationship with Mingus, bringing a superior musicality and inventiveness with which the bass player quickly grew to rely upon and interact. Dolphy's style and multi-instrumentalism emerged as a main ingredient to Mingus's compositional fusions of large, suite-like structure and improvisation, and as James Newton has observed, 'Mingus said Dolphy could play lead alto saxophone in a small group, flute or bass clarinet in a chamber group. If we extend the exponential growth that occurred between 1961 and 1964, he would have been beyond our imagination by 1970.'[18] Aside from his Prestige contract, joining Mingus may have been the best thing that could have happened to Dolphy at this career juncture.

According to Curson, Mingus went with him and Dolphy to see Ornette play at the Five Spot, where the trumpet player said Mingus sat in on piano. However, a club regular who witnessed the incident added that Mingus's unsolicited attempt to join the band during Cherry's solo was met with consternation from Coleman. Later that evening, Mingus asked the two if they could play like that. 'Of course we could,' Curson replied, making light of the challenges and exaggerating the outcome. 'I'd just got my pocket trumpet. Eric said okay. We rehearsed a bit, and soon we were playing that style, and just as good.'[19]

Freeform improvisation was not entirely new to Mingus. The quixotic bandleader's creative antennae were pointed in all directions, including the future. As early as 1954, the composer had presented nearly unstructured group improvisation on recordings that became the ten-inch Savoy album *The Moods Of Mingus*. On the swinging hard bop of 'Purple Heart,' horn players John LaPorta, Teo Macero, and George Barrow subtly emerge from the arrangement, sounding not unlike polyphonic Dixieland voices. A thick counterpoint of multiple free-sounding lines launches that album's 'Getting Together.' Eric Porter cites this disc as a significant step by the bassist toward 'unplanned group improvisations,' quoting Mingus as saying, 'If and when these present constructions are accepted, I will venture to delve a little more into the so-called dissonance of free form improvisation—which one may then label atonal.'[20]

The jazz press played up the sometimes-friendly rivalry Coleman and Mingus developed, while a biographer noted that Mingus would 'bristle whenever contemporaries compared Coleman and Dolphy,' extolling Dolphy's wide-ranging virtuosity and adding that he valued Coleman's ideas about free jazz more than he did his playing.[21] Mingus, whom Robin D.G. Kelley characterized as being an important yet reluctant figure of the emerging movement loosely termed free jazz, famously quipped, 'I'm not saying everyone's going to have to start playing like Coleman, but they're going to have to stop playing like Bird.'[22]

Eric learned a great deal from Mingus, re-entering the forward-thinking composer's life following nearly twenty years of Mingus's conceptual and procedural development of group interplay and 'workshop' methods, some of which he claimed were gleaned from classical music ensemble technique at Los Angeles City College. The bassist's experiences with Collette in the collectively run Stars Of Swing back on Central Avenue of the 1940s had also produced a spark in these regards. He also famously collaborated with Charlie Parker, the legacy of Mingus altoists therefore bringing Dolphy closer to his musical hero and thus to jazz's top tier. Mingus the composer had discovered an expressive power in conjoining Western concert music's techniques of thematic development and modernistic contrasts of tempo and character with the raw immediacy of improvisation, drawing from a plethora of jazz styles. His artistic complexity, restless activism, and universalist desire to compose beyond the limits of jazz, while celebrating its traditions and improvisational allure, are revealed in some of his Jazz Composer Workshop pieces from the late 1950s (he later dropped 'Composer' from the name). They express his compositional sensibilities while simultaneously relying on the spontaneity of skilled improvisers to complete the musical form. Eric Dolphy proved the most accomplished of this long list of musicians.

Mingus's work at this time incorporated inventive post-bop and what some might call free jazz into compositions juxtaposing a panoply of African American music styles reaching back to the blues and original jazz. An emblem of Mingus's regard for tradition is his showcasing of Jaki Byard's phenomenal modernist survey of stride piano in the unaccompanied 'A.T.F.W' (Art Tatum, Fats Waller), which he performed during quintet concerts going into 1964. When necessary in freer material, the bassist, though successfully experimenting with group improvisation during this time, often expected players to hear his lines as conduits of ensemble sound, sonically conducting, in a sense, the general nature and direction of improvisation. His suite-like tunes featured at the Antibes Festival the coming summer—an expansive program transcending his previous work in terms of enlarged form and improvisational process—work as overarching surveys of jazz history: 'Wednesday Night Prayer Meeting,' 'Prayer For Passive Resistance,' 'Folk Forms 1,' and 'Better Get It Into Your Soul' strike the listener like a freight train delivering revitalized gospel inflections, blues, and hard bop—timely material for the broadening Civil Rights Movement. 'Prayer For Passive Resistance' honors the sit-ins in Greensboro, North Carolina, where peaceful Black protesters sat at whites-only lunch counters and faced violent reprisals.

Mingus's Workshop modeled how freedom could be represented in a collective, approaching structured improvisation and the ideals of collaboration with less regard for the worn, categorical labels placed on Black artists but rather in stylized charts and post-bop and free soloing in discursive parallel to the Civil Rights Movement's struggle for social and political freedoms.

However, Mingus's potential for personal vindictiveness proved difficult for many, and Eric would leave and return to his group several times. The chaos that occasionally reigned in the Mingus kingdom rubbed Eric the wrong way, as it did other collaborators, and the two can be seen as attracted opposites. The comparatively quiet, respectful Dolphy was mostly spared the public abuse Mingus meted out to nearly everyone else. He tolerated Mingus's personal excesses as the bandleader encouraged improvisational freedom, allowing his iconoclastic style to flourish. It is within the context of Mingus's harmonic worlds, demanding formal structures, and driving rhythmic sensibility that some of Dolphy's best sideman work shines brightest. Along with his live performances with Coltrane, and Ornette's *Free Jazz* disc, Dolphy's work with Mingus forms the pinnacle of his sideman playing.

Years later, in an interview with Raymond Horricks, Britt Woodman claimed that Eric's joining Mingus was 'sort of a second best,' and that his first goal was quite different: 'He had gone [to New York] with the idea of trying to get into the Miles Davis combo.'[23] Though his friend Ron Carter and Dolphy quintet member Herbie Hancock would both gain entry to the quintet Davis that ran from 1963 to 1968, Woodman adds, 'Eric failed to impress Miles, who even made some disparaging remarks about his new-style playing. Anyway, he ended up playing with Mingus.'

Miles Davis set himself apart from other great jazz musicians with his supreme technique, artistic vision, and ear for talent. Like Mingus, however, he famously trashed those he did not like, subjecting them to public invective and mocking critiques. Eric was a very public victim of Davis's ire in print, most notably during the final weeks of his life. Regardless, Dolphy gained plenty from the structured group dynamics in Mingus's hard-won equilibrium of composition and improvisation. That approach included little games Mingus played with his musicians, such as once providing Lateef not with a lead sheet but with a small drawing of a coffin from which he was expected to draw inspiration, or restructuring his established tunes with spontaneous verbal directions live onstage in front of a paying audience.

Dolphy would also be influenced by, and be part of, the bassist's growing activism and desire to agitate against racial prejudice and unjust business practices in the entertainment industry. For his *Out There* album, Dolphy penned 'The Baron' as an homage to Mingus and covered the bassist's challenging composition 'Eclipse.' But now the multi-instrumentalist was about to take center stage, as the time came for the world to hear this voice uninhibited by sideman status.

04 OUTWARD BOUND, OUT THERE

APRIL–AUGUST 1960

The flurry of activity during Dolphy's first months in New York obscures the Carlton house rehearsals and preparations for his first recording session as a leader, held on April 1. His debut album, *Outward Bound*, billed to 'The Eric Dolphy Quintet Featuring Freddie Hubbard,' was released by Prestige that August, featuring Tucker, Byard, and drummer Roy Haynes. Each brought their best game across the George Washington Bridge to legendary recording engineer Rudy Van Gelder's studio in Englewood Cliffs, New Jersey, who also mastered the album, pressing and cutting the lacquer on the premises.

Eric plays alto on his aggressive and gutsy originals 'G.W.,' 'Les,' and '245,' each with strong solos by the group—tunes that remained in his club sets until his last days in Paris and Berlin. He chose bass clarinet for 'On Green Dolphin Street' (Kaper/Washington) and 'Miss Toni' (Charles 'Majeed' Greenlee), and laid down a flute masterclass on 'Glad To Be Unhappy' (Rodgers/Hart). Also recorded that day, but not included on the album, was 'April Fool,' a four-minute-plus freeform flute solo over a moderately up-tempo A-flat blues, complete with Byard's incomparable quilt of rhythmic, shimmering clusters that never seem to get in the way. Prestige later found a home for 'April Fool' on the posthumous *Here And There* (1966) and on its expanded RVG Remasters series reissue of *Outward Bound* forty years later.

Haynes's crisp eight-bar intro of rim shots, snare strikes, intermittent hi-hat, kick drum, and press-roll pick-ups opens the first track, 'G.W.,' which Eric composed three years earlier in honor of mentor Gerald Wilson. Welding alto and trumpet to curiously unstable contrapuntal intervals and formal asymmetry, the two-voice dissonances of the head are contoured more as oddly phrased questions than statements. There is a conversational quality here, of secret agents of change speaking in ebullient code as they re-map the musical landscape. This musical rhetoric is cast in a familiar AABA format, but with its twelve-bar A section truncated to eight bars in its final return, and an eleven-bar B section. The tune is a conundrum from which Eric's solo bursts forth in an assault on expectations, with double-time flurries, sequences ruptured by leaps and vocalizations, and his signature phrase of jumping to repeated high-register, on-beat accents followed by twirling descent.

Sudden jabs aside, this is a remarkably cohesive improvisation, with arch-like plateaus from which Dolphy then jumps. Sympathetic listeners find driving, dizzying meanings; detractors looking for traditional phrasing and echoes of the tune distrust the disjointed unpredictability. A beautiful mutation has formed in the jazz family tree. Hubbard answers with clarity, rhythmic vigor, and joy, creating the space to converse with himself—then an effusive rhythm section backs Byard's thoughtful romp, answering his own rhetorical questions with left-hand interjections punching clanging dissonances. The 1982 Prestige compilation album *Dash One* is titled for its inclusion of the first takes of 'G.W.' and '245' from this session.* That equally successful alternate take of 'G.W.,' with Dolphy's solo covering four choruses, clocks in at over twelve minutes, swamping the taut, eight-minute version on *Outward Bound.*

'On Green Dolphin Street' finds Dolphy on bass clarinet, while Hubbard channels Miles's timeless 1958 take of the number. From the arrangement's celebratory cha-cha-cha ostinato, supporting the trumpeter's wickedly muted melody, the bass clarinet's low-register reed tone whacks the listener with a new sound palette for jazz. In his solo, Dolphy coaxes radiant, sustained notes from the thin, difficult-to-produce upper register, his high, counterintuitive pitches fashioned into coruscating, liquid runs that stretch to cover the instrument's full three-octave range. The exclamatory solo, steps ahead of Dolphy's use of the instrument with Hamilton, speaks as incisively as a bass clarinet can, with post-bop pathos and humor to equal what listeners had just heard on 'G.W.' Byard's backing is loaded with complex contrary motion, a jeweled thickening bringing sonic depth to the number, as does his playful elan on the tune's fade out.

* The Swedish label Metronome released a 45rpm single containing 'G.W.' and '245.'

Named for trombonist Lester Robertson—Eric's Los Angeles friend and future co-founder, with Horace Tapscott, of the Pan-African People's Arkestra—'Les' drives the unison angularity of its opening statement with lots of altered harmonies, an up-tempo head consisting of two six-measure phrases capped with a two-measure turnaround tag for a fourteen-measure F blues form that then repeats. The alto solo stays a fanciful, unrepentant step ahead of the rhythm section's chase, bravely followed by what is perhaps the disc's best Hubbard solo. Byard's presence is strong throughout; after his mercurial solo, Eric and Hubbard trade eights with great results. Sax/trumpet hits, smears, and squawks mark the number's close, carving out strata against piano arpeggios and the rhythm section's suspended animation. One can imagine first listeners not flipping over their new vinyl record just yet but instead choosing to give these three numbers an immediate re-hearing.

Side B launches with '245,' a cathartic blues in F with film noir gusto, its twelve-bar melody a squeezed-down trumpet-and-alto unison. (The first take heard on *Dash One* is a full minute longer.) The alto's initial gesture stretches the upper extremes of the instrument. The title is the street number of the Carlton house, and the tune has a feel-good foot in jazz's most conservative terrain of the blues. Hubbard holds forth with rips and growls, keeping it lyrical whenever he wants, getting inside his resilient brass tone. It's Eric's piece, but he blows last, pouring on a bluesy rawness while wrapping up select, ornamented phrases with graceful rhetorical flourishes. *DownBeat* managing editor Don DeMicheal, one of Eric's most influential early supporters, described Dolphy's '245' solo as capturing 'the melancholy spirit of deserted streets.'[1] With the rhythm section, it's everything in moderation, giving lots of space and time, including an understated Byard whose tasteful solo contrasts the stormy blues let loose by the barroom horn wizards. The pianist's skilled encyclopedism and stride eloquence were partially honed during tough stints with Mingus and as arranger/pianist with Maynard Ferguson's big band.

Flute tour de force 'Glad To Be Unhappy' de-escalates the intensity into an interiorized world defined not only by Dolphy's absolute control of tone and technique but by his extraordinary range of singing emotions. The middle section's torrid double-time cascades reveal a musician who wants listeners to know that he can play, with crystalline runs, trills, tremolos, and flutter-tonguing with snappy brilliance. The entire album is such a calling card on three instruments. Widely recorded trombonist Charles Greenlee composed 'Miss Toni,' and this version isn't the throwaway number it has sometimes been made out to be; Eric's bass clarinet solo purposefully incorporates the guttural cry, the broken shriek, the staccato punctuations, and the holler, as he moves away from the confines of phrasal expectations. This is a snippet of unbridled if not free jazz, framed by the arrangement's odd voicings and the solo's 'honk like a goose' testimony. And it is how Dolphy chooses to end his first outing as leader, an unspoken invitation to the next one.

Byard recalled the session over two decades later:

> His approach to everything was different, but it was most evident in his music. The tones and chords were laid out on paper, but his music at that session was simple. What made it special was Dolphy … [he] played great and took care of everything. He picked us for the date and Freddie was pretty innovative for that time. My playing was the same as usual, but he made you feel involved … He made sure we knew it was his first date and there were rehearsals.[2]

Continuing his five-star review, DeMichael wrote, 'Although Dolphy varies his conception on all three instruments—his flute is less like his bass clarinet than is his alto, there is a taut wire binding them all together: the power to transmit emotion from the player to the listener. And that's the mark of a real artist.' The review ends with, 'This album is life.'[3]

The late-blooming thirty-two-year-old from the then-misunderstood, near-mythic West Coast was an untested new voice for the East Coast jazz establishment, one easily heard as mature yet with room to grow. Confident and convincing as Dolphy's bass clarinet is on 'Miss Toni' and 'On Green Dolphin Street,' listeners can hear over the course of his very short recording career a steady improvement on the instrument, not just in tone and technical mastery, but more importantly in the increasingly daring material. Likewise, the flute work on 'Glad To Be Unhappy' shines on its own as surely as his later work on the instrument expands, moving to incorporate special effects, timbral experiment, birdsong microtonality, and more frequent attempts at the streetwise jazz expressivity that emerges more easily on reeds.

Richard 'Prophet' Jennings's striking painting *The Prophet* stares out from

Outward Bound's original, green-tinged cover, presenting a Dalí-esque nocturne of Afro-futurism depicting a dreaming, closed-eyed Eric, a rustic wooden 'Outward Bound' sign pointing to the starry night sky, a dark surrealism tethered to Earth only by the 'New Jazz 8236' catalog designation. The space-age scene is a precursor in some ways to Sun Ra's stellar ruminations. Sonny Rollins tells the story: 'My friend, Prophet Jennings . . . painted a nice portrait, a big oil painting of Eric . . . [who] had to come by my house in Brooklyn to get it. Prophet had left it with me . . . we became good friends.'[4]

From now until September of 1961, Eric would be a Prestige artist, appearing as leader on five albums during his lifetime, and as sideman on eight more of the label's releases. Bob Weinstock's label had emerged originally from his record store and had grown by early 1960 to include six subsidiary labels. Prestige's recent signing of early 'soul jazz' practitioners Jack McDuff, Richard 'Groove' Holmes, and Charles Earland indicated the management's desire to push the edges of the genre.

GUNTHER SCHULLER AND THIRD STREAM

Eric entered the Atlantic studios less than three weeks after the *Outward Bound* session to record numbers for R&B queen Ruth Brown, though none were released. He sat with A-list musicians, many of whom he would see again in further sessions with Brown in August: Ernie Royal, Julian Priester, George Coleman, Tommy Flanagan, and Kenny Burrell, among others. If the rest of April seemed slow, the latter half of May proved otherwise. On May 20, Eric appeared at Greenwich Village's Circle On The Square theater to perform with Ornette Coleman in the final spring installment of Gunther Schuller's *Jazz Profiles* concert series.

This was the beginning of an enduring, productive relationship with Schuller, as the two became close musical friends. The classically trained Schuller's interest in jazz conflated with the hybrid jazz-classical sensibilities of John Lewis, who in the early 1950s founded the classically infused Modern Jazz Quartet and co-founded the Lenox School Of Jazz (1957–1960). Lewis championed Coleman, inviting him to Lenox and helping to arrange his Atlantic contract. Dolphy too became one of third stream's primary soloists and multi-instrumentalists, appearing on many Schuller and Lewis projects.

Schuller had been on the inside of a 1950s jazz juggernaut, playing French horn for Miles Davis's *Birth Of The Cool* sessions, released in 1957. That same year, Schuller gave a watershed lecture at Brandeis University in which he spoke of an emerging sensibility of cross-fertilization between jazz and contemporary classical that he termed 'third stream.' In concert settings, various ensembles led by Schuller also played works by Stravinsky, Ives, Babbitt, Henze, Webern, and others, with some of their scores remaining among Eric's possessions at the time of his death. The composer/conductor incorporated Dolphy's well-rounded multi-instrumentalism and explosive post-bop style, and Ornette's free jazz blowing, as improvisational expansions of modernist concert music imbued with jazz techniques and instrumentation.

That Friday night in late May at Circle On The Square, Eric played flute, bass clarinet, and clarinet in the premieres of Schuller's music under his baton, including 'Abstraction,' 'Variants On A Theme By John Lewis (Django),' and 'Variants On A Theme By Thelonious Monk (Criss Cross).' Rounding out the ensemble was the Contemporary String Quartet, two drum sets, and a vibraphone augmenting the core quintet. Notable was the presence of pianist Bill Evans, who had recently formed his history-making trio with Scott LaFaro and Paul Motian and was enjoying a post–*Kind Of Blue* spotlight. Ornette played on 'Abstraction,' and in the same September *DownBeat* issue in which DeMicheal reviewed *Outward Bound*, George Hoefer shared his observations of the *Jazz Profiles* concert, writing that toward the end of that performance, 'There was a frantic ensemble sound when Dolphy, playing bass clarinet, joined Coleman.' The two friends who had met in Los Angeles's underground incubator of experimentation were now holding forth in New York as part of a chamber orchestra, where 'Dolphy's simultaneous improvisations wove in and out of the shrill alto sounds.'[5]

Later in the year, Dolphy had words for early critics of this creative path: 'It's just music, and it's good music. I wish people would quit saying jazz musician, and just say musician. If you can play jazz, you can play other things. There's so much good music that isn't being heard. Schoenberg and Berg and Bartok and Webern, they're just beginning to be heard.'[6] It is notable how Dolphy conjoins Schuller's third steam serialism with those big names of European modernism, exposing his self-perception of having moved closer to that tradition—of becoming part of New Music, the concert hall, and chamber orchestra circles, albeit of a jazz type.

MINGUS'S *PRE-BIRD*: 'BEMOANABLE LADY'

Four days later, Eric was again under Schuller's baton, recording Mingus's *Pre-Bird* album at Plaza Sound Studios, the instrumentation of which amounted to much more than a glorified Workshop club ensemble. With several reed players doubling—including Dolphy on alto sax, flute, and bass clarinet—the large ensemble comprised five trumpets, four trombones, tuba, three tenor sax, two alto sax, baritone sax, three flutes, oboe, clarinet, bass clarinet, piano, cello, and of course Mingus on bass. In addition to the drum kit were three percussionists, including Max Roach. 'Bemoanable Lady' spotlights Dolphy's unique sound, with scored melodic themes and clear sonic space reserved for his exquisite alto work, marking the first high-profile sideman solo in his post-Hamilton period. He stands close to the microphone, heard intimately within the big, near-orchestral charts, locking in his association with Mingus's jazz genius, the first of their many recordings both live and in the studio. (Martin Williams's original album liner notes mistakenly call attention to Eric's work on 'Do Nothin' Till You Hear From Me,' a tune on which he does not solo.) A *DownBeat* reviewer later wrote, 'A solo vehicle for Dolphy, *Bemoanable* contains the merest hint of a further genuflection toward Ellington. Dolphy is more appealing than I heretofore have heard.'[7]

That tune was one of three recorded on May 24, with five more set to tape the next day. His flute work shines on 'Weird Nightmare,' from that second session, in exchanges with fellow Workshop member and flutist Yusef Lateef, adding composed, supportive lines. Discographer Uwe Reichardt notes that for the second session, Eric played B-flat clarinet, but on which tune it is difficult to determine (Simosko and Tepperman do not list clarinet). Schuller, having heard Dolphy at Circle On The Square a few nights earlier, was now witnessing again his agile musicianship and fertile imagination in Mingus's thorny compositions. The 'Pre-Bird' concept refers to Mingus's creative period before Charlie Parker, its material and orchestration speaking not anachronistically to the cool revolt of the 50s but to the youthful Romantic universalism from which his compositional vision nearly forms a proto-third stream, predating Schuller's crossover ideals. 'Half-Mast Inhibition' attests to an expressionistic taste for dissonant sonorities and circuitous formal contrasts lying somewhere beyond jazz. Mingus believed in the authenticity of the soul and its direct expression through music improvisation, in the vibrancy of African American music culture and of jazz rhythm and harmony, but also in orchestral colors and fully notated composition.

OLIVER NELSON'S *SCREAMIN' THE BLUES*

The week of Circle On The Square and the *Pre-Bird* session was not yet over when Dolphy returned to the Van Gelder Studio on Friday, May 27, as a Prestige contract member of the Oliver Nelson Sextet for the aptly titled *Screamin' The Blues*. It was his first of three appearances on Nelson-led discs; in less than a year, he would also take part in the majestic *The Blues And The Abstract Truth* (Impulse) and *Straight Ahead* (not to be confused with Abbey Lincoln's Candid album of the same name, on which Dolphy also performs).* This three-album Nelson collaboration produced some of Eric's most important studio work as a sideman.

Born in St. Louis in 1932, Nelson came from a musical family, learning several instruments before coming under the spell of twentieth-century concert music. He decided to compose and arrange for large ensembles while serving in the military in Japan, after hearing live symphonic music for the first time at a Tokyo Philharmonic Orchestra concert featuring works by Ravel and Hindemith. Nelson wrestled with the racial segregation from which he emerged as a young musician, social and artistic barriers depriving him of even the dream of formal concert music participation, let alone of becoming a composer. 'Back in St. Louis,' he stated, 'I hadn't even known that Negroes were allowed to go to concerts.' As with so many other African American musicians who desired classical music training and opportunity (such as Mingus and Dolphy), these paths had been kept out of his reach. After completing his musical studies in Missouri, Nelson became a top arranger for the biggest names in jazz and house arranger for Harlem's Apollo Theater. His growing list of original compositions carried him into a busy Prestige contract, and he appeared as leader or sideman on eleven albums between 1959 and 1961.

Working on *Screamin' The Blues* also meant Dolphy would collaborate with Roy Haynes and George Duvivier. Haynes had just played on *Outward Bound* and would appear on Dolphy's two other albums as leader that year. The drummer also briefly included Dolphy in his own working club group with bassist Reggie Workman. Duvivier contributed bass to *Out There* and would join Eric on three other albums, including two tracks of Ron Carter's debut as leader, the 1961 LP *Where? Screamin' The Blues* trumpeter Richard Williams was a top-call player who

---

* For *Blues And The Abstract Truth*, Oliver Nelson and Eric Dolphy both appeared by arrangement with Prestige.

had sat in with Eric a few weeks earlier at the Ruth Brown date, then again at Mingus's *Pre-Bird* recordings. The two would get to know each other at future sessions with Brown, 'Lockjaw' Davis, Mingus, and during the recording of Hubbard's marvelous *The Body And The Soul* in March 1963. Nelson's session pianist, Richard Wyands, later joined Eric on two more recordings.

Screamin' The Blues is an essential part of Dolphy's sideman discography, particularly notable for his extensive use of alto. (There is also bass clarinet on one track, but no flute.) While some of these soulful numbers have the surface simplicity of the blues, their folksy pentatonic themes, gospel flavors, and pared-down harmonies fitting the form, Nelson's refined directness as tunesmith is heartfelt and rarely falls back on cliche: this is hard bop with roots music at the edges. The title track showcases Eric's bass clarinet, tearing at the blues fabric and pushing the instrument's technical and stylistic envelope. He first milks the testifying air with human cries, whispers, and speech-like acclamations; then, allowing for more silences than typically found in his solos, he dives into scurrying runs and scalar exploits covering the instrument's rich low end, emphasizing tones and timbres unusual in jazz. His 'Screamin' The Blues' solo compliments *Outward Bound*'s 'On Green Dolphin Street,' and 'Miss Toni,' continuing Dolphy's exploration of the bass clarinet's possibilities. Nat Hentoff described his solo as 'startlingly unexpected,' yet 'going back to the early jazz tradition of highly vocalized horn playing.'[8]

Producer Esmond Edwards's compositions 'March On, March On' and 'The Meetin'' are solid, joyous vehicles for Dolphy in particular, further solidifying this album as one crucial to his sideman legacy. On the former, he just jumps in with a magical, miniature workshop on innovative improvisation. It would be too easy to criticize Eric for playing beyond these tunes, or for hijacking their wholesome folksiness: he was hired to light the fireworks. Here he enters big and winds down with no time for a build-up, the sharp solo's rocket launch quickly readjusting toward a trill that fades into Wyands's solo.

'Three Seconds' is a compositionally self-conscious number, the clumsy arrangement and restless sensibility of which just waits for Eric to pierce the atmosphere with lightning. The alto starts with fire, but it is ultimately one of his less-than-electric moments, throwaway sequences juggling too many awkward tones that fail to connect. The three-way trading fours following Wyand's solo offers a chance at redemption, though Dolphy mishandles the opportunity with a shrill abruptness, lacking direction and luster. Such lesser performances are rare, his work on a shaky 'Three Seconds' revealing a risky flipside to his improvisation strategies.

Simosko and Tepperman accurately characterize Dolphy's 'striking' presence on the album as contributing to an 'experimental sound,' and *Screamin'* has far less of the (arguable) imbalance some would soon hear on Ken McIntyre's *Looking Ahead.*[9] For Nat Hentoff, Eric here is an example of a 'non-embalmed sidemen… Dolphy is, along with Ornette Coleman, the most venturesome and original young alto saxophonist in jazz. He plays with unremittingly fierce emotion and often daring imagination.'

Written with Dolphy in mind, Nelson's 'Alto-Itis' echoes Eric's 'G.W.' and 'Les,' its head a thorny, angular two-voice counterpoint with post-bebop aggressiveness. The leader's warm alto tone and comparatively reserved solo contrasts sharply with Eric's variegated tone and fearlessly independent approach. 'The Drive' has a near-commercial appeal with an easygoing yet powerful tunefulness. Here, Eric stabs the air with invective and sustained onslaughts, using his signature riff as a sign-off as he hands things over to the underrated Wyands. Appealing and warm, 'The Drive' comes off as the optimistic, homogenous work of a cohesive, long-standing band.

Screamin' The Blues was released in January 1961 and subsequently reissued in 1964, following Eric's death. The 1967 pressing by the UK label Xtra features on its cover a full-bleed portrait of Eric. Nelson's successes led to film and television positions as composer and arranger, precipitating his move to Los Angeles. He would maintain a vital career in the jazz world with big-band and saxophone performances. He died of a heart attack at age forty-three in 1975.

LATE SPRING/SUMMER 1960

In 1958, Hentoff and fellow jazz writer Martin Williams, both early supporters of Eric's, founded the short-lived magazine *The Jazz Review*. In the June 1960 issue, Williams interviewed Dolphy for his feature article 'Introducing Eric Dolphy' and elicited some technical detail from the newcomer: 'Yes, I think of my playing as tonal. I play notes that would not ordinarily be said to be in a given key, but I hear them as proper. I don't think I *leave the changes*, as the expression goes; every note I play has some reference to the chords of the piece.' Williams presciently continues, 'Comparisons between Dolphy's work and Ornette Coleman's are probably inevitable and will just as probably plague both of them from now on.'[10]

Following his work with Nelson, and before his upcoming role with Mingus at the Newport Jazz Festival, Eric had time to address his own work, composing, rehearsing original ideas, and further perfecting his sound. The Prestige artist was preparing for August's *Out There*, his second disc as a leader, to which he would bring four originals and arrangements of three pieces by Mingus, Hale Smith, and Randy Weston.

In May, the fast-rising John Coltrane headlined the Jazz Gallery, splitting bills with the Chico Hamilton Quintet. *Daily News* reviewer Don Nelson described Dolphy's old unit as 'vastly more swinging than former Hamilton groups . . . Carrington Visor, a tenor sax, clarinet, and flute man, is a standout.' Eric's time with Hamilton was his most financially secure, and those days were long over. He had moved on, and though it is possible he gigged around town before the June 28 recording date for Ken McIntyre's *Looking Ahead*, there are no such reports, reviews, or concert announcements.

Good times perked Dolphy up, such as when, about this time, Los Angeles friends Lester Robinson and Horace Tapscott stayed at his place while on tour with Lionel Hampton, but such dry periods began to unnerve; waves of club and studio activity followed by weeks during which the telephone did not ring.

Eric Sr. and Sadie remembered their son calling and writing home frequently, and on several occasions during the remaining years of his life, he would fly home to Los Angeles unannounced. There waited with his parents and old friends, the bedroom he called home from the ages of six to thirty (save for his Army stint), and a backyard shed full of memories. No doubt his inner flame welcomed such rekindling before he returned to a sometimes lonely New York. More than anything else, the ambitious musician practiced. Some of his technique and exercise books included H. Klose's *125 Daily Studies For Saxophone*, *The Developing Flautist* by Norman Dello, and Arban and Vanasek's *Daily Drills for Clarinet*; his collection of scores included, among other works, 'Rag-Time' by Igor Stravinsky, 'In The Inn' by Charles Ives, 'Partita In A Minor For Flute' by J.S. Bach, and Milton Babbitt's 'All Set.'[11] If during June Dolphy did become a bit lonely and worried about his career, he patiently shook it off and looked to summer: a June 28 recording date with fellow Prestige artist Ken McIntyre; some personal, creative studio time dedicated to learning classical Indian music; the Mingus/Roach–led 'rebellion' at Newport; his first trip to Europe for the Mingus ensemble appearance at the Jazz à Juan Festival in Juan-Les-Pins, Antibes, France; and, at the end of July, further work on John Lewis's Third Steam music with *The Wonderful World Of Jazz.*

LOOKING AHEAD

The original Prestige/New Jazz album cover for *Looking Ahead* presents McIntyre as leader and Dolphy as featured sideman, with a photo of the two side by side, Eric's name beneath his collaborator's in a slightly smaller font. Producer Esmond Edwards advocated for McIntyre, an unknown twenty-nine-year-old who had submitted to the label an unsolicited, self-produced audition tape. The newcomer recalled of the session that, 'I could not at times help feeling a bit left out of all the qualitative nuances that I felt while Eric and the rhythm section were playing,' adding that 'they had the New York feel … I was in fact an outsider.'[12] The rest of the line-up appearing at Van Gelder Studio on that Tuesday, June 28, included pianist Walter Bishop Jr., bassist Sam Jones, and Art Taylor on drums. The altoist McIntyre doubled on flute and composed all the material, save for Gershwin's 'They All Laughed.'

'Lautir' ('Ritual' spelled backward) starts off with an introverted twist, a unison melody in a staid, off-kilter rhythm, an asymmetric series of plain, unadorned notes in twelve bars that are then repeated. McIntyre's arguably academic-sounding compositions (he studied at Boston Conservatory and Brandeis) tend to be mismatched by Dolphy's technical skill, expressive passion, and modern style, and on this opening track, Dolphy's flute instantly makes one forget the alto solo McIntyre has just played.

'Curtsy' is a fun, aggressive tune that matches the two altoists. As with Nelson's alto challenge on *Screamin' The Blues*, these two sound miles apart in tone, range, and improvisational gravitas. McIntyre later stressed that Prestige stipulated Eric's presence on the disc. What else could explain his comments in an interview with *DownBeat's* Don Heckman, who wrote, 'Like many young musicians who have arrived on the scene after Ornette Coleman, McIntyre has been bunched into a group casually labeled the jazz avant-garde. But even a cursory hearing of McIntyre's music reveals that his melodic and rhythmic conceptions are far removed from the work of Coleman, Eric Dolphy, Don Ellis, et al.' McIntyre then frankly added, 'There is basically no difference in my approach from that, say, of Johnny Hodges with his small group, or any mainstream or traditional group.'[13]

'Geo's Tune' is a soulful, riff-based riddle of harmonizing altos, its long theme delivered in two parts. The exuberant deluge of Dolphy's solo seems to overpower the studio, and in the following trading section, broken up by Taylor's drums, McIntyre and Dolphy each rant through an admirable exchange that finds the former holding his own. On a fine version of 'They All Laughed,' Eric again excels on alto, playing through conservative sequences before relaxing into real singing passages traversing his new thing vocabulary.

'Head Shakin'' is a swinging, laid-back R&B romp, with Bishop taking the first sweet solo. The gutsy presence of Eric's deep alto blues grows into astonishing pyrotechnics, including an exceptional, extended set of short riffs that constitute for him a rare process of rhythmic variations and rephrased repetitions with a shotgun array of metric displacements, perhaps hinting at Coltrane's technique of extrapolating from limited intervallic and rhythmic gestures. The narrow passage gradually widens to include cries and blues wailing straight from Central Avenue.

'Dianna' plays out with McIntyre's lead flute riding high above a restless bass clarinet before the leader takes an overly careful solo. This track sees Dolphy's restrained 'singsong' lyricism change gears in the last chorus as he plays super-facile runs, arpeggios, and highly ornamented melodic gestures. It is from plateau tunes such as 'Dianna' that one can gauge his development on the instrument and his increased daring on what to play (even jumping in early with his solo when McIntyre had one more chorus planned). In the trading before the refrain, one hears him alternate purely chordal melodic figures with sharp-edged humoresque shouts and polite explosions of farewell.

To some listeners, the *Looking Ahead* material does not consistently hold up in comparison to Eric's soloistic provocations, its numbers too straight for post-bop divergences. Notwithstanding such imbalances, the album remains a strong testament to Dolphy's artistic spirit and growing stature as a sideman. According to McIntyre, producer Edwards dictated who soloed and for how long. *Looking Ahead* later appeared as one disc of Dolphy's double-LP Prestige 24000 series reissue album *Fire Waltz* (1978), its cover given over entirely to Dolphy's name and image, with the added cover acknowledgment, 'Featuring Ken McIntyre, Booker Ervin, and Mal Waldron.'* His *Looking Ahead* solos have been transcribed by Andrew White and published through Andrew's Music.

* The other disc in the Dolphy *Fire Waltz* reissue is *The Quest*, originally attributed on its release in 1962 to leader Mal Waldron, 'with Eric Dolphy and Booker Ervin.'

THE NEWPORT REBELS

The adventurous, devil-may-care Dolphy provided an elemental edginess and avant-garde depth to Mingus's music. In turn, rather than corralling Eric's sound, Mingus encouraged his progressive explorations. Like other post-bop musicians, he and Dolphy were promoting jazz as art music, redefining and transcending entertainment, establishing new contexts for flights of freedom and controlled doses of free jazz.

The healthy aesthetic challenge Mingus was so willing to deliver to audiences was not compromised when he learned that July's Newport Jazz Festival was offering less pay and disadvantageous daytime schedules to progressive, Black jazz acts. Mingus contacted Max Roach and producer Nat Hentoff to coordinate a response to festival producer George Wein's unsatisfactory offers. To assist in producing an alternative stage in protest, Hentoff contacted festival board member Lorraine Lorillard, the recently divorced wife of Wein's most prominent financial backer. She helped enlist the Cliff Walk Manor Hotel as an alternate stage location and the hotel grounds as a camping space for musicians, near the official festival site at Freebody Park. Tents were pitched to house the protesting musicians; even while welcoming their music, the segregated hotel had denied accommodation for Mingus and others because they were Black. (In an unrelated incident that weekend, white teenagers attacked official festival grounds with bottles and cans in a drunken riot against the establishment.)

In addition to the Mingus Quintet, the festival walkouts included a generous sampling from the jazz community: Ornette Coleman and his group with Don Cherry, Ed Blackwell, and Charlie Haden; the Max Roach ensemble, including Abbey Lincoln, Ahmed Abdul-Malik, Booker Little, Walter Benton, and Julian Priester; Wilbur Ware, Art Taylor, Allen Eager, Kenny Drew, Teddy Charles, and all of Kenny Dorham's group; plus others including Jimmy Knepper, Coleman Hawkins, Jo Jones, and Roy Eldridge. Collectively, they protested both the diminishing of festival standards and the unjust compensation. With a seating capacity of less than five hundred, the old oceanfront hotel attracted roughly two hundred concertgoers over the weekend. The performances went unrecorded. Wein later called the rebel action 'a masterpiece of public relations. . . . When I came back to Newport in 1962 to restart the festival, the first person I hired was Charles Mingus.'[14] The white riot got the press, however, with few mainstream outlets covering the alternative stage and its backstory.

In the meantime, *DownBeat* editor Gene Lee scouted festival shots with his camera, looking to capture some of the weekend drama, and spotted a pensive Eric Dolphy practicing flute by the seashore near the Cliff Walk Manor:

> I took several photographs before he saw me and broke the mood. He said he had found this secluded place among the rocks and had been coming here to practice in quiet. He said he hoped to buy an alto flute soon because of its warm, haunting tone. I left after that. … Eric stayed on the rocks, his flute seeming to whisper to the waves, and the waves whispered back. And that's what music is all about, really.[15]

The image was a balm of sorts, smoothing over acrimony with peaceful imagery, and it made the cover of the issue dated August 18, 1960, alongside the title 'Newport Festival: Trouble And Aftermath.' From those long-ago backyard bird conversations, Eric now conversed with the Atlantic Ocean, across which he would soon travel.

The Newport action can be seen in the context and contours of the Civil Rights Movement, the period 1955–60 witnessing dramatic successes and gruesome retaliations. The year following the court victory of Brown vs. Board Of Education in 1954, the nation came face to face with newspaper photos of the ghastly Emmett Till murder. The Montgomery bus boycott that grew from the Rosa Parks incident was followed by 1957's Little Rock Central High School integration battlefront. At the time of the Newport rebellion, non-violent sit-ins at segregated diners introduced a broad movement, gaining the general public's attention. That August, New York's Village Gate hosted a 'Jazz Sit In' fundraiser sponsored by the New York chapter of the Congress Of Racial Equality (CORE). It included Monk's quintet, Clark Terry's quintet, and others, all in support of the Southern student movement. The 'Newport Rebels' name and protest atmosphere extended to a Hentoff-produced November recording and subsequent Candid album that overlapped with the short-lived Jazz Artists Guild.

'IMPROVISATIONS & TUKRAS'

Dolphy's journey beyond jazz tradition rebooted at the start of July's second week, when he entered Stereo Sound Studios to record with tabla player and dancer Gina Lalli and tamboura player Roger Mason. Lalli was, like Eric, a brilliant child of immigrants, born to Italian parents in Upstate New York in 1929. At twenty-three, she began studies in Indian dance and religion in New York City after seeing Uday Shankar's 'Hindu Ballet' tour, featuring his younger brother Ravi on sitar. Lalli then studied Sanskrit and spent long periods in India, learning the classical dance techniques of *Kathak* and *Bharatanatyam*—North and South traditions, respectively—as well as the *veena* lute and the tabla.

Never intended for commercial release and thus incongruously included on Blue Note's 1987 Dolphy album *Other Aspects*, 'Improvisations & Tukras' was a recorded lesson focusing on cadential tabla patterns known as *tukras*. Eric plays a cyclically repeating, non-improvised flute obligato while Lalli plays and vocalizes *tukra* cadential approaches to select *sam* (or downbeats) of the sixteen-beat pattern. The session was likely an outgrowth of at least one previous lesson, though there is no further background on their relationship. The flute part demands stamina and focus, yet is a didactic template for further practice.

Dolphy's ideal next step would have been to internalize the *tukra* phrases (ultimately embedded in the music itself, rather than vocalized, as Lalli demonstrates on the recording), adding them to the structural cadences of improvised melody, employing an appropriate raga, and adapting the technique for his own music. In studying Indian music, he was seeking technique and inspiration from a culture he knew something about, having listened closely to recordings and having met Ravi Shankar. He wanted to go inside the theory and practice and play with Indian musicians and instruments. Dolphy knew of Yusef Lateef's advances in cross-cultural music, and like Coltrane and other jazz musicians of his day, he felt some degree of commonality with various non-Western and ancient music systems as invigorating, culturally appropriate alternatives.

Lateef left the Mingus Workshop in June, giving Eric plenty of time to gather what he could of that artist's fascinating global sounds. These are certainly topics he discussed with Coltrane and took up in informal rehearsals. He later shared with Leonard Feather:

> So, with them [musicians from India], like in talking to Mr. Shankar, Ravi Shankar, they study for quite a while to get enough material to even work with. So, like, not to say that the musicians are just doing this to keep up with the Indian musicians, but I think that it's a little connection there, because, classical Indian music is the Indian music of the people, and jazz

is the music of the American people, especially the American Negro, and it's their music, so quite naturally, there's something of a connection there, of people expressing themselves in the same way.[16]

MINGUS WORKSHOP AT ANTIBES

Dolphy's first trip abroad was fast approaching: five days after the tukras recording, he would be onstage with the Workshop at the Antibes Jazz Festival on the South of France's Côte d'Azur. From the Showplace group via Newport, the Workshop continued with Dolphy and a very solid piano-less quintet including Curson, Richmond, and Booker Ervin as Lateef's replacement, taking the festival stage at Juan-les-Pins on July 13. The well-rehearsed band tore up the place, and Bud Powell, the heralded bebop giant who had moved to Paris in 1959, joined for a rare appearance on a whimsical 'I'll Remember April.' The recordings went unheard for years, however, leaving jazz fans unaware of the entirety of this phenomenal live work until 1976.*

Soloists that afternoon left no stone unturned. 'Wednesday Night Prayer Meeting' finds Eric playing what some have referred to as his best alto on record, steering the group sound into a searing melting pot of intense musical ideas. Critic Robert Palmer would describe him as 'burbling volubly like an entranced, tongue-talking devotee over the band's sanctified-style handclapping.'[17] The prescient, socially conscious 'Prayer For Passive Resistance' is an off-kilter blues that starts with a funky repeating bass riff and horn jabs. Then it's Booker Ervin's moment, and he sails into a meditative solo against curiously busy Dolphy/Curson background interjections. A volatile suite of blues-based ideas as sectional and episodic as any Mingus piece, 'Prayer' relies on the soloist's angularity to ward off any sign of normalcy. Mingus brings the dynamics down to intense intimacy before blasting the crowd once more with soulful, tutti choruses to close.

Playing to an audience that had never seen such a spectacle, 'What Love' finds Eric on bass clarinet joining Mingus's bass solo, the two creating a compelling, conversational duet with Richmond's polite punctuation. Eric had stumbled across

---

* Jean Luc Young was with Barclay's Music in 1960, and as a founding member of the French label BYG, he helped release a Japanese printing of *Charles Mingus Live With Eric Dolphy* in 1974. Barclay's recorded the concert for Atlantic Records, as did the French national radio network ORTF for its own ORTF broadcast. In 1976, sixteen years after the performance, Atlantic released a double album, *Mingus In Antibes*.

'What Love' at Mingus's apartment and 'remarked on how much like Ornette Coleman's music it sounded.'[18] Mingus then shaped the tune's presentation to meet free jazz head-on. Legendary are the Mingus and Dolphy 'conversations,' which got their start when Eric responded musically to being mocked by Mingus during a Showcase gig, the back and forth subsequently developing into a well-planned improvisational schema. In October, they would record over four minutes of a further cultivated 'conversation' embedded in 'What Love' for Candid's *Charles Mingus Presents Charles Mingus.* Yet the Antibes audience does not know what to think; some initially whistle their displeasure at what they likely interpreted as the bass clarinet's strangeness while others whoop encouragement then shout in acknowledgment of the music's provocative discourse. Ultimately, applause drowns out the tense reception of what amounted to a rarely heard before free duo. Adding to the moment are the surprising compositional elements of 'What Love,' an episodic journey with stark contrasts of tempo, textural density, themes, subthemes, and developmental variations telescoping in and out of purifying improvisational flair, and structured moments of stylistic reference to gospel, blues, swing, and bebop.

'I'll Remember April,' notable also for Powell's presence, features a playful, sometimes reserved alto solo from Dolphy, who then spices up the extended trading with Ervin as the tune bends to accommodate the freewheeling duo. The number closes with a party of sound. The funky blues of 'Folk Forms No. 1' blossoms into a polyphonic maze of curt riffs soon pared down to a super-focused Dolphy, who unfortunately steps away from the mic a bit too much. The old-school pentatonic free-for-all gives way from old New Orleans to a wistful bass solo. In steps Eric with Richmond, soon supported by a muted Curson, then a pensive Ervin. It's a barnburner when they all turn on at once, a mad dash through gut-bucket jazz history. Mingus guides them to the end of his many-sided piece, in and out of exposed solo material followed by joyous, saloon cacophony. The French applaud the old-time music.

Eric walks across the stage to the microphone at the five-minute mark of 'Better Get Hit In Yo' Soul' to talk some sense into those who want to listen, cutting loose with dangerously outlandish playing. His alto spits out sparks; he's playing as percussively and vehemently as he's ever played on a recording. The violent attack employs all of the strange words that nobody uses, then tapers down to a Richmond drum break as onlookers cheer the dynamite explosion they've just witnessed. Mingus, it seems, has harnessed the wind, fire, water, and air, and he eggs them on into a finale for the ages. Backstage, the Workshop greeted passing members of Hans Koller's band, including pianist Karl Berger, who four years later would invite Eric to play in Berlin.

African American artists had been touring, visiting, and relocating to parts of Europe for decades, some finding more socially welcoming racial conditions, better economic opportunities, and more freedom to explore their disciplines than what they had in the USA. One cannot help thinking of Miles Davis's Paris sojourn in 1957, filled with love, hope, a broad sense of unquestioned stardom, and personal awakenings—much of which was squashed on his return to racist America. There is simply no denying the role of Europe in the tragic envelope of Dolphy's life: he would return several times as a citizen of the world to find appreciative audiences and colleagues within new musical horizons, and a hopeful life full of plans with fiancé Joyce Mordecai. Returning to New York after Antibes in mid-July of 1960, he savored the applause, and he had no reason to question the brightness of the coming months of late summer: a July 29 session for John Lewis's *The Wonderful World Of Jazz* (released on Atlantic in 1961); more work with the Mingus Workshop throughout August, in the Jazz Artists Guild's concerts; an East Coast reunion with his parents and New York family; a move out of 245 Carlton (following noise complaints) to a lower Manhattan apartment on South Street; and making the cover of *DownBeat* three days after recording his second album as leader, *Out There*.

On August 7, the *New York Daily News* announced the East 74th Street Theater's Jazz Artists Guild concert series starting the following evening: 'Two concerts nightly from August 8th thru August 28th at 8 and 11:30pm. Matinee at 2:30 on Saturday and Sunday.' The title of the ambitious schedule of performances was 'Music In The Clift Walk Manner' (with 'Cliff' intentionally misspelled by Mingus), meaning that the rebellious spirit of the Newport Jazz Festival's alternative Cliff Walk Manor rebel concert would imbue these performances and include some of those musicians. While not openly referencing the intensifying Civil Rights Movement, the Mingus/Roach–led series was an attempt to break free from the jazz industry's standard business model and to gain some independence and control for African American musicians.

Working on *Out There* and the Latin Jazz Quintet's *Caribé* in early August, Dolphy took a breather from Mingus's Workshop, which in addition to the Jazz

Artists Guild concert series appearances played two weeks at Pep's in Philadelphia. The *Out There* liner notes mention (but with no further details of his involvement) that Dolphy attended at least two rehearsals that late summer for a Max Roach–led pit orchestra pulled together for an off-Broadway production of Jean Genet's radically inflammatory play *The Blacks: A Clown Show*. After a delayed opening on May 4, 1961, the show, originally written for an all-Black cast, ran for 1,408 performances at the St. Marks Playhouse before closing in late September of 1964, making it at the time one of the longest-running theater productions not on Broadway. Though he opted out after preparing to participate, it is noteworthy that Eric signed up for this confrontational production of avant-garde theater, featuring among other great African American actors Cicely Tyson, Maya Angelou, Roscoe Lee Browne, James Earl Jones, and Louis Gossett Jr.*

OUT THERE

For his second Prestige album as leader, Dolphy created a piano-less quartet with cello, inviting the rhythm section of Haynes and Duvivier back to Van Gelder's studio on August 15. The disc's avant-garde material and timbral darkness represented a new direction in jazz, with a nod to the Chico Hamilton Quintet's chamber-like qualities and the last bassist Eric worked within that group, twenty-three-year-old Ron Carter, on cello. As Joe Goldberg states regarding their time in that quintet, Carter 'would jam on the instrument whenever he got the chance, and Eric was highly impressed with what he heard—he had found, if you wish, a soulmate in the group.'[19] When he met Dolphy, Carter was just out of the Eastman School Of Music and was now on his first major label studio gig while working on a Manhattan School Of Music master's degree.

With no second horn or piano the quartet foregrounded and exposed his flute, alto saxophone, and bass clarinet, foregoing two-voice wind/wind or wind/brass arrangements (regarding the lack of a harmony instrument on this album, it is interesting to note that Dolphy never invited a guitarist to any of his album sessions). Rather, the cello doubles, harmonizes, or counterpoints Eric's lines, its

* The play—an expressionist drama on the hypocrisies of racial politics, racial stereotypes, and colonialism—was published in 1958 to commemorate Ghana's declaration of independence in 1957. The cast shockingly re-enacts the violent murder of a white woman, a ritualistic play within a play of then-tasteless dialogue performed for other Black cast members made up in white-face and portraying stock figures of colonial authority, including a bishop, a judge, and the queen.

mid-to-high range speaking more quickly and clearly than its lower range, and for scored melodies this creates a convincing composite sound with Dolphy's instruments. Its mid-to-low register is slower to emerge, but its rich harmonics blend effectively with the winds in a wider range of timbral results. Dolphy's bass clarinet on 'Serene' and 'The Baron' brings the deeper range of the *chalumeau* register to meet Carter on his own sonic turf.

'Out There' is Dolphy's driving title track, an asymmetric array of strong-willed, hard-bop melodic lines pairing Eric's alto with bowed cello, set into an oddly numbered AABA pattern of 7+7+9+7 bar sections. It is somewhat reminiscent of 'Les' with its playfully unexpected accents; some of the cello's bowing tangles with the reed instrument's immediate attack, creating an experimental stamp for the album. At the time, the cello was on the rise as an outlier jazz instrument, and Carter gets his first solo over the bouncy yet exacting walking bass, his early long, held notes wavering beyond a wide vibrato, in and out of tune. With Haynes and Duvivier holding down a clockwork grid, the faster tempo is a challenge for the cellist's slower-sounding attack. Eric swings and plays into a lot of on-beat hits in his solo, adding to a rounder collaboration with Duvivier's pulsating bass and Haynes's brushes. He is playing it somewhat straight throughout his moment in the spotlight, considering this is the title track on his album as leader: he's not 'out there.' The handful of special effects—such as sliding through a smear of pitches, obsessing on a short rhythmic riff, and blurting out metrically stressed non-chordal tones—are politely caged as his melodic onslaught plays out. But before he passes the mic to Duvivier, his insistent statements break a bit more toward the fragmented and unpredictable. (Ripe for interpretation is the fact that 'Out There' would later be rescored, renamed, and rerecorded as a new title track, 'Far Cry,' in December.)

Like Mingus, Carter played cello first before mastering the bass. During his many fine moments on this album, his cello excels at defining this new sound world, though intonation problems briefly undermine the quality of several tracks. Simosko and Tepperman would later confirm that 'a statement attributed to Carter indicates that in fact he was not well that day, and was having some difficulty playing,' adding that Carter's sound is diffuse, at times faltering, and that 'one can conclude that many of these effects were unintentional.'[20] Bill Kirchner indirectly acknowledges this issue by noting that most jazz bassists who double on cello limit themselves to pizzicato technique, adding, 'If Carter's arco execution on the cello was sometimes less than exemplary, this is to be expected from a doubler; I know of no one who has managed to play both cello and bass at a world-class level.'[21] The same author would note that Prestige owner Bob Weinstock demanded one-day sessions without time for rehearsal, the label's philosophy holding that 'unrehearsed jazz was superior in terms of improvised freshness.' If true, this policy also might account for the lack of second takes of problematic performances.

Another *Out There* tune later rerecorded for *Far Cry* is the timeless Dolphy composition 'Serene,' its wandering, lazy twelve-bar blues feel slowly unfolding with bass clarinet and cello in unison. This is the shining star of the August session due to the theme's intangible character, the high quality of soloing, and instrumental balance. In the head, Eric blends his instrument's tone as if it were a baritone sax while exploring its upper mid-range with command, his solo welcoming listeners back from where he left off with *Outward Bound*'s final track, 'Miss Toni.' Van Gelder's recording is crystal clear and captures the richness of the instrument's low end, with the artist showing off post-bop mannerisms and a conversational method of speech-like utterances and human cries. 'Serene' gently pokes listeners with humorous innuendo and bewildering virtuosity. In the background, Haynes lifts and carries Duvivier's expressive bass essay, and, in one of the album's high points, Carter's pizzicato cello joins in this forest of plucked, low strings. These moments make *Out There* the special work that it is. And, to the composer's credit, the drums and bass clarinet exchange wonderful eights before the tune's limpid magic returns.

As on 'Serene,' Eric goes with bass clarinet and welds his sound closely to Carter on 'The Baron,' the cellist quickly launching his best solo of the album. The theme is a thorny musical profile of Mingus, who, during his youthful devotion to Duke Ellington, adopted his own noble title of 'Baron.' It may have been the first musical homage to the composer, adumbrated in the uneven AABA form of 9+9+8+9—as perplexing as Mingus himself, yet also as entertaining and endearing. One cannot help but imagine the expressive amalgam of Eric's brief solo as a salve, as much as a homage, offered to Mingus, who throughout the year had been staging his bass/bass clarinet confrontations to the delight of Workshop audiences while also pestering and verbally confronting the reedman. 'He writes very strong, daring music,' Eric said of Mingus, 'and it's a ball to play with him.'[22] Carter's false entrance during Eric's solo is strange, as is the cut's brevity.

As the album further explores the shadows of new jazz sonics, the group tackles Mingus's pungent 1948 ballad penned for Billie Holiday, 'Eclipse.' Though 'not representative of Mingus's best writing,' according to Goldberg, 'Eclipse' 'most approximates the way Eric feels about him.'[23] It was also the first time that a Mingus piece was recorded without his presence as a performer. In Dolphy's otherworldly arrangement, which includes his B-flat clarinet, a short, flowering intro of ascending low notes brings in the gravely slow opening in which Duvivier's bowed double bass is sometimes a pedal point, sometimes a moving line pitched well below the cello and clarinet as they carefully navigate the melody. Haynes casually ticks out sporadic time on his ride cymbal. The tune then slides into a slightly brisker pace, with Carter providing an improvised, sometimes wavering countermelody to Eric's super-clean tone. Duvivier walks slowly and simply through the progression's chords. This little gem of a third stream piece, as effective as any chamber work by Schuller or Lewis, finds in its final line a superbly mysterious air of clarinet and bowed string harmonics and a general shift to 'out there.'

'17 West' is another admirable example of Dolphy's penchant for driving, post-bop angularity in up-tempo heads, capturing a roving sense of freedom where flute and cello map wonderfully over a tight rhythm section. The title, notes Goldberg, 'is part of a former Manhattan address.'[24] The closing cadence of the head's repeated sections has Carter effectively jabbing double stops, playing a riff that comes back to punctuate Eric's luminous solo. Carter's agility is showcased in a playful, technically demanding solo, while his arco comments on Duvivier's soulful bass solo bring his instrument into an effective light. Haynes provides a fun solo break before the head's reprise. The outro fades like a pop tune, Van Gelder throwing an excess of reverb on the disappearing quartet.

Two tracks remain on the album side. Randy Weston's 'Sketch Of Melba,' a touching ballad dedicated to the remarkable trombonist, composer, and arranger Melba Liston, develops into a flute vehicle occasionally touched by the cello's intonation problems. As is the case on more than a handful of Dolphy tracks throughout his career, his passionate, authoritative soloing wins the day, a vital composition within a composition.

Hale Smith's 'Feathers' is one of the album's most solid musical tracks, a dark tone poem brought alive through each player's unique contribution and achieving its compositional goals with expressive clarity. Dolphy's solo brings listeners back to the album's post-bop alterity and purpose as a heterogeneous deviation from the jazz norm and tradition—a vehicle for cathartic expression. As with 'Eclipse,' this short chamber piece equals the best of what Lewis and Schuller promulgated as third stream. One wonders how a Dolphy album of Hale Smith works would have landed in the jazz world. For his second album as leader, Eric chooses again to close side B with a restless musical question, a gesture quietly asking audiences to come back for the next show. That will be December's *Far Cry*.

Prestige took over a year to release the album. When they did, *Out There* received mixed reviews while solidifying Dolphy as an innovative avant-garde outlier due to the album's glowingly dark, chamber-like instrumentation and moody atmosphere, in which he delivers artful, burnished solos on all three of his instruments. The album embraces a challenging sliver of what some may consider third stream compositions by Mingus and Smith. Molly Sants comments that, in this music, Dolphy 'reveals a shadowy side, but also depth and purpose that were unprecedented and remain singularly unique.'[25]

There are forty-four known *Out There* reissues: five by Prestige in the USA during the 1960s, nine by Prestige Japan, and multiple others by international labels. Its darkly sepia, Dalí-esque album cover, again by Richard Jennings, is a classic bookend to his stunning *Outward Bound* artwork, portraying an otherworldly sci-fi landscape of determined solitude: a starship of bass, cello, flute, and giant cymbal sailing through space, carrying Eric, jamming on his alto, approaching a planetary surface's lonely metronome and music score nestled in a square hole. Sheets of music score are blowing off the starship, pages drifting and curling in the glare of a new morning—or is it a bronze twilight?

This music's daringly thick and lurid new sound doubled down on *Outward Bound*'s originality and brilliant breadth of compositional and improvisational ideas. But 1960 was far from over, and Dolphy would sprint to its finish line, leaving a historically impressive wake of sound.

05 CANDID, *FREE JAZZ*, *FAR CRY*

AUGUST–DECEMBER 1960

At some point during the late summer of 1960, Eric vacated 245 Carleton, at least partly due to neighborhood noise complaints, heading across the East River to a loft on South Street in Lower Manhattan that lacked a functional heater. The Brooklyn home had been an unusually productive musical haunt—a bright spot on the cultural map of jazz history where tunes were written, rehearsals held, and ideas exchanged among masters of their art. '245' is part of *Outward Bound*, as it was most of Dolphy's live sets thereafter, a bluesy marker of that legendary social space. In turn, 'South Street Exit' would emerge as a new Dolphy tune in 1962.

The relocation echoed Dolphy's first year in New York, moving upward and outward, seeking and finding, landing on his feet with horns in hand. He had a visit from Sadie to look forward to, his mother traveling from Los Angeles the second week of August with plans to rendezvous in New York with a friend returning from a Caribbean tour. Sadie's sister Luzmilda and her family were certainly part of the reunion; her sixteen-year-old son Lorenzo was already a budding poet and writer steering toward the African and Afro-Caribbean roots he later celebrated in work associated with New York City's Black Arts Movement and the Umbra writing workshop. Sadie may have been in New York during the *Out There* session, a few days before Eric appeared on *DownBeat*'s cover in the enigmatic seaside photo from Cliff Walk Manor's rocky shore at Newport.

This exposure and artistic acknowledgment validated Dolphy's sense of mission, confirmed his aesthetic path, and illuminated the way in his search for new sounds. Mysteries of the little-known multi-instrumentalist were conveyed in that photograph; he was not a lone artist playing to no one but an element of nature blowing for the world to listen. The magazine cover delivered a vision of this jazz Pan's love for his beautiful Syrinx, mythically transformed into panpipes. The image of Dolphy's calm and introversion juxtaposed the cathartic fires he set on the stages and recording studios wherever he performed. He moved out of Brooklyn and into the view of a curious, international jazz audience.

Sadie stayed in New York long enough to attend another family get-together including Joyce, Dolphy's real-life Syrinx. She remembered meeting him in the fall of 1960, 'when his family came to my home, it's like an old family relationship from generations back. So when we met, I just assumed that he was one of my cousins.'[1] She was one of ten children of Jamaican immigrants Ross and Beryl Mordecai, who arrived in New York via Panama in 1920. Joyce grew up in Brooklyn, studied dance, and embarked on a performing career in the early 1950s. During 1953–54, she toured the USA extensively as a cast member in stage productions of *Carmen Jones* and *Salome* and appeared on a CBS-TV broadcast featuring Jackie Gleason. In 1955, she studied in France with members of the Paris Opera.

The *DownBeat* cover presaged a new thing storm that would include Dolphy's close musical friends and free jazz acquaintances. It was around this time that Roy Haynes hired Eric and Reggie Workman for a regular gig near the Village Vanguard. They attracted the attention of Coltrane, who watched their shows and would hire all three within a year. McCoy Tyner and Elvin Jones joined Coltrane and his new soprano saxophone, recording the *My Favorite Things* album over five days that October. It was a smash hit that enabled Coltrane to call many of his own shots, while the title track became a flute solo vehicle for Dolphy after he joined Coltrane's group.

With his bombshell album *Change Of The Century* released that June, Ornette signed a personal management contract with Monte Kay sometime in September and was busy scheming for a December recording of an even bigger change in the *Free Jazz* album. Coltrane and Ornette were friends, and the former frequently visited the Five Spot to hear the latter's quartet during the close of 1959. 'He would grab Ornette by the arm as soon as we got off,' bassist Charlie Haden recalled of Coltrane's presence at those gigs, 'and they would go off into the night talking about music.'[2]

Meanwhile, Albert Ayler had just been discharged from the military after serving in Europe and was struggling to find places to play free jazz in Los

Angeles, then briefly in his hometown of Cleveland. He left the USA for Sweden out of frustration, playing and recording there during 1962–63 (including with Cecil Taylor) before relocating to New York in 1963 and establishing his brief and brilliant career in avant-garde jazz. His and Eric's paths crossed later that year, and Dolphy promised to form an ensemble with him in the months before his death.

CARIBÉ

Eric's summer was far from over. Four days after the *Out There* session, he returned to Van Gelder's New Jersey studio to play on a Prestige contract recording, guesting on the Latin Jazz Quintet's *Caribé*. The album requires attention from Dolphy fans as his soloing is further proof of his incisive artistic direction, even as a sideman.

In early July, Van Gelder had hosted this new pick-up ensemble in their first recording session, backing organist Shirley Scott for her quickly released *Mucho, Mucho* album. Like that album's fourteen-minute-plus title track, 'Caribé' is not so much Latin jazz as an expertly played middle-of-the-road blues jam over a rhythm section featuring Juan Amalbert's stylish congas. *Caribé*, billed to 'The Latin Jazz Quintet And Eric Dolphy,' also features Bill Ellington (bass), Manny Ramos (drums, timbales), Gene Casey (piano), and Charlie Simons (vibraphone).

At the time, Prestige was fumbling around with a faux-Latin sound, settling later on more focused Latin Jazz Quintet recordings led by Amalbert on the label's gospel subsidiary Tru-Sound, allowing for more Latin percussion while emphasizing vibraphone and flute-based jazz over blues. It is in this context of Prestige's search for consumer-friendly, easy-listening, commercial jazz that we encounter Dolphy on *Caribé*, bending over backward to fit label expectations. Though the band rarely warms up to his presence, the musicians are really tight, the intensity and expressive imagination of Eric's solos grabbing the spotlight.

On the title track, his alto sax solo initially sticks to blues phrasing, but by the second chorus he is leaping out of those traditional riffs, coyly accenting the unusual pitch here, the odd metric placement there. The entertaining result is celebratory and in keeping with the upbeat feel of the track, a 'groovy' atmosphere lightheartedly passed along to vibraphonist Simons.

'Blues In 6/8' starts with gusto, introducing a feel-good bluesy theme, but the piece is in four, and Casey's vamping behind Simon's solo soon gets in the way of the fun. Dolphy launches a restless sax that does not do much before having to come back down, reluctant to go into orbit. A percussion break saves the track and reminds listeners that there are two fabulous, genuine Latin players in the studio, who like Eric, seem at times to be in straightjackets. What is notable on the subdued 'First Bass Line' is neither the tune itself nor the looseness of the extended jam session feel, but Ellington's unique bass explorations with Eric, and the gripping bass clarinet solo that emerges at the halfway mark. At times convulsive, it twists around itself several times before finding a way back to the scored doubling of the bass riff.

The attractively up-tempo 'Mambo Ricci' lets Eric blow alto right off the mark; he plays consistent yet restrained lines before he hits a more expressive pace and finds a set of unique pitches and timbral colors that set off a structural high point before the solo loses its balance and devolves into strangely cautious passages. Casey's technically solid piano solo that follows also falls back on his standard, tried-and-true, blues-inflected bop. 'Spring Is Here' is fronted by the flute in an unusual ballad arrangement that finds the rhythm section's various propulsive devices and patterns awkwardly juxtaposed and foregrounded. Eric's brief musical journey tests not the limits of the stylistic situation but rather the homogeneity of his sound, saving the session's best flute work for 'Sunday Go Meetin',' in which he romps and wails at will.

Caribé is a miniature treasure of Dolphy's solo work, for on all three of his instruments he manages to play his way out of a box, sounding like a reluctant group leader in charge of neither hiring, nor arrangements, nor song selection. A widely read May 1961 *DownBeat* review excoriated him for not fitting in. The Latin Jazz Quintet would be forever linked to the Dolphy name, and curiously he would record the following January with a completely different line-up on the 1961 United Artists Records release *The Latin Jazz Quintet.**

On Tuesday, August 30, Dolphy arrived in the studio to read charts for two more singles by Ruth Brown. The seven-inch 45rpm records 'Taking Care Of Business'/ 'Honey Boy' and 'Anyone But You'/ 'It Tears Me All To Pieces,' arranged and conducted by Howard Biggs, brought together Julian Priester, Ernie Royal, Kenney Burrell, Tommy Flanagan, and other first-call professionals first

* Nearly every decade since its first release, Prestige has reissued *Caribé*, including the early 1980s black-cover reprint with a giant 'Dolphy' banner swathed across the top of his profile photo, flipping the order of contributors ('Eric Dolphy With The Latin Jazz Quintet'). The Italian jazz boutique reissue label Honey Pie, founded in 2020, released a widely distributed new pressing of the album in 2021.

encountered at the Brown session earlier that year. Dolphy's versatility took him back into the studio on September 8 (some sources state September 9) as an important alto soloist on John Lewis's 'Afternoon In Paris,' a track featured on his Atlantic album *The Wonderful World Of Jazz*, to be released the following year and featuring Gunther Schuller on French horn among an all-star cast. Eric doesn't compromise here on flirtations with the unusual as he emerges from the thickly scored background to briefly double Jim Hall's guitar. With Benny Golson and Jimmy Giuffre on the other saxes, Gunther Schuller on French horn, and Herb Pomeroy on trumpet, the reed and brass quintet swells and stabs with the best of them, lushly recorded by Tom Dowd in the Atlantic studio. Dolphy swoops in with his own kindling solo and jumpy restlessness, his leaps, vocalizations, and filigree runs providing a complete departure from Lewis's laid-back solo. Dolphy's voice then gives way to a swinging, minimal Jim Hall.

Eric's refusal to fit in actually fits in: Lewis and Schuller were both banking on the legitimizing unpredictability of avant-garde voices to spice up what were sometimes staid arrangements. In this rarefied arena of third stream chamber-jazz royalty, listeners expecting a laid-back, moody 'Afternoon In Paris' are asked to welcome Dolphy's curiously post-bop style. He also read through his alto part on Gary McFarland's 'Night Float,' which would appear on the 1962 John Lewis album *Essence*, completed in three sessions over a three-year period. (Eric returned to the project in October of 1962, making rare appearances on alto flute on 'Tillamook Two' and 'Another Encounter.')*

One can easily question Lewis and Schuller's aesthetic goals in including Dolphy's outlier sound of edgy improvised jazz in their concert hall respectability. A litany of criticism has been raised in response to third stream, with Robert Palmer noting that the 'sterile and pretentious' fledgling genre was 'perhaps more controversial than Ornette's music.'[3] Purists on both sides posit that this blending of musical cultures was at best a packaging of conflicting genres and traditions, an inauthentic manipulation branding divergent authenticities in work that was more false than true. Raymond Horricks characterizes third stream as something Eric 'got caught up in.'[4] Regardless, Dolphy thoroughly embraced the role,

---

* Alan Saul lists 'The Stranger' rather than 'Night Float' as having been recorded on September 8, while noting that 'If You Could See Me Now' and ''Round Midnight' from that same session were never released.

taking advantage of the artistic opportunities and willingly participating in the experiment, while becoming Schuller's close friend and productive collaborator.

Polemics aside, a master musician reading the notated score as musically and reliably as a professional classical musician, and then performing truly inspirational, original, contemporary jazz solos on the spot, is the performative key to the conjoining of original, notated composition with innovative improvisation drawn from the jazz experience. Matching Dolphy's eagerness to define the edgy side of third stream are Lewis's leanings toward less aggressive jazz in his Orchestra USA performances, for which he eventually froze Eric out of soloing in favor of Phil Woods's alto. Furthermore, Lewis would never have invited Dolphy's individuality into, for instance, the straightlaced environs of his Modern Jazz Quartet. Nonetheless, Eric and Ornette rejoined this crowd in December to record two tracks for the album *John Lewis Presents Contemporary Music: Jazz Abstractions.*

DON DEMICHAEL ON *OUTWARD BOUND*

The September 1960 issue of *DownBeat* arrived on New York newsstands containing managing editor Don DeMichael's rave review of *Outward Bound,* the disc's five-star reception offering a laundry list of accolades. 'I firmly believe that this man will be one of the most rewarding jazzmen of the coming decade,' DeMichael wrote. 'It's possible to draw a parallel between Dolphy and Ornette Coleman—similar harmonic conceptions being the most cogent—but to me, Dolphy's message is the more coherent, and his is the greater talent.'

The review emphasized the music's cutting-edge status and the immediacy of its emotional impact, with DeMichael keenly linking this success to Dolphy's multi-instrumentalism:

> Sometimes sounding as if it is boiling with rage, Dolphy's music is filled with sharp, jagged lines that lift the listener as they spiral to peak after peak of raw emotional expression. The impact of his work is in his startling display of these emotions. I know of no word that would neatly categorize the emotional content of Dolphy's work, but it would have to encompass fury, frustration, and all the other twisting emotions…
>
> Although Dolphy varies his conception on all three instruments—his flute is less like his bass clarinet than is his alto—there is a taut wire binding them all together: the power to transmit emotion from the player

> to the listener. And that's the mark of a real artist... his bass clarinet is the most intriguing. I've never heard a sound quite like the one he gets on this neglected instrument... but Dolphy produces a more tortured tone than one is used to hearing from bass clarinet.

DeMichael continues by embracing the bass clarinet 'yelp,' which 'may be a quirk of Dolphy's, but whatever the reason behind this yelp, the effect is marvelous.' The laudatory rant was not over: Dolphy is 'more like the source from which the others draw sustenance—a well of life. Life. That's it. This album is life.'[5] (DeMichael's enthusiasm would gradually diminish in the coming years, in the face of growing criticism of Eric's work, and Dolphy would never again receive such a favorable review from the magazine.)

September slowly rolled in as the summer of 1960 cooled to Dolphy's first New York autumn, his romance with Joyce blooming with seasonal colors, his temporary victories in the jazz press filling his sails. He played with the Mingus Workshop's piano-less quartet opening at the Showplace on September 4. The gig came at a time when both Dolphy and Curson had openly complained to Mingus, asking for increased pay in the face of other offers, leaving the leader unhappy and feeling betrayed: he had been paying Eric $175 per week—$40 more than the others. Mingus biographer Gene Santoro advances a notion that the bassist also felt miffed because 'he'd encouraged Eric's bass clarinet work, his eccentric note choices, and angular lines when most others thought the young reedman was out of tune or crazy'—misguided comments typical of even present-day writers still selling the 'crazy' moniker despite Mingus's full embrace of Dolphy's virtuosity.[6]

On September 20, Eric was called to the Van Gelder Prestige session for Eddie 'Lockjaw' Davis's *Trane Whistle*. This was a big band with big names and some old friends, though it resulted in a disc on which he played no solos and took second alto behind Oliver Nelson, who penned the charts including a prominent bass clarinet line in 'Stolen Moments.' It was the first of seven sessions running well into 1963 where Dolphy met up with his former Los Angeles mentor Jerome Richardson, who appeared as a sideman, band member, and studio musician on countless recordings between 1955 and 1992. By the time Eric moved to New York, Prestige/New Jazz had released two albums with Richardson as leader. Alan Douglas, who signed Dolphy to FM Records for 1963's *Conversations / Iron Man* sessions, produced the Richardson Quintet's 1962 United Artists album *Going To The Movies*.

Bennie Maupin recalls seeing Dolphy play in Detroit about this time, hired on alto by trumpeter Talib Dawud (born Alfonso Nelson Rainey) for the band backing his wife, singer Dakota Staton (also known as Aliyah Rabia). Staton played Detroit's Birdland Supper Club on October 5–9, Wednesday through Sunday. At an after-hours jam session at the West End Motel, Maupin heard Dolphy jam with former Mingus Workshop colleague Yusef Lateef. 'He would play some stuff and Yusef would look at him and they'd laugh,' he recalled. 'There was an exchange of some magnitude going on between those two minds.'[7]

Dawud had played trumpet since the 1940s, including stints with Dizzy Gillespie's big band, while from 1959 onward he dedicated himself to an African-import retail store in New York City and to spreading the word of Ahmadiyya Islam, in defiance of Elijah Mohammed's Nation Of Islam teachings. Dawud converted both Yusef Lateef and Ahmad Jamal to his brand of Islam. Malcolm X would denounce both Dawud and Staton for engaging in sinful popular music.

THE CANDID EXPERIENCE

By the second week of October, Charles Mingus was very angry that his bass had been damaged while stored between gigs at the Showcase, with management refusing to pay for repairs. Legend has Mingus pulling strings out of the club's piano to exact revenge. Group tension was also rising, with Dolphy and Curson continuing to request higher wages from their boss, who then took the Workshop 'on tour,' first to the Half Note, then to Philadelphia's Showboat. An October 12 *Daily News* article stated, 'Charles Mingus, whose current Showboat gig is the first out of New York in more than two years, engages in an uproarious comic dialogue with Eric Dolphy's bass clarinet.'

Escape from New York only fomented anticipation for their return and what proved to be a highly regarded October 20 recording session. The bassist had been talking up material for the group's next recording projects, which ultimately produced two exemplary Candid albums, *Charles Mingus Presents Charles Mingus* and the dryly titled *Mingus*. November also netted for the label the Jazz Artists Guild album *Newport Rebels*.*

---

* Years later, British jazz producer Alan Bates revived the Candid name and developed the reissue imprint Barnaby to release some of its titles. Beginning in 1995, Candid became an independent, award-winning UK jazz label distributed by Germany's ZYX Music.

Candid's Nat Hentoff got his start in Boston radio, hosting jazz shows in the 1940s and expanding into print journalism and jazz criticism, rising to the position of New York City editor for *DownBeat* and soon founding *The Jazz Review* magazine with Martin Williams. The two became Dolphy's most ardent supporters in print. *DownBeat* fired Hentoff in the late 50s for insisting on hiring a Black writer, and his weekly *Village Voice* columns revealed a civil rights-oriented political progressive arguing for social activism. He championed the political dimensions of jazz, particularly as an anti-racist weapon for social change. As Eric Porter details, Hentoff 'argued that "the art of today" came out of particularly political contexts and should not be devalued for reflecting it [politics]. Art was not beyond ideology, Hentoff argued: even the "evasion" of politics reflected a certain "attitude."'

In 1960, Hentoff accepted Bob Altshuler's offer to become a recording supervisor and A&R director for the newly founded Candid label, duties that were overshadowed by his writing career. Originally a Cadence Records subsidiary named Coda, the short-lived Candid label produced over thirty titles in its first year, specializing in blues and new jazz, including Mingus, Cecil Taylor, Steve Lacy, Booker Little, and Abbey Lincoln. The label suspended new recording projects within three years, releasing its remaining albums in 1963.

Eric's fine work is all over Mingus's two Candid albums, and he played on three more of the label's first batch of jazz releases, appearing on Booker Little's *Out Front*, *Straight Ahead* by Abbey Lincoln, and the October 1961 compilation album *The Jazz Life!* Select alternate takes and unreleased recordings from each of his 1960–61 Candid sessions appear on 1989's *Candid Dolphy*.* Another early Candid release not involving Dolphy, *We Insist! Max Roach's Freedom Now Suite*,

* *Candid Dolphy* includes alternate tracks from six different NOLA Penthouse studio sessions dating from October 1960 to April 1961. From *Charles Mingus Presents Charles Mingus*: 'Re-incarnation Of A Love Bird' (take 1) and 'Stormy Weather' (take 1), both recorded on October 20, 1960. From Abbey Lincoln's *Straight Ahead*: 'T'aint Nobody's Business If I Do' (take 3), recorded on November 1, 1960; 'Body And Soul' (take 2), recorded on November 11, 1960; and 'African Lady' (take 4), recorded on February 2, 1961. And from Booker Little's *Out Front*: 'Quiet, Please ' (take 1), recorded on March 17, 1961; and 'Moods In Free Time' (take 5) and 'Hazy Hues' (take 5), both recorded on April 4, 1961. Six of these tracks were previously unreleased. The album was licensed by Candid to Phonoco (Germany, 1989) and to AO! (Artists Only, 1989). Black Lion also licensed some of Eric's Candid recordings to the French label Editions Atlas for its Les Génies Du Jazz series (vol. 6 no. 1) release *Eric Dolphy: Stormy Weather* (1991).

helped to spread the voices of political protest and the Civil Rights movement's brewing cultural milieu. *We Insist!* was recorded at New York's Nola Penthouse Sound Studio on the top floor of the Steinway Building on East 57th Street, where, on October 20, the Mingus Workshop quartet (without Booker Ervin) held three separate sessions. The studio had catered to small and large jazz ensembles since 1945, with a storied history of hosting progressive voices, such as the sessions for Cecil Taylor's first album.

On this day, Nola captured *Charles Mingus Presents Charles Mingus*, released that January, including these future juggernauts for live shows: 'Folk Forms No. 1' and 'Original Faubus Fables' (released together in edited versions on a seven-inch 45rpm single in 1961), plus 'What Love' and 'All The Things You Could Be By Now If Sigmund Freud's Wife Was Your Mother.' Featuring prominent roles for Eric, the album has enjoyed over fifty international pressings.

'Folk Forms No. 1' finds the bassist speaking to imaginary club-goers, telling a nonexistent studio audience that their applause is not welcome until the end of the set, reminding them that the players onstage find their noise annoying. The toying monologue echoes Mingus's confrontational club banter: this is art, not mere entertainment. Faux introductions follow, during which the 'brooding Zeus,' as Hentoff called Mingus, exaggerates the list of instruments Dolphy plays, asking if he mentioned them all. This cut opens the album with enthralling blues, free-for-all Dixieland-ish shout-outs, and celebratory polyphony. Eric channels hot jazz and takes his alto out for a walk, throwing in his signature riff, with Curson keeping tabs on him through interlocking intrigue. This is as free as Mingus had let things get in the studio, the group having perfected the piece even well before their high-quality Antibes rendition that summer.

Candid agreed to something Columbia Records would not: to record the 'Original Faubus Fables' lyrics, which drew from the fallout of Arkansas governor Orval Faubus's refusal to allow court-ordered desegregation of Little Rock schools. Three years after the 1954 Brown vs. Board Of Education decision on integrating public schools, Faubus had called out National Guard troops to prevent Black students from entering Little Rock High School. Here, the Old South redneck is scandalized with jazz invective, including spoken word, shouts, commentary, and Eric's outstanding soloing, with which he executes radical vocalizations while satisfying Mingus's equally demanding compositional devices, sharp tempo changes, and formal complexities. Poignant are the repurposed 'Johnny Comes

Marching Home' references, haunting indications of past, present, and future battles over racial injustice on American soil.

'What Love' was performed on the Antibes stage the previous July; here it is sharp and exacting, a vehicle for both a solid Curson solo and a bass clarinet/bass dialogue that remains a classic moment of recorded jazz history. Richmond knows the routine and adds perfect percussive support for the contours of tensions the low instruments throw back at one another. Eric's wildly free solo curiously transcends the freedom he gave himself on any of his three 1960 albums as leader. Kudos to Mingus for positing a role for this fiery brand of music, and for relying on masters to carry the improvisational side of his compositional structures.

Though he later turned radically against Eric in his *DownBeat* commentary, the widely read Ira Gitler wrote of *Charles Mingus Presents The Charles Mingus Quartet*:

> Dolphy is one of the most daring of today's new players. He is working on a 'vocal' conception that bears similarities to Ornette Coleman but I find him more coherent. In the past, I have also enjoyed his bass clarinet, too. Here, on 'What Love,' he engages Mingus in an out-of-tempo conversation that is described in the notes as Dolphy's telling Mingus that he is leaving the group. The argument is quite intense. Dolphy sounds like a cross between an aardvark and some species of fowl ancestry (perhaps a pterodactyl). This may be emotionally valid, but I don't feel compelled to re-hear it very often.[8]

'All The Things You Could Be By Now If Sigmund Freud's Wife Was Your Mother' launches with an aggressively jagged head, and Curson obliges with a searching, hard bebop solo. 'All The Things' indeed: Eric's alto solo is an encyclopedic investigation of improvisational vocabulary, with sustained altissimo notes bending among ultra-fast Parker-esque figurations, sounding like the mixing of sonic matter in a high-speed post-bop blender. Curson's motoric background ostinato pushes him toward intense unison passage work marking the finale. Hentoff shared in his liner notes that Dolphy, 'an exceptionally alert, unpretentious and self-critical musician, was grinning throughout the playbacks,' further stating, 'The album was recorded during a crisis of personnel. After many months with Mingus, Dolphy and Curson had decided to leave.' Though the split came two months later, in December, Eric reflected on their superlative studio efforts, 'I don't know what happened, but we never got together like this in the club. Maybe it's because we were leaving, and the tension was off.'[9] Many have commented that their bass and bass clarinet 'conversations' over many club nights might have been a hashing-out of this conflict in musical dialogue.*

An exceptional take of 'Stormy Weather,' as featured on *Mingus*, was captured during the first session on October 20, Dolphy's consummate alto gracing the standard with minimal accompaniment.† Glissandos and blues-inflected cries shape the well-known theme into something new over a simple, halting bass line, with Curson's modest counterpoint adding support the second time through. Dolphy's solo spins out an entirely new atmosphere for the storm, briefly sloughing off the tune's introspective consternation to reveal free passages and abstract textures, contributing several paragraphs to the saxophone technique book. Curson's brief tone exploration leads to a painterly arrangement of the theme, the soulfulness emerging from the moody cloud before a rigorous outro.

Trombonists Britt Woodman and Jimmy Knepper were brought in for Mingus's madcap 'MDM' for ten players, a track also found on *Mingus*. 'MDM,' for Monk–Duke–Mingus, is a long suite treating thematic material from these composers, with Dolphy laying out an admirable alto solo plus exceptional bass clarinet work, the latter solo full of humor, rhythmic angst, and striking individuality. The same line-up also recorded a studied version of Mingus's 'All The Things You Are (All),' with Eric on arranged bass clarinet—an 'unheard' track that even went unregistered with Mingus's publishing company and missing from subsequent anthologies, including Mosaic's 1989 release of Mingus's complete Candid recordings. It finally came out on Candid's Charlie Mingus *Incarnations* album in 2023.

---

* In 1971, Barnaby reissued the album as *Charles Mingus Presents The Charles Mingus Quartet Featuring Eric Dolphy*. A 2018 Jazz Images reissue cover features a full-bleed William Claxton photo of a foregrounded Dolphy in shades and floral African cap, looking back toward a seated Mingus facing the camera. The Cliff Walk Manor hotel grounds shot was taken at the Newport festival protest and was also used for that label's reissue of *Newport Rebels*.

† 'Reincarnation Of A Love Bird' (the first of two versions recorded that fall and known as the 'session one' version) emerged from the second October 20 session, which added to the quartet Lonnie Hillyer (trumpet), Charles McPherson (alto sax), Booker Ervin (tenor sax), and Nico Bunink (piano); followed by 'Vassarlean' (also titled 'Weird Nightmare,' which may stem from the November 11 session) with Booker Ervin joining in an octet, and which appeared on the compilation album *The Jazz Life!*

The Workshop spent October's final week north of the border recording for the Canadian Broadcasting Corporation, returning to New York before month's end. As an outgrowth of the Newport Jazz Festival alternative stage protest, Mingus and Roach joined drummer Jo Jones in organizing the Jazz Artists Guild as a short-lived answer to the jazz industry's unfair, racially biased business practices, and to promote artistic and economic independence. On November 1, the *Newport Rebels* session captured two versions of the Robbins/Grainger number 'Tain't Nobody's Bizness If I Do,' featuring Abbey Lincoln on vocals and Eric ripping up the blues on alto sax, sharing solid solos with trumpeter Benny Bailey. (An alternate take appears on *Candid Dolphy*.)

Eric appears on one other rebel track, Mingus's 'Mysterious Blues,' recorded on November 11, a session that transitioned from Mingus's sextet and octet, to the Artist Guild line up. Roy Eldridge brings his marvelous old-school game, blowing a cool muted blues before Eric enters with his inspired choruses before Jimmy Knepper's work.* According to Hentoff, Eldridge appeared startled by Dolphy as he started his solo, though he 'kept nodding, his smile broadening and pointed to his ear, mouthing the words, *He can really hear*!'[10]

The *Mingus* album needed one more track, and on November 11 the bassist directed the intense 'Lock 'Em Up,' without a Dolphy solo. The other track from that session, featuring Eric on flute, is 'Reincarnation Of A Lovebird' (second session), which appears on *Candid Dolphy* (1989) and the Mosaic label's 1984 four-LP album box set *The Complete Candid Recordings Of Charles Mingus*. As internal conflict led to the Guild's disbanding, the original *Newport Rebels* cover featured a photograph of the Cliff Walk manor grounds, boasting 'Charles Mingus, Max Roach, Eric Dolphy, Roy Eldridge, Jo Jones.'

LEAVING MINGUS, RECORDING WITH RON CARTER

John F. Kennedy was now President-elect, and Eric had been playing with Mingus for nearly a year. Candid session work rounded out what he felt to have been an underpaid Workshop experience, and Mingus was wearing him down. On Sunday, December 11, the *Oakland Tribune* announced Mingus's upcoming San Francisco Jazz Workshop club gig, stating that the group 'includes Eric Dolphy, an

---

* That session produced two versions of 'Body And Soul' and 'R&R,' as included on *The Jazz Life!* Both tracks appear on the 1988 Candid CD *Charles Mingus: Reincarnation Of A Love Bird*.

outstanding young saxophonist.' By that Friday, Dolphy's name was missing from the follow-up report; his enrollment in what Hentoff called Mingus's 'radically re-energizing university' was over for now. Curson also left, with talented substitutes Lonnie Hillyer and Charles McPherson traveling for that West Coast tour instead. 'By that time, Dolphy had notified Mingus of his intent of leaving the group,' Simosko and Tepperman comment simply, citing a January *DownBeat* article claiming Dolphy had suffered from an 'undisclosed accident.'[11] This is an odd absurdity, since Eric was preparing for an unprecedented two-day run of recording sessions the very next week—part of a remarkably productive December that produced career milestones still resonating in jazz history. The standing account is that Eric simply did not want to tour and was fired. Regardless, Dolphy and Mingus had certainly not seen the last of each other.

Until now, Eric had yet to join a music licensing agency in connection to his compositions and recordings; before November's end, he duly became a member of BMI. This was roughly when he and Ron Carter entered the aptly named Esoteric Sound studios, their duets and solos expertly recorded by Jerry Newman. Blue Note later released several of these pieces as part of *Other Aspects*, a 1987 album drawing from Dolphy's personal belongings; the album's subtitle reads, 'Newly discovered recordings from Eric Dolphy's private collection.' Eric possessed either the original tapes of the Esoteric Sound recordings or a high-quality copy of the master. An acetate album was pressed containing five of these tracks, for which Hale Smith provided titles following Dolphy's passing.

The small collection of pieces includes Carter's five-minute solo, balancing Eric's two takes of unaccompanied flute, later titled 'Inner Flight #1' and 'Inner Flight #2.' There are arresting aspects to the track eventually called 'Dolphy-N,' an alto sax and bass duet for which Alan Saul claims an unissued alternate take exists. In this strong musical essay, the two move through loosely organized tonal areas and free material as Carter's inventive muscle dialogues with Dolphy's explorations of sonic smears and piquant scalar runs. The improvised piece includes an intriguing bass solo with strong compositional directions, the two closing with intertwining stylistic and textural twists and turns. Avant-garde jazz would see more of this kind of work as creative music scenes developed throughout the 1960s and beyond, experimenting with structured improvisation, open composition, new approaches to group interaction, and the sonic capabilities of an increasing variety of instruments.

For 'Triple Mix,' which first appeared on the Italian label Jazzway's 1987 album *Eric Dolphy: Naima*, Eric overdubbed flute and bass clarinet on top of Carter's bass. Though this was a simple studio overdub, tape music was a new compositional direction in the cutting-edge New Music world. Out of pure conjecture, one could imagine Dolphy engaging or collaborating further with tape processes, exploring a more avant-garde direction than third stream. In Paris in 1963, composer Terry Riley recorded Chet Baker's quartet performing their individual parts of Miles Davis's 'So What,' subjecting the tapes to a variety of loop delays and manipulations for the theater work *The Gift*. The bassist on those sessions was Luigi Trussardi, with whom Eric would play in September 1961 at the Club-Saint Germaine in Paris during his first solo tour of Europe.

Dolphy was often in creative proximity to this brand of new music, and occasionally inside it. Sometime in May 1962, Hale Smith brought Eric to meet with French American composer Edgard Varèse, to coach him on his performance of the composer's 1936 solo flute work 'Density 21.5' that month at the Ojai Music Festival in Southern California. Among Varèse's three electronic tape pieces, *Poème électronique* (1957–1958) famously premiered in the Philips Pavilion at the 1958 World Fair in Brussels, its first commercial release coming on the 1960 Columbia Masterworks LP album *Music Of Edgar Varèse*. That disc was Eric's first exposure to 'Density 21.5.'

JAZZ ABSTRACTIONS

The Tuesday and Wednesday before Christmas Day that Sunday witnessed an unprecedented forty-eight hours in Dolphy's life, during which he appeared at recording sessions for three remarkable albums: *Jazz Abstractions: Compositions By Gunther Schuller And Jim Hall*; Ornette Coleman's juggernaut *Free Jazz*; and his third Prestige/New Jazz title as leader, *Fry Cry*.

Free Jazz and *Jazz Abstractions* are Atlantic Records catalog numbers 1364 and 1365, respectively, with Ornette, Dolphy, and bassist Scott LaFaro playing on both. The Tuesday found them in Atlantic Records studio with a twelve-piece chamber orchestra recording the Schuller album, a reprise of the May 20 premieres of these works at Circle On The Square. Ornette solos on 'Abstraction' (on which Eric does not play) and 'Variants On A Theme By Thelonious Monk (Criss Cross),' but without the improvisational duet with Dolphy's bass clarinet that Schuller worked into May's performance.

Schuller's variations on Monk—a piece Dolphy would perform in concert many times—make for a challenging set, with a modernist introduction anchored by a string quartet, with doubling from vibes and saxophones. Components of Monk's melody are worked out in complex ways in 'Variant I,' capturing elements of contour and rhythm and reflecting Monk's quirky originality. Ornette's solo touches some strange bases yet it is reserved overall. Listeners hear why Schuller again wanted Dolphy's bass clarinet; his timbral richness speaks to the music in ways other instruments and players could not. To follow Dolphy's solo, Schuller scored a curiously evocative string quartet passage behind Eddie Costa's vibraphone solo as a means of formally balancing Dolphy's aggressive individualism.

'Variant II' has Eric's flute paired with that of Robert DiDomenica, their sustained timbres and occasional melodic fragments blending with a picturesque atonal string quartet and Ornette's sporadic inflections. 'Variant III' offers the virtuosic pairing of bass clarinet and LaFaro's unmatched sensibility, a duet notably defined against crisp swing drumming and minimal backing. Bass clarinet lip smacks and reed 'kisses' add a never-before-heard percussive element to the instrument's vocabulary. The two continue alone, together, on this essential track from the growing number of bass duets that Dolphy records throughout his career.

'Variant IV' launches with a brief bass clarinet statement setting up the sustained string sonorities and vibes introducing Jim Hall's guitar solo with walking bass, soon joined by Dolphy's flute and Costa. It gets thick even before Ornette's entrance, which ushers in a taste of free jazz before the piece ends abruptly with big, weighty chords. Overall, 'Variants On A Theme By Thelonious Monk' succeeds where other third stream compositions fail: the material and scoring are original, dramatic, and commanding, placing dissonant elements of atonal modernism among atmospheric, moody passages intersecting with radical flashes of improvised jazz. Ornette's and Dolphy's solos are beautifully balanced by Costa's vibraphone textures, contours, and stylistic integrity, transforming and transitioning reed-based energy back into Schuller's successfully blended orchestral colors.

Dolphy's friendly relationship with Schuller grew closer as they shared interests in crossover, genre-bending conflations of classical concert music, avant-garde jazz, and improvisation. Third stream found one of its most compelling documents in *Jazz Abstractions*, a work programmed for formal concert hall performances with Dolphy in mind, including those at Syracuse, Carnegie Hall, and Chicago in 1962–63. He'd also meet up again with John Lewis to record more of Gary McFarland's music, and ultimately join them and Schuller in the 1963 debut recording of Orchestra USA. (A founding member of that organization's chamber music spinoff, Sextet Of Orchestra USA, Eric died six months after recording tracks for their first disc, *Mack The Knife And Other Berlin Theater Songs Of Kurt Weill*, released by RCA Victor in 1964.)

THE *FREE JAZZ* ALBUM

Dolphy and Coleman's only shared studio sessions came on consecutive days for different projects. 'I get bugged when people compare us,' Eric stated earlier in the year. 'I've known Ornette a long time, and we agree about a good many things. But I'm just playing myself, the same as he is. Of course, so many people aren't interested in the music, but in the person.'[12]

Coleman brought traditional blues and R&B riffs into radically new contexts, and his free jazz often echoes these contours in asymmetric phrases, truncated melodic cadences, and new harmonically free mannerisms, both in terms of vertical chord voicing and linear chord progressions. Of course, to most listeners, his powerful and expressive musical elements emerged in surprising and suspenseful ways. Unlike Ornette's, Dolphy's so-called 'free' playing was anchored in complex chromatic relationships to harmonic concepts and his sound world of human speech and birdsong, his aesthetic and stylistic goals, though wildly diverse, unified by his sound on three instruments, as witnessed by the range of his work through 1960.

Free Jazz sounds as revolutionary today as it did when the double quartet entered New York City's A&R Studios on December 21, the two quartets captured in their respective stereo channels by legendary recording engineer Tom Dowd. Left channel: Ornette (alto), Don Cherry (pocket trumpet), LaFaro, and Billy Higgins. Right channel: Dolphy (bass clarinet), Hubbard, Charlie Haden, and Ed Blackwell. Two years earlier, Sonny Rollins had introduced Hubbard and Ornette in Los Angeles.

Aside from attitude and a willingness to break all the rules, the only real preparation for *Free Jazz* came in the form of previous collaborations between some of the players. Of course, Ornette's key quartet and their familiarity with one another formed an essential element, and Hubbard, Dolphy, and Higgins had also played together extensively. Yet despite these histories, LaFaro—the player least involved with the others up to that point—is clearly one of the stars of the album, adding sensitive, intense bass lines throughout.

The ensemble played through and recorded the structure twice; the much shorter 'First Take' was released with that title on *Ornette Coleman/Twins* (Atlantic, 1971). This version clocks in at seventeen minutes and is quite different from the second run-through, a recording that lasts over thirty-seven minutes. Both retain what might be described as static intensity with unique dynamic interplay, color, and rhythmic vitality. Ornette's description of the process appears in the original liner notes: 'The most important thing was for us to play together, all at the same time, without getting in the way.' The cues are very brief passages introducing soloists, with coalescences of parts leading into a new player's soloistic foregrounding. Otherwise, all musical elements are at play. Upon close listening, multiple simultaneous tempi, wild polyphony, and divergent emotional tangents intermingle, along with radically shifting textures and density, but without predetermined moments of reprieve, climax, or architectural differentiation rendered through planned musical elements.

Following a cued tutti introduction of held notes and sustained freneticism, Dolphy's bass clarinet solo emerges, bubbling amidst the pulsating fabric of two rhythm sections, and brings ice-breaking humor early on. Ear-catching from the get-go is the complexity arising from Haden and LaFaro's compelling bass lines, each punching out separate time in contours supporting, and at times contesting Dolphy's solo lines. This is likely one of the sources for Coltrane's subsequent experiments with two bass players, though those arrangements are more streamlined. As he comes to understand that he is in the driver's seat, Eric's work grows increasingly individualized and directional, while background melody players jab their way into the texture. The drumming provides a forest canopy, a collective scrim corralling sound into the center. The aural debris field of snares, toms, rim shots, kick drums, and their polymetric swing sometimes separates from the sizzling and buzzing of busy cymbal work. Into the fourth minute, Dolphy reaches closer to the podium, taking a stance with his vocalizations, shortening his mid-to-low-register shamanistic chant of concentrated iterations. On bass clarinet, he is not screaming at a high register to gather attention; rather, he's playing intensely into the texture while leading. His bluesy riffing attracts catcalls from the other horn players; the 5:10 announcement for a transference of soloist brings a wicked sonority of held notes to rein in the jungle of sound as Hubbard takes the torch.

Again, with three of four melody players briefly quieted, the buoyant ocean of rhythm and driving bass lines propels the collective. Eric's gestures starting at 8:00 echo Coleman's tiny fragments. Ornette's solo ushers in a different type of group energy, and the others render smears of sounds that break up just as quickly. Bassists and drummers are stretching out a canvas onto which the others assist Ornette in painting a picture using couch pillows, toothbrushes, and mops as brushes. Ornette, more than the other melody players, creates his own world, standing alone then stepping out of the painting, detaching only to then reconvene with a beat, a timbral wisp, a tone, or a moment growing simultaneously from the mass. He steps back into a different painting, working his way into intense runs, emphasizing directions of ascent and descent, always nipping the phrase in the bud. At 14:50, the rhythm sections seem to jibe in a fat groove just as Eric dives in with gutsy swing riffs alluding, one might imagine, to a tune only he is hearing. He is trying his best to realize *Free Jazz*'s framing principles, listening closely but distancing his line from others, simultaneously spinning his own web of moments; he drops out only to return with echoes of his secret song a minute later.

Cherry takes the mantle above the bass duo's polymetric interjections as the drummers steer their grooves closer together. Soon, an Ivesian moment conjures postmodern New Orleans, where two pairs of municipal band miscreants march into a midnight alley from opposite ends, playing similar songs at different speeds in different keys. It gets heavy, and Dolphy drops out of the business, followed by Ornette. LaFaro and Haden are locked in, but to what? Their loopy, devil-may-care complex of contours, plucks, and snaps, has the drummers coming way down to reveal clean fresh sounds of cymbal scrapes and closed hi-hat ticks. The bassists hold forth with gasps and double stops, quick arpeggios in the highest position. The piece's last section begins after another snarling attack, and sustained tutti dissonance brings in Higgins's cymbal cadenza against Blackwell's super crisp swing. Heads are bobbing, minds are making their own way, counting down through their heartbeats and envelopes of breath as the *Free Jazz* universe ends with the big bang that brought it in.

Free Jazz, so hip and cool to hardcore Dolphy fans enamored with this groundbreaking recording, was arguably more the outlier of Dolphy's career than was third stream. He would never again play with Ornette in a studio; and in his own subsequent recordings as leader, Eric leaned toward far more restrained methods of free playing, shaped by harmonic changes and predetermined structural elements. He very rarely borrowed this recipe for his own projects, never made his own version of *Free Jazz*, and avoided extended passages of simultaneously improvising horns or radical group improvisation. However, moments of *Iron Man*'s 'Burning Spear' and the articulated boldness in his final album as leader, *Out To Lunch!*, suggest that this direction was not wholly abandoned. In overembellishing his association with Ornette historically, Eric Dolphy's name and reputation have perhaps been mythologized as an equal partner in *Free Jazz*, suggesting that their limited joint work in free playing shared similar techniques and goals. Neither was the case. The notion that Dolphy held a symbiotic position in the free-jazz pantheon adjacent to Ornette diminishes the accomplishments of both players and overstates the role each had in the other's life and work. Though fortuitous circumstances brought them together, they were as different as night and day.

FAR CRY

Immediately following the *Free Jazz* session, Eric loaded three instrument cases into his car and journeyed through the winter cold to New Jersey in a VW Beetle warmer than his apartment. Leaving Manhattan, his head buzzed with the complex yet fresh aural flashbacks of the double quartet, a sonic souvenir from the planet Ornette had just helped humankind discover.

Dolphy's second album session that day was for *Far Cry*, in part a tribute to Charlie Parker he had been planning for months. His bass clarinet briefly recuperating from the trial by fire that was Ornette's session, and his flute and alto sax were waiting to play with Jaki Byard, Ron Carter, Roy Haynes, and his new friend, the young trumpet virtuoso Booker Little.

Born in Memphis in 1938, Little had studied music with the great pianist Phineas Newborn Jr. before moving to Chicago in 1954 to earn a bachelor's degree. There he roomed with Sonny Rollins, who soon joined Clifford Brown and Max Roach. Following Brown's sudden death, Booker was invited to record with Max Roach + 4, later appearing with them at the 1958 Newport Jazz Festival, when Eric played there with the Chico Hamilton Quintet.

Little and Dolphy were two peas in a pod, the trumpeter unknowingly echoing Dolphy's words: 'I can't think in terms of wrong notes—in fact, I don't hear any notes as being wrong. It's a matter of knowing how to integrate the notes and, if you must, how to resolve them. Because if you insist that this note or that note is wrong, I think you're thinking conventionally—technically, and forgetting about emotion.'[13]

Little was so strong and original a voice that United Artists signed him and immediately recorded *The Defiant Ones*, an album billed to the Booker Little 4 And Max Roach (UA, 1959), featuring, from Roach's band, Art Davis on bass and George Coleman on tenor sax. Little left Roach for a year-long sojourn as a sideman with artists including Teddy Charles, Luis Smith, and Slide Hampton. *The Defiant Ones* was the first of four Little albums, and his sophomore effort, Time Records' April 1960 release *Booker Little* (also known simply as *Quartet*), is dominated by his original compositions and sharp, modernist trumpet, with critics noting his brightness and effective composing.

The Far Cry session finds two tunes wandering in from *Out There*: "Serene" (first released on the 1974 Prestige compilation Twenty-Five Years of Prestige), and "Out There" reconfigured as a new title track, 'Far Cry.' Byard's B-flat blues 'Mrs. Parker Of K.C. (Bird's Mother)' launches side A with its thorny hard bop head spelled out by bass clarinet and trumpet doubling on the composer's keen piano stabs. Byard recalled that the group's only rehearsal was to 'talk through the tunes.'[14] Carter and Haynes are in uncanny sync as Little's searing tone takes flight, his chops nimbly negotiating this Parker frenzy. Byard's intellectualism is a living, breathing element to his solo, thick with ideas yet pruned down to single-note iterations when necessary. His freedom with chromatic sequences and near-atonal gestures is colored with clusters and wide dissonances. Eric's bass clarinet has been hot all day, here finding its way into a rich jumble of licks, his solo entering a bit over halfway through this first track. Byard's accompaniment is a quixotic spiral, Carter and Haynes setting a crisp table for Dolphy's masterclass. Carter's solo is bowed and florid, and Haynes's brief drum solo leads to an unusual coda of composed bluesy one-offs.

'Ode To Charlie Parker,' also by Byard, presents a dreamy intro of flute filigree and shining trumpet, leading to the lyrically reflective, multi-section, twenty-bar tune. Dolphy's first solo on flute, fast and florid, closes with blurry punctuations of overblowing and multiphonics.

The title track, 'Far Cry,' is a slight reworking of 'Out There' refitted for the precise attack of trumpet in place of cello for a post-bop two-part dissonant counterpoint recalling 'G.W.' and the hard-driving aggressiveness of 'Les.' A brilliant new take of his delicate blues vehicle for bass clarinet, the *Far Cry* session's version of *Out There*'s 'Serene' would not be released until 1974.* These two new versions in quick succession of the originals are evidence of Dolphy's secret disquiet with *Out There*, with Carter now recast as bassist rather than sharing the front seat on cello. Little gets the first 'Far Cry' solo, a bit conservative and restrained in contrast to Dolphy's alto—burning, sometimes chopped up, there is a deliberateness to Dolphy's phrasing.

Eric explains his composition, and the album's message:

> The title's meaning is that it's a far cry from the impact Bird had when he was alive and his position now. I wrote this to show that I haven't forgotten him or what he's meant to me. But the song also says that as great as he was, he was a far cry from what he could have been. And, finally, it says that I'm a far cry from being able to say all I want in jazz.[15]

That is, Parker's name should have been held higher in 1960, and the jazz world has too short a memory of its heroes. Acknowledging his influence so directly, Dolphy is testifying to Bird's long-term, ongoing impact, as is Byard, whose tunes are dedications to him. If there was a theme to Dolphy's early critical reception, beyond negating his harmonically outside and free playing, it was that he too closely modeled Parker. He provides rich musical evidence with *Far Cry* that he has indeed taken from Parker and is openly proud of the fact; the twist being that he has layered on top of that influence so much personal style and originality that it is now necessary to reacknowledge Parker as a core element of his own complex sound.

Another dimension of *Far Cry's* meaning is Dolphy's laying bare his constant drive to perfect artistic goals, recognizing that there is so much more to say, and thus a poignant declaration from an artist who would die nine days after his thirty-sixth birthday.

Dolphy's 'Miss Ann' has a fast, aggressive unison of twists and turns compressed into a fourteen-bar head, as clever as *Outward Bound's* 'Les' yet more disjunct and restless. This is one of the most satisfying tracks, not only for the imaginative solos but for Carter and Haynes's remarkable interplay. The alto solo's

---

* 'Serene,' from *Out There*, appeared first on the 1974 anthology *25 Years Of Prestige*, and again on the 1982 album *Eric Dolphy: Dash One*.

whimsical freedom is characterized by adventurous combinations of rhythmic work, curiously probing fragments, and dramatic leaps. Dolphy throttles his lines against metric and phrasal expectation, cavorting with ascents and descents in unusual ways. This is also the album's best showing for Little, who equals Dolphy's depth of inventiveness and imaginative flurries. Byard rides the powerful Carter/Haynes wave with two-part mosaics of contrary motion and unusually independent hands. The Dolphy/Little cutting exchange following Byard's inventive solo inspires pyrotechnics, and the tune stops on a dime with a sharp unison. That intensity then meets Mal Waldron's beautiful ballad dedicated to Billie Holiday, 'Left Alone,' here a flute essay with soft piano and Carter's upper-register pizzicato. Haynes's crisp work and the rest of the ambiance is perhaps one of Van Gelder's better productions of Dolphy. The tune tackles a similar format to 'Glad To Be Unhappy' (sans Little), a touching ballad transformed into a flute showcase; he takes one more round before the head's return, ending with overblowing and multiphonics in the codetta.

The Lawrence/Gross number 'Tenderly' appears out of the blue to the unsuspecting listener, an unaccompanied alto solo that fades out at just under 4:20, swaying from sentimental reflection to exploratory new music, from pure tonal interpretation to spontaneous investigations of timbre via thorny chromatic variations. Perhaps one of the first such commercially released unaccompanied solos for jazz alto sax, 'Tenderly' helped usher in a legacy of highly individualized, unaccompanied solo work from avant-garde and free jazz musicians. Bill Kirchner accurately suggests Eric's emulation of Sonny Rollins here and on the next track, the Conn/Styne number 'It's Magic.' This closing number is a vehicle for serious bass clarinet explorations, faintly outside playing, and a touch of intonation problems. The solo's flurries, counterintuitive cadential figures, and weird registral journeys are effective in their juggling of both playfulness and sentimental depth. 'It's Magic' says goodbye to the album listener, ending *Far Cry* with a perplexing statement—a taste of charm found on *Outward Bound* and *Out There*, on which the playfully mysterious 'Miss Toni' and 'Feathers,' respectively, play similar roles.

The end of Dolphy's artistically rich and productive 1960 overlapped with the dovetailing of the Eisenhower years into Kennedy's Camelot. Things were cooling off and heating up at the same time. In the coming April, Martin Luther King Jr. would issue invitations for a conference at Shaw University in Raleigh, North Carolina, ultimately attended by over 120 student delegates from all over the country. Those youthful voices would coalesce in the Student Nonviolent Coordinating Committee (SNCC), an organization formed and empowered by the inertia of sit-in strikers fighting racial inequality and segregation. At first advancing actions such as boycotts, sit-ins, and other public demonstrations, SNCC and Civil Rights organizations such as CORE and the Southern Christian Leadership Conference (SCLS) would help to organize Freedom Rides into the Deep South in 1961, with subsequent campaigns including voting rights initiatives in 1962, and the March on Washington for Jobs and Freedom held in August 1963.

Heard faintly in these challenging winds, Eric Dolphy's first three albums as leader and sideman performances at festivals, clubs, and on recordings helped form a backdrop to the first year of a decade of radical change.

06 THE LATIN JAZZ QUINTET, MAL WALDRON'S *THE QUEST*

JANUARY–JUNE 1961

The jazz revolutionary's first full year in New York proved a triumph. Following *Far Cry*, Eric's next studio sideman project was United Artists Records' *The Latin Jazz Quintet*, but no one knows if this recording took place in late 1960 or early 1961, with the otherwise unflappable discographer Uwe Reichardt calling it 'this obscure session.'[1] The ensemble was a sextet with Dolphy, but 'quintet' appears on the cover, without acknowledging him either as a featured soloist or as a designated sixth man.*

Latin jazz had grown in popularity since the late 40s when a younger Eric first listened to Charlie Parker on 'Mango Mangüé' by Machito & His Afro-Cuban Orchestra. His involvement now with two entirely different Latin Jazz Quintet outfits came with a waning of the mambo craze. *The Latin Jazz Quintet* album is closer to the genre than *Caribé*, the latter enjoying more printings and reissues while lacking the well-rounded authenticity one would expect from an ensemble carrying the name. *The Latin Jazz Quintet* is a more stylistically fluent collection, equally ripe with convincing yet brief Dolphy moments. The band is tight, the percussion high in the mix, and the effervescent timbales player Luis Ramirez does not split time on a standard drum kit, as Manny Ramos does on *Caribé*, because there is no drum set on *The Latin Jazz Quintet*. Instead, Ramirez is coupled with soulful conga player Tommy Lopez on every tune, joining bassist Bobby Rodríges, Arthur Jenkins on piano, and vibraphonist Felipe Díaz.

---

* Of the nine reissued versions of *The Latin Jazz Quintet*, only the 2015 unofficial release by Jazz Wax includes Eric's name on the album cover. Discogs.com states the recording year as 1961.

Dolphy's bass clarinet is showcased on the opening track, 'You're The Cutest One,' a fanciful cha-cha on which he branches way out, exploring a set of funky riffs and rhythmic gestures. 'Speak Low' presents a carefree flute solo (listen for 'Pop Goes The Weasel'), and in 'I Got Rhythm' he dispatches staccato bass clarinet and a doggedly inventive, turbulent, Parker-channeling solo. The scored melody arrangement of 'Night In Tunisia' includes snarky flute/vibraphone dissonances and what might be extended technique with simultaneous vocalizations. For his solo, he switches to alto sax for a mid-tune rumpus ride: he's not holding back, but he does stick to conventional cadence points. 'Cha Cha King' is a jaunty salsa adaptation of Edvard Grieg's 'In The Hall Of The Mountain King' from *Peer Gynt*. (Talk about third stream!) The Hart/Rodgers standard 'I Wish I Were In Love Again' features flute through the head, then shoots out a freewheeling bass clarinet solo, cutting into Jenkins's *montuno* with serrated fortitude. The disc's remaining three titles featuring flute are serious takes: scored and solo work on Rodgers and Hart's 'Lover;' a curiously pungent 'outside' solo on the montuno-heavy 'Mangolina'; and his most commercial approach on Diaz's meandering 'April Rain.'

Amid the questionable aesthetic landscape of the late mambo craze and the afterlife of 50s-era easy listening, *The Latin Jazz Quintet* seems to have slipped through the cracks of Dolphyphile attention, as the first of seven imported reissues did not appear until twenty-eight years later. Remarkably, the disc has yet to be reissued in the USA. Eric made no big compromises for the recording's commercial purpose except that most of the solos, though pliant and of best intentions, are short, curtailing longer forays into his expanding post-bop language. The multi-instrumentalist's comments on *Caribé* can also be applied to *The Latin Jazz Quintet*: 'Every different kind of music is its own particular challenge. In my own group I concentrate on playing my own compositions, and this [sideman in a Latin jazz project] requires a different approach.'[2]

It is worth remembering that Eric was a bilingual Spanish speaker with Latino heritage, although there is no evidence of a deeper musical cultural connection; no sign that Caribbean, Panamanian, or Costa Rican music was important enough for the Dolphys to pass down such tastes to their son. As a youngster, Dolphy may even have veiled his own Latino traits and interests from his circle of African American friends, downplaying his parent's West Indian and Hispanic roots and Eric Sr.'s multi-racial background. In this regard, one thinks of the cruelties Mingus faced in his Watts upbringing as a mixed-race 'yellow' child with Asian ancestry in a Black community, and over conflicting modes of racial identity within his family. Regardless, Dolphy held an undying interest in world music, an intellectual concern and artistic passion emboldened by the global intersections he discovered in Los Angeles, New York, and Europe.

The Latin Jazz Quintet sessions aside, Eric appears to have had some downtime between *Far Cry* and the start of another intense recording period from late February to mid-March, when he participated as sideman on four albums. Simosko and Tepperman state simply that, after his last December recording, 'he dropped out of sight for the next two months,' overlooking the *Latin Jazz Quintet* sessions.[3] Raymond Horricks, on the other hand, suggests that Eric was sitting in on a lot of club jam sessions during this period. 'In one Harlem jam session,' he writes, 'Eric was heard blowing chorus after chorus on alto in the earlier straight swing style of Tab Smith,' the then-popular swing and R&B saxophonist.[4] In comments attributed to Dolphy about these appearances, it is said that he quipped, 'You can hear two hundred saxophone players around New York blowing just the same. On records it's important I become Eric Dolphy again.'[5]

RECORD REVIEWS

Dolphy's hard work throughout 1960 as album leader and notable sideman was paying off, and by early spring 1961, more reviews of his recordings began appearing. The *Bergen Record* cited *Screamin' The Blues* as an important album 'due in large part to the strong musical personalities of tenor/alto saxist Nelson and bass clarinetist/alto saxist Eric Dolphy. Anyone who thinks Ornette Coleman is saying new things should listen to Dolphy whose playing is experimentation and individualism personified.'[6] The four-star *DownBeat* review of the same album mentioned Eric only in passing, however, with no reference to his playing. Meanwhile, *Looking Ahead* earned praise as 'highly progressive' and 'far out,' with the *Pittsburg Courier* touting the album as 'one of the most significant releases of 1960' and remarking on Eric's genuine swing and synthesis of Ornette's 'pointless meanderings.'[7]

Caribé also caught the attention of the *Courier*, which noted that Dolphy 'is an accomplished saxophonist whose ideas are full of the froth of avant-gardism ... the insistent and consistent force which motivates his technique is the thing which sets him several pales above the journeyman.'[8] The paper's Harold L. Keith, in his

'Data 'Bout Discs' jazz column, was perhaps Dolphy's biggest supporter among the mainstream East Coast press, heaping superlatives, noting recording details, and following the player's development. His Chico Hamilton Quintet recordings were still being described as groundbreaking and definitive of a new West Coast sound, and in April, *Los Angeles Valley News* jazz writer Mike Davenport commented that, on *Charles Mingus Presents Charles Mingus*, 'Dolphy is probably the outstanding performer on the album. While he sounds somewhat like Ornette Coleman, his playing is much more logical.'[9]

Not all press exposure at this time was positive. A public upbraiding came in Rex Stewart's March *DownBeat* blindfold test with Leonard Feather. After listening to Ornette's 'Eventually,' from *The Shape Of Jazz To Come*, the Ellington horn man who'd frequented Lloyd Reese's Los Angeles home during Dolphy's student days responded, 'Wow! Protest! That reminds me of sitting in with Charles Mingus, I think the name is Eric Dolphy… I'd like to give him a lot of credit for trying real hard [but] frankly it did not appeal to me. No stars.'[10]

Feather would prove to be a thorn in Dolphy's side simply by giving so much space to jazz musicians denouncing his playing. A brewing critical storm would spill over into 1962, after Dolphy made his name with three Prestige releases as leader, his recorded and live work with Mingus, and on club stages with Coltrane. Dolphy's playing and musical relationship with the latter would be challenged by British jazz press invective clouding the quintet's tour there in November 1961. Ken McIntyre recalled *DownBeat*'s late-1960 review of *Looking Ahead*:

> A reviewer for *DownBeat* wrote, 'Don't listen to this record if you have the slightest hint of headache.' Later in the review he wrote about our 'libido,' called us the 'terrible twins,' and finally stated, 'All in all this is not a bad album.' He rated it at two and a half out of a possible five stars. How much influence this had on both our careers I do not really know, but it obviously did not help, because Eric subsequently left the country, and in October 1961 I started my public school teaching career at PS 171 in Manhattan.[11]

Not incidental to Eric's critical reception was the early 1961 folding of Hentoff and Williams's *Jazz Review*. Both founders extolled Dolphy's artistic virtues, but their short-lived publication did not survive to applaud any of his recordings.

LINCOLN'S *STRAIGHT AHEAD*, NELSON'S *BLUES AND THE ABSTRACT TRUTH*

A photograph dated February 22, 1961, captures Thelonious Monk standing next to a seated Coleman Hawkins during the Nola Studio sessions for Abbey Lincoln's powerful Candid album *Straight Ahead*. The pianist had been invited to give his blessing to her newly penned 'Blue Monk' lyrics. Hawkins looks apprehensive, as if waiting to see what type of day Monk is having; the pianist is still wearing his winter coat and hat and appears happy to be there, only a few weeks after a fire severely damaged his Harlem apartment. The musician in the foreground is likely Eric, an acolyte gazing away from the camera toward his musical hero.

On *Straight Ahead*, Dolphy joins Booker Little, Julian Priester, old Los Angeles friend Walter Benton, Mal Waldron, bassist Art Davis, Max Roach (then Lincoln's fiancé), and Roger Sanders and Robert Whitley on congas. According to Hentoff:

> Monk was quite pleased. He stuck around for most of the session, enjoying Lincoln's interpretation of Randy Weston's 'African Lady' ... Monk listened intently and danced to at least one number. . . . As Lincoln tells it, 'He whispered in my ear, Don't be so perfect. He meant, Don't be afraid to make a mistake.'[12]

That tune, originally from Weston's 1960 LP album *Uhuru Afrika* (*Freedom Africa*), sets Langston Hughes's culturally conscious, Black nationalist poetry to surges of melodic expression. One wonders if Monk enjoyed Eric's piccolo work on that track, a silvery, high-register obligato supporting both Lincoln's edgy vocals and Hawkins's moody solo. Dolphy's lines paint a wildlife menagerie of natural splendor suggesting an African exoticism. An alternate take of 'African Lady' is found on *Candid Dolphy*; they are the only known recordings of Eric playing the instrument. 'When Malindy Sings' features Dolphy's flute in a similar manner, playing filigree passages way back in the mix, echoing the bluesy mood of the last verse. These two tunes feature Dolphy's only exposed parts on the album; on other tracks, his alto sax and bass clarinet blend deep into scored arrangements.

Even when considering its cultish popularity, Oliver Nelson's *The Blues And The Abstract Truth* remains an underrated Impulse! album, with its original cover shouting out the names Bill Evans, Roy Haynes, Eric Dolphy, Oliver Nelson, Paul Chambers, and Freddie Hubbard. Subsequent covers did more justice by headlining Nelson, whose poignant, expressive arrangements here launched his name everywhere it hadn't already been heard. The forward-sounding clarity of Nelson's compositions and arrangements soon influenced much popular music with their economic and mood-inducing instrumental writing.

The blues, the thirty-two-bar form, and the 'I've Got Rhythm' chord progression dominate Nelson's materials here, with themes variously dressed in folksy, bebop, and hard-bop attire. Solos by each participant hit satisfying heights, and the recording presents the legendary Dolphy/Hubbard pairing in a new light. 'Stolen Moments' delivers a lyrical and commanding Hubbard solo that sparks something special from Dolphy, who follows with a mercurial flute passage, spryly compositional and seasoned. If the main theme of 'Hoe Down' seems a bit hokey, listen to how Nelson answers his opening with sectional contrasts, and how Hubbard's sharp brilliance gives way to Dolphy's 'beautifully projected and controlled, interesting alto saxophone solo,' as Nelson observed in his liner notes. Bill Evans delivers refined and adventuresome solos on every tune on which he plays. Other defining moments for Dolphy include 'Butch And Butch' and a zealous, parading solo on 'Yearnin''—'one hell of a solo,' according to *DownBeat*'s reviewer.

On the questioning 'Teenie's Blues,' with its quirky dual alto sax voicings, Dolphy's fantastical solo rips a hole in the speaker, squeaking, squawking, and leaping off the beat, defeating every listener's expectation, with a twisted 'Camp Town Races' quote to boot. Nimble bird chirps and stubby riffs alternate with strident howls sculpted into a miniature composition. It is one of Eric's finest studio solos of this period. *The Blues And The Abstract Truth* packs a punch thanks to the arrangements, its original material, and the soloists: it remains an exceptional document of Dolphy's progress and quickly emerging status as the high priest of post-bop invention. Rock legend Frank Zappa later shared that Eric's work on the album awakened him to the potential of free jazz within his own compositions, and Dolphy, Mingus, Cecil Taylor, and other jazz figures appear on a list of influences on his debut album, *Freak Out!* (Verve, 1966).*

---

* This author first learned of Eric Dolphy's name through that often-satirical composer's work 'Eric Dolphy Memorial Barbeque,' from the Mothers Of Invention album *Weasels Ripped My Flesh* (Bizarre/Reprise, 1970). From that first exposure I was prompted to explore Dolphy's albums from the local library during my high school years.

SUN RA

At some point during the winter of early 1961, New Yorkers started to catch glimpses of Herman Poole Blount, aka Sun Ra, walking about in space-age stage attire. Stranded in the city with a broken-down car and members of his Arkestra settling in the East Village, he and the group began performing locally. Relocating from Chicago, they occasionally performed at the Playhouse coffee shop. But it wasn't until January of 1962 that the Arkestra, billed as The Outer Spacemen, began gigging regularly at the Cafe Bizarre. Mingus came to hear them, as did Coltrane, the latter acknowledging the Arkestra's John Gilmore as a saxophonist whose playing, like Dolphy's, encouraged him to open up to new notions of improvisation and experimentation. The gig led to the Arkestra performing at film screenings at the Charles Theater, Greenwich Village's avant-garde film mecca. Soon, a full-fledged concert there was advertised in the *Village Voice* as Le Sun Ra & His Cosmic Jazz Space Patrol performing 'Outer Space Jazz,' a 'combination of Monk, Ellington, and Ornette Coleman.'[13] The jacket of the group's 1963 recording *When Angels Speak Of Love* (released in 1966) includes a poem by the bandleader that concludes, perhaps with a nod to Dolphy's first album as leader:

They speak of cosmic waves of sound
Wavelength infinity
Always touching planets
In opposition outward bound.[14]

Afro-futurism, space travel, alternative consciousness, and science-fiction tropes drew surface parallels between Sun Ra and Dolphy's album covers and titles: *Outward Bound*, *Out There*, and even *Out To Lunch*. Prestige ran a full-page ad that included *Outward Bound*, its sci-fi cover, and a blurb about the emerging figure: 'He has been acclaimed as one of the great jazzmen of the future . . . the bridge between Coltrane and Coleman, but he sounds like no one but Eric Dolphy, and that means daring, depth and power.'[15]

The Marvel Comics character Iron Man debuted in the March 1963 *Tales Of Suspense* no. 39, the same month Eric premiered his new tune 'Iron Man' at a concert in Illinois, and three months before the recording sessions for the *Conversations* and *Iron Man* albums, later released on the Douglas label. The sci-fi-enmeshed Cold War–era comic book story adds, in a peculiar way, to the fantasy dreamscape of this space-age avant-garde, where the emerging new age of consciousness and hallucinogens intermixed with Civil Rights and Black identity, the free speech movement, Eastern mysticism and Egyptology, the founding of NASA, early rumblings of the Vietnam War, and the promise of new worlds.* The avant-garde provocateurs of this circus's celebration of the celestial and earthbound underground played increasingly free music, escaping traditional jazz restrictions and racist America, reimagining creative processes of ensemble interactions, and declaring new directions in music. The Sun Ra Arkestra charted a way to the stars. James Newton's liner notes to *Eric Dolphy: Musical Prophet* are appropriately titled 'From The Field Holler To Outer Space.'

ANOTHER *STRAIGHT AHEAD*

Less than a week after the *Straight Ahead* and *Blues And The Abstract Truth* sessions, Dolphy returned for yet another *Straight Ahead*: Oliver Nelson's Prestige album recorded on March 1 with Haynes, Duvivier, and Wyands. The *Screamin' The Blues* rhythm section once again filled Van Gelder's studio with inspirational backing on five Nelson compositions, several with extended scored passages. The intimate 'Images' brings close, secundal harmonies and dissonances to the alto and bass clarinet for the opening track's tenebrous, eerie mystery. The arranged theme stretches nearly two minutes before solos, as Nelson builds thematically from the tune's simple intervals and distant mood. Dolphy's brief, exuberant solo strikes a fine balance between pensive, low-register angularity and graceful gestures that spin up and out of the number's self-conscious character. 'Images' reveals a technically demanding solo, his instrument's copious timbral variety receiving a thorough examination. Simosko and Tepperman make the wholly inaccurate statement that Eric's solos on this album are 'relatively conservative'; *Straight Ahead* remains essential to the Dolphy discography, with performances of enigmatic power and musical expressions marking new plateaus of abstraction, ferocity, and freedom. In his extended commentary on the recording, Bill Kirchner comments that, though it is less renowned than *Abstract Truth*, *Straight Ahead* accomplishes as much in terms of artistic integrity.[16]

The album's 'Six And Four' juxtaposes multi-measure sections of six and

* The story of *Iron Man*—the first capitalist businessman superhero—begins with the anti-communist battling Vietnamese revolutionaries.

four beats. The opening blues figure is in six (with the piano's left hand in funky unison with the bass); a separate walking bass section is in four. The tight and springy rhythm section imparts a push-me, pull-me feel to the six-beat line that is then broken by the contrasting passage's smooth walking bass. Nelson, on alto, employs thematic development in his reserved solo, then swings over the walking bass. No part of *Straight Ahead* showcases the contrasts between the saxophonists as does the first part of Eric's alto solo played over the riff in six. It is deliberately 'out there,' halting and jumping, fooling around with the metric holes in the tune, filling them with gasping, rifled passages and marked convulsiveness. He then goes to town over the walking bass, smearing the soundscape with hellfire runs and licks, coming back to his 6/4 solo strategies through the repeat with even more exaggerated leaps and frantic excitement. Here he earns Goldberg's comments that 'his most notable musical quality is powerful force of conviction, which comes through on this album with almost stunning force.'[17]

Nelson's older sister inspired the third track, 'Mama Lou,' with Eric playing a plaintive flute melody in the slow introduction, then switching to alto to represent her other side: 'She's one of those people who displays two different moods,' explained Nelson in his liner notes. But the flute/alto handoffs don't illustrate Mama's moods as much as Dolphy's brief alto explosion, a fiery flipside to Oliver's work on the same instrument.

Milt Jackson's 'Ralph's New Blues' (written for Ralph Gleason) gets a rave send-up, featuring Nelson's clarinet on scored passages and what may be Eric's finest studio solo on bass clarinet: he gives an encyclopedic tour of his lexicon, a fleet treatise of dexterous upheaval drawn from his own terms and definitions, notwithstanding 'the blues.' It's an epic journey of idiosyncratic, labyrinthine expressions. In the second chorus, Haynes responds with oblique answers to a string of Dolphy's outpourings. Listeners need to stay on board for Nelson's superb tenor solo as we imagine how someone would follow this masterpiece of improvisation.

'Straight Ahead' is a mad rush of two altos, 'the humorous flag-waver of the set,' as Nelson states, and the leader takes a rip-roaring solo—his best on the album. He is glad, however, to have gone first, as Eric blisters on his watch, not unlike a volcanic eruption, and the trading fours between the alto men following Haynes's inspired solo is certainly one for the books, leading to an ornately arranged closing, an obstacle course of a finale.

Contributing to the street-address-as-song-title subgenre, Nelson's '111-44' closes *Straight Ahead* with spirited bass clarinet and alto doubling in the head. It is a tune dabbling in a pointed edginess that is arguably dulled by overly clever writing—and, like so many of Dolphy's sideman tracks, is far too brief of a musical moment for how much he had to say.

This short session (all tracks were first takes) brought an end to Eric's music-making with Nelson. That the two men recorded all three of their collaborative albums in less than ten months stands as a milestone not just in Dolphy's storied career as a featured sideman but in the whole of early 60s jazz. Prestige reissued their two albums as the 24000 series title *Images*. 'Oliver was sufficiently confident of his blowing capacities by this stage to choose the explosive Eric Dolphy to share these flights with him,' wrote Hentoff. 'Each, as it turned out, sharply stimulated the other, and they also complemented each other to considerable effect.' The stately Nelson, with his full, round saxophone tone so well-versed in jazz lore, from swing through the 50s moderns, embraced his fellow reedman's 'quite new grammar of jazz.'[18]

For some time, Dolphy had been facing a drought of performance opportunities for his quintet. He unsuccessfully hustled for club engagements at the start of the year, only to return to his spot in the Roy Haynes Quintet. They traveled to San Francisco's Jazz Workshop on March 5 for an engagement with Haynes as leader and Eric billed in the local press as the new sensational saxman. A rare and thus notable March gig for a Dolphy-led group was a brief Copa City club residency in Jamaica/Queens, playing opposite the Mingus Workshop until March 15. Complimenting the jazz reunion, the Copa sat close to where both Eric's aunt Luzmilda and Mingus's uncle Fess Williams kept their homes.

Eric was due back at Nola Studios on March 17 to record three numbers for Booker Little's Candid release *Out Front* with Julian Priester, Don Friedman on piano, bassist Art Davis, and Max Roach (the same personnel as for Abbey Lincoln's *Straight Ahead*, but with Friedman replacing Waldron). An April 4 follow-up session for that disc found Ron Carter on bass. Though it contains quality original compositions by Little and stellar performances, the album offered little space for Dolphy's soloing, save for brief alto exposure on 'We Speak,' 'Moods In Free Time' 'Quiet Please,' and a snippet on 'Hazy Hues.' Nonetheless, the *Out Front* date reinforced Dolphy's friendship with the younger Little, cementing their post–*Far Cry* collaboration and further securing the Eric Dolphy/Booker

Little Quintet's historical appearance at the Five Spot in less than four months' time. They would become partners in adventure—artistic soulmates feeding off a shared energy and exuberance.

Dolphy worked out on his alto a pungently free-sounding, one-minute-long set of contrasting gestures for 'Moods In Free Time' that at first sound inimitably abstract yet are closely reproduced on the alternate take found on *Candid Dolphy*, not unlike a structured composition. After a dramatic leap to the altissimo range, a sweep of microtonal smears descends, balanced by ghostly vocalizations and a rhythmicized, shaking emphasis on a few notes, taking the listener from lyrical extremes to a rather intense focus. Eric brings flute and a hot alto solo to 'Hazy Hues,' an alternate take of which also populates *Candid Dolphy*. On 'We Speak,' he follows Little's brilliant opening solo with an evanescent alto working of the tune's harmonic edges, wherein Little's expert use of three wind/brass voices creates tight harmonies that ring true to Eric's sense of composition. An alternate take of 'Quiet Please' also earned its way onto *Candid Dolphy*, and for good reason: he blows more daring contours and inventive, risky lines, offering a powerful solo elemental to this enlivened, edgy version.

GEORGE RUSSELL, 'ANGRY YOUNG CANNONBALL,' AND A TRIP HOME

Where *Out Front* offered listeners a too-brief glimpse of Dolphy's soloing, his April session for Ted Curson's *Plenty Of Horn* (Old Town), held at Bell Sound Studios, resulted in even less: flute obligato on two numbers, 'The Things We Did Last Summer' and 'Bali H'ai.' Pianist Kenny Drew rounded out the first-class rhythm section of Haynes and Jimmy Garrison; Eric would later hook up with Drew in Paris during the last weeks of his life.

The *Plenty Of Horn* bit part epitomizes Dolphy's periodic slippage into the background as a sideman when he should have been fronting his own group in clubs and readying his new compositions; springtime in New York and the *Outward Bound* session's first anniversary found him with little to do but plot the future. During this time, Dolphy began planning his solo tour to Europe, which would begin with an appearance in Berlin on August 30. Advance contracts, itineraries, and bookings were finalized by the time he flew back to Los Angeles in mid-May to visit his parents, following a session with a new collaborator.

The George Russell Sextet played various Birdland dates early in the year as their 1960 Riverside albums *Stratusphunk* and *Space Age Jazz* garnered positive reviews. Critics added Russell to the list of experimental modernists forging new paths of technical composition in jazz, and he won *DownBeat*'s 'New Star' poll that July. He brought detailed charts for his exceptional *Ezz-thetics* album, recorded at Plaza Sound Studios on May 8 and featuring Dolphy, trumpeter Don Ellis, Dave Baker on trombone, bassist Steve Swallow, and Joe Hunt on drums. The album commands attention in part due to Dolphy's zealous soloing, Russell's welcoming 'out there' atmosphere, and exceptional work from the other players.

Eric brought his alto sax and bass clarinet to the session, soloing on every tune, with particularly momentous work on ''Round Midnight.' Russell's avant-garde scoring of the introduction leads Dolphy in from special-effects-filled passages, for what Martin Williams would later describe as 'a decidedly exterior monologue':

> 'I try to get the instrument to more or less speak—everybody does,' Dolphy once said. The startling introduction here—a kind of instrumental imitation of electronic sounds—is a fine contrast to Dolphy's words-on-Monk.[19]

Eric carries the head without Ellis, slow and easy, full of gasps and less-than-predictable outpourings in a highly exposed alto line, his solo coming after the arrangement's three-and-a-half-minute mark. His long, uninterrupted playing is maintained into the melody's reprise, offering another example of the cutting-edge freedoms being enjoyed during this golden age of post-bop flirtations with free jazz. His ornaments zip and swirl around the theme's closing statement, to the heightened background of brass stings. The codetta is a fine example of composed new music meeting free jazz.

The title track, 'Ezz-thetic,' features a hard-driving chromatic line in challenging unison and doubling for Dolphy on alto, Ellis, and Baker. The up-tempo, disjunct tune is a drawn-out study in restless modal centers, with uniquely punctuating counterpoint from Russell's piano, taking the listener right into a set of blistering solos.

'Honesty' is the disc's jazz circus show tune, Baker's feelgood send-up à la Mingus, and Dolphy takes the first solo against this arrangement's many out-of-tempo breaks. Poetic license in full force, his alto shouts with wit and athleticism. Russell's 'Thoughts' balances its demanding score of juggling riffs, thorny head-like lines, and mood-contrasting subsections with the free improvisation provided by soloists. The band makes unusually dissonant parts and rugged harmonization sound easy, weaving in and out of successive solos, Dolphy's bass clarinet stepping out on its own without venturing too far.

With its clever reference to the tune's mode and Russell's Lydian theory of harmony, 'Lydiot' presents a cool yet demanding unison and doubled line among the three horns. Russell sets himself up for a deserved solo, breathing pianistic life into his chromatic concept against an effective rhythm section, the horns quietly emerging with shimmering clusters of tremolos. Dolphy's alto gets a short solo, tearing up Russell's scalar material. On bass clarinet for a brief workout of Miles's 'Nardis,' Dolphy reads through a moody, otherworldly passage and sets of interior gestures arranged for these three superb horn players, each then soloing. Finally, Al Kiger's hard bop 'Kiger's Tune' presents a healthy Dolphy alto solo and an excellent arrangement by Russell.

Russell got Eric's ear by talking up his *Lydian Chromatic Concept Of Tonal Organization*, a jazz theory book first published in 1953. In late November 1961, during Eric's European tour with Coltrane, he sent Russell a postcard from Baden-Baden, Germany, reading, 'Trying to play the new concept with an outward bound feeling.' By 1962, Russell's book was advertised with a blurb by Dolphy:

> 'Gives you so much more to work with.'
> —Eric Dolphy, New Star Poll-winner.[20]

The theory locates the power of harmonic progressions and modal pitch arrays in scales derived from the Lydian mode.* Some jazz musicians use the theory to discuss structures found in the music of Bill Evans, Miles, and Coltrane, among others. Regarding Dolphy's sophisticated interests in scalar resources, harmonic language, and challenging concepts of music theory, James Newton reminds us, 'There was this beautiful and rigorous dialogue going on between Yusef Lateef, John Coltrane, George Russell, and Eric Dolphy,' noting they were 'theoreticians of the highest order that were sharing their found information with one another

* The Lydian mode is like the major scale but with a raised fourth degree. Its rearranged seven pitches result in a circle of perfect fifths, which when sounded together can be voiced to sound as a major thirteenth chord with a raised eleventh. In the *Lydian Chromatic Concept*, systemic arrays of derivative scales and harmonic progressions are graded for their 'gravitational' effect and usefulness.

and impacting one another's art in profound ways.'[21] His interactions with Russell may have been limited, yet the intellectual bond was set. Dolphy's attraction to learning and his interest in musical theories like Russell's remained characteristic of the master musician throughout his life. But as a skilled and adventurous creative musician, Eric would never limit himself to a system. Before his sudden death in Berlin, he was scheduled to play with Russell in London later that summer.

Riverside quickly released *Ezz-thetics*, generating reviews such as the lengthy *Pittsburgh Courier* piece by Dolphy supporter Harold Keith, who also plugged the newly released *Out There*, recorded almost a year previous: 'One of the most dynamic forces involved in getting over to the public new ideas has been Eric Dolphy, a truly versatile exponent of so-called "atonal" jazz . . . [he] blows with complete abandon [and] plays with the aplomb of a virtuoso.'[22]

Sideman gigs indirectly paid extra when positive reviews shined a light on his playing, such as when the *Minneapolis Star Tribune* called him 'a major force in the success' of *Ezz-thetics*. *DownBeat* praised Russell's 'compelling voice' yet panned Dolphy as flamboyant and unconvincing, accusing him of producing an 'unlikely pastiche of too many other currently fashionable saxophonists . . . I get the impression of an angry young Cannonball.'[23] 'Angry,' of course, had become a veiled racist put-down from jazz critics skeptical of, for instance, Coltrane's fast flurries of dissonance and outside playing, his 'sheets of sound' carrying, according to cynical naysayers, a threatening undertone akin to 'uppity-ness' and resistance to the order of things: now Dolphy's name was added to the 'angry' list. (In the coming months, after their *Africa/Brass* and *Olé* sessions, Coltrane would begin inviting Dolphy to join his quartet at the Village Gate.)

In the midst of his second New York spring, Dolphy was no doubt proud of his uncompromising artistic accomplishments, a fast-track accumulation of recordings, many of which have entered into jazz history. Since breaking away from Hamilton and their four 1959 albums together, he already had six albums in stores and being reviewed: *Outward Bound*, *Looking Ahead*, *Charles Mingus Presents Charles Mingus*, *Screamin' The Blues*, and *Caribé*. Coming in the remaining months of 1961 would be twelve more titles: *Ezz-thetics*, *The Blues And The Abstract Truth*, *Free Jazz*, *Out There*, Coltrane's *Africa/Brass* and *Olé*, Booker Little's *Out Front*, Schuller and Lewis's *Jazz Abstractions*, volume one of *Eric Dolphy At The Five Spot*, Lincoln and Nelson's *Straight Ahead* albums, and *Newport Rebels*. Prestige delayed releasing *Far Cry*, recorded in December 1960 but in stores only in the spring of

1962. By the end of 1961, there would be twenty-two extant albums featuring Eric, his role varying from leader to featured soloist to ensemble member simply reading charts. Despite these accomplishments, he knew that his own group was not finding a footing in New York's club world. Playing onstage as a bandleader this infrequently was not even close to a viable livelihood, and record company royalties were not cutting it.

Eric Sr. and Sadie had last seen their son during their late summer trip to New York the previous year. Following the *Ezz-thetics* session, Eric flew back to Los Angeles to visit his parents, an event noted in Bill Smallwood's society column in the *California Eagle*: 'Sadie Dolphy's son, Eric, came out from Manhattan to visit awhile with her; later, he'll be Europe-bound.'[24] It was a needed respite with family and old-time friends, a chance to breathe before heading back out to new challenges and existential horizons. The Dolphy family reunion in the old Los Angeles neighborhood came about immediately before his only studio recordings with Coltrane, Eric no doubt sharing New York stories and detailing upcoming work with his famous musical partner.

JOHN COLTRANE: THE *AFRICA/BRASS* AND *OLÉ* SESSIONS

Coltrane's debut sessions under his new Impulse! contract resulted in the albums *Africa/Brass* and *Olé*. The large *Africa/Brass* ensemble proved to be a one-off for Coltrane, the sextet behind *Olé* a far more familiar sound to the leader. Coltrane continued to signal a post–*Giant Steps* period, turning away from those explorations into some of jazz's most advanced harmonic progressions and focusing instead on melodic and rhythmic development. In his earlier work with Miles and Bill Evans, Coltrane had assimilated the partly 'cool' harmonic landscape, emerging with so-called modal jazz's slower rate of harmonic change and elongated sonorities over which he often played the stacked arpeggiated chords comprising his 'sheets of sound.' The new approach fostered comparatively static harmonic landscapes, offering less deterministic, more open-ended support for solos, often presenting a polyrhythmic fabric spearheaded by drummer Elvin Jones. Dolphy and Coltrane met regularly at the latter's Queens apartment to rehearse, practice, and share ideas.

The first *Africa/Brass* date at Van Gelder's on May 23 (May 25 erroneously appears in various sources, but was the *Olé* album recording date), produced four tracks: 'Greensleeves' (two takes), 'Song Of The Underground Railroad,' 'The

Damned Don't Cry,' and 'Africa' (what became known as version one). Eric reads his parts, never soloing on an album given over to Coltrane and his core quartet with a big band background. This was the largest ensemble Coltrane would ever call forth, and was one full of mellow brass.

With McCoy Tyner's name misspelled as 'Turner' on the liner notes, his role as arranger was overshadowed for many years by the mythologizing surrounding Dolphy's role in this regard. Trane had enlisted Eric to orchestrate Tyner's piano voicings (a recording studio photo shows Dolphy consulting with Tyner at the piano), making Tyner the arranger and Dolphy the orchestrator and ultimately conductor of the session performances. Eric is quoted in the original liner notes as clarifying all of this from the very start, 'Actually, all I did was orchestrate. Basically, John and McCoy worked out the whole thing. And it all came from John: he knew exactly what he wanted. And that was, essentially, the feeling of his group.' The credits were eventually adjusted to reflect Coltrane's subsequent summarizing statement—'We've taken what McCoy was to have played at the piano and arranged it for orchestra'—resulting in this wording: 'Arranged by John Coltrane and McCoy Tyner and orchestrated and arranged by Eric Dolphy.' That final arrangement credit was likely an attempt at providing Dolphy with a trickle of royalties. The original album cover mentions only the John Coltrane Quartet, without identifying other musicians. Two weeks later, a second Englewood Cliffs session completed the *Africa/Brass* project when, on June 7, a smaller ensemble recorded two takes of 'Africa' (second version) and 'Blues Minor.'*

Coltrane had been listening to recordings of traditional African music, likely from the Folkways catalogue, which included *Music Of Equatorial Africa* (1949), *African Drums* (1954), *African And Afro-American Drums* (1954), *Bantu Choral Folk Songs* (1955), *Drums Of The Yoruba Of Nigeria* (1956), and a 1957 reissue of the 1939 78rpm title *African Music: Rhythm Of The Jungle*. The Baka (Pygmy) music so many authors mention in relation to Dolphy and Coltrane's exposure to African field recordings was likely heard on Lyrichord's recently released *Music Of The Rainforest Pygmies*. But perhaps the biggest influence on Coltrane in these

* The first take of 'Africa' from June 7 was later used for *The Africa/Brass Sessions: Vol. 2*, produced under the guidance of Alice Coltrane and released in 1974, where it appeared alongside May 23's second take of 'Greensleeves' and that session's 'Song Of The Underground Railroad.' In 1995, Impulse! incorporated all of the tracks into a two-disc set entitled *The Complete Africa/Brass Sessions*.

regards was Nigerian drummer Michael Babatunde Olatunji's 1960 Columbia album *Drums Of Passion*, a hugely popular title recorded in New York during the summer of 1959 and an international hit promoted among the label's jazz releases. Clark Terry, Yusef Lateef, George Duvivier, and other jazz notables performed on the recording, the success of which garnered Olatunji many club performances, including Birdland that March, bringing his music to jazz audiences.

Dolphy's playing on the *Africa/Brass* sessions is buried in a cavernous sound and commemorates the creative conjoining of two friends more than documenting Dolphy's voice within the Coltrane project. Rather, *Olé* sonically inaugurates the Dolphy/Coltrane pairing and was recorded in between the two *Africa/Brass* sessions on May 25, with Eric credited as George Lane due to Prestige contract limitations (a pseudonym that appeared on Atlantic reissues until 1976). On the *Olé* sessions, held at A&R Studios, Eric plays flute on the title track and 'To Her Ladyship' (the latter released only in 1970 on Atlantic's *The Coltrane Legacy*) and handles alto sax on 'Dahomey Dance' and 'Aisha.'

'Olé' is a vehicle for melodic exploration and rhythmic development, and one that beckons the future with free-jazz lines despite its strong tonal center. Coltrane even dispenses with a fully scored head, with Dolphy and Hubbard sitting out the opening passage. Dolphy's strongly tonal solo—in which he settles into whole, pure sustained notes from the tonic chord—alternates arpeggios and modal runs, with surprisingly restrained melodic phrases embedded in the modality and sonorities Tyner incessantly pounds out of the piano and that are bubbling up from the bassists' handiwork. Dolphy's playing is rather uninspired and conservative—surprisingly so, compared to what he and Coltrane would soon unleash during live club dates. Inaccurately describing the flute solo as 'rather free,' Simosko and Tepperman elaborate rightly on its sense of disassociation: 'Unfortunately, his and Hubbard's solos sound as if they were inserted into "Olé" rather than integral with it.'[25]

'Olé' is also a powerful study in the two–double bass idea, here featuring Reggie Workman and Art Davis, that Coltrane designed to enrich harmonically static numbers focusing on melody and rhythm. Broadcasting nightly from Chicago's Sutherland Hotel Lounge on radio station WSBC-FM for the first two weeks of March, the Coltrane Quartet was joined by second bassist Donald Garrett, with 'Equinox' including a Garrett/Workman bass duet. Both Garrett and Coltrane were consciously recreating a composite sound to mimic the East Indian water drum, whereby the stratification of low- and high-register basses creates stable, pulsing tones. In addition, it is important in these regards to consider Coltrane's positive impressions of the spectacular Haden/LaFaro pairing on Coleman's *Free Jazz* double-quartet format. At the Half Note for a March 16 gig, Coltrane invited Art Davis into his quartet for another two-bass experiment.

'Dahomey Dance' is a harmonically static work of moderate tempo that finds Dolphy's exuberant alto vocabulary solo celebrating the pan-African theme on a track anticipating the territory he will expand upon in future Coltrane quintet performances. In several distinctly 'outside' instances, Eric executes a spontaneous-sounding set of thinly connected blues gestures, and in making little effort toward overall developmental cohesiveness or performing long contiguous lines he sets up a highly episodic time reckoned with pauses, truncated phrases, and sudden leaps. The formal ambiguity of his 'Dahomey Dance' solo stems from a deep sense of structural freedom and a compositional nature defined by multiple motivic development. Moreover, Dolphy leans into intonational variation, tweaking pitches so that his tone palette and phrasing benefit from microtonal inflections. Compare this to Coltrane, who establishes a strong modal center and spins out spectacular riff-based phrasal development.

As with 'Olé,' Dolphy plays it fairly straight on the first released version of 'To Her Ladyship,' keeping within Tyner's harmonic field, shaping his phrases toward standard balladry, and playing it safe though passionate. The coda features what the head lacks, a scored passage with all three melody players. In 1989, Atlantic Jazz released a 'complete' *Olé* CD album featuring a second take of 'To Her Ladyship,' erroneously named 'Original Untitled Ballad.' If this far better take with Dolphy leading the tune had somehow found its way onto the original album, he would have been appreciated by a far wider audience early on. *Olé* was massively popular, reprinted ten times for the US market before the end of the 1960s. The disparity of Eric's performance on the posthumously released second take is a pre-echo of the even longer wait audiences endured before hearing the complete Village Vanguard recordings in 1997: Dolphy's best work from these Coltrane sessions remained hidden for many years. And he would never again join Coltrane in the studio for the purpose of releasing a commercial recording.

Dolphy's upcoming role as Coltrane's partner in live shows would slowly emerge over a ten-month period following the *Africa/Brass* and *Olé* projects. Found in this first stage of their venture is arguably the seed of what would soon become one of progressive jazz's existential crises: applying freer jazz and avant-garde exploration to an otherwise clearly structured tune format with a rhythm section keeping time. Eric was a contrasting yet compelling voice, a multi-instrumentalist capable of answering Coltrane's soaring solos with his own powerful and intricate work night after night live onstage. Their live solos elongated as they turned toward the freedoms Coleman, Ayler, and others had been investigating, including adventurous leaps among registers and a focus on the rhythmic complexity and metric placement of phrases less encumbered by concerns with tune structure, harmonic changes, and traditional melodic form.

RON CARTER'S *WHERE?* AND MAL WALDRON'S *THE QUEST*

Following the last *Africa/Brass* session, Eric returned to his apartment, knowing he'd be back in the studio for Prestige on June 20 for Ron Carter's album *Where?* and Mal Waldron's *The Quest* the week following. Waldron and Carter appear on each other's discs, the latter returning to play cello for Waldron, with Joe Benjamin covering on bass. Charlie (later Charli) Persip, whose work with Dizzy Gillespie began in 1954, played drums at both sessions.

Where? received a four-and-a-half star review from *DownBeat* and launches with an up-tempo unison of bowed cello and fat bass clarinet on the head of 'Rally.' This exciting, adventuresome piece foregrounds superb timing and a playfulness that recalls *Out There*. The low-register pairing proves once again that bass clarinet and cello can create wonderful jazz. A spot-on Duvivier handles bass on the tracks featuring Carter's cello. Eric's 'Rally' solo contains many of his increasingly legendary traits: serpentine sixteenths, outrageous leaps, snippets of 'Pop Goes The Weasel,' and melodic twists and turns defying phrasal expectations. That work fits perfectly into the track's joviality, complementing the tune's curious songfulness and contributing to its success as a timbral outsider.

Along with an obligatory dig at Eric's style, *DownBeat* noted the album's experimental nature, adding that the recording 'contains some excellent work by Dolphy at both the more conventional and the tortured extremes of his style.'[26] With a punch-less arrangement, 'Softly As A Morning Sunrise' finds Eric's throw-back vibrato cutting into the ballad with old-school panache before his alto solo takes us to unfamiliar new thing places dressed with blues cadences and romantic sensibility. But his solo becomes a mishmash, struggling with form and direction—a situation made worse by Carter's unusual cello attack and intonation, which makes for an unsettling sonic collaboration. Surprisingly, *DownBeat's* Pete Welding disagreed:

> This latter piece contains a stunning Dolphy alto solo, to my mind one of the finest he has recorded. It is a flashing, forward-moving improvisation of power and warmth, and it, too, possesses a contrapuntal character—in fact, Carter picks this up from Dolphy, as the cello follows the alto in order of solos. It is a strong, virile statement, sweeping and fully realized, and somewhat Bird-like at times.[27]

The number is underlined by the shock of its closing: Dolphy's trading fours with Persip is suddenly a shining delicious icing on what was to be a cake but popped out from the oven as something else. The title track, sans Dolphy, is somewhat ill-conceived, with piano, bass, and cello all wrestling for sonic attention within similar ranges. 'Yes, Indeed!' shines because of its tuneful clarity, an imaginative flute solo, and Carter's evocative upper register pizzicato solo over Duvivier's expert bass playing. Sticking with flute on 'Saucer Eyes,' Eric plays with authentic abandon above Carter's rightful instrument, the bass. 'Saucer Eyes' and 'Rally' are the true standouts of the session, and Waldron is superb throughout, as is Persip's soulful sensibility, economic groove, and swing. The album was reissued five times in the USA within two years of its 1962 release and helped solidify the experimental side of Dolphy's association with the darkness and brilliant timbral variety of Carter's cello.*

By the summer of 1961, pianist and composer Mal Waldron had recorded over seventy albums with some of the biggest names in jazz, including important Mingus Workshop discs for which he helped develop a freer sensibility. About that experience, Waldron shared that Mingus changed 'because the times changed … we were talking freedom and getting out of jails. Bar lines was like going to jail for us. So everyone wanted to escape from that. There was a general feeling that everyone wanted to be free.'[28]

---

* Prestige's 1971 reissue packaged *Where?* as a Dolphy disc with a full-bleed cover portrait of the pensive wind player, with 'Eric Dolphy' appearing prominently above Carter's name. *Where?* was then soon paired with *Far Cry* as the 1975 two-LP Prestige 24000 series reissue *Eric Dolphy/Ron Carter: Magic*.

Waldron and Dolphy first recorded together on Abbey Lincoln's *Straight Ahead* back in February and would share a recording studio on eight more occasions, all in 1961. On June 27, Waldron brought in a sextet of Dolphy, Persip, Booker Ervin, bassist Joe Benjamin, and Carter on cello for his stylistically transitional album *The Quest.* The pianist was already rehearsing with the Dolphy/Little Quintet for a two-week residency at the Five Spot, due to start on July 4. Waldron composed *The Quest*'s seven titles, each of which is realized here with a penchant for post-bop eclecticism. Dolphy offers a rare B-flat clarinet performance on 'Warm Canto,' a delicate chamber work featuring Carter's superb upper-register cello pizzicato soloing over Waldron's pensive chords and Benjamin's probing bass line (reminiscent of Carter's 'Yes, Indeed!'). The multi-instrumentalist inserts just-so sustained tones as scored pedal points in this reserved, thoughtful arrangement. There's a film noir edge to 'Status Seeking,' its stark dissonances, Benjamin's exposed bass line, and Persip's slicing hi-hat lifting the curtain on an urban nocturne of wet city streets and paranoid mystery.* Dolphy's intense alto solo bites right into that theme, advancing with pincers into the darkness, a rogue element running on electric rails, flashing futuristic sparks. This is a great track because Dolphy's virtuosic solo is followed by similarly incisive solo work by Ervin, Benjamin, and Waldron, each laying down energized musical lines constructed from a similar vein.

The up-tempo storm of 'We Diddit' gets off to the races with a blistering but brief alto solo, followed by convincing bowed cello and quality solos by Ervin and Waldron. 'Warp And Woof' brings Carter's bowed cello out over a cool, R&B-ish blues/swing lick. Dolphy's alto solo is a must-hear as he seizes the opportunity to carve out his own space in the spirit of a Mingus revival: he and Ervin shout out a chorus together before the riff returns. Scored reed parts support a moving cello line in the wet, plodding ballad 'Duquility,' while the quasi-serial composition 'Thirteen' is a near-cinematic curiosity, providing Dolphy's alto sax with opportunity. Waldron created the piece from a series of thirteen pitches subsequently used as chord roots, with unique polymetric layering

* The Dolphy/Little Quintet reprised 'Status Seeking' at the Five Spot, yet the track would miraculously not find its way onto either volume of *Eric Dolphy At The Five Spot*, eventually appearing instead on the posthumous LP *Here And There* (1966) and on yet another Prestige 24000 series two-LP reissue, *Status* (1977).

of parts. Carter's unmeasured tremolo bowing is delicate, and, along with his cello work on 'We Diddit,' is perhaps his best work on the instrument in all his Dolphy collaborations.

Pete Welding's acknowledged Eric's contributions in his four-and-a-half-star *DownBeat* review of *The Quest*:

> Dolphy, heard here almost entirely on alto saxophone, plays with his usual blistering force and thrusting passion, but on several of the numbers—Status and Warp most notably—he seems to be merely skittering across the surface of the chords, sputtering instead of speaking. He runs into some trouble on Canto, on which he plays clarinet, and hits a couple of clinkers during the course of an otherwise well-ordered and thoughtful solo.[29]

Waldron's 'Fire Waltz' appeared tailor-made for the reed man's sensibility: it's a Monkish number, uplifting and melodic, yet with no room for Eric to blow. This situation was remedied in spectacular fashion at the Five Spot the following week. Like other important albums featuring Eric as a sideman, Prestige reissued Waldron's album with reordered credits headlining Dolphy; the 1969 cover has 'Eric Dolphy And Booker Ervin' in a large font and 'With The Mal Waldron Sextet' smaller below. In 1978, the label reissued the disc as part of the 24000 series two-LP *Fire Waltz*, paired with Ken McIntyre's *Looking Ahead*, the cover of which has 'Eric Dolphy' in the largest possible single-line font size over a large format photo of him.

One might wonder how Eric's career would have played out if Prestige had displayed this respect for him during his life. Rather, the label would drop his contract in less than three months.

07 THE DOLPHY/LITTLE QUINTET, SOLO EUROPEAN TOUR, VILLAGE VANGUARD WITH COLTRANE

JULY–NOVEMBER 1961

In *DownBeat*'s June 22 issue, its 'Combo Directory' noted, 'Booker Little–Eric Dolphy (Ind.): Little, one of the most promising young trumpeters of recent years, and Dolphy, as a man of many reeds and much experimental music, make their new group a combination of much interest. A Candid album is due.'[1]

The group's parenthetical 'independent' status meant that they had neither professional management nor agency representation; the two frontmen handled bookings themselves. To any Dolphy or Little fan, the teaser about a Candid album adds to the tragedy of Little's death in the coming October, as a studio session tied to his contract would have greatly complimented the highly praised live concert Prestige recorded at the Five Spot that July. Dolphy's reputation as a temerarious soloist blazing a new path was cemented in the jazz world, and though there would be no forthcoming Dolphy/Little studio album, their live performances helped define the year in jazz.

Bassist Richard Davis was scheduled to play on Little's *Out Front*, only to be replaced at the last minute by Ron Carter. Serendipitously, Eric ran into Davis on a subway platform and introduced himself, as the bassist recalled:

> I said, 'Well, pleasure meeting you.' And he said, 'What are you doing this weekend?' 'Nothing.' He said, 'Would you work with me this weekend?' I said, 'Sure.' And that was the beginning of a beautiful, heavenly relationship.[2]

Davis walked into the Dolphy/Little Quintet, which he felt was certainly Eric's group. 'I don't think we ever rehearsed. We just got together and started playing,' the bassist recalled at one point, though over the years his recollections changed, as he later stated, 'We had time to assess the music because we played it at my house, at his house, and at the Five Spot during the daytime ... I felt good about the music then, but when I heard it years later, I was able to understand how far ahead of his time Eric was. I felt he knew exactly where he wanted to go with the music he was playing.'[3] Pianist Mal Waldron remembered two weeks of solid preparation, commenting that the rehearsals were 'very inspiring too, because it made you think, and it moved you in different directions for your own personal way of writing music when you got back to it. And it was very educating.'[4]

Growing up in Chicago, an underaged Davis snuck inside blues joints such as the 708 Club, hosting the likes of Memphis Slim and Muddy Waters, and fell in love with the bass. As a journeyman he attended what he termed the University Of Sarah Vaughn, playing for the singer yet ultimately leaving for more adventurous jazz in order to play the notes and rhythms in his head. Film director Spike Lee's father, Bill Lee, encouraged him to use a bow. With Dolphy, Davis later said, 'That was exactly where I knew these sounds fit ... it was free.'[5] Later, he would often find it best to play down his widely recognized bass work on hundreds of non-jazz projects, such as Van Morrison's watershed 1968 album *Astral Weeks*, a timeless cross of folk, rock, and light jazz.

In the meantime, the final week of May brought a poor, three-star *DownBeat* review of *Caribé* haranguing Dolphy's tone and style:

> The inclusion of Dolphy as a guest in this set is not completely successful. The raw, jagged attack he is currently using on alto saxophone seems out of place.... He turns to bass clarinet on 'First Bass Line' [on which] his own solo becomes a wildly wiggling thing expressed with a strained intonation that breaks the easy atmosphere. . . . Dolphy's apparent determination to be different destroys what might have been an excellent piece. . . . It's unfortunate that Dolphy is such a conditioning influence on this disc.[6]

LIVE AT THE FIVE SPOT

DownBeat's 'Strictly Ad Lib' gossip column rarely mentioned Eric, though that same May issue noted the Dolphy/Little group's formation. The *New York Daily News* also sported a short plug on July 4th: 'Five by Five: The Booker Little Quintet, featuring Eric Dolphy, opens a two-week stand tonight at the Five-

Spot Café.' Five days into the residency, the same newspaper's Don Nelsen cited Dolphy as one of only a few contemporary alto saxophonists who 'have been able to get out from under the immense shadow of the late Charlie Parker.'[7]

With a cooperative attitude, the group prepared three works by Little, two by Waldron, and two by Dolphy, plus the Burke/Van Heusen standard 'Like Someone In Love' and 'God Bless The Child' by Billie Holiday and Arthur Herzog Jr. The latter, transformed into Eric's signature piece for unaccompanied bass clarinet, was destined to be captured on several live recordings but never in the studio.* The drummer that night was an active member of Ornette's quintet, Ed Blackwell, who brought a vast vocabulary of inventive percussion, forming an axis with Dolphy and Little, two capable, abstract players looking to distance themselves from complacency. Waldron brought power and elegance to the rhythm section, was up for experimentation, and, with Davis, formed a firm yet flexible backbone.

As word of the residency spread, musicians flocked to the club, the curious, the skeptical, and supporters alike crowding into the small venue. Driving to New York from Los Angeles that early July, in part to meet Dolphy and follow in his footsteps, saxophonist Sonny Simmons and flutist Prince Lasha went straight to the Five Spot the first night they arrived in the city.† Scattered across four albums over five years, the label's initial releases of ten Five Spot numbers include several long tracks taking up entire album sides. Below is a breakdown of the releases. Titles 1–6 are Prestige releases and account for all ten tracks.‡

1. *Eric Dolphy At The Five Spot Volume 1* (1961): 'Fire Waltz,' 'Bee Vamp,' 'The Prophet'
2. *Eric Dolphy At The Five Spot Volume 2* (1963): 'Aggression,' 'Like Someone In Love'

---

* 'God Bless The Child' was recorded for German television (*The Berlin Concerts*, Enja, 1978), in Copenhagen (*Eric Dolphy in Europe, Vol. 1*, Prestige, 1964), and in Stockholm (*Stockholm Sessions*, Enja, 1981). Dolphy's performance of the number at the University Of Illinois in 1963 was released decades later on *The Illinois Concert* (Blue Note, 1999).

† The two would meet their idol and participate in Eric's 1963 *Conversations / Iron Man* sessions while contributing one of their own, 'Music Matador,' to the project. Prior to that, Dolphy had heard Simmons play alto on Lasha's album *The Cry!*

‡ Prestige's remastered three-LP box set *The Great Concert Of Eric Dolphy* (1974) collates the first three albums dedicated to that evening's music. The 1982 Prestige album *Dash One* includes the second version of 'Bee Vamp.'

3. *Eric Dolphy & Booker Little Memorial Album* (1965): 'Number Eight,' 'Booker's Waltz'
4. *Here And There* (1966, Side A): 'Status Seeking,' 'God Bless The Child'
5. *The Great Concert Of Eric Dolphy* (remastered three-LP box set of albums 1–3 above, 1974)
6. *Dash One* (1982): second version of 'Bee Vamp'
7. *Eric Dolphy/Booker Little Quintet At The Five Spot: Complete Edition* (Essential Jazz Classics double CD, 2011)

For listeners at home, 'Fire Waltz,' Little's 'Bee Vamp,' and Eric's 'The Prophet,' written for Richard Jennings, comprised *Live At The Five Spot Volume 1*, released by Prestige that December. Emanating from the dimly lit club's small stage, 'The Prophet' announces a wandering, expressionistic ambiguity. Blackwell immediately adds a new inflection to the tune, his gestures accenting and complimenting Dolphy's contours and expressive points proving definitive. The tempo is pensive: a grave, somber time frame in which sustained dissonances from sax and trumpet are lifted by Waldron's precise, rich chordal vamps and Davis's punctual line. The head returns after a brief chorus of Eric's restrained explorations and Blackwell's colorful attacks, and then it's into Eric's solo, celebrating his presence on a New York club stage as the elder co-leader of a fine band: excited vocalizations, bird calls, guttural exaltations, buzzing melodic fragments, and outrageous leaps to outside pitches. His alto extemporaneously reimagines form and is compositional as much as it is a mere solo: backyard bird conversations from Los Angeles, conversational outpourings perfected with Mingus, and playful rhythmic tirades, all mixed in with polytonal sheets of post-bop free association. Yet Waldron and Davis are playing through a chord progression to which Dolphy frequently returns, touching base, cadencing a sub-phrase, or sustaining a chordal tone. Richard Cook and Brian Morton of the *Penguin Guide to Jazz* note that 'The Prophet' is 'quite clearly autobiographical piece, an insight into Dolphy's own quicksilver personality and forward-looking intelligence.'[8] Blackwell masterfully shadows Dolphy, commanding a unique direction and breaking free from Waldron and Davis before laying back into a pocket.

Dolphy's 'Number Eight (Potsa Lotsa)' explodes from Waldron's low-end riff, the tune's rhythmic two-part head for alto and trumpet pronounces its dissonant voicings in tense contours. The catchy number takes us to Little's concise, bright solo; the twenty-three-year-old has something masterful to say.* Dolphy seems to resume the whirlwind he displayed on 'The Prophet,' a carefree virtuoso journeying with the magnificent support of Davis and Blackwell.

Following Waldron's succinct piano gestures, the introduction to 'Like Someone In Love' features a well-thought-out polyphony of bowed bass, trumpet, and flute, lyrically entwined in gracefully suspended meter. Moderate-speed walking bass emerges after Eric's staccato transition, and his long solo is a marvel, though its length raised the ire of a few influential critics.† The track closes in on twenty minutes as everyone gets to stretch out.

'God Bless The Child,' released in 1966 on *Here And There*, is a revelation: emotionally lyrical yet gutsy unaccompanied bass clarinet in remarkable contrast to the quintet's big new thing sound that careened onstage every night of its Five Spot residency. Earning the club's rapt attention that night, a few squawks and squeaks emerge from a purely human realm, happy imperfections embedded in daring perfection. Dolphy was thirteen when Okeh first released the tune by Billie Holiday with the Eddie Heywood Orchestra; now, riffing off the theme with fluid arpeggios, the lone musician ventures into a compositional arena. Its five and a half minutes pass too quickly. This performance helps explain what Eric was doing at home during those sometimes lonely stints: namely, practicing and working up this rarified masterwork's triumphant undertow. As Colin Fleming commented on this performance:

> His attack is all swoops, dives, and bench-pressing of geological plates, as if coming from inside the earth and then pushing against a canopy of stars, before raining back down in droplets of indigo and liquefied rubber. You're not going to find a more demanding piece, but he underpins this dialogic wonder, as Holiday did, with the blues. It is a blues both ancient and modern, incorporating ageless rhythms of Africa with the Mondrian-

---

* The posthumous 1965 Prestige album *Eric Dolphy And Booker Little: Memorial Album/Recorded Live At The Five Spot* features 'Number Eight (Potsa Lotsa)' and 'Booker's Waltz.' In justifying using an entire album side for one tune, Prestige insisted on printing a seventeen-minute duration for 'Number Eight (Potsa Lotsa),' though it actually runs a few seconds over fifteen minutes.

† Alun Morgan of the UK's *Gramophone* magazine stated, 'Surely no jazz student would have objected to slashing cuts being made in the solos of Little and Dolphy … rarely have we had to endure so much musical filibustering.'

> like coloristic staccato of the city. At some intervals you might think of it as sci-fi, and then—two clicks of Dolphy's tongue later—as a hymn that has enfolded the earth since long before we got here.[9]

Little's 'Aggression' pulls in the listener with trumpet and bass clarinet, the sectional tune in rhythmic unison until Eric's sustained pitches fade out and the younger front man strides into his bristling, challenging solo. Dolphy answers with daring spaces of furious monologue, and the two leaders execute a timeless trading eights section with Blackwell before the tune's reprise. Waldron's 'Fire Waltz' is a fun romp, Eric's opening alto work blistering with halting rhythmic figures and unexpected turns, taking playful revenge for having been skipped over on *The Quest's* studio version. It also offers one of his best alto solos from this stage of his career. Little enters with a simple descending counterpoint to Dolphy's delicate juggling of fragmented, speech-like vocabulary with out-of-the-blue, ranting exclamations, a passage barely pulling back from the edge of blessed mania.

The first version of Little's 'Bee Vamp' seems to have caught the bass clarinetist off guard: there are delayed entrances, intonation issues, and sometimes awkward voicings of the tune across registers. An entertaining solo attempts to redeem those missteps, however, and both versions of 'Bee Vamp' are must-hear tracks. Uneven mic placement, an out-of-tune piano, and Blackwell's overly elastic approach unsettle 'Booker's Waltz,' the band struggling to gel despite Dolphy's fancifully acrobatic bass clarinet solo. It is the stomping 'Status Seeking' that remains this quintet's calling card: up-tempo, gritty, a rhythm section off to the races, and unforgiving, brazenly hot soloing from both frontmen. Davis pushes the group, laying down stubbornly powerful bass lines as Dolphy manages to carry his playing past 'Fire Waltz' intensity.

But the Five Spot recordings also present questions. As this was a professional session run by Esmond Edwards and Van Gelder, why does the instrumental mix suffer from poor mic placement? Why didn't Prestige recording supervisor Edwards have the club's piano tuned prior to the performance? The band had started its residency on July 4, and the recordings were made on July 16; was the piano out of tune the entire two weeks? Did it gradually go out of tune during the engagement? Few listeners have failed to hear sour notes in exposed upper-register passages. Yet the jazz world is fortunate Prestige recorded the show.

Dolphy and Little met again in the studio during four sessions for Max Roach's *Percussion Bitter Sweet* album in early August. Little died from uremia less than two months later, on October 5, 1961. Fellow musicians had noticed the young trumpeter sitting down at gigs to catch his breath. His *DownBeat* death notice states that a form of arthritis afflicted his right hand, making it difficult to play. He was hospitalized, with blood tests likely revealing anemia and blood clotting, and a call went out for blood donors. These symptoms of untreated lupus—an autoimmune disease causing fatigue, joint inflammation, muscular cramps, and skin rashes—can advance to include kidney failure, as in Little's case.

The Dolphy/Little Quintet Five Spot residency and recording made a huge impact, though the ensemble would never play or record again. Critics called the group a 'role model for all progressive jazz combos to come' and 'a quintet that could have become very basic to modern jazz but didn't.'[10]

In early 1962, *DownBeat*'s Harvey Pekar reviewed *Eric Dolphy at the Five Spot: Volume 1*, praising the group's breadth while directly panning Dolphy's performance. His playing 'has deteriorated badly,' is 'compelling by virtue of its violence,' is not 'concerned with the melodic content of his solos and repeats several pet phrases ad nauseum,' 'has little contrast in it,' and achieves only the level of 'screaming intensity.'[11] Along with Gunther Schuller, Don Heckman, and others, Pekar contributed to Nat Hentoff and Martin Williams's *Jazz Review*, published from 1958 to January of 1961, and would later gain cult fame as an underground author and collaborator, with renowned illustrator R. Crumb, on the self-deprecating autobiographical comic book series *American Splendor*. Though he later championed out-of-mainstream artists as a music and film critic, at twenty-five he was trashing Dolphy with all his might.

NEW STAR ALTO AWARD

During July, forty-one critics from ten countries voted Eric the 'New Star' on alto sax in the *DownBeat* International Critics Poll, which was published on August 3. He placed second in both flute and 'miscellaneous' (bass clarinet), with critical commentary from Europe and Japan notably favorable. On alto sax he beat out Jackie McLean, Leo Wright, John Handy, Charline Mariano, and Hank Crawford. Though his Prestige contract ended in September, the label went the extra yard in the magazine, boasting of their man's award by running a full-page ad promoting *Outward Bound*, *Out There*, and *Screamin' The Blues*:

> Starting with Lester Young, continuing through Charlie Parker, and coming down to the present day by way of Sonny Rollins and John Coltrane, there is a tradition that the lasting innovations in jazz always appear first on the saxophone. The latest proof of that tradition is Eric Dolphy. He plays alto, flute, and bass clarinet—there are more, but he will only record on those three—but versatility is the least of his accomplishments. He has been acclaimed as one of the great jazzmen of the future by such esteemed critics as Nat Hentoff and Martin Williams. He has been called the bridge between Coltrane and Ornette Coleman, but he sounds like no one else but Eric Dolphy, and that means daring, depth, and power. His first album, appropriately called OUTWARD BOUND, adds one more name to the impressive roster of those greats who were first recognized by Prestige. It has created the greatest critical stir in recent years.

Announcing the release of *Out There*, the ad emphasizes Dolphy's edginess, claiming that '*Out There* is certain to be the most controversial album of 1961.' Promoting work by Oliver Nelson, Eric, and Richard Williams in *Screamin' The Blues*, the ad states that if 'the careers of those three gentlemen go as the way they should, someday *Screamin' The Blues* will have the same status of classic that the Miles Davis sessions enjoy.'

The 'New Star' award sent ripples through the jazz world, perhaps more as an acknowledgment of the iconoclastic musician's total virtuosity than of the radical stylistic synthesis revealed in his imaginative post-bop language. *DownBeat*'s blurb acknowledged a late bloomer, noting, 'Eric Dolphy is considered one of the young Turks among jazzmen—although since he was born in 1928 (in Los Angeles), he is only two years younger than, for instance, Ray Brown. But Dolphy is a member of a fiery generation of new jazzmen.'[12]

The award appeared as a rebuke to the multi-instrumentalist's growing number of detractors in print, reluctant club owners choosing not to hire his groups, and fellow musicians openly dismissing his work. Ira Gitler placed Eric third in a vote that marked that critic's slide into outright anti-Dolphy vitriol, though he later claimed to have touted Eric as a future great when others did not. Later in the year, Gitler joined John Tynan, Leonard Feather, and others in condemning Dolphy's work as heard in recordings and in the Coltrane Quintet. In a March

1962 *DownBeat* review of Booker Little's *Out Front*, he went out of his way to badmouth Dolphy, despite his near absence from album soloing: 'It is fortunate that Dolphy does not get any more solo space than he does. I used to be one of his champions, but he is hard to tolerate anymore. I like to think that it is he, rather than I, who has changed. He has taken his worst characteristics and amplified them.'[13] Such negative press helped to further sink Eric's slim chances of making a living playing his music.*

Dolphy's prescient words in response to the 1961 *DownBeat* award signaled an increasingly ominous reality: 'Does that mean I'm going to get work?' The tragic answer is that he would get very little as a leader. Regardless, the fall of 1961 would find him on a European solo tour, then at the Monterey Jazz Festival with Coltrane, and finally back in Europe with Coltrane's Quintet—the latter tour coming on the heels of their heralded Village Vanguard residency in November. Along with those with the Mingus Workshop, these recorded appearances produced a legacy of some of his best performances captured live.

In the face of awards and negative criticism alike, by August Eric was juggling several roles, including that of cutting-edge yet struggling bandleader, A-list session musician preparing for Max Roach's *Percussion Bitter Sweet* album, and soon-to-be European traveler on a solo tour headlining performances with both all-star and lesser-known pick-up groups. Immediately following his Five Spot engagement, Eric rounded out the Coltrane Quintet on a Village Gate bill split with Aretha Franklin, with club owner Art D'Lugoff booking them for an August return. In the meantime, that quintet started August's first Friday at Detroit's Minor Key—a repurposed westside furniture store—for an engagement attended by twenty-year-old local Bennie Maupin and his friend pianist/arranger Alice McLeod, soon to be Coltrane's wife. As Maupin recalled:

> Eric came to Detroit during the period he was playing with Coltrane ... they had established this thing that was really upsetting a lot of people

* In 1974, Prestige failed to find an appropriate candidate to write liner notes for the box set *The Great Concert Of Eric Dolphy*: for this historically important reissue, none other than Gitler wrote effusively of the artists and about how he had encouraged Prestige to sign Dolphy, a musician who had 'carved out a sizable reputation as an innovator and strong personal voice.' As late as 1987, Gitler was again inaptly tasked with writing rose-colored rearview mirror liner notes for *Eric Dolphy & Booker Little Remembered Live At Sweet Basil* (ProJazz).

> because it was so incredibly powerful, unlike anything that had ever been presented, unlike anything I had heard. . . . Alice and I went to hear Trane. . . . They played, and at the end of the night I went over [and] Eric was standing there as people were saying hello, musicians were just gathering around. I told him that I had just started to play the flute. He just looked at me as he held his flute and says, 'Here, play something for me.' He gave me the flute and proceeded to give me like a thirty- or forty-minute lesson, right there at the end of his gig. . . . I'll never forget that moment because that was my moment, my only moment with him. It was amazing.[14]

Coaching Maupin on balance, fingering, and embouchure, the master musician commented, 'You'll be okay. Just practice a lot of long tones and play every day.' The moment also marked the first time Maupin witnessed the bass clarinet performed Dolphy's way. Eight years later, Maupin played the instrument on Miles Davis's watershed album *Bitches Brew*.

Some in the jazz world were beginning to propound Dolphy as the 'reputable' learned explorer of free jazz who incorporated chord changes and retained links to musical elements that Ornette, Taylor, and other pioneers tended to ignore, visiting a densely chromatic plethora of notes as a soloist, per Litweiler, 'with a sense of harmony and a free association of solo form that often came much closer to atonality than Ornette.'[15] Dolphy had already arrived to carry part of the free-jazz banner, and in the late summer of 1961, he emerged as one of the parade leaders. He challenged 1950s conformity, like Ornette musically and Mingus rhetorically, appearing as an uncompromising cultural militant, an avant-garde urban minstrel speaking a different language. (Over the next few years, Ornette would gradually recede from the limelight and temporarily closed shop, choosing to not play clubs rather than to play for peanuts: he also rejected the 'free jazz' label, stating much later that, 'the word *free* indicates just that, but I haven't been able to acquire that kind of freedom to say it's free. Because I've spent a lot of time working things out.'[16])

Despite his recordings as leader with Prestige/New Jazz and later Blue Note, the role of sideman would dominate Eric's livelihood from his discharge from the Army to his last days—a little over a decade between the ages of twenty-five and thirty-six. He made little from royalties or by playing original material from his albums in clubs with groups under his name. The growing ranks of his American fan base were not nearly enough to sustain him financially, and, save for a brief stint at the Jazz Gallery that August (one performance of which Sonny Rollins attested to attending), he was not getting any gigs for his group. His music was heard by some as a guidepost from the future, yet day-to-day struggles forced his eyes overseas. A European tour was set to kick into gear at the end of the month, with two weeks of club dates, television, and radio broadcasts. Overseas rewards, exposure, and challenges awaited the man who now had an international following in Europe and in Japan (where, at the time of his death, he had plans to tour). In European capitals, he would be received as an artist worthy of immediate attention, yet his work, while percolating to core followers and believers in the new thing, did not command the American jazz stage.

Despite Prestige's promotions that summer, the label soon dropped him and would long delay the posthumous release in three volumes of his September 1961 Copenhagen recordings. While Ornette was turning down gigs because management refused to pay his groups adequately, Eric had very few to turn down. He would not meet up with Albert Ayler until 1963, in part because Ayler had already fled the inhospitable US club environment for Scandinavia. Despite winning awards in 1961, Dolphy failed to place higher than fourth in any *DownBeat* poll category in 1962.

AUGUST 1961

Roach's Impulse! album *Percussion Bitter Sweet* uses a core of musicians from the Candid period sprinkled with Dolphy's friends and collaborators, including Mal Waldron, Clifford Jordan, Julian Priester, Booker Little, Abbey Lincoln, and bassist Art Davis, in addition to Latin percussion specialists Carlos 'Patato' Valeler on congas and Carlos 'Totico' Eugenio on cowbell. Tragically, this would be twenty-three-year-old Booker Little's final recording.

The four sessions were stretched over nine busy days. On Tuesday, August 1, they cut 'Garvey's Ghost' and 'Mendacity'; on August 3, 'Mama' and 'Tender Warriors,' a session quickly followed by the weekend with Coltrane in Detroit; on August 8, 'Praise For A Martyr,' with Eric joining Coltrane that night to launch the quintet's second Village Gate run; and on August 9, 'Man From South Africa.' *DownBeat*'s Pete Welding found the Roach album singularly unappealing, yet added, 'Dolphy is stunning in several spots and for several different reasons. His bass clarinet solo on *Warriors* [sic] is in his most bristling, angry, snappish manner.' The reviewer continued by contrasting 'his limpid, fluid flute work in that piece's theme, and in Mendacity, his long, sinuous, and strongly individual alto solo (incorporating the human cry effect) follows Miss Lincoln's doltish treatment of the tune.'[17]

The 'Tender Warriors' theme finds Eric's exposed flute scored above the full ensemble. He unslings the bass clarinet for the solo, executing a sinuous upheaval, an exemplary sample from his sideman portfolio. His alto work on 'Mendacity' rewards repeated hearings for its idiosyncratic elasticity, waves of sound, blues executed with expressive alacrity, and head-turning acrobatics. His alto solo on 'Man From South Africa' is a more-than-usually focused hard-bop essay designed to fit the tune's mood and cool riff, and to reflect the other soloist's work; though soloing on alto, he begins and ends the tune's arrangement on flute. The track reminds us how convincingly Dolphy could fit in stylistically. But in the same *DownBeat* review, one finds a good example of that publication's condescending social commentary amid crucial moments of the Civil Rights Movement: 'Another of the tedious essays in race-consciousness that apparently Roach has appropriated as his special province in the last year.'[18]

Starting August 8, the Coltrane Quintet returned to four weeks of Village Gate performances, sharing bills with the Horace Silver Quintet and Art Blakey & The Messengers with Wayne Shorter and Curtis Fuller. The quintet featured Tyner, Jones, and both Art Davis and Workman on bass, and at some point during the engagement they performed a thirty-five-minute version of 'My Favorite Things' with Eric on bass clarinet. This extended length was not new to Coltrane; an unissued recording of that tune from the previous month ran a reported forty-five minutes.[19]

'My Favorite Things' became a major vehicle for Dolphy's flute during the European tour. Using long-misplaced recordings of their first New York club engagement, Impulse! released *Evenings At The Village Gate: John Coltrane With Eric Dolphy* in July 2023.* Workman recalls Dolphy's entrance to the group that summer:

* Their Village Gate set list included 'My Favorite Things,' 'When Lights Are Low,' 'Impressions,' 'Greensleeves,' and the only known live renditions of 'Africa.'

> [Coltrane] was always reaching for new sounds and Eric being in the group was part of that. They were very close in concept . . . I remember John sitting off to the side of the stage, listening to him doing a lot of different things. He loved Eric's sound on the bass clarinet. 'When Lights Are Low' is a great example of that, John giving the stage to Eric . . . when Eric jumped into it, he was very free with it.[20]

Dolphy programmed 'When Lights Are Low' throughout his subsequent European tour.

Workman continues by noting how Coltrane gave Eric long solo spots on some tunes, and that 'John would come after him and take a much shorter solo than he would normally take and let Eric's voice be prominent.' As revealed in recordings of their subsequent live sets, Coltrane assumed first solo and rarely backed away from longer excursions. On the *Evenings At The Village Gate* recording of 'Impressions' from mid-July, Dolphy's standard-length bass clarinet solo comes second and focuses on a set of hard bop ideas. He switched to alto for this number later in his tenure with Coltrane, and while he takes a bass clarinet solo on this set's 'Greensleeves,' he would sit out both takes of that tune on the Village Vanguard recordings made that November, the number having developed into a major vehicle for Coltrane's soprano sax.

Coltrane and Dolphy challenged each other physically as well as musically, and the quintet would in the coming months turn jazz on its head, earning the 'anti-jazz' invective, killing it at the Village Vanguard, and venturing out on a sweeping tour of European capitals via England. Raymond Horricks writes, 'When I saw Eric and Coltrane live I was only a few feet away from them. And I have never seen two musicians punish their bodies more in the act of creation. Their music was not just an affair of the head, the heart, the togetherness; it required an enormous effort physically to blow the way they did.'[21]

The two men played quite differently yet were both introspective, private individuals utterly dedicated to their horns. In the broadest sense, Coltrane's welcoming of his friend marked his first transition to exploratory solos that were no longer necessarily conceived as successive choruses but rather expressive journeys cutting loose from the tune's structural and emotional boundaries, emphasizing melodic elaboration with stretched-out, comparatively static harmonic landscapes. Their collaborations on *Africa/Brass*, *Olé*, and *The Africa Brass Sessions Vol. 2* (their only studio work together), exemplified by the tune 'Africa,' are remarkable for their harmonic stasis. This is particularly striking when compared to the tonal complexity and breakneck harmonic rhythms of 'Giant Steps,' recorded on April 1, 1959.

On the only known live recording of 'Africa,' found on *Evenings At The Village Gate*, Dolphy uses bass clarinet tremolos and leaps to simulate the wildness of the studio version's opening horn section and rhythmic accents he conducted during the studio recording. After dropping out, he returns on alto sax in a foray into an expressionistic solo. The tune finds Art Davis joining Workman (as he did for one of the number's studio versions) and includes Elvin Jones revisiting his studio work's extended drum solo.

Experimenting with post-bop styles further from his roots, Coltrane openly adopted more dissonant material in newfound modal freedom, challenging casual listeners and conservative critics with an intensified rhythmic feel that transcended swing. It was a radical departure from his earlier voice (pitch arrays, phrasing, timbre, and aesthetic goals), which had proven so popular since his rise in the Miles Davis Quintet. He had been establishing his own quartet since before Dolphy relocated to New York, and now, once in control, Coltrane began putting into practice non-Western approaches to soloing increasingly free from harmonic progressions, experiments in two-bass textures partially inspired by Indian percussion, and the transcendent, ecstasy-laden potential of unrestrained melodic exploration in extended soloing.

Born in Philadelphia, where Coltrane's family had moved in 1943, McCoy Tyner had been playing with the Art Farmer/Benny Golson Jazztet before replacing Steve Kuhn in Coltrane's group, doing so after Elvin Jones replaced Billy Higgins in the fall of 1960. When bassist Steve Davis left, Philadelphia-born Reggie Workman joined on club dates in early 1961 and remained for the rest of the calendar year, also working in a group led by Dolphy. By August, Coltrane had been experimenting with the two-bass idea for over five months, during which time Art Davis and Reggie Workman played on *Olé*'s title track and 'Dahomey Dance,' and on 'Africa' from *The Africa Brass Sessions Vol. 2.*

Coltrane became comfortable fitting specific bassists for certain tunes, for instance using Workman and Jimmy Garrison together on 'India' and 'Miles' Mode.' In 1962, Garrison's permanent inclusion would provide the final piece in Coltrane's 'classic quartet.' Coltrane had wanted Art Davis all along, but the bassist was so in demand and deeply trained that he had more opportunities elsewhere. He turned Coltrane down for a third time at the end of 1961, around the time he broke the color barrier at NBC-TV as a staff bassist. That September, it was Workman who played in Coltrane's residency at San Francisco's Jazz Workshop with Wes Montgomery and Dolphy, the latter joining immediately upon return from his European tour, making a sextet that went on to appear at the Monterey Jazz Festival.

TWO WEEKS IN EUROPE

Stanley Robertson's August 17 *Los Angeles Sentinel* review of Abbey Lincoln's *Straight Ahead* referred to his old friend Dolphy as 'a local boy who has made it big in New York.'[22] No doubt Eric had been keeping his parents briefed on his progress via telephone and cards. And though seeing his name in a local paper must have been reassuring for hometown friends and fellow musicians, the biggest and latest news was his departure for Europe to headline clubs and play on radio and television broadcasts for the first time as a leader.

Less than two weeks following the start of the Berlin Wall's construction, Dolphy flew into Tempelhof airport and performed in West Berlin's reverberant TV/Radio Funkturm Exhibition Hall on August 30 with a band consisting of expat trumpeter Benny Bailey, pianist Pepsi Auer, George Joyner (later Jamil Nasser) on bass, and drummer Buster Smith. Germany's SWF (Südwestrundfunk) television program *Jazz—Gehört Und Gesehen* ('Jazz, Heard And Seen') was shown every two months for seventeen years starting in 1955. By the fall of 1961, episodes recorded on 35mm film for later broadcast were being produced by *DownBeat*'s German correspondent, Joachim Ernst Berendt, who had hosted over a dozen major American jazz musicians, including Ellington, Armstrong, and Miles Davis.

The resulting live recording, commercially released over sixteen years later, was the thirty-three-year-old Dolphy's first as a sole group leader. As might be expected, the ad hoc rhythm section can sound rusty, with a stiffening of expression contrasted by Dolphy's energized performance celebrating a newfound freedom.

Originally from Cleveland, Benny Bailey was touring Europe with Lionel Hampton in the late 1950s when he chose to stay in Sweden, then moving to Berlin in 1960. He played with Dolphy on Lincoln's *Newport Rebels* track 'Tain't

Nobody's Bizness If I Do,' and that night on *Jazz—Gehört Und Gesehen*, his brilliant trumpet shines on Dolphy's 'G.W.' and '245.'* Later that day, the group relocated to another SWF venue and audience, the more intimate Club Jazz Salon, recording there a nearly twenty-minute version of Tadd Dameron's 'Hot House,' Benny Carter's jaunty 'When Lights Are Low' (a tune Eric had been playing with Coltrane), 'I'll Remember April,' and Randy Weston's 'Hi-Fly.' Fearing poor audience response to Dolphy's avant-garde style, Berendt removed him as the show's headliner, forcing the group into a shorter time slot following the British trad jazz showman Humphrey Littleton's band and vocalist Billie Poole.†

On *The Berlin Concerts*, released by Enja Records in 1977, Dolphy's succinct version of his unaccompanied bass clarinet arrangement of 'God Bless The Child' has the impact of a stunning concert hall work, and, though it is over two minutes shorter, closely echoes his Five Spot rendition captured earlier in the summer with the Dolphy/Little Quintet. Randy Weston's 'Hi-Fly,' arranged here as a trio with bass and drums, contains ephemeral flute work seasoned with jabs of overblown dissonance, agile blues runs, and florid sequences and arpeggios. Sustained, wispy half-tones highlight his timbral investigation, finding a place alongside an imaginative collection of bird calls. Eric as frontman is here moving noticeably toward non-pitch-related phenomena in his flute playing, employing timbral effects and affording structural importance to vocalizations, birdsong fragments, and animal sounds. Traded bars anticipating the tune's reprise catch Smith's drums in effective discussion with the flute—a telling human exchange, as is the Joyner/ Dolphy dialogue during the equally conversational coda.

'When Lights Are Low,' like 'Hi-Fly,' is set for a trio with drum and bass, here transformed into a spectacular bass clarinet vehicle with husky growls and vigorous convulsions interweaving deadpan references to tune fragments run

---

* 'G.W.' and '245' are misidentified on the Enja Records and Inner City album issues of *The Berlin Concerts*, the first as 'Gee Wee,' the second as Oliver Nelson's 'The Meeting.' Enja, a Munich-based label founded in 1971 by jazz enthusiasts Matthias Winckelmann and Horst Weber, released the seven titles on the double album *The Berlin Concerts* in 1977, licensed the following year to Inner City in the USA. The 2006 Impro-Jazz DVD *Eric Dolphy In Europe 1961–1964* features four of these numbers: 'G.W.' (mislabeled as 'GeeWee'), 'God Bless The Child,' 'Blues In The Closet,' and '245' (mislabeled 'Blues Improvisation'). A video of the TV show segment appears on Alan Saul's website.

† The Essential Jazz Classics reissue of the 1962 Debut Records release *Eric Dolphy In Europe* features three previously unreleased tracks from the September 8 concert at the Studentenforeningens Foredragsaal, Copenhagen.

through a joyously haywire circuit. Following Joyner's less-than-thrilling bass solo, Eric trades unwavering humor and racy riffs before returning to the now more freely blown tune. A highly edited 'G.W.' clocking in at a little over two and half minutes is far up-tempo from the original *Outward Bound* version, its breakneck dare pushing Dolphy's alto maelstrom through the ceiling. This quickened version is followed by a slowed-down '245' that finds Dolphy and Bailey blowing fun, expressive blues. An extravagant alto sax hijacks 'I Remember April' for a hard-edged post-bop ride, pulling out in front of the rhythm section and executing overblown split-tone passages.

Dolphy had a long weekend to get from Berlin to Sweden, from Thursday, August 31, to Sunday, September 3. Embedded within the Soviet-controlled German Democratic Republic since the end of WWII, West Berlin was now completely isolated, as were East Germans wishing to leave. Regarding these early September activities, Alan Saul has stated that there was likely a radio broadcast on either September 3 or 4, probably including a longer 'Serene,' 'Don't Blame Me,' and a 'very up-tempo' 'Les'. As discussed below, these broadcasts suggest that some of the posthumously released *Stockholm Session* recordings were completed during these first few days of the month rather than on the dates indicated.

Dolphy traveled to Uppsala for an appearance on Monday, September 4, at a student 'nation' sponsored by the local university jazz club. He arrived at the hall a few hours before the show to rehearse with a too-youthful rhythm section consisting of nineteen-year-old Rony Johansson on piano, Kurt Lindgren on bass, and twenty-one-year-old Rune Carlsson on drums. That night, the quartet recorded an hour and a half of music covering nine tunes, including a marathon version of '245' complete with an audacious thirteen-plus-minute alto solo. That was it for his originals, as the group relied on standards for common ground. Never intended for commercial release, the poorly recorded performance captures an often roughshod rhythm section at times barely holding it together in support of their summer guest (sonically, sporadic piano can be heard behind the rest with muffled drums, and Eric steps away from the mic on occasion). Simosko and Tepperman do not mince words in their annotated discography: 'The rhythm section is the least attuned to Dolphy of any with which he is known to have recorded.'[23]

Eric here tackles David Raskin's film score theme 'Laura' as a seven-minute unaccompanied alto solo akin to his bass clarinet arrangement of 'God Bless The

Child,' wrapping the timeless ballad's key melodic passages in scalar runs, fast sequences, and fluid arpeggios, with expositional passages juxtaposing cadenza-like flourishes in a performance that rarely loses focus. 'Laura' was again programmed two days later in Copenhagen with full group accompaniment (*Eric Dolphy In Europe Vol. 2*), the only two recordings Dolphy made of the tune. Following a short, throwaway version of Monk's '52nd St. Theme' (a second, shorter version was played as a coda later in the show), the trio offered decent support for Eric's spacious and abstract flute work on 'Bag's Groove.' Five of the Uppsala tracks have durations over twelve minutes (alto on 'Out Of Nowhere,' 'I'll Remember April,' bass clarinet on 'When Lights Are Low'), and while it is certainly worth hearing Eric, the jam session's uneven tempi, lack of cohesive ensemble, and the meandering of others' solos are hard to take. Over five hundred audience members packed the small hall, their ambient buzz during quieter passages complimenting the hearty applause following each number.*

Before traveling to Copenhagen for three separate performances, Dolphy played in nearby Stockholm the next day, September 5, in a television studio for a show titled *Eric I'stan* ('Eric In The City'), joined by trumpeter and expat Stockholm resident Idrees Dawud ibn Sulieman (born Leonard Graham).† Sulieman had attended bebop's original sessions at Minton's and joined Monk's first Blue Note recording band in 1947, following a stint with Earl Hines's group. He had relocated to Stockholm only a few months prior to the Dolphy gig, deciding to stay while on tour. No doubt Dolphy's contact with the Black expat jazz community helped plant the seed of his own relocation to Paris in the spring of 1964.

The 'Eric In The City' rhythm section—a distinct improvement over the previous evening—included pianist Rune Öwferman, former Ellington bassist Jimmy Woode, and drummer Sture Kallin. The 1981 Enja Records release *Eric Dolphy Stockholm Sessions* (and the Inner City label's licensed US version)

---

* In the late 1980s, the French label Serene was the first to release this material, on two CDs (*The Uppsala Concert Vol. 1* and *Vol. 2*). The European labels Jazz Door, Gambit, Naked Lunch, and others followed beginning in 1993, including a picture disc from Japan's collector's market label Marshmallow Records. At some point during 1962, Eric was interviewed in New York by Claes Dahlgren, the audio released by Marshmallow on its *Vol. 2* CD.

† Simosko and Tepperman suggest Eric played for additional television broadcasts in Stockholm after his Copenhagen appearances on September 6 and 8, and before the Paris concert on September 14.

misdates these recordings as September 25 (when Eric was in San Francisco with the Coltrane Quintet), and November 19 (when he played two concerts with the Coltrane Quintet in Amsterdam).*

After wrapping up the Swedish television spot, Eric packed for a three-hundred-plus mile trip to Copenhagen and the Berlingske Has television studio that very next day for filming and recording in front of a small audience. Joining him there on Wednesday, September 6, were pianist Bent Axen, bassist Erik Moseholm, and drummer Jorn Elniff—a more cohesive rhythm section than Öwferman's Stockholm group, but without the horn. From this session, take one of 'Don't Blame Me' (flute) and 'When Lights Are Low' (bass clarinet) appear on *Eric Dolphy In Europe Vol. 3*; two takes of 'Miss Ann' (on which Dolphy alternated between alto and bass clarinet) went unreleased. Eric fastens 'Don't Blame Me' (first found on *Vol. 3*) with meditative, crystalline sonics and sticks to strong tonal patterns for the first half of his four-minute-plus flute solo before briefly visiting abstract fragmentation and timbral variations. He regularly falls back on energetic, Parker-esque runs and arpeggios. Following solos by Axen and Moseholm, Dolphy dresses the finale with impressive filigree. 'When Lights Are Low' is a nostalgic trip hijacked by the leader's effervescent bass clarinet, juggling celebratory fun with outrageously entertaining acrobatics in an uninhibited highwire act dripping with humor, trills, and surprising explosions. The party atmosphere seduces Elniff, who then graffitis the margins with percussive commentary during Eric's five wanton minutes of freedom.

The touring American had a rare day off on Thursday, September 7, then played with the same rhythm section the following day at the Studenterforeningen Foredragssal, a cultural space at Copenhagen University where Chuck Israels sat in on bass for 'Hi-Fly.' Denmark's Debut Records recorded that day's session and quickly released *Eric Dolphy In Europe* in 1962, featuring 'God Bless The Child,' 'The Way You Look Tonight,' 'Oleo,' 'Hi-Fly,' and 'In The Blues' (take 4) mislabeled as 'I Don't Know Why.' The show's exceptional take of 'Glad To Be Unhappy'—Eric's flute vehicle dating to *Outward Bound*—was not included on

* The *Stockholm Sessions* album's 'God Bless The Child,' 'G.W.,' 'Miss Ann,' and an alternate take of 'Serene' are from the September 5 television broadcast. In addition to the incorrect recording date, the Enja label provided mistitled compositions on various issues of *Stockholm Sessions*: 'Les' appears as 'Loss,' 'Miss Ann' becomes 'Ann,' 'Left Alone' is rendered as 'Alone,' 'G.W.' is 'Geewee,' and 'Serene' is mislabeled 'Soriono' or 'Sorino.'

the Debut release but appeared on Prestige's *Eric Dolphy In Europe Vol. 1* three years later.*

Eric then took this group to a television studio for a third Copenhagen performance, with William Schlopffe substituting for Elniff on drums; Simosko and Tepperman state that there exists an uncirculated audio recording. Initial Prestige releases from this tour include the following:

1. *Eric Dolphy In Europe Vol. 1* (1964): 'Hi Fly,' 'Glad To Be Unhappy,' 'God Bless The Child,' 'Oleo'
2. *Eric Dolphy In Europe Vol. 2* (1964): 'Don't Blame Me,' 'The Way You Look Tonight,' 'Miss Ann' (actually 'Les'), 'Laura'
3. *Eric Dolphy In Europe Vol. 3* (1965): 'Woody n' You,' 'When Lights Are Low' 'In The Blues' (takes 1–3)
4. *Here And There* (1966) 'Don't Blame Me' (take 2 from September 6)

Debut's release of the September 8 Copenhagen gig scooped Prestige, the latter's belated mid-60s releases helping to solidify Dolphy's name posthumously among connoisseurs of the emerging jazz avant-garde. Like other jazz greats of his era, Dolphy held a place in his creative spirit for Copenhagen. He would return to the city with Coltrane that November, later with Mingus, and in the week before his passing booked a residency there that he would not live to fulfill.

Dolphy had a week off after his Copenhagen engagements with no account of his activities. Arriving in Paris, he played the Club-Saint Germaine on September 14 with the young Swiss drummer Daniel Humair and bassist Luigi Trussardi, the latter seen in a well-known Jean-Pierre Leloir photograph playing behind Eric on the Parisian stage. Trussardi, incidentally, participated in Chet Baker's quartet for Terry Riley's 1963 experimental tape piece *The Gift* (see chapter four).

* That Debut disc was reissued in 2019 by Essential Jazz Classics with three bonus tracks: a previously unreleased second take of 'When Lights Are Low' (from the 6th), a second take of 'Laura,' and '52nd Street Theme,' which is Dolphy's impromptu coda to 'The Way You Look Tonight.' Prestige quickly purchased Debut's recordings made at both the Berlingske Has and the Studenterforeningen, releasing them posthumously across four volumes. 'Les' is mislabeled as 'Miss Ann' on *Eric Dolphy in Europe Vol. II*. In 1973, Prestige reissued volumes one and three of *Eric Dolphy Live In Europe* as the 24000 series two-LP album *Eric Dolphy Copenhagen Concert. Vol. II* and *Here And There* were conjoined for that series' double LP *Status Seeking*.

Little is known about this unrecorded club show, and Simosko and Tepperman do not mention it. The pianist may have been Jacques Diéval, who, like Humair, collaborated with Eric in Paris during the final weeks of his life.

Within days following this tour, Dolphy rejoined Coltrane's quintet at their Jazz Workshop residency in San Francisco and the Monterey Jazz Festival. Despite his outstanding playing and growing stature, Prestige did not renew Dolphy's contract that month.

WITH THE COLTRANE QUINTET ON THE WEST COAST

A September 24 *Oakland Tribune* plug read, 'Eric Dolphy, one of the outstanding figures in the jazz avant-garde, flew into the Bay Area from New York last Tuesday [September 19] and joined the John Coltrane Quartet. With Wes Montgomery sitting in during the group's stay at the Jazz Workshop—well, one must hear it to believe it. Dolphy, a virtuoso instrumentalist, plays alto sax, flute, and bass clarinet.

Coltrane's expanded line-up played three consecutive nights at the club, prepping for the festival opening that Friday in Monterey. Promoting the launch in his column that day, *San Francisco Examiner* jazz writer John Bryan noted of the Jazz Workshop performances that 'the power of the group stunned audiences.'[24] Duke Ellington MC'd the festival's opening bill, which he shared with Johnny Hodges & The Modern Mainstreamers with Dizzy Gillespie, Ben Webster, Earl Hines, Harry Carney, Stuff Smith, Jimmy Rushing & Big Miller, and Terry Gibbs & His New All Star Big Band. Coltrane and Dolphy took their time soloing, filling a one-hour slot with just three tunes, not coincidentally showcasing Eric's three instruments: 'My Favorite Things' (flute), 'Naima' (bass clarinet), and 'So What' (alto sax). The *DownBeat* review noted both players overcoming intonation issues throughout the set, and that while Dolphy's flute playing was generally good, 'part of his solo sounded as if he were trying to imitate birds. His use of quarter tones on Things led nowhere. And this seemed his greatest hang-up; none of his solos had a clear direction,' yet adding, 'if Coltrane is able to keep this group together, it could turn into one of the most interesting in jazz.'

Keeping in mind the remarkable popularity of Coltrane's studio recording of 'My Favorite Things'—a hit record Atlantic re-released as a 45rpm single in April 1961—it is worth emphasizing the capacious opportunity Dolphy embraced during that number's many live performances. Even in the original 1960 studio version—from an album of the same name that sold over five hundred thousand copies and has since been elected to the Grammy Hall Of Fame—Coltrane takes the tune on a nearly fourteen-minute journey, stretching the number out with solos soaring over not the chord changes but rather the singular chords of what were originally structural interludes in E major and E minor. Coltrane transforms the upbeat, fairytale children's song and its themes of whiteness as purity into an introspective epic journey beyond the boundaries of the Western canon—a stylistic metamorphosis befitting the compelling zeitgeist of the Civil Rights Movement and the Cold War's threat of nuclear annihilation.[25] A stage musical's populist waltz, now hypnotized by the tonic E, becomes a polyrhythmic essay on freedom facing off with a dangerous world. Dolphy's flute graced the Coltrane Quintet's live performances into 1962.

Montgomery turned down Coltrane's invitation for a longer hitch in his group, the primary reason being the guitarist's brightening career and the horn men's incredibly long solos. He had received a wave of awards and accolades from jazz publications over the previous two years and had just released *So Much Guitar* on the Riverside label, a noteworthy album featuring Ron Carter on bass and Elvin Jones's brother Hank on piano. Montgomery was at the top of his game and wanted his share of the spotlight and solo time.

In Coltrane's idealized yet conflicted view, Dolphy, Montgomery, and Art Davis would have helped form his dream sextet, yet the addition of guitar would have also complicated his musical goal of diminishing the role of harmonic progressions: at that juncture, what jazz sextet with piano and guitar would venture into material characterized by harmonic stasis? And what about Coltrane's misgivings over arranging for just two horns, which he shared regarding questions about his quintet with Dolphy? How would he have managed such musical decisions in a sextet with Montgomery?

Not all clubgoers were prepared for the fantastical explorations Coltrane, Dolphy, and company had begun at the Village Gate earlier that summer and continued now on the West Coast in late September. This was music empowered by a focus on melody and rhythm, an approach to jazz improvisation conjuring transcendent experience, and the journey-like potential of extended, soul-baring solos drilling into the interior of hearts and minds. From Monterey, a Los Angeles excursion allowed Eric to catch up with family and old friends, all of whom could be regaled with tales from his solo European tour. The family reunion came with

Coltrane in tow as he and Dolphy reflected on the progress in their artistic paths since first meeting here in 1954, when Dolphy was readjusting to post-Army life and Coltrane had hit rock bottom with Hodges.

The quintet then began a highly anticipated October residency at Hollywood's Renaissance Club, the owner of which, Ben Shapiro, had recently hired as an assistant local newspaper critic Mike Davenport. As a cub journalist writing jazz reviews in a local newspaper, Davenport had praised Dolphy's playing and recordings until mid-to-late 1961, when he began bashing the jazzman's name at every opportunity. But the young writer's badmouthing paled in comparison to the widely read, brutal review of one of those Renaissance Club performances penned by *DownBeat*'s Los Angeles–based associate editor, John Tynan: 'I heard a good rhythm section go to waste behind the nihilistic exercises of the two horns. Coltrane and Dolphy seem intent on deliberately destroying [swing]. They seem bent on pursuing an anarchistic course in their music that can but be termed anti-jazz.' Tynan denounced the avant-garde and new thing trend, of which Coltrane's group was a 'horrifying demonstration,' and whose horn solos were nothing if not 'musical nonsense currently being peddled in the name of jazz.'[26]

Tynan's tirade, published that November, would cost Eric plenty. Until Dolphy's death, the 'anti-jazz' smear haunted *DownBeat*'s reviews and articles concerning his playing, with other writers invoking the absurd label as they too piled on their target. The publication would attempt to even the playing field in the spring of 1962 with a cover story rebuttal from Dolphy and Coltrane, but several of its influential critics never stopped the attack. More than simply delaying Coltrane's turn toward free jazz during his last years, the controversy led to Impulse! producer Bob Thiele rethinking the jazz giant's increasingly controversial profile.

DownBeat was the classic establishment ogre of the time in its sporadically confrontational, sometimes vindictive stance toward the jazz avant-garde's early 1960s innovations, dishing both accolades and brutal invective, building and destroying careers, and simultaneously challenging and reinforcing racist tendencies in often flippant critical discourse about real social issues—a paternalistic trait particularly noticeable during these crucial years of the Civil Rights struggle. For instance, there was Gitler's questionable discounting of Abbey Lincoln's comments on Black racial identity and her album *Straight Ahead* (on which Eric plays), an attack that damaged Lincoln's career. Yet as an example of the push/pull tendencies of a publication with close to eighty thousand readers, the issue of the magazine current with the Coltrane Quintet's Renaissance gig included Bill Coss's favorable, sympathetic profile of new thing guru Cecil Taylor, in which the pianist stated, 'Since 1957, a change has begun—Ornette, Jackie Byard, and Eric Dolphy. Of course, there's one constant. Duke Ellington.'[27]

Regardless of the negativity and potential damage to Dolphy, Coltrane was named the magazine's 'Jazzman Of The Year' for 1961, and the critics and readers' poll winner in the tenor saxophone and miscellaneous (soprano sax) categories. Thankfully, his quintet kept to its prescient aesthetic path during their remaining 1961 tour dates, including a residency at Chicago's Sutherland Hotel Lounge, a groundbreaking engagement at the Village Vanguard, and an equally weighty European tour that—like Dolphy's spring 1964 tour there with Mingus—would bequeath a treasure of timeless recordings.

Along the way, on October 5, came Booker Little's tragic, untimely passing. His family lost a father and husband, friends lost the vigor of their youthful acquaintance, and collaborators such as Dolphy lost a creative partner. The Dolphy/Little Quintet passed into history, the grief staying with Eric during his creative ascent with Coltrane's group and beyond. Prestige later released an expanded three-LP Five Spot box set as *The Great Concert Of Eric Dolphy*, omitting Little's name entirely from the title and cover. What is more, regarding that mesmerizing quintet, in 1963 Eric would also lose the Mal Waldron he knew: the pianist barely survived a heroin overdose, suffered a complete breakdown and loss of keyboard memory, and faced years of methodical musical rehabilitation.

THE VILLAGE VANGUARD, NOVEMBER 1–5, 1961

Among those attending the Coltrane Quintet's November 5 performance at Max Gordon's Village Vanguard were Eric's Los Angeles friends Lester Robinson and Horace Tapscott, the latter stating, 'That Sunday afternoon we went there and they recorded that and immediately after, all over the country, it started happening … that sound got across … everybody thought, *Ah, music—the music* … it was the religion they felt for the music.'[28] Spirituality, meditation, transcendence—were all common terms that flowed from the positive reception of the quintet's long journeys into modal, near-free-form solos.

By now, Bob Thiele had replaced Impulse! founder and producer Creed Taylor and made the decision to record Coltrane live at the same venue where Bill Evans's most admired live album had been recorded a few months earlier, and where the Sonny Rollins Trio had recorded a highly regarded live album in 1957. After witnessing the group's opening Wednesday night performance, Thiel directed Van Gelder to record more of the shows, but only those tunes from the second sets he felt acceptable for commercial release—a decision that belied the artist's intentions of playing something new and valuable every night.

The landmark residency delivered both spiritual celebration and a joyous circus of new ideas, with Coltrane bolstering personnel with highly unique timbres by adding to his already expressive unit. On Thursday, November 2, fifty-nine-year-old Garvin Bushell joined in on 'India.' His double-reed instrument's dark timbre and low-register notes could only be those of an English horn, not what the liner notes originally identified as an oboe.*

In July of 1963, Bushell would play bassoon on Dolphy's *Conversations / Iron Man* sessions. The veteran jazzer had seen a lot of changes in his lifetime:

> We went on the road with Mamie Smith in 1921. When we got to Chicago, Bubber Miley and I went to hear Oliver [King Oliver's Creole Jazz Band, pre–Louis Armstrong] at the Dreamland every night. It was the first time I'd heard New Orleans jazz to any advantage, and I studied them every night for the entire week . . . Bubber and I sat there with our mouths open.[29]

Bushell played another traditionally Western orchestral instrument, adding contrabassoon pedal tones to the intro of 'Spiritual' and on Sunday creating with that low-register double-reed further rhythmic punctuation in accompaniment to the solos on that number. The instrument's lowest range is used here also for special percussive and timbral effects, punching out a propulsive sub-bass buzz. Tyner's left hand, Workman's bass, and the contrabassoon provide 'Spiritual' with an incredibly deep pad for the front men's already low-end instruments, tenor and

---

* These are the recorded numbers from those nights. November 1: 'Brasilia' (originally issued as 'Untitled Original'), 'Chasin' The Trane' (titled by Rudy Van Gelder), 'Impressions,' 'India,' 'Miles' Mode' (originally 'Red Planet,' composed by Dolphy), 'Naima,' and 'Spiritual.' November 2: 'Chasin' Another Trane' (Haynes on drums), 'Chasin' The Trane,' 'Greensleeves' (quartet), 'Impressions,' 'India,' 'Softly As A Morning Sunrise' (quartet), and 'Spiritual.' November 3: 'Greensleeves,' 'Impressions,' 'India,' 'Miles' Mode,' 'Naima,' and 'Spiritual.' November 5: 'India' and 'Spiritual.'

bass clarinet, the unusual sound palette augmenting Coltrane's experiments in low-register intensity.

Appearing on 'India' every night but Friday was the bassist in Monk's 1957 quartet with Coltrane, Ahmed Abdul-Malik, here playing the tamboura, a resonant drone instrument used in classical Indian music, and not the Near Eastern oud (short-neck lute) designated in the original notes. 'India' includes Garrison and Workman on simultaneous bass parts, Coltrane on soprano sax, Dolphy on bass clarinet, Tyner, and Jones.

For 'Impressions,' Coltrane opted for Garrison, who tends to outshine Workman in finding an individual path within Elvin Jones's oceanic energy. Garrison pairs with Workman again on 'Miles' Mode,' a tune discussed below as 'Red Planet.'

Recording selectively over four nights, Van Gelder amassed thirteen reels of tape from which two original Impulse! albums emerged over the next two years. *Coltrane Live At The Village Vanguard* (1962) features Eric on 'Spiritual' (from November 3), though unfortunately, his solo is nowhere near his best. This high-profile release thus presents a comparatively weak bass clarinet outing, particularly after Coltrane's heartfelt, soulful excursion on tenor (who returns to finish the tune on soprano with spiritually zesty blues). Dolphy attempts lyricism and sinuousness with lackluster bluesy riffs, various plays at color, a rather ineffective sequence, and repetitive licks that struggle for lack of imagination and verve. Ironically, this is one of the few examples of Eric sounding tentative, if not adrift, with a shortage of intensity, little build-up, and a lack of immediacy.

'Chasin' The Trane' (from November 2) is a nearly sixteen-minute-long, groundbreaking Coltrane solo on tenor that does not feature Eric's playing, even on the head, as is the case with the third number from *Coltrane Live At The Village Vanguard*, 'Softly As In A Morning Sunrise.' For his classic 1963 album *Impressions*, Coltrane chose only 'India,' from the same November 3 set, with Eric's solo bass clarinet offering a less convoluted essay as he explores distinctly abstract directions, less focused and more volatile than Coltrane's learned, passionate mysticism. Coltrane projected little of Dolphy's unpredictability, creative fragmentation, humor, and instrumental range; Dolphy reflected less of Coltrane's obsessively developmental approaches to constructing solos, connection to swing, or emotionally effective use of spiritual blues. Neither of these album releases from 1962 and 1963 feature Dolphy's alto or flute. And, though it would be a staple of the quintet's European shows to follow, Coltrane did not call Dolphy's flute vehicle 'My Favorite Things' at the Village Vanguard. In fact, Eric left his flute at home for the entire residency.

One can perhaps imagine a different critical reception of early Dolphy if his best work from these performances had been released before his death. Instead, in August of the following year, the *DownBeat* reviewer of *Impressions* rightly concluded that 'Dolphy opens his spot well (on India), but it degenerates as he begins to employ the vocal cries and tired melodic ideas that have been his stock in trade recently.'[30] Hearing the same cut, a sympathetic Paul Horn was honest and accurate in a spring 1964 blindfold test:

> Eric is very much of an individual, as Coltrane is, and these two don't necessarily blend. The feeling of continuity dropped away when Eric came in. Eric is in a bad spot there; Coltrane had set up a certain intensity, and how are you going to follow him and pick up where he left off? I would rather have heard the composition end at that point and hear Eric by himself on something else.[31]

It is in this sense that *Coltrane Live At The Village Vanguard* and *Impressions* arguably fueled criticism of Dolphy's presence in the quintet. These two albums were all that anybody would hear of the shows for fifteen years, during which time the remaining outtakes sat nearly forgotten in ABC corporate storage, from where it was not uncommon for such unissued tape reels to be discarded. Esmond Edwards, the Prestige recording supervisor responsible for Dolphy's first albums as leader, and in 1976 an ABC producer, later oversaw a small trove of additional releases from those dates.* But fans would not hear the complete recordings until the 1997 Impulse! four-CD set *The Complete 1961 Village Vanguard Recordings*, for which each evening's program was painstakingly reconstructed by David Wild, with assistance from Michael Cuscuna and Reggie Workman.

---

* The following Prestige releases include Village Vanguard tracks: the two-LP *John Coltrane: The Other Village Vanguard Tapes* (1977), *Trane's Modes* (*The Mastery Of John Coltrane Vol. IV*, 1979), and *From The Original Master Tapes* (1985). *The Other Village Vanguard Tapes* includes crucial Dolphy work. However, on *Trane's Modes*, Edwards cut Dolphy's solo from 'Miles' Mode.' Dolphy's bass clarinet solo work on 'Naima,' recorded twice during the quintet's Village Vanguard gig, first came to light on *The Mastery Of John Coltrane Vol. IV*.

In contrast to the 1962–63 Coltrane issues, the 1997 release showcases superlative examples of Dolphy's work. 'Chasin' The Trane' from the first night, with Garrison on bass, includes a solid Dolphy alto sax effort exploring sustained upper register pitches and sounds, transformational sequences, and Coltrane-esque variations of closely repeated fragments. The same night's 'Spiritual' contains a far more successful bass clarinet solo than what Eric played November 3, displaying an overall gravitas, vivid blues, and exquisite shaping of thematic material; his work on a second take of 'Spiritual' recorded on the final night is equally engaging. His alto sax on 'Brasilia' is both exploratory and playful in its celebration of human vocal cries and speech-like conversation, not unlike a monologue (or dialogue, as he assumes multiple personae, proving that he didn't need Mingus onstage to musically converse). In 'Brasilia,' released along with six other never before heard tracks on *The Other Village Vanguard Tapes* as 'Untitled Original' (its proper title later identified by Anthony Braxton), he turns on the pyrotechnics at will, stepping outside of the piece to form his own ring of fire.

This treasure of recordings fully exposes what Coltrane and his quintet were about to unleash on their European tour—recordings from which further establish the great strides they took with Dolphy.

08 EUROPEAN TOUR WITH COLTRANE, RESPONSE TO CRITICS, A LONG SUMMER

NOVEMBER 1961–AUGUST 1962

Eric's deepening collaboration with Coltrane had taken on a spirited glow. *Africa/Brass* and *Olé*, the Village Gate residency and other summer club appearances, the weeks leading up to and including their Village Vanguard gig and the European tour; all helped mark his densely active, high-profile period as an innovative sideman. He was sewing up his second year in New York in consummate musical style, having walked away from Mingus for the first time nearly a year earlier, finding his own way following that productive phase of Workshop residencies, the Antibes and Newport festivals, and breakthrough recordings with the bassist. Later, he coyly shared, 'Well the thing is there are two different bags. Coltrane is another type of playing and Mingus is another type of playing and so like each of them have something very interesting and something to go after.'[1] In Europe during his two-week solo tour in September, a core contemporary-jazz audience embraced him as a leader headlining pick-up groups with sets filled with his compositions. Some of those fans welcomed him back less than two months later with Coltrane's group.

Another sign of Dolphy's solidification in the jazz world came with the flood of career-defining recordings filling record-store bins over the last four months of 1961. In addition to his work as leader on *Out There*, he appeared as sideman on nine new releases: *Free Jazz* and *Africa/Brass* (each released in September, as was *Out There*), Booker Little's *Out Front* (October), *Olé* and *Jazz Abstractions* (November), Lincoln's *Straight Ahead*, Nelson's *Straight Ahead*, *Newport Rebels*, and Max Roach's *Percussion Bitter Sweet* (December). Each title offered listeners unique slices of his talents.

Within the week following their Village Vanguard glory, the Coltrane Quintet performed 'My Favorite Things' for a Westinghouse television spot promoting the group's European tour, aired by PM West and hosted by San Francisco critic Terrence O'Flaherty. Norman Granz, who that year sold his Verve label to MGM for $3.1 million (close to $29 million in 2024), produced a three-week 'Jazz At The Philharmonic' caravan with Dizzy Gillespie's outfit through England and Scotland, and from Paris to Helsinki, consisting of an ambitious thirty appearances in large halls. Coltrane's first trip to Europe the previous year had come at the end of his stint with Miles's first great quintet, sharing the bill with Stan Getz and Oscar Peterson. Granz wanted a repeat of those mildly controversial scenes of French, German, and Scandinavian audiences dramatically applauding to drown out the boos and whistles following some of Coltrane's longer solos. Now Coltrane was getting a $300 weekly bonus as leader. These European audiences, however, had no access to recordings of Coltrane's new aesthetic turn with Dolphy, and little inkling of what the quintet was about to unleash. In turn, the general jazz public would not hear a taste of these concert recordings until 1987, when Italy's Jazzway label released the mono LP *John Coltrane Quintet Featuring Eric Dolphy—Live In Paris 1961*, with extensive solo work from Dolphy on 'Blue Train,' 'Impressions' and 'My Favorite Things.'

As the tour plane ascended from New York heading northeast over New England and the Atlantic, Dolphy was content with more than simply having a job. He was in the clouds both figuratively and literally. The New York to London flight is one thousand miles longer than one back to Los Angeles, where his parents sat at home, hoping for the best for their only child and looking forward to his telephone calls and a spring '62 visit. For the third time in less than two years, Eric was visiting Europe playing as he wanted and building a following of his own. A creative gel had set with Tyner, Jones, and Workman, all of whom remained with Coltrane. Though the harsh criticism of forthcoming *DownBeat* articles would do more than dampen his mood, they would be neither the first nor last journalistic bullets aimed at his head. In the meantime, he was staying ahead of the game by working, practicing, gaining recognition, and honing his position as one of the leaders of the jazz avant-garde—albeit for now as a sideman to one of the greatest emerging international stars.

The British tour leg launched from London's massive Gaumont Cinema/State Theatre in Kilburn, then headed out for six dates before returning to London on Friday, November 17, for two more shows. Hard-blowing numbers 'Blue Train,' 'My Favorite Things,' and 'Impressions' remained the athletic bulwark of engaged, extended soloing for the two frontmen, with 'Naima' and a few other ballads appearing throughout the tour. The itinerary pushed ahead: Birmingham's Hippodrome; St. Andrew's Hall, Glasgow; Newcastle City Hall; Leicester's De Montfort Hall; Brighton Dome; and London's Granada Theatre in Walthamstow. A few accounts would leak out from concertgoers later associated with the avant-garde, such as that of a seventeen-year-old Bristol lad named Evan Parker, who managed to catch the last London performance. As an added twist, no one will ever hear these British performances, because no recording was made of any of the concerts. This maddening fact brings to mind Eric's comment that music disappears into the air once it has been played. Into that void flowed little positive critical response, audiences instead wallowing in an ambivalent cloud tinged with barely polite hostility. Brits were having none of it, perhaps expecting quaint renditions of 'Greensleeves.'

The week-long series of concerts brought confused, indignant, sometimes unruly crowds and jaundiced critical response. With 'Baffled, bothered, and bewildered' as an opening line to a *Melody Maker* concert review titled 'What Happened?' in which Coltrane and Dolphy's playing is described as 'extraneous noise,' one can almost hear Bob Dawbarn's smug condescension in his Coltrane interview published a week later: 'I found your quintet's music completely bewildering. Can you explain what it is you are trying to do? Surely, you and Eric Dolphy are not following the normal chord sequences?'[2] *Jazz Journal*'s Benny Green took offense at Eric's work, stating, 'The twelve-minute flute solo of Dolphy's at the Gaumont State, Kilburn, represented the low water mark of jazz in this country.'[3]

Concertgoer Wellington Holliday deserves mention as he physically confronted Coltrane backstage at the Glasgow concert (and later wrote about it boastfully), accosting him with the accusation that 'Elvin Jones sounded like the worst professional drummer I had ever heard.'[4] Letters to the editor of *Melody Maker* recall the hilarious *Monty Python's Flying Circus* television skits incorporating stuffy, indignant correspondence from eccentric readers whining about banal, inconsequential problems while revealing ultra-conservative, bigoted viewpoints: 'I came to the conclusion that, for this particular concert, he was playing "joke" music,' reads one such letter, earning an editor's response that 'scores of other readers have been equally puzzled.'[5]

Having inherited the 'moldy fig' mantle from mid-century journalists ranting against bebop, British jazz writers such as Alun Morgan and Charles Fox, uninterested in progressive change, would prove prickly posthumous critics of Dolphy's best work. Neither Coltrane nor Dolphy would ever again perform in Great Britain (though it was rumored that, at the time of his death, Eric was considering joining a George Russell engagement in London). The British tour dates prove wrong the often-told legend of Dolphy's involvement with Ornette's double quartet during the Cincinnati 'free jazz' fiasco on November 17, when Coleman refused to play the Taft Auditorium because the promoters had advertised the concert as 'free,' misunderstood as no admission charge.

If the Paris recordings are any indication of the group's playing in Great Britain, one wonders how those audiences were so turned off by these passionate, dedicated musicians. By contrast, the City Of Light welcomed Eric's return. With Joyce Mordecai soon to live here in pursuit of her dance career, Paris looked more and more to Eric like a future expat's home away from home. Throughout this new European adventure, his alto, bass clarinet, and flute solos began revealing increased direction and verve without compromising his uncanny vocabulary and humor. There was a resoluteness in his playing at this time, but never a somberness to dampen the playful ingenuity expected by dedicated listeners. Some of this maturity arguably came from his regular performances with Coltrane, whereby confidence and improvisational direction grew night after night and week after week following one of the greatest jazz soloists who had ever set foot onstage. Tyner, Workman, and Jones were equally responsible for helping Eric sharpen his axe without killing the wildness. Inhabiting his space as a soloist on three instruments, the sideman added structural, arranged lines to 'Naima,' 'Impressions,' and other classic Coltrane tunes.

Two sets at Paris's L'Olympia on November 18 provided more gems for this quintet's crown, performances heard again only decades later, on *John Coltrane Quintet Featuring Eric Dolphy, Live In Paris 1961* (Jazz Way, 1987). Amid the audience's cavernous roar of approval for Coltrane's masterful ten-minute solo on 'Blue Train,' the first notes of Dolphy's alto emerge as if from the middle of an already developed frenzy. Biting, acerbic lines mingle with daredevil attacks on high notes and perfected leaps all fitting into a smattering of phrases going every which way. He cuts out after a compact, precise two minutes, passing the torch to Tyner as L'Olympia is drenched in a sound propelled by the enmeshed driving force of Jones and Workman. Dolphy rests on Eckstine's 'I Want To Talk About You,' a ballad Coltrane would call again at the Helsinki show in four days' time. Next in the set, 'Impressions' is lit on fire by his alto, a rage of notes and incandescent flourishes closing in on the three-minute mark with a sense of compressed energy and vital renewal.

Dolphy sat out the first show's 'My Favorite Things'; the second show's flute solo on the tune is at the outset relatively reserved in terms of tonal experimentation save for a handful of 'outside' gestures that, even given their harmonic tension, are rendered smoothly and formally complacent. Dolphy, however, has deeper explorations in mind and soon advances into a landscape of overblown multiphonics, split tones, and adventurous escapes. Many of his flute solos set out this way, proving less biting than his reed work and more tonally centered. Coltrane's dovetailed re-entrance, signaling an end to Eric's compelling musical world, is accompanied by eager applause and earnest shouts. In the Magnetic Records releases of 1961 European tour performances by the quintet, *John Coltrane Quintet Featuring Eric Dolphy: The Complete Paris Concerts*, one clearly hears a ready, general applause for Dolphy's soloing (even more for Coltrane).* One must wonder again how this group was, in the meantime, being branded anti-jazz in the country of their origin.

The group traveled to Amsterdam for two shows on November 19: first at the Concertgebouw, followed by the Hague's Kurhaus, thirty miles away. The Dutch schedule spotlights the Enja label's second erroneous date for Eric's *Stockholm Sessions* tracks that were actually recorded during his solo tour on September 4 and 5. This was Eric's Netherlands debut, and the first of three eventual appearances at the Concertgebouw, where he would return twice in the spring of 1964, with Mingus and as soloist with the local Boys Big Band.

The tour's next stop was Copenhagen's Falkoner Centret on November 20, an unofficial recording of which was released by Magnetic Records in 2009. Following Norman Granz's announcement, the group launches into the oddly chosen 'Delilah' by Victor Young, Coltrane's curious soprano sax work followed by Eric's mediocre bass clarinet solo. His unaltered vocabulary fails the ballad's

* More of the Paris performances were released in 1991 on an unofficial double CD issued by Magnetic Records of Luxembourg, *John Coltrane Quintet Featuring Eric Dolphy: The Complete Paris Concerts*. The same label also released *John Coltrane Quintet Featuring Eric Dolphy: The Complete Copenhagen Concert*.

optimistic, bouncy mood, his awkward attempts at standard bebop licks falling short as he struggles with overly fragmented repetition and unsatisfactory sequences. The group had never before performed this number on a recorded date, and they never returned to it. The program also included 'Naima' (in a version discussed below) and Cole Porter's 'Ev'ry Time We Say Goodbye.'

Following the November 21 show at the Konserthuset in Sweden's west-coast port city of Gothenburg, the next evening's performances at Helsinki's Kulttuuritalo duplicated the Paris program and witnessed another standout 'Impressions' solo from Dolphy. 'My Favorite Things' (always featuring Tyner's extended solo) finds Eric's exceptional explorations of scalar runs, arpeggios, and leaps early on, his flute clearly expanding the tonal boundaries of this modal-minimalist hit. After restating the theme, he returns to playfully angular, asymmetric melodic fragments outside the piece's super-reiterated tonal center. He holds forth for seven minutes in a rendition that lasts for over twenty-eight minutes and ends with wild applause.* The tour then landed in Stockholm for two well-recorded concerts at the Konserthuset. The wealth of recordings from this tour shows the liberties the group took in arranging solos, their varying intensity from night to night, performance to performance, player to player.

The group zig-zagged back to Copenhagen on Sunday to play the extra date Granz booked after their sell-out there the previous week, with no known recordings of that latter concert. They then flew to Hamburg on Saturday, November 25, performing three unknown tunes, quickly followed by shows in Stuttgart's Liederhalle Beethoven-Saal and Frankfurt's Kongresshalle on November 29.† Alan Saul would later share an account by US Air Force serviceman and musician Lamont Johnson stationed at Rhein-Main Air Force Base, who recalled

* In 1972, the Swedish label Historic Performances Records released the oddly titled *Eric Dolphy Quintet Live On Mount Meru, Featuring John Coltrane* in two volumes. *Volume One* is the second show and *Volume Two* the first. It features 'My Favorite Things' with its distinguished flute solo, stunning alto work on 'Blue Train,' the lyrical bass clarinet of 'Naima' (one recorded version omitting Dolphy), and two versions of 'Impressions,' one with Dolphy's solo cut. The following year, Japan's BYG Records released the same material as *Coltranology*. Full versions eventually emerged in Pablo's *Live Trane: The European Tours*. In 2015, the Trapeze Music imprint Acrobat Records released the privately recorded Helsinki concert as part of the four-CD set *So Many Things: The European Tour 1961*; that set is not found on the Pablo label's 2001 seven-CD release.

† The Pablo label's 2001 seven-disc set *Live Trane: The European Tours* mistakenly presents the group's Birdland recordings from February 10, 1962, as being from this Hamburg show.

playing with Eric and members of both bands sans Coltrane after the Kongresshalle performance at an afterhours Frankfurt club, Jazz Kellar.*

The musicians played Munich on the night of December 1, with only Dizzy's group being recorded. Dolphy, Tyner, Workman, and Dizzy's drummer Mel Lewis split after the show to play an after-hours set, again without Coltrane, at German bandleader and drummer Freddie Brocksieper's club Studio 15/Uni-Reitschule. Contesting narratives speculate as to why Elvin Jones did not play that night (passport problems, illness, early departure from the tour), but there is no evidence that there was even an issue; perhaps Jones, like Coltrane, simply did not join his cohorts at the impromptu. Poorly recorded bootlegs of this jam session include 'On Green Dolphin Street,' 'Softly, As In A Morning Sunrise,' 'The Way You Look Tonight,' and 'Oleo.'† Despite claims by several sources, neither Lalo Schifrin nor Bob Cunningham performed on this recording.

The Coltrane quintet played their penultimate tour date the next evening, December 2, at Berlin's Auditorium Maximum at Freie University, with a powerful and utterly fluid Dolphy solo on 'Impressions,' the only number captured on tape, albeit in very poor quality.‡ The excellent Baden-Baden Sudwestfunk TV performance often dated November 24 was in fact the tour's last date, December 4.

BACK IN THE USA

Soon after the fruitful tour's return to New York on December 5, Dolphy likely attended, and may have performed at, the Jazz Gallery benefit concert for the late Booker Little's family. Eric often thought of the trumpeter, their close musical relationship, the young man's tragic end, and the Five Spot concert recordings that remained the only sonic document of their creative quintet. Memories of artistic

---

* Poor-quality amateur recordings drawn from Frankfurt, Stuttgart, and Berlin are found on RLR Records' 2010 release *The Unissued German Concerts*, with error-ridden track listings and notes.

† The first LP album release of the Munich after-hours club performance was the 1981 Musidisc release *Eric Dolphy: Quartet 1961* (France). Subsequent CDs include, among others, Rare Live Recordings' 2006 LP *Eric Dolphy Quartet With McCoy Tyner: Munich Jam Session December 1, 1961.*

‡ Regarding the December 4 Baden-Baden performance, an undated bootleg issued by the Jazz Connoisseur label, *Coltrane: Quartet And Quintet In Europe*, includes 'Ev'ry Time We Say Goodbye,' 'My Favorite Things,' and 'Impressions,' the latter also a bonus track on RLR's 2006 *Munich Jam Sessions* CD. That television appearance is also included on a 2005 German DVD from the Jazz Door label, *John Coltrane Quintet With Eric Dolphy + Lennie Tristano, In Europe*—an odd pairing that also presents Tristano's 1965 solo piano concert at Tivoli Gardens, Copenhagen.

success tightly associated with Dolphy's name as a group leader intertwined with his perpetual sideman hustle for session work and the defining axis of activity with Mingus, Coltrane, and Ornette's *Free Jazz*. Dolphy then returned to the Workshop, and, at one of his first Jazz Gallery gigs with Mingus that winter, said hello to Roy Haynes, who was being interviewed by LeRoi Jones (aka Amiri Baraka) for a *DownBeat* feature as the drummer waited to take the stage with a headlining Stan Getz group.

Coleman had Dolphy on his mind when he was interviewed in Oakland that week, stating that he was writing new material for another double quartet and envisioned himself playing again with Dolphy, Bobby Bradford, Freddie Hubbard, Art Davis, Jimmy Garrison, Roy Haynes, and Ed Blackwell.[6] *Free Jazz: A Collective Improvisation* had been in the stores for only two months, yet Ornette was openly discussing a follow-up. Imagining more Dolphy/Coleman collaborations is yet another haunting 'what-if.'

A surprise came in the form of Pete Welding's five-star review of *Free Jazz* in the mid-January 1962 issue of *DownBeat*, extolling the 'gripping five-minute exploration by Dolphy in his most waspish acerbic manner' and leaving the readers with, 'I, for one, have been completely won over and look forward to more pieces of this nature.'[7] Not surprisingly, the magazine also enlisted John Tynan, fresh off his indignant attack on Dolphy and Coltrane, to offer the 'con' side of the review in the same issue. 'Where does neurosis end and psychosis begin?' Tynan wondered. 'This witches brew is the logical end product of a bankrupt philosophy of ultra-individualism in music.' The reactionary journalist continued by attacking the idea of collective improvisation, adding, 'The only semblance of collectivity lies in the fact that these eight nihilists were collected together in one studio at one time and with one common cause: to destroy the music that gave them birth.'[8]

As 1962 dawned, it seemed possible Dolphy would launch into even higher circles of creative collaboration. He had a Carnegie Hall New Year's Eve concert with Coltrane to look forward to, occasionally took the stage throughout January with the quintet at the Jazz Gallery and Philadelphia's Showboat, and appeared with them for two separate television sessions taped for a January broadcast. The engineer/bootlegger Boris Rose recorded Coltrane Quintet performances of 'Mr. P.C.,' 'Miles' Mode,' and 'My Favorite Things' from a February 9 WADO-AM radio broadcast from Birdland, with Garrison on bass.

The reason for so many unofficial reprints of this bootleg from multiple labels is the high quality of playing: Jones, Garrison, and Tyner do not fall by the wayside as Coltrane and Dolphy dish their virtuosity.* Eric's flute solo on 'My Favorite Things' suffers a bit from recurring intonation problems in the first half (before his formal restatement of the theme), subsequently focusing on an extraordinary array of ideas, ultimately gaining momentum for an improvised 'piece within a piece' complete with overblown timbral experiments and jagged, polytonal statements. With its hard-edged unison head on tenor and alto, 'Mr. P.C.' did not appear on the European tour; here, Coltrane steps way out of his comfort zone toward a Dolphy-esque collage of daring, craggy passages and leaps. Eric follows with a deep exposition of his lexicon, juxtaposing madcap flourishes. That evening's rendition of 'Miles' Mode,' another piece avoided throughout the European tour, is excitingly executed by the group, particularly Coltrane's passionate forays into quarter tones, smeared pitches, and overblown timbres. Eric follows, exploring microtonal inflections on many held tones. While Reggie Workman's youthful work with Coltrane through 1961 is to be applauded, Garrison's seasoned sound broadened the group with more exploratory low register work, arguably inspiring an uptick in playing among what became known as Coltrane's 'classic' quartet, sans Dolphy.

Eric eased back into session work the following week when he entered New York's Epic Recording Studios on February 16 for saxophonist Pony Poindexter's album *Pony's Express*, produced by Teo Macero and released later that year. Poindexter had left his hometown of New Orleans for the San Francisco Bay Area, and as a professional sideman had played with Billy Eckstine, Lionel Hampton, Stan Kenton, Charlie Parker, Nat King Cole, and Bay Area bassist and bandleader Vernon Alley. Dolphy's former bandleader Roy Porter drummed for an Alley/Poindexter group in the early 1950s. Poindexter relocated to Paris in 1963, a year before Dolphy made the same move, and while in Europe made both Spain and Germany his home before eventually returning to Oakland. It was not the greatest of sessions, artistically speaking, for Eric; he read his arranged *Pony's Express* alto parts on 'B Frequency' and 'Lanyop,' soloing briefly on the latter. Benefiting from the paycheck and camaraderie, he mingled in the studio with Pepper Adams, Ron Carter, Charlie Persip, Elvin Jones, Tommy Flanagan, Clifford Jordan, Dexter Gordon, and Jimmy Heath.

---

* Only in 1976 did the French label Musicdisc issue the album *John Coltrane/Eric Dolphy: Two Giants Together, Rare Live Performance 1962*, the first of many unofficial releases of that evening's performance.

THE COLTRANE/DOLPHY LEGACY

Dolphy's membership of the Coltrane Quintet marks one of the definitive chapters of 1960s jazz history. Their musical relationship has been routinely misconstrued, primarily due to Coltrane's fame and his controversial stylistic shift to freer playing, but in the broadest sense, Coltrane's welcoming of Dolphy had less to do with friendship than with his performance/practice transition, his 'Dolphy era' marked by stylistic departures from the soulful style that had proven so popular since his rise with Miles Davis. Their expanded, exploratory solos were no longer about counting choruses but were rhythmically revitalized, expressive journeys cut loose from the tune. Coltrane's dissonant material emerging from modal freedom includes a rhythmic sense transcending swing and the employment of timbral variety, reinvigorated articulation techniques, and formal aspects of phrasing and melodic gestures as groundwork for expressive development.

Three sources confirm the impact of this collaboration: recordings, Coltrane's own words, and scholarly analysis of their musical relationship. The first source is the live recordings that emerged during and after their period together onstage, from the summer of 1961 through the Village Vanguard engagement and the European tour, and Dolphy's sporadic appearances with the group throughout 1962 until early 1964. If Miles once said of Coltrane's playing that it's like explaining something five different ways, then in Dolphy's work we hear five entirely different things being explained. Yet the two clicked musically, with Coltrane's diverging genius well documented in Impulse! releases at the time. However, many of Dolphy's most accomplished live recordings with Coltrane were not released for decades.

For instance, in addition to the many bootlegs emerging from the Coltrane Quintet's European tour cited above, the night following his Poindexter session, Eric played Birdland again with Coltrane, with recordings of that Saturday night's performances of 'The Inchworm,' 'Mr. P.C.,' 'My Favorite Things' appearing only in 2009, on Gambit Records' unofficial *John Coltrane Quintet With Eric Dolphy: The Complete 1962 Birdland Broadcasts*. Releases such as this one and the complete Village Vanguard recordings reveal a whole new world of Eric's innovative playing, documents pointing to a flourishing collaboration. In Copenhagen as at the Village Vanguard, Dolphy's bass clarinet solo on Coltrane's 'Naima,' the *Giant Steps* album track European audiences would have strongly associated with Coltrane's tenor saxophone, was enthusiastically applauded. Bill

Cole calls it 'a must for any collector,' adding, 'I don't think Trane ever played this piece as well as Dolphy does here.'[9] 'Naima' closed that show, in fact, and one hears the entire auditorium erupt in applause, concertgoers clapping in unison in hopes of bringing the entire quintet back on stage, not just Coltrane, and certainly not the 'old' Coltrane.

The second source spotlighting their mutual impact is Coltrane's own testimony regarding this collaboration. He adamantly expressed this sense of absorbing and reflecting upon Dolphy's performances on several occasions, dating their artistic exchange to 1954 while noting their shared interests in developing new musical ideas. When Eric stopped playing regularly with the quintet sometime in early April 1962, one of the greatest jazz musicians in history had this to say about his tenure:

> That was perfect. He's the only soloist who gives me complete satisfaction. . . . He's the kind of musician I'd like to have again. . . . I don't see anyone at the moment who truly pleases me. . . . I don't see anyone who I would want to have in my group.[10]

From the April *DownBeat* article:

> I told [Dolphy] to come on down and play, and he did—and turned us all around. . . . He'd found another way to express the same thing we had found one way to do. . . . We began to play some of the things we had only talked about before. Since he's been in the band, he's had a broadening effect on us. There are a lot of things we try now that we never tried before. This helped me, because I've started to write. . . .
>
> Eric Dolphy is a hell of a musician, and he plays a lot of horn. When he is up there searching and experimenting, I learn a lot from him, but I just haven't found exactly what I want yet.'[11]

There is much more of Coltrane's commentary on this subject.

The third source revealing the impact of this collaboration is the work of a short list of jazz scholars attempting to clarify Dolphy's presence at this juncture of Coltrane's playing. It was as supportive as it was influential: with Eric's wilder chromaticism and increasingly explosive style, Coltrane had found a partner in experimentation and advancement toward new plateaus of soloing. This meant easing a path of using harmonic, key, and scalar resources not derived from the tune's chords played by Tyner, or the harmonic implications of Workman's bass lines. What is more, those harmonic frameworks had already been greatly simplified by Coltrane along the way, as in 'Africa' and 'Impressions.'

Lewis Porter rightly attributes Coltrane's personal growth toward 'free' playing to the ultra-chromatic material of 'Giant Steps,' but played over simple modal harmonic changes such as those comprising 'Impressions.' Though he erroneously postdates the pair's work together from that summer, Porter states, 'By late 1961, when Coltrane was performing with Eric Dolphy—no doubt encouraged by Dolphy's example—he interpolated whole phrases that were outside the key.' The author further comments on this transformation, suggesting that 'Dolphy was a thrilling and unique player and composer whose influence is as strong as ever. The unbridled freedom of Dolphy's harmonic approach made a strong impact on Coltrane and stimulated the tenorist to search for his own avenues of exploration.'[12]

Pianist and scholar Geri Allen added to this interpretation:

> Coltrane's overall stepwise and arpeggiatic, or 'vertical' approach, as David Baker refers to it, began to break down during the period when Eric Dolphy joined Coltrane's band. . . . This shift from a preoccupation with basing his improvisations off the implications of difficult harmonically structured compositions such as 'Giant Steps' and 'Count Down' was perhaps greatly affected by Dolphy's approach. Dolphy's usage of large skips from low register to high, along with articulation of difficult and unpredictable rhythmic combinations, sometimes phrasing across the bar line, as well as the use of intervallic relationships and bitonality were some characteristics of his improvisational work.[13]

Bill Cole further observes in his Coltrane biography that Dolphy's 'jumping style had a tremendous effect on Trane, for it was at this time that Trane began playing patterns in the upper and lower registers simultaneously through the use of harmonics.'[14] He adds, 'From this specific year—working with Dolphy—all kinds of musical situations evolved . . . even in their playing in unison, there seems to be something about the connecting forces of Trane and Dolphy—whose styles of playing were really dramatically different but whose need to make music was absolutely on the same level.'[15]

Ekkehard Jost refers to the Village Vanguard recordings in suggesting that, 'In *India*, the mode is treated much more freely than in Coltrane's earlier modal pieces. This is perhaps due to the influence of Dolphy, who tends to stray from a strict observance of the mode: even the entrance to his chorus has a distinctly bitonal character.'[16] And, as Simon Spillett argues, 'Although Dolphy's brief tenure with Coltrane appears to have left little direct impact in the music the quartet would play after he left, his spirit continued to be an inspiration to Coltrane, helping in preparing him to embrace the new wave of avant-gardists on the horizon.'[17]

Coltrane's controversial embrace of free jazz toward the end of his life was an even more notable move away from his most admired playing in the three years between *My Favorite Things* and 1964's *A Love Supreme*. Skeptical critics and some Coltrane enthusiasts routinely point to his last period as a wrong turn, with many simply dismissing his free jazz output. Dolphy's name often arises in this conversation, appearing as one of the culprits, along with Ornette, Pharoah Sanders, Archie Shepp, and others who misguided the master. The accomplished, insightful jazz critic Ben Ratliff, for instance, has painted Dolphy's inclusion in the quintet as 'foolish sponsorship' on the part of Coltrane.[18] Referring to the jazz great's period following *My Favorite Things* as one of 'trial and error,' he suggests that 'Coltrane's uneasiness could have been part of a defensive reaction because what he brought to his public through 1961 with Dolphy, including the Vanguard engagement and the subsequent European tour, provoked the strongest negative reactions he had yet experienced.'[19] Echoing what many traditionalist Coltrane fans think of Dolphy, he continues, '[Coltrane] was testing the integrity of his jewel of a group with Eric Dolphy, a saxophonist who would not engage popular interest. This is not business; from a commercial standpoint, these are almost perverse decisions.'[20] Ratliff describes Pharoah Sanders, who joined the tenor man in the mid-60s as, 'Coltrane's new Eric Dolphy, a wilder trip wire who helped the leader more than he helped the group as a whole.'[21] He joins the many critics who have discounted Dolphy's style even if it meant casting aspersions on the master, concluding, 'Coltrane . . . had become interested in a kind of babbling style of improvising in Charlie Parker's tight, bouncing rhythmic phrasing. Dolphy played it, too, though more pronounced, more over-the-top; but instead of intensifying the music, Dolphy's presence made it slacker.'[22]

Dolphy upset the Coltrane cart and thus took the heat for their musical hijinks. The accused troublemaker's inimitable technique and his uncompromising approach to expanding post-bop language with freer jazz earned him praise in avant-garde circles—and in Mingus's arena of social militancy—while securing him a bad reputation elsewhere as one who soured Coltrane. Dolphy's role in jazz history is perhaps obscured simply because of this alleged 'spoiler' role. Likewise, with his departure, the group became Coltrane's classic quartet, releasing a string of 'post-Dolphy' masterpiece recordings.

These concerns aside, their association was immensely fruitful for both. A few days before Coltrane and Dolphy opened their epochal Village Vanguard engagement, Cecil Taylor commented in a *DownBeat* interview, 'See what happens when Coltrane and I play together. He and Dolphy can hear me.'[23]

Despite the growing acceptance and appreciation for Dolphy's work today, his impact on Coltrane and their mutual influence remains a muddled topic for two conflicting reasons. The first is simple: Coltrane as a cultural juggernaut is seen as a master of his own domain on a strongly self-determined path, a trajectory of technical ability and creative verve that would have been realized with or without Dolphy. The second orbits the view that Coltrane, despite his vaunted standing, ended his career producing wildly free music—a mistake to many, and erroneously blamed on the likes of Dolphy, among others.

1962: STRUGGLES AND OPPORTUNITIES

Long periods of 1962 proved difficult for Eric. With no recording contract and the damaging Tynan criticisms haunting him, he left Coltrane to face a hand-to-mouth freelance existence. Never one to tread water, he re-engaged with Gunther Schuller's third stream activities, developed a club connection in strait-laced Washington DC, and met avant-garde composer Edgard Varèse.

The trajectory of his seven-month membership in Coltrane's group had a shelf life partially determined by its own established high points, and by *DownBeat*'s reopening of the Tynan wound in April, with Coltrane and Dolphy gracing the cover of an issue containing interviews prompting the two to 'explain' themselves. The following issue included poor reviews of the Village Vanguard recordings.

During the second week of March, Eric traveled upstate to Syracuse's Everson Museum to play in Schuller's Twentieth-Century Innovations series. There, on Saturday, March 10, the composer conducted the Syracuse Friends Of Chamber Music in a program of his works including 'Night Music,' with Dolphy on bass clarinet, Barry Galbraith on guitar, 'Stick' Evans on drums, and both Art Davis and Chuck Israels (who had sat in with Eric at his Copenhagen University gig last September) on bass. 'Night Music' is a short piece evolving from a moody, quiet double bass duet, Galbraith emerging with dissonant sonorities, and Dolphy's dark, searching explorations. The piece then opens up to jaunty improvisational sections foregrounding Eric's engaged soloing against quieter scored effects. A big, dynamic point of arrival gives way to a misty passage of shifting colors, a sound field that simply fades to a close. The convincing piece is over in less than four minutes. Schuller's 'Variants On A Theme By Thelonious Monk' finds Eric playing all three of his axes. Recordings of these two performances were first released on *Vintage Dolphy*, a 1986 compilation album on Schuller's GM Recordings label. They would reconvene with the same program at Carnegie Hall in April.

Perhaps the oddest recording on which Eric appeared was Benny Golson's *Pop + Jazz = Swing*, a 'Triple Play Stereo' album on Audio Fidelity, recorded in early April with an all-star line-up: Paul Chambers, Ron Carter, Charlie Persip, Jimmy Cobb, Bill Evans, Wayne Shorter, Curtis Fuller, Grachan Moncur, Bill Hardman, and Freddie Hubbard. The album cover boasts, 'POP music on the left, JAZZ music on the right.... The Triple Play miracle.... Using regular stereo controls you can create infinitely variable blends of lilting pop music with spicy jazz or you can create separate pop or jazz concerts.' The left channel's pop tunes are paired with different jazz tunes that share the same chord changes. For example, the standard 'Whispering' is paired with Dizzy Gillespie's 'Groovin' High.' The long-standing jazz practice of writing new tunes over existing chord changes ('I Got Rhythm' is the archetype, serving as the model for Monk's 'Rhythmning,' Sonny Rollins's 'Oleo,' and countless others) is taken here to an explicit extreme.

Even within this experimental novelty production, Dolphy's playing is as serious as ever, as with his leaps and fragmented riffs in the right channel's 'Quicksilver' against the 'pop' arrangement of 'Lover Come Back To Me' playing on the left. His solo on 'Donna Lee' (paired with 'Indiana') is absolute poetry. He shares the limelight with Bill Evans on 'Ornithology' (paired with 'How High The Moon') and takes the plaintive lead alto melody for 'If I Should Lose You,' followed by an exacting solo. He cuts through with his easily recognized style, here drenched in bebop solos inaccurately described by Simosko and Tepperman as being his 'least inspired' and 'among the most conservative solos he ever recorded.'[24] Neither claim is accurate, though this work is not his best. The original disc was pulled soon after its release, the isolated right-channel jazz versions reissued in 1965 (in stereo) as *Benny Golson—Just Jazz!** In the liner notes, Sara Casset incisively states, 'The contributions here by the late Eric Dolphy are as valuable for their perception of composition as for the aspect of memorabilia.'[25]

'JOHN COLTRANE AND ERIC DOLPHY ANSWER THE JAZZ CRITICS'

The Poindexter, Schuller, and Golson gigs were a sobering return to Eric's itinerant sideman duties as Coltrane's classic quartet crystallized without him. But his career was about to take an unusual and high-profile turn. An April 12 cover story interview with *DownBeat* editor Don DeMicheal, 'John Coltrane And Eric Dolphy Answer The Jazz Critics,' ostensibly allowed the two jazzmen to rebut John Tynan's November attack.[26] Soon after the appearance of Tynan's original article, prominent jazz writers Ira Gitler and Leonard Feather joined in the discursive bullying, disparaging Dolphy's struggling career as a leader and sideman. DeMicheal, who had thrown full critical support behind *Outward Bound*, waved a peace flag in the issue before this cover story, using his review of Oliver Nelson's *Straight Ahead* to praise Dolphy's soloing, originality, and humor: 'I think that sometimes he plays those squeaks and ripping figures as leavening for his more serious passages. And it knocks me out when he sounds as if he's swallowing his bass clarinet.'[27]

For his cover feature, DeMicheal gave the master musicians a forum but did not engage them with any follow-up questions that might have led to further illumination. Regarding what was perceived as 'extra-musical' or 'non-musical' elements in Dolphy's playing, the issue of bird calls quickly entered:

> Dolphy smiled and said it was purposeful and that he had always liked birds. Is bird imitation valid in jazz? 'I don't know if it's valid in jazz,' he said, 'but I enjoy it. . . . Birds have notes in between our notes—you try to imitate something they do and, like, maybe it's between F and F#, and you'll have to go up or come down on the pitch.'

* Those same tracks were released as *Groovin' High* for a mid-60s Dutch mono reissue billed as 'The Greatest Soloists/First Time Out Together.' Subsequently, the tracks were remastered for a 1997 reissue by Spain's Fresh Sounds Records as *Benny Golson And His Orchestra: Walkin'*. The Jazz Beat label's 2009 reissue, highlighted as 'The complete Triple Play Stereo Sessions,' includes the *Just Jazz!* album in stereo plus the original Triple Play Stereo mix, with the pop/dance band in the left channel and the jazz ensemble in the right.

In his running commentary on the interview, DeMicheal noted several moments when Coltrane and Dolphy made faces, sat silent, or appeared reluctant to jump into what were often mundane questions. 'What I'm trying to do I find enjoyable,' Dolphy said. 'Inspiring—what it makes me do. It helps me play, this feel. It's like you have no idea what you're going to do next. You have an idea, but there's always that spontaneous thing that happens. This feeling, to me, leads the whole group.'

Coltrane then stepped up to help define their creative partnership: 'Eric and I have been talking music for quite a few years, since about 1954. We've been close for quite a while. We watched music. We always talked about it, discussed what was being done down through the years, because we love music. What we're doing now was started a few years ago.'

The line of questioning next switched to criticisms the two received regarding stylistic detail, such as the charge that they don't swing.

> 'I don't know what to say about that,' Dolphy said. 'Maybe it doesn't swing,' Coltrane offered. 'I can't say that they're wrong,' Dolphy said. 'But I'm still playing.' Well, don't you feel that it swings? he was asked. 'Of course I do,' Dolphy answered. 'In fact, it swings so much I don't know what to do—it moves me so much. I'm with John; I'd like to know how they explain "anti-jazz." Maybe they can tell us something.'

Dolphy pointed out the damage critics could cause to the careers of struggling musicians:

> 'It's kind of alarming to the musician,' he said, 'when someone has written something bad about what the musician plays but never asks the musician anything about it.... But he doesn't feel so bad that he quits playing. The critic influences a lot of people. If something new has happened, something nobody knows what the musician is doing, he should ask the musician about it.... because a musician not only loves his work but depends on it for a living. If somebody writes something bad about musicians, people stay away. Not because the guys don't sound good but because somebody said something that has influence over a lot of people.'

A 'double review' of Coltrane appeared in the magazine's very next issue, featuring

DeMicheal's review of *John Coltrane 'Live' At The Village Vanguard*, with responses by Ira Gitler and assistant editor Pete Welding.[28] Gitler reluctantly gave the album two and a half stars and injected Tynan's 'anti-jazz' epithet in his third sentence before making the uniquely uneducated quip that Coltrane's soprano sax timbre 'sounds much like his tenor's,' obtusely adding that it is unimportant which instrument he plays. Though often supportive of the new thing, Welding contributed the bewildering observation that 'the very intensity of the feelings that prompt it [Coltrane's solo] militate against its effectiveness as a musical experience. It's the old problem of the artist's total involvement as a man supplanting his artistry, which is based, after all, to some greater or lesser degree in detachment.'[29] He punctuated his three-and-a-half-star review by labeling the album 'one of the noblest failures on record.'

The jazz-industry ogre that was *DownBeat* of the early 1960s continued its petty debasement of Dolphy. In the June 21 issue's 'Annual Combo Directory'—a professional listing providing contact information, descriptions, and representative recordings—Eric's entry stated simply, 'Reed man Dolphy has formed his own group, probably in far orbit around the jazz world.'[30] Once the surface humor subsides, one easily senses the flippant, condescension. The put-down was a damning way of saying that his group was not getting gigs and suggesting that his music was too distant from the jazz world to be relevant. The directory revealed that he was 'independent,' without professional representation, two and a half years into his New York career.

'Saxist Eric Dolphy and his quartet do a one-nighter at the Jazz Gallery Monday [May 14],' read the *New York Daily News*, offering further evidence of the musician's struggles to land extended club residencies. As Coltrane later stated, 'It hurt me to see him get hurt in this thing,' referring to the invective aimed at Dolphy and the detrimental effect on his career.[31] In evaluating this 'anti-jazz' fallout, George Lewis notes that Dolphy 'had attracted negative notice despite his strong connections with third stream composer Gunther Schuller,' perhaps suggesting that such a connection to the 'uptown' classical music establishment should have cast a protective aura over the talented cross-over musician.[32] It is ironic, then, that reviews of Schuller's performances featuring Dolphy often inverted this critical reception, his solos credited with saving the music or somehow authenticating otherwise questionable concert music repertoire. Here, it was Dolphy who to some degree validated Schuller.

VARÈSE, OJAI, AND THE LAST CALIFORNIA JOURNEY

The Twentieth-Century Innovations series Schuller directed at Carnegie Hall the evening of Wednesday, April 18, was a partial echo of the Syracuse outing the previous month. Atlantic Records had released Schuller and Hall's *Jazz Abstractions* in November 1961, with a *DownBeat* review the following May giving the third steam classic four and a half stars. The reviewer zeroed in on Eric's role, observing that, 'Coleman and Dolphy are fascinating together. The basic differences in their phrasing are, here at least, tellingly dramatic. ... The cadenza by Dolphy and LaFaro [who had died the previous July] in the third part should command several paragraphs in the most meager discussion.'[33]

With the assistance of both Schuller and Hale Smith, Eric spent an hour with the iconoclastic Franco-American composer Edgard Varèse at his apartment in Greenwich Village, receiving coaching and insight in preparation for his upcoming performance of 'Density 21.5' at the May 19 Ojai Music Festival. Composed in 1936 for George Barrère, the solo flute piece's title refers to the density of the platinum-iridium alloy from which Barrère's flute was made. The roughly four-minute work, its two parts characterized by the composer as 'modal' and 'atonal,' respectively, was revised in 1946 and themed around angular non-diatonic intervals, emphasizing them in a series of unresolved melodic dissonances. The piece's musical elements, sculpted with formal purpose, include register (extreme high and low ranges), articulation, dynamics, abstract rhythmic gestures, timbral effects, and extended techniques. Performing such a demanding, thoroughly modernist solo work was new to Dolphy, and Schuller claimed to have coached him on its performance.[34] With his and Smith's assistance, the jazz musician was stepping fully into the arena of twentieth-century concert music. After he learned the piece, one can imagine Dolphy having to be talked out of playing it in jazz clubs, such were the musician's universalist tastes.

His performance came during Saturday evening's opening program, *Experimental Music And Jazz*, following a first half of John Cage and Luciano Berio. Dolphy filled the second half with a set subtitled 'Jazz Profiles,' featuring bassist Jimmy Bond and drummer Milt Turner. The group was mistakenly identified as 'his trio' by the *Los Angeles Sentinel* in an article that neglected the local-boy-makes-good angle, noting only that Eric 'studied clarinet in Los Angeles and played with various groups in the early fifties.'[35] The trio was followed by Schuller's work.* A social visit came on the day of his Ojai performance, accompanying festival official Cassius Stewart to his home, where Eric met eighteen-year-old Zan Stewart, an up-and-coming saxophonist and writer who had studied with Dolphy's first clarinet teacher, Ola Ebinger.

While in Southern California, Dolphy visited his parents in the old West 36th Street neighborhood. His previous return home the previous October had come about during the Coltrane Quintet Renaissance Club engagement that prompted Tynan's *DownBeat* tirade. Then, Eric was on a cloud, looking toward the Village Vanguard residency and returning to Europe with his friend's group. Unbeknown to him and everyone else in his world, this would be the last time he'd see his parents, his hometown, and his old friends. Dolphy then left for San Francisco, to play with an expanded Coltrane group for their final day of a Jazz Workshop residency alongside Wes Montgomery and violinist Michael White.

LONG HOT SUMMER

Back on the East Coast, Dolphy participated in a variety of Washington DC events, both as sideman for the JFK Quintet and for a curious series of performances over several days at the first Washington DC International Jazz Festival. The 'international' element came in the form of visiting musicians from Poland, Germany, Sweden, Belgium, and France. At Cramton Hall on the evening of Saturday, June 2, Dolphy's quintet joined in a group improvisation with Lee Becker's ten-person dance troupe and painter Paris Theodore in a simultaneous improvisation titled *Jazz Ballet Theater*: the musicians and dancers, with Baby Lawrence billed as a dance soloist, did their thing while Theodore painted abstract designs on a large backdrop canvas. Becker was fresh from directing *West Side Story* on Broadway.

Eric brought in Charlie Persip, Don Ellis, Ron Carter, and vibist Eddie Costa—the same instrumentation used for his 1964 masterpiece album *Out To Lunch!* How close to pure collective improvisation the ensemble came is unknown, though the work was well received. Here, Dolphy directed the addition of jazz to a

---

* Along with Dolphy's trio, the chamber orchestra performing 'Variants On A Theme By Thelonious Monk (Criss Cross)' consisted of Paul Horn, John Pisano, Larry Bunker (vibraphone and piano), David Frisna and Nathan Ross (violin), Howard Colf (cello), Milton Thomas (viola), and Peter Mercurio (bass).

multimedia concept, drawing perhaps from the avant-garde legacy of John Cage's 'Theater Piece No. 1,' a 1952 'happening' presented at Black Mountain College, combining dance, painting, music, and film into one experience and artistic space. In stark contrast to *Jazz Ballet Theater*'s edgy, improvised aesthetic was the festival's young audience at Constitution Hall for Saturday morning's 'Children's Introduction To Jazz.' Eric played in a BMI-commissioned work by Schuller and Nat Hentoff, the latter's text read by singer Bobby Darin. Leonard Bernstein later produced the piece for a 1964 television broadcast featuring Dolphy and other jazzers with the New York Philharmonic. Adding to the contrast of avant-garde mixed media and a children's show, he then performed the following evening at Ed Summerlin's jazz vesper service, televised from the Church Of The Epiphany, for CBS's *Look Up And Live*, appearing with Slide Hampton, Ron Carter, and Charlie Persip, among others.

Such versatile performances kept him busy, but there were no New York gigs for his band. Shows such as a Sonny Rollins/John Lewis concert at the YM-YHCA in June were one-offs—in this case, playing flute for the second half of an awkward concert. The audience listened to a striking Rollins quartet during the first half, followed by Lewis conducting Dolphy, Rollins, drummer Ben Riley, Jim Hall, Richard Davis, and the Contemporary String Quartet in a five-part concert version of his score to that year's film *A Milanese Story* (*Una Storia Milanese*), the directorial debut of Luchino Visconti's nephew Eriprando Visconti. *DownBeat*'s Martin Williams, one of the avant-garde's best jazz-press friends, pulled no punches in describing the work as naively scored, adding, 'Much hasty commercialism has shown better craftsmanship… and it is no pleasure to say so.'[36] Though he gladly accepted this paid gig among friends, Dolphy should have been leading his own group anywhere else rather than waiting in the wings to play through a scored flute part. (This soundtrack material would form much of the first recording made by Lewis's Orchestra USA in early 1963 on which Dolphy appears.)

The summer of 1962 found Dolphy in DC again, filling in for reed player Andy White of the JFK Quintet, the Bohemian Caverns' house band, likely in July. Drummer Joe Chambers recalled Eric sitting in for two or three weeks at the club, adding that he brought some of his own music to play. Studio gigs and opportunities for his own ensemble were drying up, and worry added to the unambiguous weight of career drought until his quartet was booked for a Village Gate residency on an August bill with Monk. However unrelated it may seem, the crossover breakthrough of Brazilian bossa nova emerged as a serious contender for the jazz world's attention in 1962, at a time when marginalized avant-garde figures such as Dolphy were already being shut out of clubs. As Brazilian-flavored jazz swirled about, a thirty-four-year-old Dolphy won *DownBeat*'s International Jazz Critics poll in the 'New Star' flute category, beating out Roland Kirk, Yusef Lateef, and Paul Horn, while also placing on alto sax, bass clarinet, and strangely enough, standard flute, in a four-way finish covered in the magazine's August 2 issue. 'Dolphy may be heard in many settings, from mainstream to "new thing",' read the award blurb.

This brief bout of attention helped Dolphy along as he traveled to Philadelphia to sit in with Coltrane's group at the Showboat for five hot summer nights. There, the two continued their so-called 'anti-jazz' onslaught, giving audiences what they came to hear while doing their best to ignore critics. This was hard to do, as Dolphy read in the late-August *DownBeat* a review of the *Live At The Five Spot Vol. 1* album recorded a year earlier, in which Harvey Pekar once again lauded everyone's playing except for Eric's, openly panning and ridiculing his work on an album given three and a half stars.

At the end of a challenging summer, Dolphy took note of wider social developments. Dr. Martin Luther King, who had ventured to Albany, Georgia, for nine long months of grassroots work and activism to raise awareness of a stalling Civil Rights Movement, finally abandoned the project. The action was portrayed by the media as the movement's failure, temporarily taking the wind out of the sails of justice. Over the coming weeks, the fight would move to Mississippi, where news emerged of African American student James Meredith enrolling in the whites-only Ole Miss, the segregated campus of the University Of Mississippi in Jackson. The battles for racial justice that ensued in Jackson, Birmingham, and countless other towns and cities across the United States provided a painful, proud, and poignant backdrop to Eric Dolphy's final years. In the third week of August, President Kennedy spoke to reporters about Republicans blocking his nominee to the US Court Of Appeals for the Second Circuit, Thurgood Marshall, who in 1967 would become the first African American seated on the US Supreme Court. Also during August, Soviet Prime Minister Nikita Khrushchev was nearing the completion of ballistic missile deployment in Cuba, and, over the next two months, the world seemed to teeter on the verge of destruction. That fall, Dolphy's career trajectory once again veered back toward the composer of 'Don't Let Them Drop That Atomic Bomb On Me,' Charles Mingus.

09 PICKING UP THE PIECES

AUGUST 1962–JUNE 1963

'Eric Dolphy's Quartet opens a three-week engagement at the Village Gate tomorrow night, sharing billing with Thelonious Monk quartet,' read an August 13 *New York Daily News* blurb. With 1962 proving to be the most challenging time in Dolphy's career, such headline engagements represented momentary relief, a chance to showcase set lists of originals and to solo freely. With him were Jaki Byard, Richard Davis, and drummer J.C. (John Curtis) Moses. Davis stayed on into October for Dolphy's Gaslight Cafe quintet performances with a young Herbie Hancock and trumpeter Ed Armour and would return to the studio with him on eleven more dates during 1963–64. Moses began with brothers Stanley and Tommy Turrentine in their hometown of Pittsburgh during the late 50s and appeared on albums by Clifford Jordan and Kenny Dorham before playing with Dolphy. In the 1970s he would return to Pittsburgh and play with Nathan Davis, one of Dolphy's last collaborators in Paris.

At the Village Gate that August, Dolphy and his group enjoyed good times with favorable audiences and Monk's unpredictable buzz. Ed Monck, later the MC at the Woodstock rock festival, was at the venue one of those nights, recording the Monk quartet for Xanadu Records; *Thelonious Monk Live at the Village Gate* was very likely recorded there during Dolphy's stint. Among the other groups coming and going on the bill before Eric's run ended on September 1 were Herbie Mann's Afro-Jazz Sextet and the Max Roach Quartet.

In the meantime, a curious *DownBeat* blurb about the Village Gate engagement claimed, 'Dolphy now finds himself besieged by record companies with offers of contracts.'[1] Without a contract since September 1961, label affiliation would in fact elude Eric until he signed with FM Records the following April. With Dolphy standing closer to a career abyss, the magazine's odd suggestion of business as booming was a facetious falsehood at best, since nothing could have been further from the truth. By the end of 1961, Eric had appeared on twenty-three albums as leader or sideman, but during 1962, his recording sessions thinned to a trickle, and releases of new albums declined. Dolphy's anemic New York schedule meant traveling to Washington DC for paid live performance opportunities.

Joyce Mordecai visited Los Angeles that August, possibly for dance performances, staying briefly with Eric's parents, though it is not known if the thirty-something lovers had become engaged. Well before departing with Mingus for Europe in 1964, Dolphy knew he would be leaving the group after the tour and staying behind in Paris with Joyce, as she had relocated there in the months or perhaps year prior. A small handful of comments regarding his social life give little insight into his personal relationships, his love life, or his thoughts on career ups and downs. A few musicians have stated that Eric frequented jazz clubs on a regular basis, watching, listening, and witnessing the swirl of New York activity.

The wife of Eric's good friend, the composer Hale Smith, Juanita Smith remembered a different Dolphy, sharing that he was a bit of a loner who would 'often come out to our house [on Long Island] in his Volkswagen and spend the day. He just wanted to be with a family; he was an only child who didn't really know many people in New York. He didn't hang out in clubs. He was basically a family person.'[2] Eric would visit the Smith family 'whenever he was in town'; Hale was like the brother he never had. The two musicians would engage in deep discussion about music, sharing books and ideas.

Eric lived for music while craving family togetherness. Buddy Collette remarked that when visiting New York, they'd hang out, practice, and not go out too much, with a similar emphasis on music dominating passing comments from other friends and colleagues. Mingus recalled him practicing along with Charlie Parker records while at a party. Gunther Schuller's accounts of his time with Eric always revolve around practicing music and rehearsing. During Vi Redd's visit to New York in the fall of 1962, Eric took her to an Orchestra USA rehearsal before the two dropped in at the apartment of the remarkable Melba Liston, a Los Angeles transplant at that time freelancing as a trombonist and arranger.

Dolphy returned to Mingus. The cantankerous bassist's Workshop, or 'Sweatshop' to some musicians—'Gargantua' was Mingus's joke name among the band—loomed large again in Eric's life while he was still fronting at the Village Gate. The old Five Spot had booked Mingus as the final act for their August 27 closing, where Dolphy stood with fellow altoist Charles McPherson in an expanded line-up. Like so many talented musicians entering and exiting the Mingus galaxy, Dolphy did his best to stay above the bassist's worsening outbursts. According to Curson, Mingus rather sadistically called out tunes requiring Dolphy to change instruments, only to purposefully switch him up by calling yet another tune, forcing Eric to change instruments again as the rest of the band and audience looked on. Dolphy left the band repeatedly, as he would again in early January 1963.

When one speaks of Eric's struggles in hardscrabble 1962, one speaks of him rejoining Mingus instead of fronting his own group, though he did take a quartet to headline Pittsburgh's friendly Crawford Inn around this time. Nonetheless, the Workshop was more than an economic lifeline to Eric. He made the most of his place in Mingus's spotlight and growing fame, tolerating his extremes while flourishing artistically, playing uncompromisingly, and extending his vocabulary while easily handling Mingus's challenging pieces.

The Village Gate engagement and the Five Spot closure ran concurrently with a brace of rehearsals for Mingus's infamous Town Hall premieres of 'Epitaph,' 'Osmosis,' and other pieces for jazz orchestra. Mingus prepped his growing ensemble on this spate of new works at Birdland, in his own apartment, on off-nights at various clubs, and at Carroll Studios, where practice recordings were to have been made to speed along the learning process but were never realized.

As summer turned to fall, Dolphy was also called upon to play another third stream project. *Essence: John Lewis Plays The Compositions & Arrangements Of Gary McFarland* had its first session on September 9: 'Night Float,' the only track completed, features the theme's bold alto sax/trumpet unison by Dolphy and Herb Pomeroy. October 5 found Eric under McFarland's baton for a second *Essence* session recording 'Tillamook Two,' 'By My Side,' and 'Another Encounter,' the latter with Eric on scored alto flute—his only recording playing the instrument.

GASLIGHT CAFE

Dolphy took a fresh quintet to New York's Gaslight Cafe on Sunday, October 7. Decades later, a bootleg of their performance would emerge as the only live recording of a Dolphy-led group during a two-and-a-half-year period between the

Five Spot performance in the summer of 1961 and the March 1963 Carnegie Hall concert—a gaping hole not just in the aural record but in the struggling musician's livelihood.

Three new names join the Dolphy discography here, the most notable being twenty-two-year-old pianist Herbie Hancock, who'd recorded his Blue Note debut album *Takin' Off* the previous May and recently earned Grinnell College degrees in both electrical engineering and music. Hancock would play with Dolphy on several more dates but was destined to enlist in Miles Davis's great second quintet early the following year. Trumpet and flugelhorn player Ed Armour appears as perhaps the most mysterious if not shadowy of all Dolphy collaborators. Coached by trumpeter Herb Pomeroy at Boston's Berklee School Of Music, where he studied with fellow students Gary McFarland and Hungarian guitarist Gabor Szabo, Armour quickly rose through the Mingus Workshop ranks. He played with Mingus at both the Town Hall concert and the well-known Birdland performance of October 26. The following March, he recorded several tracks with Eric on Freddie Hubbard's underrated Impulse! album *The Body And The Soul.* He would become a crucial presence in Dolphy's quintet until soon after the group's next Crawford's Grill gig in 1963, when he abruptly and angrily walked out of a rehearsal and disappeared back to Chicago. Finally, the unavailability of J.C. Moses for the Gaslight gig led to the recruitment of the little-known Andrew Bateman, who drummed for Walt Dickerson and would play with Ken McIntyre, Ted Curson, and John Handy, among others.

The bootlegged radio broadcast of the Gaslight performance includes a live interview made at the scene during which Dolphy states that the group had just played Pittsburgh. He doesn't announce upcoming gigs because there are none to mention, though the group would play Town Hall the next month, and in 1963 in Boston, at the Village Vanguard, and without Hancock at Carnegie Hall. Eric's work that evening was striking, as were many aspects of the group's performances. Following a convincing unison head, 'Miss Ann' reveals a tight, aggressive alto solo propelled by Hancock's powerful block-chord punctuations, Dolphy condensing diverse ideas and familiar gestures into feverish directions. An extended version of Waldron's 'Left Alone' launches with a conversant flute/bass duet graced with chamber-like introspection. He then pours on filigree woodwind exclamations, breakneck scalar runs and arpeggios, dramatic trills, leaps, overblowing, half-tones, flutter tongue, and vocalizations. When Dolphy returns with a second, brief solo,

Hancock mirrors it and ornaments several flute gestures in a unique, near-duet fashion; the young pianist's splashy accompaniment to the closing restatement of the tune is gracefully all over the place.

The scope of 'Left Alone' is matched by the sprawling 'G.W.,' gasping a bit with Bateman's hard-edged accents and with Armour hanging on for dear life. Dolphy at first takes a reserved, focused path on his alto solo, exploring familiar vocabularies before surprising listeners with twists and turns emphasizing the altissimo register with precise, extraordinary leaps, transforming his signature call-out into a series of wild exclamations.* One can easily make out the fine work of Davis and Bateman, who provide a strong underpinning to the pickup group that would gel for a handful of future gigs.

It is not hard to imagine what a fall 1962 studio recording featuring Hancock, Davis, Moses, and Armour might have sounded like, led by Dolphy on an album of his originals—a fantasy he himself likely coupled to the simple dream of landing a regular club engagement with the group. He had walked away from Mingus in December of 1960 but was now being coaxed back to a bittersweet opportunity, yet a lifeline for which he was grateful.

MINGUS'S TOWN HALL CONCERT

It was perhaps with some degree of foreboding that Eric prepared for the Mingus's Town Hall concert originally scheduled for November 15, now moved up to October, and where he had the opportunity to play with Jerome Richardson, Jaki Byard, and Buddy Collette (whom Mingus insisted United Artists fly out from Los Angeles). His Gaslight trumpeter Ed Armour was in the brass section. Regardless of his bad behavior surrounding the event, Mingus had a point: the label had moved the demanding project up an entire month, forcing the composer into a far tighter, perhaps unmanageable preparation schedule. He wanted a live audience

---

* Italy's illicit live jazz recording label Unique Jazz first released *Gaslight Inn* selections on the undated album *Eric Dolphy: Quintet USA*; Japan's Stash label released the full recording as *Live In New York* in 1990. Another Italian bootleg label, Ingo-Fourteen, added that evening's 'Oh Lady Be Good' for its *Live At Gaslight Inn*. 'I Got Rhythm,' with Dolphy's admirable bass clarinet solo and Joe Carrol on vocals, found its way onto another Unique Jazz release, the erroneously titled *3 Dolphy Group's: Previously Unreleased*. Though it is billed a compilation of three separate 'Dolphy' groups, two of the four tracks are by the John Coltrane Quintet, taken from the February 9, 1962, Birdland radio broadcast, originally released in the 1970s.

for a recording session featuring a full program, including a massive new work for jazz orchestra that was, quite literally, still being completed at showtime, with copyists working at offstage tables. An exhausted Mingus left the podium near midnight, signifying an end to the show, but the band played on, to a cheering if not confused audience.

In a related incident two days before the concert, Mingus slugged old friend Jimmy Knepper in the mouth, causing dental problems that limited the trombonist's future playing, for which the aggressor was successfully sued.* The event fared badly in the press, prompting reviews as surly as the garbled United Artists album *Town Hall Concert* itself (1962), made from improperly mixed tapes that obscured several players (including Eric) and drawn from mediocre versions of multiple alternate takes made throughout the evening. The three-track tapes from the 'live workshop' recording session were bungled and mislabeled; barely more than one half-hour of music was issued on the original album, which made no mention of the personnel.

Alan Douglas, soon to sign Dolphy to FM Records, was the United Artists A&R representative assigned to the project; Mingus unsuccessfully sued UA, claiming he was owed $18,000 for the concert and recording. Somehow it got worse. Douglas botched crucial audio equipment needs, failing to secure monitor speakers for the recording engineers, who then had to emerge in tragicomic fashion through a stage door to engage Mingus in session interactions, all in front of a live, paying audience. Douglas was immediately fired by UA for gross negligence.[3]

Regardless of the surrounding chaos, this near fiasco deserves attention because of Eric's work on two takes of 'Epitaph (Part 1),' in notable conversation with the bassist, the human speech contours of which showcase the alto saxophonist's immediacy and sense of humor. Bill Coss referred to the Mingus/Dolphy exchange in his *DownBeat* review of the concert as one of the evening's bright spots, 'a fascinating musical dialog between Mingus and reed man Eric Dolphy.'[4] Eric carries on, holding forth on his solo above orchestral clouds, squeezing out sparks within an out-of-tempo dreamscape. Unfortunately, the mix used for the

* Mingus was found guilty of assault in New York's Criminal Court and received a suspended sentence. At the sentencing hearing, Mingus berated his own lawyer for calling him a jazz musician: 'Don't call me a jazz musician. To me the word jazz means ... discrimination, second-class citizenship, the whole back-of-the-bus bit.'

original album severely shades his sound (engineers used only two of the three original tracks), and the UA release skipped some of the better takes altogether.

A more complete accounting of Dolphy's performances and a new appreciation for the entire concert later came to light thanks to the work of Mingus biographer Brian Priestley. Thirty-two years following that evening, with the assistance of Priestly, Blue Note released *The Complete Town Hall Concert*, featuring a mysterious alternate take of 'Epitaph (Part 1).' Here, the 'conversation' is much more of an evocative Dolphy solo than the original version's back-and-forth with Mingus, the primary reason being that Mingus had left after trying to end the concert. The lyricism of Dolphy's work exploiting microtonal smears and pedal tones is presented for the first time and is captured more clearly in Blue Note's digital remix using the original three-track tape. Dolphy's work on the alternate take receives rousing applause, much of the audience having remained after Mingus disappeared. He also blows a chorus of '52nd Street Theme' following an impromptu rendition of Ellington's 'In A Mellotone,' launched by Clark Terry after Mingus's departure.

Despite going down in history as a flop, the concert ultimately produced formidable, satisfying recordings of important Mingus compositions, with 1962's bad press now appearing misleading. Compared to Blue Note's complete, digitally remixed issue exhuming the music from history, however, the original album release was a highly inaccurate, poorly mixed document. The British periodical *Jazz News* interviewed Dolphy soon after for a story about Mingus. 'You never know what he is going to do because every night he comes on the stand with something different,' he said. 'He's so creative, and in that way it was so stimulating to work with him.'[5]

Dolphy next returned to Coltrane for a stint at Philadelphia's Showboat beginning October 15. Such night-and-day contrasts were not lost on the career sideman as he transitioned from the psychologically complex Mingus and his vexing expectations and behavior to the quietly centered Coltrane and his adventurous formats for extended soloing. But before his week with the quintet ended, he took a rain check from Coltrane and traveled to the University Of Chicago for a Friday 19 chamber orchestra concert programmed by Gunther Schuller titled 'Simultaneous Music.' There, Eric once again played the Monk variations, 'Abstraction,' and a curious work by Charles Ives, joined by among others Richard Davis and future collaborator Bob James on piano. A *Chicago*

Tribune reviewer noted, 'With Eric Dolphy the obvious standout for pedal notes, high-low skips, rapid melismas, on saxophone and bass clarinet, and real melodic ingenuity. Most fascinating: the way Mr. Schuller's serial wisps of melody set the soloist off.'[6]

Schuller's eclectic program included Stravinsky's 'Ragtime,' excerpts from Mozart's *Don Giovanni*, Renaissance composer Giovanni Gabrieli's 'Canzon In Echo,' and the 'Set For Theater Orchestra' by Ives (misidentified in the review as 'Second Set For Theater Orchestra'), on which Eric played B-flat clarinet. The grandfather of America's classical avant-garde, Ives assembled this three-movement work around 1914 from small works completed between 1899 and 1906. As Schuller later shared, 'I did some Ives music, some of his proto-jazz ragtime music from his "Sets" ... full of jazz licks ... so I had [Eric] play the "jazz" parts on the clarinet.' The piece brings to programmatic life a wild 1890s revival meeting utilizing Ives's own 'Four Ragtime Dances' and the hymn 'Bringing In The Sheaves.' One can imagine Dolphy trying his hand at Ivesian ragtime.

DownBeat's Pete Welding reviewed that concert along with the recently released 'Abstraction' recording, sharing that

> the most successful was the last ['Abstraction']. [It was] distinguished for Dolphy's speech-like saxophone at its most acerbic and vituperative . . . with the strings participating as foils to Dolphy's leaping, corrosive improvisations. ... Perhaps it was the lacerating strength and iconoclastic frenzy of Dolphy's playing that emphasized most fully the disparity between the written and extemporized sections of the works.[7]

That fall, Dolphy became an original member of John Lewis's Orchestra USA, which had its first meeting at Atlantic Studios in November. The orchestra's premiere concert, in which Dolphy did not perform, was unceremoniously trashed by Bill Coss on both a national level in *Time* magazine and belittled in *DownBeat*. As Simosko and Tepperman remark, the ensemble aimed to transcend third stream by performing 'contemporary compositions and to reach into the past for other non-jazz literature reflecting the full range of music available to such an organization.'

Schuller, as a friend and direct witness to his achievements, foregrounded Dolphy's commitment to the crossover vision:

> Eric was one of those rare musicians who loved and wanted to understand all music. His musical appetite was voracious yet discriminating. It extended from jazz to the 'classical' avant-garde and included, as well, an appreciation of his older jazz colleagues and predecessors. He was as interested in the complex surfaces of Xenakis, the quaint chaos of Ives, or the serial intricacies of Babbitt as in the soulful expressiveness of a Coleman Hawkins, the forceful 'messages' of Charles Mingus, of the experiments of the 'new thing.'[8]

Citing Schuller's observations, ethnomusicologist Paul Austerlitz argues for recognition of Dolphy's contribution to music in a book chapter subheading titled 'Dolphy's Consciousness,' pointing to the musician's unique stature within African American, and American, 'jazz consciousness':

> Dolphy's musical vision is notable for his not necessarily distinguishing between bebop and these other styles. Instead of ossifying various types of musical thinking into mutually exclusive camps, he saw a holistic aesthetic universe that traversed bop, new music, classical music, and other influences.[9]

One might consider that Dolphy did not necessarily distinguish an overly contrasting sense of meaningfulness, nor observe hierarchical 'cultural values,' between jazz and other forms of music he passionately engaged in as a musician. He embraced a sense of freedom in doing so.

REFLECTIONS AND ENTRANCES

During the fall of 1962, Dolphy was cultivating yet another artistic collaboration. His Gaslight quintet returned to Town Hall on November 20 for a headline show with Greenwich Village fixture and poet Ree Dragonette (born Rita Marie Dragonetti). Dragonette organized West Village readings at Les Deux Megots, the Harlequin, Goody's, and Le Metro, and had already read her poetry in conjunction with jazz performance at the Village Vanguard. The event with Dolphy at the Town Hall was organized by Martin Mitchell and Ross Fagin. The collaboration reached beyond anything Dolphy had previously done with music, providing deeply personal compositions based on Dragonette's poetry and improvised interpretive responses to her poetry during live performances.

In a pre-concert interview, he reported having dedicated hours to reading Dragonette's poetry and that they worked out material and structured their collaborative performance. 'It was the first time I had ever done that kind of thing,' he said of the project. 'What was most important to me was what she meant by each of the words. It was tough, but it was a wonderful experience, and I must say that it never would have come off unless all the musicians played marvelously.' Dragonette then explained:

> Dolphy's approach is original, perhaps radical, but it is so structured, and it goes back into so much jazz that went before. I feel that we are much alike, and his response to my work has been greater and better than I would normally find from some other poet.... In any case, there are very few metaphysical poets around. Eric is working in a new field, and so am I. We're breaking ground. Here we will do it together.[10]

The two performed *Reflections And Entrances* in three program sections with two intermissions. The first portion featured the 'free-blowing' Dolphy Quintet, the second recitations of fourteen poems, and the third found Dragonette joining the quintet for four numbers, 'singly and in tandem,' as Bill Coss described them in his *DownBeat* review. This final section called for Dragonette to join the quintet onstage and was comprised of four pieces: 'To Tonio, Dead' (flute and bass duet), 'Song For The Ram's Horn,' 'The Mandrake Sleeps The Panther Walks,' and 'Like Pharoa's Eye, Like Onyx Stone,' each a poem title also used for Eric's original tunes.* No further titles are mentioned in the program, yet Alan Saul states that Dolphy wrote six pieces for the concert. Robin D.G. Kelley suggests that he composed five new pieces to specific poems, plus a premiere of his flute vehicle 'South Street Exit,' which according to Saul enjoyed a long rendition, along with 'G.W.,' in the concert's opening section.

Dragonette penned 'The Mandrake Sleeps The Panther Walks' in honor of Black writer Calvin Hernton, a member of the Umbra poetry workshop group that emerged from Lower East Side readings launched that summer. Another Umbra member was Eric's cousin Lorenzo Thomas. Dolphy soon retitled this alto-

* Dragonette self-published her poetry book *Like Pharoa's Eye, Like Onyx Stone* in 1962 in a limited edition of five hundred copies.

based composition 'Mandrake' for the album *Iron Man*, though the Fontana label used the original title on the 1964 album *Last Date*. Dolphy carried 'Mandrake' and 'South Street Exit' into some of the very last performances before his death, conjoining the tunes in what he called the 'Two Part Suite.'

Dragonette's poem 'Like Pharoa's Eye, Like Onyx Stone' was matched with a new composition dedicated to Monk and retitled 'Hat And Beard.' That tune appeared on *Out To Lunch!* alongside another November 20 program number, 'Something Sweet, Something Tender,' characterized in part by the opening's delicate bass clarinet duet with bassist Davis. The program was recorded and posthumously broadcast on New Jersey's WBAI within two months of Eric's death. Alan Saul confirms that a recording of the *Reflections And Entrances* concert exists, while Geri Allen claims that Dolphy's group 'often performed in conjunction with the poet.'[11]

Despite clumsily saddling Dolphy with the 'anti-jazz' epithet, Coss gave *Reflections And Entrances* a general thumbs-up:

> The first big league combination of the two art forms that has had moments of true brilliance. . . . [Dolphy] has sometimes been accused of anti-jazz . . . he does show the signs of what has been outlined as his crime. However, here, given the chance of matching compositions to poetry, he wrote in a way that for all times must prove his real ability.

Heaping praise and poison in the same review, the journalist rebuked Dolphy for 'nonsplendored' choruses but reined in his invective to observe that when composing and performing in accordance to poetic structure, Dolphy was 'nearly always unique' and 'the compositions were tight.' Regarding 'Like Pharoa's Eye, Like Onyx Stone' ('Hat and Beard'), he added, 'The bass clarinet-bowed bass portions were strong, fresh, angular—everything that might fit the portrait. It was an unusual success.'

A few days following the Dragonette performance, Eric was disappointed to read Dom DeMicheal's mediocre three-and-a-half-star review of *Far Cry* in *DownBeat*'s second November issue. Readers were told of the work's ambiguity and humor and that it was interesting 'yet not wholly successful,' with the compositions holding together more than his playing. 'There should be little doubt of Dolphy's importance or talent by now,' the review continued. 'Most of his solos here strike me as being questions instead of statements. This may be intentional since Dolphy's humor sometimes gets the upper hand.... He appears to depend on phrases instead of individual notes.'[12]

Eric once again escaped back to planet Coltrane in mid-December, during the tenor man's residency at Chicago's McKie's club, and appeared with the group in New York later in the month for a concert at the Lincoln Center Philharmonic Hall. For this uptown gala, Dolphy missed the premiere performance of the Orchestra USA—not a surprise, given his crass treatment by Lewis, who had asked him in rehearsals to mellow out and play closer to the tune, then pointed to Phil Woods for alto sax solos. He replaced Eric with a last-minute classical flute ringer before another concert.[13]

The Coltrane Quintet played the Carnegie Hall New Year's Eve jazz concert on a bill including Sonny Rollins, 'The Amazing' Nina Simone, and Thelonious Monk & His Band. Dolphy had participated in a similar December 31 show with Coltrane's group the previous year within weeks of returning from their thirty-day European adventure. The following year, they would play together again on New Year's Eve to close out 1963—his last such celebration.

1963

The icing on the New Year's Eve cake came in the form of more Coltrane gigs, first in Chicago, again at McKie's, until January 6. McCoy Tyner's wife gave birth on opening night, so the pianist missed the gig. The brief tour then visited Penn State Jazz Club, Cleveland's Jazz Temple, Babe Baker's Jazz Corner in Cincinnati, into February at Gino's in St. Louis, and finished with a return to McKie's, where Dolphy was billed in the *Chicago Tribune* as 'Eric Dauphine.' There, the quintet reportedly played 'So What' for an hour and twenty minutes, thumbing their noses at critics deriding long solos. Then, for what was likely their first gig since the Dragonette collaboration, Dolphy brought his Gaslight group with Hancock up to Connolly's Stardust Room in Boston's Roxbury district. The group was still assimilating his recently penned tunes, perhaps along with the new compositions 'Iron Man' (to be performed in early March in Illinois) and 'Half Note Triplets' (retitled 'Burning Spear' for the *Iron Man* album), both tunes performed at Carnegie Hall on April 18.

Orbiting Mingus when necessary, jumping onto the Coltrane bandwagon whenever invited, and waiting by his telephone for session calls were lifelines that

Eric juggled along with his third stream connections. Intermingled with sideman club performances were a set of recording dates for Orchestra USA's first album, titled *Orchestra USA Debut* (Colpix, 1963), engineered by Tom Dowd at Atlantic studios, the first session coming on February 4. Much of the music was from Lewis's film score for *Una Storia Milanese*, music premiered in concert form the previous June at the YM-YHCA, with Dolphy in the ranks.

A wide shot of the orchestra fills the original Colpix album cover, with Dolphy seen at his second flute chair. The aesthetic dichotomies between third stream material (as found on this disc) and Dolphy's vanguard position had never been so notable. Eric's imaginative solo can't save McFarland's riff-based 'Milesign,' on which Lewis's overly spartan piano solo nearly collapses. Characterized by thumping and pointedly brash brass charts drawing out a repetitive blues groove, the number thrashes about before giving way to Lewis's wispy ballad 'Milano.' 'Donnie's Theme' first finds Eric blowing a bit of a solo against Phil Woods in the intro to this strange tune's psychological thriller landscape. Soon Dolphy cuts loose, once again bringing the album some of its few shreds of vitality. Schuller's liner notes describe the piece as 'largely a vehicle for Eric Dolphy, who in his impassioned solos captures some of the violent atmosphere of the drama.' Dolphy's style is thus not included here for its own musical value but exploited to programmatically represent the film's disturbing narrative of insanity. Eric reads through his parts for the last two numbers: McFarland's weirdly eclectic and moody 'Grand Encounter,' and Schuller's orchestration of a strait-laced, patriotic 'Star-Spangled Banner.' It was, after all, Orchestra USA.

Also in February, Albert Ayler passed through New York, returning from Europe on his way home to Cleveland to visit his parents and recharge his free-jazz battery. When he returned to New York later in 1963 is not exactly known, though he began playing wherever he could, including with Ornette, Coltrane, and Dolphy. Briefly that March, Ayler sat in with Cecil Taylor and bassist Henry Grimes at the small Greenwich Village coffee house Take Three, when, it is claimed, Dolphy was sitting in with Coltrane at the nearby Village Gate. The two would occasionally leave after their set and walk over to the Take Three to watch and listen to free jazz. Richard Koloda claims, 'Ayler acknowledged that, even though they [Coltrane and Dolphy] did not grasp the music Taylor was playing, they realized that a new sound was developing,' though Dolphy was known to have owned Taylor's records and had already appreciated his playing.[14] Coltrane followed up several of his Half

Note shows by catching Ayler and Dolphy laying down scorched-earth sounds together at an unidentified nearby club later in the year (the specific dates are lost).[15] By December, Ayler was regularly jamming at Ornette's house. As Sonny Simmons recalled, 'The brothers changed things, but Albert Ayler was the only brother I know, other than Eric Dolphy, who shook Coltrane up. I was there. I witnessed it.'[16] Ayler impressed Dolphy, the latter talking up plans to bring his free-jazz friend to Paris in the weeks before his sudden death.

Dolphy's creative road from late February 1963 to the early July recording sessions for *Conversations* and *Iron Man* started with an engagement at the Village Vanguard. On Friday, March 1, his quartet—'exponents of the more experimental school,' according to the *New York Daily News*—launched a shared, perhaps awkward, weekend billing with Lewis's Modern Jazz Quartet, 'noted for its freshness and spontaneity.'[17] By referencing 'Eric Dolphy and his quartet,' the *Daily News* plug indicated either a piano-less group (without Hancock) or a full rhythm section without Armour. The headline role was a rare, top-club acknowledgment of Dolphy's sound.

Dolphy's schedule then assumed a series of eclectic music-making experiences: three separate recording sessions, beginning March 8, for Freddie Hubbard's underappreciated album *The Body And The Soul* (Impulse!, 1963), its charts arranged by the up-and-coming Wayne Shorter; the eleventh Festival Of Contemporary Arts at the University Of Illinois, Champaign, the following Sunday, March 10, where he had been asked by Ornette to replace him as the sole jazz musician featured among concert-music academics; two Carnegie Hall performances as part of Schuller's Twentieth-Century Innovations concert series, one of which featured the Dolphy Quartet (without Hancock); a recording gig for an odd Cold War–era album by Teddy Charles & The All-Stars, *Russia Goes Jazz—Swinging Themes From The Great Russian Composers* (United Artists, 1964); and two residencies for his quintet, first at Pittsburgh's Crawford's Inn, and in June at New York's Take Three. This wild array all led to the *Conversations* / *Iron Man* recording sessions, held during the first week of July.

FESTIVAL OF CONTEMPORARY ARTS

To Illinois Dolphy brought Moses; Kahn, as a replacement for Davis; and Hancock, soon to depart for the Miles Davis Quintet. Following rehearsals and Eric's afternoon roundtable discussion, the quartet performed as part of an evening concert. Beckoned from run-throughs with students preparing his arrangements, Eric arrived late for the panel discussion on 'Approaches To Improvisation,' which became, by account, an argumentative exchange. The other panelists were of the young and progressive, avant-garde phalanx of academia. Though each went on to well-deserved stellar careers in music, at the time they were an unproven bunch; Dolphy likely knew nothing about them or their performance practice because none of their music was available on record. The thirty-year-old bassist and composer Bertram Turetsky, a specialist in contemporary chamber music who at the time also played swing jazz, went on to a rich career developing avant-garde techniques, improvisation, and advanced composition; the now-heralded modernist composer Robert Erickson, four years later the founder of the music department at the University Of California, San Diego (where he eventually hired Turetsky), had written the formalist book *The Structure Of Music: A Listener's Guide* in 1957; Rhodes scholar and self-taught composer Barney Childs won the Koussevitzky Award at Tanglewood in 1954 and was two years out of a Stanford PhD in English, now teaching at University of Arizona. It is not known how Dolphy—an apparently token African American jazz musician among academics, with the only proven artistic record among them—would have been expected to interact with his fellow improvisation panelists.

'Students and faculty who were there recalled that Dolphy returned from the panel in an agitated state,' states Vladimir Simosko. 'Whether this was due to the intellectual argument or, more likely, to the faculty's response to Dolphy's opinions and credibility is unclear.'[18] The talented, privileged members of the panel likely held forth with what was (and often still is) the typical entitlement academics afford themselves in the presence of cultural practitioners outside their limited academic circles. While Dolphy's frustration could have stemmed from any number of issues or incidences, his position as a highly trained professional musician on the frontline of avant-garde performance practice was probably discounted, ignored, or questioned. Struggling without institutional support and facing serious challenges of livelihood for braving the artistic path he had undertaken, Dolphy felt deeply the abyss between himself and the academics speaking that day on *his* specialty: improvisation. Once berated for ruining the 'color scheme' of his Los Angeles City College orchestra and denied a USC summer music camp scholarship due to race, Eric that afternoon likely felt again the vast distance between his reality and theirs. At such times, Dolphy certainly appreciated Schuller, an academic but one who sincerely appreciated Eric's sensibilities and methods of improvisation beyond jazz, growing to lean on them for the success of his own compositions.

J.J. Johnson had just played the Urbana–Champaign campus's brand new eighteen-thousand-seat assembly hall days earlier to commemorate the venue's opening. This evening's concert began with professor John Garvey's student big band, followed by Dolphy's quartet; the second half featured two Dolphy arrangements for large ensembles, his group joined by a nine-piece brass ensemble (six French horns, two baritone horns, and tuba) for a performance of 'Red Planet,' followed by a return of the big band playing an arrangement of 'G.W.' In discussing the event, Simosko rightfully points out Dolphy's other large-ensemble arrangements made in Los Angeles for his ten-piece band and those later completed in Paris, to which can be added his orchestrations for the two volumes of Coltrane's *Africa/Brass*. Though a clear recording of the quartet found its way to *The Illinois Concert* (Blue Note, 1999), poor mic placement and stage management mar the results. His instruments are often badly off-mic throughout extended solos, behind Hancock's piano and Moses's cymbals. Regardless, the performances are brilliant; the musicians whip through 'Softly, As In A Morning Sunrise' and 'Something Sweet, Something Tender,' the latter number also finding its way onto *Out To Lunch!* Here, the tune segues into a rich set of important material: the unaccompanied bass clarinet arrangement of 'God Bless The Child,' 'South Street Exit' (mistitled by the local newspaper reviewer as 'Blues In A-flat'), and the first known performance of 'Iron Man' (misidentified by the same reviewer as 'Bombs').

The original university tape of the quartet's portion of the show was copied by Brian Sanders, a jazz radio producer who occasionally aired the recording. Thirty-three years after Dolphy's appearance on campus, Sanders contacted Alan Saul, who assisted in clearing the recording's release with family, friends, and fans and submitted the music to Blue Note producer Michael Cuscuna. Former University Of Illinois students and faculty—including composer Ben Johnston, campus officials, the Eric Dolphy Memorial Foundation, and members of Alan Saul's 'Dolphy-L' email list—assisted with the information necessary for release.

'RED PLANET'

It is not incidental that Dolphy programmed 'Red Planet' for the Illinois concert, for which publicity materials stated that the work was composed by him. Onstage that night, the piece was a righteous vehicle for a fantastic, exploratory alto solo, including tricky altissimo-range gestures full of quarter tones and whispery harmonics. Listening to Dolphy solo, one might think of his saxophone as addressing his fellow panelists from that afternoon, a performance/ sonic lecture on how to keep jazz alive with innovation and experimentation while expanding the possibilities of what can be played on the instrument. After seven minutes of holding forth, Eric drifts off with a sweet, lyrical melodic phrase and turns things over to Hancock. Until that point, the accompanying brass ensemble has been responsible for a few dynamic swells and pads.

Among the piece's curious features is its head. Very unlike most jazz heads, its twelve notes include every pitch in the chromatic scale, making them a 'tone row,' a hallmark of modernist classical 'twelve-tone' or 'serial' composition. Eric was well aware of this compositional school, pioneered by composer Arnold Schoenberg, but no further serial technique is employed beyond the bop-inflected head's retrograde form of its tone row. The piece is not subsequently subjected to any of the usual serialist transformations. Though 'Red Planet' nods to serialism, it is no more serial than Bill Evans's likeminded 'Twelve Tone Tune.'

Title and authorship were the number's real perplexities. 'Red Planet' entered the Coltrane Quintet leading up to their Village Vanguard residency in November 1961, and was included in club sets following their return from Europe at gigs such as the bootlegged Birdland show on February 10, 1962.* It is not known why, then, Coltrane recorded the number with his quartet as 'Miles' Mode,' claiming authorship and releasing it in the summer of 1962 on the Impulse! album *Coltrane*. That new title refers to the Dorian mode used in 'So What' and employed by Coltrane for his solos on this number. Impulse! followed suit by retitling 'Red Planet' as 'Miles' Mode' in subsequent Village Vanguard issues. Alan Saul notes that Michael Cuscuna has speculated that the set of twelve ordered pitches 'may have been a Coltrane line that Dolphy arranged for brass ensemble, perhaps for the *Africa/Brass* sessions (but unused),' thus bolstering Coltrane's claim as author, though this speculation lacks evidence.

---

* Simosko states that in these performances, 'each time it was referred to as "Red Planet."'

If Dolphy picked up a discarded excerpt from Tyner's arrangement of *Africa/Brass* verbatim, that makes Coltrane a 'serialist' composer—something very few would agree with. If Dolphy reshaped such an excerpt into 'Red Planet' (an unlikely scenario), that makes him the composer, and many thus find the piece's structure to be proof of his 'serial' technique. But neither is the head associated with Coltrane's highly contrasting modal approach to soloing, and his shallow relationship to serialism differs from Dolphy's proximity to it through work with Schuller and Hale Smith.

Schuller, who worked with Dolphy closely and retained possession of some of his personal manuscripts following his death, stated:

> At the end of his life, [Eric did] try to write twelve-tone music. I have them; they remained in sketches or in manuscript at his death. . . . So for him atonality was not a problem of any kind—he heard that way, and one can hear in his playing, I mean it isn't twelve-tone because it isn't organized into a tone row, but is certainly atonal in the use of the intervals and the continuity. He could go back and forth, though.[19]

The brief tune could have been a Dolphy/Coltrane collaboration, depending on how they worked 'Red Planet' into the Coltrane Quintet repertoire. As Simosko states, 'A four-bar ascending passage [after the serial material] establishing tonality [is] more along the lines of something Coltrane might have invented.'[20] But it is nearly obvious that the two never sat down to hammer out a finalized title with rights. It just so happens that Coltrane was the first to break away with the material on his own, renaming it 'Miles' Mode' based on his own Dorian explorations on the *Coltrane* album (recorded in April and June of 1962).*

Dolphy kept the title 'Red Planet,' arranging something special for the Illinois concert a year later in March 1963, on the recording of which Blue Note names him as the composer. His arrangement for six French horns, two baritone horns, and tuba augmented his quartet, and his remarkable alto solo transcends any particular mode. This is certainly not Miles's mode.

---

* The Coltrane album's retitling of 'Red Planet' as 'Miles' Mode' had a domino effect throughout the 1970s. In 1997, Coltrane discographer David Wild clarified the matter in notes to the 1997 ABC Impulse *Complete Village Vanguard Recordings.*

Predating Eric's preparation for the Illinois concert, the tune's riddle was further twisted by the Pee Wee Russell Quartet with Marshall Brown, who recorded an unattributed 'Red Planet' in the summer of 1962 for their album *New Groove* (Columbia, 1963).* Regardless, the consensus now is that Dolphy wrote the tune, yet by March of 1963 he had seen the piece on two albums—neither attributed to him—with the title 'Miles' Mode' mysteriously attached to his creation by Coltrane and Impulse! Though it seems that Coltrane's recording would have settled the issue with the jazz public, as Simosko states, 'As an attractive takeoff for solos, the piece appealed to musicians in the 1960s; in those years "the word was out" among hard-core jazz lovers that it was actually a Dolphy composition called "Red Planet."' Hale Smith's 1975 letter to Eric Sr. and Sadie mentions the 'Red Planet' score as Eric's original work.

CARNEGIE HALL AND OTHER DELIGHTS

Back in Manhattan's Atlantic Studios the day after his Illinois concert, Eric rubbed elbows with old friends Melba Liston, Jerome Richardson, Reggie Workman, Clark Terry, and Ernie Royal, among others, playing Wayne Shorter's *The Body And The Soul* charts for a second Hubbard session. It was good to renew bonds and earn rent money, but quite different from that Thursday evening's 'Recent Developments In Jazz' Carnegie Hall concert, part of Schuller's 'Twentieth-Century Innovations' series, an echo of the Syracuse performances in March. The April 18 program included works by Lalo Schifrin, Andre Hodier, and George Russell. Eric played B-flat clarinet on Schuller's 'Densities' in an effective quartet with Warren Chiasson on vibes, Davis on bass, and Gloria Agostini on harp.†

Previously recorded in 1960 with Ornette in the seat, Schuller's 'Abstraction' for string sextet with two basses, guitar, and drum set, was fronted that evening by Eric's improvisational work.‡ Don Heckman, in a pointed review echoing what many audience members likely thought, commented on the crucial role played by a singular improviser, and on Schuller's questionable claims of his concert music's relationship to jazz:

---

* Subsequent reissues attribute the tune to Coltrane.

† Recordings of 'Densities' and 'Abstraction' are featured on *Vintage Dolphy*.

‡ The musicians included Matthew Raimindi and Lewis Kaplan (violin); Samuel Rhodes (viola); Michael Rudiakoz (violincello); Richard Davis and Barre Phillips (bass); Jim Hall (guitar); and 'Sticks' Evans (drums).

> Alas, the only important thing that took place at this concert was the superb playing of Eric Dolphy. It was his contribution alone, on alto saxophone, bass clarinet, and flute, that brought Schuller's pieces ('Densities I,' 'Night Music,' and 'Abstraction') to momentary life. Dolphy's alto cadenza on 'Abstraction' must surely be considered one of the finest spontaneous expressions in recent memory. Schuller is wise to use the soloists with Dolphy's powers... in his jazz works, since they bring vitality and spirit to music that frequently seems to have been devised as a technical exercise.[21]

Referencing the recording of this Carnegie Hall performance, longtime Dolphy supporter Martin Williams later offered insight into the Coleman/Dolphy roles in 'Abstraction': 'What Ornette did through an intuitive leap, however, Eric accomplished step-by-step... Coleman, who sensed it [the piece's structure], sized it up and ran a parallel course to it. Dolphy goes inside "Abstraction" and his lines become, spontaneously, an integrated part of it.'[22]

In the midst of these intense musical activities, John Tynan's reactionary jazz criticism again reared its ugly head, poking this time at the artistry of the Chico Hamilton Quintet. In the March 28 *DownBeat*, Tynan interviewed Chico Hamilton in Los Angeles with a focus on his saxophonist Charles Lloyd's 'frequently brutal tenor sax assaults,' as the drummer defended the new thing in contrast to what he thought of as the 'shackling of jazz' by the likes of Brubeck, Cannonball Adderley, and Gerry Mulligan. 'Coltrane, Dolphy, Ornette,' Hamilton emphasized, were the most significant contributors to a revitalized jazz world: 'They're playing impossible things on their instruments.'[23]

Tynan's article infuriated Hamilton's bassist, Albert Stinson, whose subsequent letter to *DownBeat* ended, 'Jazz no longer needs John Tynan. It never did. I'd relish being Charles Mingus for a while just to slap Tynan in his mouth.'[24] One could imagine the Marvel Comics character Iron Man as a Dolphy alter-ego bent on righting the wrongs of the jazz world. Tynan was lucky: Iron Man helped found The Avengers, a group who, along with Mingus and Albert Stinson, would have gladly done more than just show Tynan the door.

The 1986 GM Recordings album *Vintage Dolphy* features the April 18 Carnegie Hall installment of Schuller's *Twentieth-Century Innovations* series—the second live recording of Dolphy's working group since the October '62

Gaslight bootleg.* With Hancock gone and vibist Bobby Hutcherson not yet on board, Dolphy's quartet included Armour, Moses, and Davis. The bass clarinet solo takes its time on the well-organized 'Half Note Triplets,' with its head's compact alternation of frantic bebop and languid spaciness, a structural polarity from which Dolphy's solo explodes in celebratory shouts, jumping from melancholy lines and recombining in an extemporaneous composition within a composition. Armour's solo is less carefree and comes off as didactic; restrained in its fragmentations of melodic themes, with rather ordinary scalar runs, his exploration rarely gets beyond his trumpet's clarity and beautiful tone. Davis's solo is a mélange of driving riffs and punctuation until Eric and Moses jump in with more free material, overlapping and then fading out for a return to the head's oddly questioning intro. By this coda-like return, the audience gets the tune's pattern and politely applauds after a fade-out ending.

Byard's 'Ode To Charlie Parker,' which the pianist performs on *Far Cry*, provides sporadically polyphonic free-jazz treatments on the Carnegie Hall stage: Eric takes off on his flute flights, and Davis joins with searching lines as Moses creates a minimalist smattering of percussion. Armour works his way through a series of held notes and transitional sustained tones as Moses continues exploring his kit. Armour slowly slips away as Eric's ambitious solo continues. Davis stays in, attacking the low end of his instrument with Moses coming off as the juggler of rare gestures. Again, Armour follows Dolphy with noticeably weaker approaches to this freer atmosphere, blowing well but only tentatively building away from his meandering lines. It is toward the end of the number that the lackadaisical side of Moses emerges, and, without energy, the tune tends to sink.

'Ode To Charlie Parker'—sometimes identified as 'Ode To PC' and as often mistakenly attributed to Eric—also appears on *Iron Man*, arranged for flute and bass. 'Iron Man,' which might have premiered at the Illinois concert, wins the evening with its acerbic boldness, Moses and Davis providing strong support for Eric's incredible alto histrionics, which Martin Williams later cited as 'the most amusing, ingenious examples of a jazz soloist's toying playfully with a single musical motive.'[25] He really goes to town, and Moses tries matching his gestures, anticipating and dialoguing with the soloist. Armour finally steps up with gusto,

---

* GM Recordings was a Boston-based label founded by Schuller in 1981; Germany's Enja label remastered those recordings the following year for CD, with the copyright still held by GM.

providing an admirable solo that keeps marking new ground, and playing on the tune's open-ended message of futurism and empowerment. It is not insignificant that Carnegie Hall concertgoers applaud passionately, shouting 'Bravo!' and filling the track's fade-out with their eager reception of Dolphy's quartet. Eric's players left the stage for the concert's second half, which featured a Schuller-selected all-star group playing 'Donna Lee,' with ten soloists including Eric, Phil Woods, Nick Travis, Benny Golson, Jimmy Knepper, Don Ellis, Jim Hall, Lalo Schifrin, bassist Barre Phillips, and Charles Persip.

In writing about *Vintage Dolphy*, Martin Williams alerted readers to how the album brings together great performances by the jazzman on all three instruments, his importance in the realization of Schuller's work, and the recording's showcasing of everything Dolphy did well.[26] In considering the lack of posthumous rewards Eric's reputation received, Williams posited that he suffered mightily from poorly made comparisons to Ornette and Coltrane, adding that in a 1960 interview, Eric stated that Ornette taught him a direction: 'I wish he had said *encouraged* rather than *taught*.' The veteran writer continued by citing Mingus's observation that Eric 'absorbed Bird rhythmically,' adding that Coltrane had not. More than two decades after Dolphy's death, some critics still felt the need to do right by the legend, placing him more prominently among the greatest jazz revolutionaries of his day by suggesting that he be allowed to stand on his own and take center stage.

In the weeks following Carnegie Hall, Eric engaged his old Los Angeles friend Bobby Hutcherson, likely in response to a new recording contract. Alan Douglas approached Dolphy with a recording agreement that gave the musician total control over material and musicians. The producer had joined the Jazz Theater record production company, formed by Monte Kaye and Pete Cameron, after being fired by United Artists the previous fall for his role in the Mingus Town Hall catastrophe. The company's plan was to sell their new recordings to major labels, but they soon formed the short-lived FM Records and signed Dolphy for the sessions leading to *Conversations* and *Iron Man*. In the spirit of the company's original business model, licenses for reissuing both albums came quickly, and to multiple labels.

On Friday, April 25, Eric hung out with another old LA friend, Jerome Richardson, and others, playing on three tracks in a United Artists session for the album *Russia Goes Jazz—Swinging Themes From The Great Russian Composers* by

Teddy Charles & The All-Stars.[*] Dolphy added bass clarinet, with no solos, to the numbers 'Scheherazade Blue,' 'Love For Three Oranges March,' and 'Borodin Bossa Nova'—kitsch proof of bossa nova's arrival. He moved on to further work on Freddie Hubbard's album, entering the studio on Thursday, May 2 to help finalize the disc, still being assembled from the March sessions.[†] He read flute parts for 'Dedicated To You' and 'Body And Soul' and recorded a brief, stupendous single chorus alto solo on the crisp, up-tempo blues of 'Clarence's Place.' This tidbit maelstrom demonstrates Dolphy pulling an entire colony of rabbits out of his horn. There's a Coltrane-esque concentration here, coming from someone who has so much to say, compressed into a few seconds on an album for which he's otherwise reading Shorter's parts. For Dolphy fans, at least, 'Clarence's Place' is the cherry on top of this fine album.

The rest of May was quiet, leading one to ponder Dolphy's routine: practicing, jamming with bandmates, composing, seeing Joyce, visiting the Smiths, perhaps sitting in at clubs. Ayler may have already been back in town, as the two were soon jamming together. This was probably when Eric purchased a new alto sax, replacing his 1949 Selmer. In 2005, that older saxophone was put up for auction on eBay.[‡]

THE CRAWFORD GRILL, THE ARMOUR INCIDENT, AND THE TAKE THREE

The first week of June found the Eric Dolphy Quintet in Pittsburgh, with Eddie Khan again substituting for Davis. With them was Bobby Hutcherson for what was likely the last engagement before Armour's dramatic departure. The Crawford

---

[*] Dolphy's fellow contributors included Zoot Sims (tenor sax), Jerome Richardson (tenor sax, flute), Pepper Adams (bars), Teddy Charles (vibes, arrangements), Hall Overton (piano), Teddy Kotick (bass), Jimmy Raney (guitar), Osie Johnson (drums), and Ed Bland (arrangements).

[†] Dolphy's collaborators this time were Freddie Hubbard (trumpet), Curtis Fuller (trombone), Wayne Shorter (tenor sax), Cedar Walton (piano), and Reggie Workman (bass) with Louis Hayes (drums) replacing Philly Jones.

[‡] Guernsey's Jazz Auction February 20, 2005, Lot 272 (provenance: Carl Grubbs, 1963). Estimate $30,000–40,000. The auction was prefaced by Grubbs's statement: 'In 1963 my brother Earl Grubbs was going to New York to visit Naima Coltrane. I asked him to find me a decent alto saxophone. While Earl was in New York he met Eric Dolphy. He and Eric hung out on the scene, and he spent the night at Eric's loft apartment. Earl spoke with Eric about finding me a decent saxophone. Eric told him that he had an alto saxophone that he would give him for me. Eric stated that if he kept the horn around, he would always play it and would not play the new horn that he had obtained.'

Grill was a nationally recognized jazz venue nestled in Pittsburgh's Hill District, hosting in addition to the local practitioners of the 'Pittsburgh Sound' (George Benson, Stanley Turrentine, and Walt Harper started here) the touring groups of Art Blakey, Charles Mingus, Max Roach, Miles Davis, John Coltrane, Bill Evans, and Kenny Burrell. The restaurant and bar welcomed multi-racial audiences during a vibrant music scene from the 1930s throughout the 1960s and was renovated after a 1953 fire with an ample raised stage, colorful dining booths, and new murals. The place was busy, serving breakfast, lunch, and dinner, and staying open late for jazz performances in a building that later received a Pennsylvania State Historical Marker in 2001 and is now listed in the National Register Of Historic Places. Dolphy received ready support in the pages of the local, Black-owned *Pittsburgh Courier* newspaper. His group's set list included standard Dolphy fare, and material that looked toward the *Conversations* / *Iron Man* recordings the following month. In addition to 'G.W.,' 'Miss Ann,' '245,' and 'Les,' clubgoers likely heard newer tunes from the April 18 Carnegie Hall program, namely 'Iron Man,' 'Half Note Triplets,' and 'Mandrake.'

There are discrepancies among accounts of Ed Armour's stormy departure from the group after the quintet returned from Pittsburgh and before the Take Three Club engagement later that June. Bobby Hutcherson's account from 2008 depicts a blustery winter's day with Tony Williams on drums, mistakenly placing the breakup in the weeks leading up to the February 1964 recording of *Out To Lunch!*, the vibraphonist claiming the Armour scene led directly to Eric calling in Freddie Hubbard for that album. But it is not the case that Armour left the group in June 1963, only to return for winter rehearsals for *Out To Lunch!*, only to quit again. There is no evidence that the estranged brass player ever played with Eric again after the Crawford Grill dates. In any case, Hutcherson recalled Eric's aplomb in response to Armour's outrage:

> We were rehearsing for about an hour and a half… all of a sudden, right in the middle of the tune, the trumpet player, Eddie, starts cussing and packing up his horn. We get to the end of the tune and Eddie says to Eric, 'You're nasty.' And Eric was real sweet, just like Trane was—you know, a real sweet cat. Eric said, 'What?' Eddie says, 'I don't like you, I don't like your music, and I'm not going to play this gig. I'm out of here. F you. F this band. That's it. How do you like that?' We're all standing there

> thinking, 'My God, how can this cat say this?' And he continues to put his horn away, clip the fasteners on his trumpet case. He grabs his coat, pulls his hat down, and goes stomping to the door. He gets to the door—I mean, just yanks it open. The door hits the wall. Bam! He's just about to go out the door. Eric had just been sitting there with his head down. We're all thinking, 'Eric must feel horrible. What's he going to do?' All of a sudden, Eric says, 'Hey, Eddie.' Eddie turns around and says [in a growling voice] 'What?' Eric, with the most conviction and love, says, 'If I can ever do anything you need, please don't hesitate to call me. I'll be there for you anytime.'[27]

In sharing excerpts from a similar Hutcherson account, Robin D.G. Kelley notes, 'Armour never did call. Instead, he dropped out of the scene, returned to Michigan, and was spotted in Detroit two years later sitting in with local musicians. He was never heard from again.'[28] It is not known whether Davis or Kahn played bass at the Take Three, Dolphy's first gig with Armour's replacement, the nineteen-year-old Woody Shaw. 'Residency' might be an exaggeration, but Simosko and Tepperman mention 'appearances' at the club—an opportunity possibly related to news emerging in August that Eric had acquired a manager: 'Jean French, who manages saxophonists Eric Dolphy and Charles Davis, has added flutist Prince Lasha to her stable. Dolphy, with trumpeter Woody Shaw and vibist Bobby Hutcherson, played at the Take Three in late June.'[29]

Finding Shaw was also the start of Dolphy organizing players for the FM Records sessions. He hustled up musicians, strategizing how to best take advantage of Douglas's generous, alleged offer of long, late-night sessions five nights running: 'We stayed in the studio one week, from 3pm until 3am,' the producer recalled years later (despite the official recording dates being listed as July 1 and 3).[30]

During that summer's ebb and flow, Ornette Coleman had slowly slipped out of the spotlight, exhausted from low pay and from dodging critic's bullets. Regarding the free-jazz warrior's silence at the start of 1963, it was not just the world of hostile clubs, labels, and critics that wore him down, it was also the compromised sense of freedom. About those times Ornette commented, 'I think that's because of a certain kind of fear of offending just to get ahead. It's a fear that just tears me up. It must have something to do with being Black, or it's something instinctively in me that I can't explain.'[31] Ruminating over the dead air of his self-censorship during 1963–64, he added, 'There's always the tragedy of your not being totally understood because someone suspects some other motive outside of you expressing yourself.' Ornette's artistic plateau in 1963 was not achieved in the jazz world, but rather via a crossover work for New Music piano virtuoso David Tudor and cellist Charlotte Moorman, who premiered his *City Minds And Country Hearts* in New York.

The world was changing, too slowly for some, too quickly for others. On June 11, Alabama Governor George Wallace stood in the doorway of the University Of Alabama's administrative office, preventing African Americans from registering as part of a recent federal court order to desegregate the institution. The next day, NAACP activist Medgar Evers was shot dead in his driveway after arriving at his home in Jackson, Mississippi. Later in the year, Hoover's FBI began their most elaborate surveillance of Dr. Martin Luther King Jr., whom they codenamed 'Zorro.' He was soon named *Time* magazine's Man Of The Year, winning the Nobel Peace Prize. In November, John F. Kennedy was assassinated in Dallas.

It should not be lost that during the summer of 1963, as the violent response to the Civil Rights Movement heated up, Eric entered the last year of his life. Gunther Schuller, in commenting on the spartan, monkish life Dolphy led in his dedication to music, shared that once, after a long rehearsal at Dolphy's sparsely furnished apartment, Eric showed Schuller a large sack sitting in a closet: 'They're full of white beans; that's almost all I eat. And, you know, that's how Blacks in the South survived for years in the old days. You almost don't need anything else.'[32] He and Coltrane consumed honey as a major dietary supplement, and Eric brought a jar of honey to performances and rehearsals.

Hale Smith painfully recalled Eric's situation to Zan Stewart:

> Dolphy rarely had much money. 'It seemed that the only person who would consistently hire him was Coltrane,' says Smith, who often fed Dolphy at his home on Long Island because Eric couldn't afford to buy food. 'He had had a falling out with Mingus because of Mingus's temper. Eric didn't want to travel with him, so Mingus fired him.' Smith visited Eric at his lower Manhattan loft on South Street in 1963, when the reed player had called to say he didn't feel well and was shocked at what he saw. 'It was one of those bad winters, and he had no heat,' says Smith. 'You could see snow coming in through cracks in the walls.'[33]

Juanita Smith, like the rest of Dolphy's friends and family, later realized that he never knew he was diabetic. He shared with her that a sore on his leg had failed to heal for three weeks. In his last year, his body was slowly reacting to incredibly high blood glucose levels. According to Dolphy, the benign cyst on his forehead formed as he slept sweltering in a hot car traveling across the Southwest. Juanita noticed that, after the lump was surgically removed, the skin did not heal properly. 'Eric had several illnesses [related to diabetes],' Hale Smith recalled. 'He had a fungus in his mouth which was very painful, and he had an injury to his shin that took a long time to heal. These were all signs that something was wrong, but no one suspected diabetes.'[34]

Dolphy's sporadic discomforts likely included numbness of limbs, dry mouth, sore gums, and blurred vision. He could easily have suffered from unusual hunger patterns, fatigue, weight loss, increased thirst and urination, stomach pain, and nausea. Nonetheless, he remained undeterred by the symptoms confronting his mind and body as he stepped into the recording studio to document music resulting in two albums under his name.

10 CONVERSATIONS / IRON MAN, PREPARING OUT TO LUNCH!

JULY 1963–FEBRUARY 1964

Prince Lasha and Sonny Simmons drove from Los Angeles to New York during the first week of July 1961 and attended a Dolphy/Little Quintet Five Spot gig the night they arrived. As Lasha recalled, the two jazzmen played on the *Conversations / Iron Man* album sessions two years later, on July 1 and 4, 1963:

> I was in the record store one day [in Los Angeles] and heard this alto player, and Simmons was with me, and I said, 'Who is that?' He said, 'That's Eric Dolphy,' and I said, 'Is that Eric Dolphy in New York? Simmons, look. You gonna be ready to go in a couple weeks.' Simmons adds that Dolphy said he 'loved that composition you two wrote ["Music Matador"]; I want to record you and I'm taking you on a record date.' When we got there he said, 'We're going to play that composition you two wrote, first piece, first track.'[1]

Alan Douglas produced *Conversations* (FM Records, 1963), distributed by Vee-Jay and released by that label as *The Eric Dolphy Memorial Album* (1965), and he issued most of the remaining tracks as the posthumous *Iron Man* (Douglas International, 1968). Eric's work here is a compendium of three and a half years of new ideas since *Far Cry*, his last studio recording as leader. Audiences wouldn't hear *Iron Man* until 1968.

Side one of *Conversations* begins with Fats Waller's bluesy vaudevillian 'Jitterbug Waltz,' a fun-loving piece the great pianist recorded on organ in 1942, here given a carnivalesque stroll. Though it contains one of Eric's best, most relaxed studio flute solos, it is arguably also Woody Shaw's number, the young brass player's tone and zestful lines bringing out the old-school theme in unison with the flute, then registering a fine solo. Shaw made it easy for Dolphy to forget Ed Armour. Recording engineer Bill Schwartau's work is superb, and the rhythm section sets the table for carefree colors to flit about as they do: Hutcherson's vibes magically hover about, never clanging in attack or overcrowding anyone's sound; Kahn's bass is up in the mix throughout, keeping time and adding a punchy melodic presence; and J.C. Moses helps drive the frolic with inventive drum fills in waltz time, welded to Kahn's groove. Who says you can't dance to jazz? Eric's unusual flute gesture at the start of Hutcherson's solo, a whimsically repeated stab at ornamented intervals, and his long trill during Kahn's solo are both reminders that it's his session, his arrangement. This same, solid quintet is heard on 'Iron Man' and then with Davis on bass for 'Mandrake'—two similar, hard-driving tracks destined for the *Iron Man* album—though on many (even reputable) reissues, the personnel credits are botched for these two impressive numbers.

Lasha and Simmons's vigorously bouncy 'Musical Matador' is immediately strengthened by Dolphy's brazenly outside bass clarinet shout-outs between festive refrains. With no pianist for these sessions and Bobby Hutcherson sitting out on vibes, 'Music Matador' is all about the single-line melody soloists, their rapport coming together to attractively mark the playful form and cadential figures of this festive Caribbean number. In Simosko and Tepperman's words, this 'kind of funky calypso' features a sextet, with Moffett's minimalist drums and Davis's unceasing energy supporting soloists Lasha, Simmons, and Clifford Jordan, the last taking up the soprano saxophone, as he does on *Iron Man*'s 'Burning Spear.' Immediately after the head, Eric's bass clarinet lays down harmonically outside permutations. Simmons's fairly timid solo barely explores the inventive figures he musters on other tracks, while Lasha's solo confidently delivers a determined flute. It is Jordan who goes airborne, with a gamut of avant-garde lines and thorny curiosities playing into the freer landscape Dolphy envisioned for the number. However, no one is having as much fun as Eric on this tune, blowing a cavalcade of confrontational grunts, wailing squeals, and Latin-ish exhibitionism in the form of clave-like rhythmic gestures similar to those running through many of the solos on this track.

'Musical Matador' is the only track in Dolphy's discography featuring Charles Moffett, who grew up in Texas and played trumpet with Ornette and Lasha in their band The Jam Jivers at Fort Worth's I.M. Terrell High School. Switching to drums, he played professionally with R&B and rock'n'roll acts, including Little Richard, before settling down in nearby Rosenberg as a high-school music teacher. Ornette played Moffett's wedding in 1953 (as did Leo Wright), and Ornette returned to visit Moffett and his students in 1960. Frustrated by the music education system in Texas, and sensing limitations in his public school job after his band was denied a higher ranking in state competitions, Moffett took up Ornette's offer to come to New York and play free jazz. During the summer and fall of Eric's first year in New York, he drummed for Ornette's group with Bobby Bradford and Jimmy Garrison at the Five Spot and stuck with the free-jazz altoist when he returned to clubs in 1965.

Side B of *Conversations* presents a completely different world from side A, offering a welcome reminder of Dolphy's versatility and aesthetic ambition. 'Alone Together' is a fragmented, complex reworking of Arthur Schwartz's standard, which had already seen its share of diverse interpretations (one thinks of Miles Davis's edgy 1955 version on *Blue Moods*, with Mingus, Britt Woodman, and Elvin Jones). Here, Dolphy and Davis have no problem sitting their jazz audience down to what is arguably a New Music piece à la third stream. Bass and bass clarinet tangle in a rich dialogue shaped by free lyricism and timbral experimentalism and painted with harmonics, intonational explorations into microtonal pitch worlds, key clicks, and conversational exchanges—slow, dark reflection periodically shaken alive with vigorous flurries and inventive interplay. Highly sectional, the duet presents an esoteric multiplicity of contrasting musical elements. Polymetric passages abound, as during Davis's solo at around 10:25, when Dolphy ghosts the bassist's musical lines with his own determined digressions. The two take their time on the session's longest track, a captivating thirteen and a half minutes of sensitive ensemble. The alternative take released on *Musical Prophet* is equally epic and deep, as David Toop notes:

> In this setting it acts as ghost presence, absent and present, a new balancing of the song's melodic and lyrical functions with oblique instrumental contextualization. Implicit within this one piece were two options: one was to forget the song book entirely, the path of free improvisation (but not free jazz, which invariably retained ties to theme and variation); the other was to find greater parity between song and accompaniment.[2]

Throughout the 1960s and beyond, the so-called Creative Music arm of free jazz would make great artistic use of such intense approaches to duet and trio structures. Where 'Alone Together' is a gentle abstraction, 'Love Me' flies off the handle in the best way, toggling between exuberant abandon, utter virtuosity, and clarity of purpose. One hears the contrast between the compositional determinism of Dolphy's arrangement of this Washington/Young ballad and the endlessly imaginative, elastic freedoms he takes.

Iron Man's line-up of the title track, 'Mandrake,' 'Come Sunday,' 'Burning Spear,' and 'Ode To C.P.' presents an equally pleasing yet demanding spectrum of musical creation with *Conversations* DNA. The aggressive 'Iron Man' forges its leaping, swirling contours with alto and trumpet, the head's eight-bar theme balanced by eight bars of pedal point over which Eric adds echoing, free figurations before the two-part structure repeats. Notable in the *Musical Prophet* reissue is that there is no alternate version, suggesting the track was a one-shot first take. There's a stabbing, crazy-quilt feel to the tune, with Shaw following in unison then adding piquant dissonant seconds to punctuate the line, and Hutcherson's spot-on vibe chords chiming on off-beat accents: he pedals those sustained chords with the vibraphone motor on, creating shimmering clusters that color the moment in a magical pre-echo of his work on *Out To Lunch!* Shaw and Hutcherson hold down the tonic in the second eight bars as Dolphy lets loose. Moses athletically reinforces the disjointed melody, adding splendid fills that sculpt and sustain the tune's energy. Hutcherson's uncanny vamping is rhythmically precise with muted, clouded timbres creating an understated tension to Dolphy's blistering solo. The alto's split-tone ornaments briefly elide with Shaw's powerful solo entrance, and one momentarily hears two lines of free playing.

Half the duration of 'Iron Man,' the compact 'Mandrake' is in a similar post-bop vein, with Davis on bass pushing a bit harder than Kahn. It's a strongly voiced, angular tune with edgy harmonization between the front men, Dolphy's solo here complimenting his 'Iron Man' maelstrom. (In subsequent club dates, Dolphy often followed 'Mandrake' with 'South Street Exit,' a combination he dubbed the 'Two-Part Suite.') 'Come Sunday' is Duke Ellington's spiritual from 1943's *Black, Brown, And Beige* suite and continues the beautifully rendered Dolphy/Davis duets in a style that freely weds jazz with concert hall classicism. Davis's effective bowing and the formal patience the two dedicate to restructuring Ellington's spiritual result in moving, virtuosic chamber music. One hears

Dolphy's continuing mastery of the bass clarinet in the rapture of his tone and improvised lines.

'Half Note Triplets,' first recorded in April at Carnegie Hall, was renamed 'Burning Spear' not long before the July recording session, its new title celebrating Kenya's newly appointed revolutionary independence leader, Jomo Kenyatta.* Dolphy refashioned the tune with a new arrangement featuring bass clarinet and welcomed nine musicians to the early July sessions to record two takes, the alternate appearing on *Musical Prophet*. The ensemble consisted of all of the previously mentioned players, plus Clifford Jordan on soprano saxophone, Garvin Bushell on bassoon, and Moses on drums. Both Kahn and Davis participated too, revisiting Coltrane's use of two basses in a coordinated registral strategy avoiding muddy textures by splitting the instrument's range, alternating low and high registers with Davis occasionally bowing. The bassists propel the piece from the bottom up. After the orchestrated head, solos enter and exit with the help of something that is rare under Dolphy's leadership: group improvisation among melody instruments. While there is a looseness in the way 'Burning Spear' toggles tempi and thematic structure, a good deal of its success grows from a sense of liberation brought by the soloists. Meanwhile, the rhythm section bubbles madly, though Hutcherson is a bit too far back in the mix. An effective bass duet provides a further sense of musical purposefulness. The other winds come in with a tiny barrage of free play as the agile and imaginative Shaw enters. Hutcherson's solo emerges from the mix, augmented at first by cued, dissonant wind chords, and two pizzicato bassists plugging away. Wind trills cover Hutcherson's fade out to the bassists' duet, during which Davis begins sustained arco passages over Kahn's plucked line. The two experiment with minimalistic rhythmic cells before expanding into more broadly expressive material. Dolphy calls in Moses and Hutcherson immediately before the return of the tutti head. It's a big sound, and Dolphy's arrangement toys with the ending, teasing out the number's jigsaw close.

In contrast with the expansive energy of 'Burning Spear,' 'Ode To C.P.'

---

* That May, Kenyatta (born Kamau Ngengi) won the election for Kenya's first independent government, following over five decades of British colonial rule. He had emerged from seven years of British incarceration two years earlier and proceeded to negotiate a new constitution before being appointed prime minister in 1963.

(sometimes 'Ode To Charlie Parker') was the session's final Dolphy/Davis duet. Eric's studio performance of the Byard tune with Davis virtually matches his December 1960 recording with the *Far Cry* quintet, with nearly the same timing and very similar pitch inflection and phrasing. 'Muses For Richard Davis,' by pianist and composer Sir Roland Hanna, went unreleased until the *Musical Prophet* album.* Following an upbringing in classical music, Hanna turned to jazz and later studied at Juilliard and the Eastman School Of Music, becoming a professor of music at CUNY-Queens. A stint in the US Army during the early years of the Korean War coincided with Dolphy's, after which he played with Benny Goodman, his career soon overlapping with Dolphy's future collaborators Mingus and George Duvivier. With over four hundred original compositions to his name, his writing includes chamber works for classical instruments in an eclectic, openly mixed style akin to third stream yet typically referenced as classical jazz. (The following September, Dolphy would share the Five Spot stage with Hanna in the Mingus Workshop.)

'Muses For Richard Davis,' written for solo bass, ascends like a spiritual from the depths of bowed double bass and subdued bass clarinet, solemnly revealing peaks and valleys. With no extant duet score or description of the arrangement, one can assume that Eric used Davis's part to create his own by mirroring, playing off of, and weaving through it. The two reportedly spent an entire studio session working out 'Ode To C.P.,' 'Come Sunday,' and two takes each of 'Alone Together' and 'Muses For Richard Davis.' There is, in 'Muses,' a heterophonic quality to the players' similar contours. The moving, reflective tune's bittersweetness is set aside as Eric bolts with foregrounded flurry, at first improvisational, then uncannily close to the theme's air of endurance and survival. The runs and leaps flowing from his horn are not a detached cadenza but a personal flight deeply connected to Hanna's intertwining of mournfulness and hope. Brief solo excursions are followed by duo passages in contrary motion dressing up the motif. The theme's restatement leads to Davis's scalar run up to a steely yet poignant set of artificial harmonics. His bass's highest pitches mix with Dolphy's horn harmonics in a cloud, bringing the seven-and-a-half-minute duet to an angelic finale. It is through Davis's melodic acumen and dexterous instrumental command that such an intimately voiced,

* Roland Hanna was later awarded an honorary knighthood by Liberian president William Tubman in recognition of concerts he played in that African nation to raise money for education.

lyrical bass vocabulary is brought up to Dolphy's level as a soulful musical partner. 'Muses For Richard Davis' shines a brilliant light on Dolphy's penchant for duets with bassists, pointing toward the intro to 'Something Sweet, Something Tender,' to be recorded with Davis in February for *Out To Lunch!*

CLARIFYING THE LEGACY OF *CONVERSATIONS / IRON MAN*

The touching introspection of 'Ode To C.P.' closes the *Iron Man* album experience, and one can picture Dolphy exiting Music Maker studio after these FM sessions, turning from his musical world to a less-than-certain future. Though he was still under contract to FM Records, the label was struggling, and he would never again record with them.

Iron Man gave listeners some of Eric's most challenging studio work to date. But what should have been a timely follow-up to *Conversations* sat silent as five long years passed before Douglas Records released it, arguably reducing the album's impact; it also suffered from poor distribution by Laurie Records. The newly formed Douglas Records had fallen into an unorganized state by 1968, losing session notes and shedding institutional knowledge of the sessions over the few years following the recording. *Iron Man*'s original, unattributed liner notes are a disaster. They mislead with the notion that these tracks were too 'futuristic' to release in 1963, play fast and loose with the facts, goof the timeline, suggest that Eric's originals formed the entire basis of the project, and erroneously suggest that Alan Douglas had a creative role in the music. They also confusingly state that Dolphy's original work was performed as duets with Davis and by 'a ten-piece orchestra of young men.' In fact, the bandleader composed none of the material arranged for duet, those pieces being by Ellington, Schwartz, an uncredited Byard, and Hanna. Of the rest, only 'Burning Spear' is for a ten-piece, with an uncredited Garvin Bushell on bassoon; 'Iron Man' and 'Mandrake' are both for quintet, the personnel of which has been misidentified across most releases. Dolphy is further miscredited for Jaki Byard's 'Ode To C.P.'

The year Douglas released *Iron Man*, the label passed along incomplete notes and licensed 'Jitterbug Waltz' and 'Music Matador' to Everest Records' Archive Of Folk And Jazz Music. Everest, in turn, released the sloppy, inaccurately credited album *Eric Dolphy*, featuring 'guest artist Cannonball Adderly [sic],' and an incomplete and improper list of musicians, further graced by what the exacting Dolphy discographer Uwe Reichardt calls 'totally ignorant liner notes' by Leonard

Feather.* *Iron Man*'s publishing rights went to both Douglas and Tempo Music, and following a final printing by Douglas in 1971, it was licensed to at least nine labels for two dozen reissues, harkening back to Kaye and Cameron's Jazz Theater company's original business model: selling recordings to labels.

Douglas stated on a number of occasions, including as recently as the early 2000s, that the Music Maker sessions ran across multiple consecutive nights. 'We stayed in the studio one week, from 3pm until 3am,' he recalled, adding elsewhere, 'The recording sessions took place late at night in a very relaxed studio for five consecutive nights.'[3] Simosko and Tepperman's updated discography from 1996 includes the inaccurate session dates from the 1976 release: 'late May–early June 1963.' Confusion over recording dates is not so rare, though here the image of Douglas turning the studio over to Dolphy for a week of 'all-nighters' is hyped in contrast to the reality that the two sessions were just that. The first printing of *Iron Man* to convey accurate recording dates was the 1973 Japanese reissue on Epic (ECPM-91), which states July 1 and 4. Douglas met Frank Zappa before the release of *Iron Man* and discussed with the emerging avant-garde rock icon a series of co-produced jazz releases, including an Eric Dolphy album to be titled *Moop Record* (what became *Iron Man*), for which artist Cal Schenkel completed cover art subsequently used for the 1970 Mothers Of Invention album *Burnt Weeny Sandwich*. Thus it appears that Douglas considered redirecting Dolphy's work toward a more commercial audience by fusing avant-garde rock and jazz.

The Douglas Records label, under the aegis of Douglas Producing Corporation, reissued a jumbled reordering of *Conversations* and *Iron Man* tracks on the retitled 1976 double album *Jitterbug Waltz*. In the mid-80s, the producer himself proved unable to provide discographer Reichardt with crucial session data except that the first master of *Conversations* was completed in the weeks following the sessions, on July 26.

These missteps echo among other questions and memories of Mingus's Town Hall concert, a debacle overseen by Douglas the previous fall. The producer claimed in the original *Iron Man* liner notes to have had some sort of artistic relationship with Dolphy in which the studio became a laboratory or testing

* Dolphy appears on only those two tracks, Adderley on only one, and the two never together, despite what is implied by the album cover. Feather produced a *Conversations* reissue for the French label Fontana using excerpts of his unpublished interview with Dolphy in those liner notes.

ground. 'The early part of 1964,' the notes state, was 'when Eric Dolphy and producer Alan Douglas decided to experiment with Eric's original compositions.'[4] This is, at best, a disingenuous concoction, arguably presaging the controversy that would haunt Douglas's legacy following his blatant doctoring of Jimi Hendrix's last recordings, for which Douglas claimed co-songwriting credits. Douglas met Hendrix at Woodstock and scheduled recording sessions with the rock legend shortly before his death. Later, Douglas tampered with the tapes for the purpose of releasing them commercially, erasing certain passages and hiring studio musicians to record new material as accompaniment to Hendrix's recordings.*

Thankfully, Resonance Records's Zev Feldman, along with James Newton and his team, managed a stunning feat in 2018 by issuing the complete sessions with all alternate versions as *Eric Dolphy, Musical Prophet: The Expanded 1963 New York Studio Sessions*, featuring an additional seven outtakes totaling over fifty-three minutes of music. The reissue's liner notes quote Douglas's claim of five nights of recording but also specify the alternative two dates: July 1, when Dolphy and Davis recorded multiple takes of their duets; and July 3, when it is assumed all remaining six pieces were recorded. Unfortunately, the credits on that exquisite reissue of the complete sessions incorrectly identify Lasha, Simmons, Jordan, and Bushell as playing on 'Iron Man' and 'Mandrake,' the two Dolphy originals held down by a quintet with Woody Shaw. Resonance also left off Byard's writing credit for 'Ode To C.P.'

AFTER THE *CONVERSATIONS / IRON MAN* SESSIONS

The first half of 1963 had been a whirlwind of success; another long, hot summer brought uneasy feelings of evaporating opportunities. The community of talent coalesced for *Conversations* and *Iron Man* not surprisingly dissolved quickly: Hutcherson took up with the Al Grey/Blue Mitchell sextet in Chicago; Lasha and Simmons joined the Elvin Jones/Jimmy Garrison group for the *Illuminations* album, as well as landing other gigs; and J.C. Moses moved into what became The New York Contemporary Five, joining Archie Shepp, Bill Dixon, Danish alto

* From these heavily edited Hendrix tracks, the Douglas Production Corporation produced three controversial Warner/Reprise albums under Hendrix's name, supervised by Douglas, who emerged as the primary Warner-related litigant fighting against the Hendrix estate's eventual success in securing the rights to his recordings.

saxophonist John Tchicai, Don Cherry, and bassist Don Moore, with a premiere performance in mid-August at Harout's Restaurant in Greenwich Village. That quintet spent the next three months gigging and recording in Stockholm and Copenhagen—just one of many European sojourns where innovative players in Eric's circle found supportive audiences.

With no prospects for headlining engagements in New York, Eric went again to Washington DC's Bohemian Caverns to front their house band, the JFK Quartet. The irony was not lost on Dolphy, leaving New York to again substitute for JFK's regular altoist Andy White, an African American Howard University graduate student who was attending the Boston Symphony's Berkshire Music Center (later renamed Tanglewood) on a full scholarship. White was fulfilling Eric's adolescent dream of becoming an orchestral oboist. Back in New York in August as a sideman, and having taken on a few private students, Dolphy returned to Mingus during one of the bassist's highest career plateaus. He played multiple gigs with Mingus at the brand new Five Spot on St. Mark's Place and Third Avenue (which was twice the size of the previous venue) and joined his ten-piece band at the Village Gate for ten days. Some of Mingus's Five Spot dates later in September, with Roland Hanna at the piano, were subbing for Monk, who played the Monterey Jazz Festival during the third weekend of the month.

This was an orbit to which Dolphy more than willingly returned, in the aftermath of Mingus's successful Impulse! album *The Black Saint And The Sinner Lady*, released that July. In the meantime, everyone who was anyone had read Dolphy's international press for the month in Leonard Feather's blindfold test with Sonny Stitt in *DownBeat*'s mid-August issue. In response to a track from *Far Cry*, Stitt exclaimed, 'Take it off. I've heard enough already. No, I don't like that record. I don't even want to hear it. You can write that down too. It's got no conformity. In fact, you know what? They're trying to find something that isn't there. . . . No stars.'[5]

Martin Luther King Jr. made a different type of news on August 28 when he led the March On Washington and delivered his 'I Have A Dream' speech. A larger swath of America began paying attention to the critical issues of the nation's racial divide and the deep problems that persisted in the South, where white supremacists openly and violently opposed the Civil Rights Movement for equal rights and desegregation. Nothing could have prepared anyone, however, for what happened in Birmingham, Alabama, on September 15, when Thomas Edwin

Blanton Jr., Herman Frank Cash, Robert Edward Chambliss, and Bobby Frank Cherry—white supremacist terrorists of the local Ku Klux Klan—placed nineteen sticks of dynamite with a timer under the stairs of the 16th Street Baptist Church. They murdered four girls, Mae Collins, Carol Denise McNair, Carole Robertson, and Cynthia Wesley, and injured twenty-two other parishioners.* America's long history of bloody violence continued, ripping the heart out of society, with the forward steps of the Civil Rights Movement shadowed by threats, police brutality, and retaliatory murders.

THE LAST NEW YORK AUTUMN

With Sonny Rollins substituting, Eric took a short leave from the Workshop immediately after the Birmingham bombing, while also juggling two short recording sessions for *The Individualism Of Gil Evans*. At A&R Studios, New Webster Hall, he joined friends Jerome Richardson, Ernie Royal, Garvin Bushell, Richard Davis, Ron Carter, Elvin Jones, and other all-star players, reading scored wind parts on 'Hotel Me,' 'Toreador,' and 'Flute Song.' The following spring, he returned to Evans's Verve album project for what would be his last commercial studio appearance in the US, days before leaving for Europe with the Mingus Sextet tour. The album was released after Eric's death.

Another Village Gate spot for Mingus's ten-piece with Eric spilled into early October, after their studio work on September 20 finalized the Ellingtonian, bottom-rich *Mingus, Mingus, Mingus, Mingus, Mingus* (aka *Mingus x5*), which they'd started in January. Here, Dolphy read his alto parts on memorable charts for 'II B.S.' (renamed 'Haitian Fight Song'), 'Theme For Lester Young' (renamed 'Goodbye Pork Pie Hat'), 'Better Get Hit In Yo' Soul,' and 'Freedom.' *Mingus x5*'s version of 'Mood Indigo' calls for a beautifully exposed bass clarinet, and Eric takes an incisive alto solo against the massive sax/brass sound of 'Hora Decubitus'—one that cuts like a well-oiled saw blade as he climbs up through registers, backed by one of the bigger band sounds Mingus had pulled together. These recordings were some of the bassist's most powerful moments, drawing from a stylistic gamut of

* Within months, FBI director J. Edgar Hoover legally blocked any federal prosecutions against the Birmingham bombing suspects, refusing to disclose to prosecutors evidence his agency had obtained. Five years later, he formally closed the FBI's investigation into the murders, with no charges filed against any named suspects, and ordered the files to be sealed.

jazz history and including throwback blues-swing and riff-based passages, shouts, gut-bucket blues, Ellington, and the stomping fun of a big band. Mingus's work here, and the ensemble's playing, is engaging entertainment sculpted from the bones, muscle, and fat of the past, several steps back from his more avant-garde leanings. *Mingus x5* was also, in the face of the Birmingham church bombing, a recognition of the power of the African American community—a sonic reflection of the March On Washington and its spirit of positive change. The album went through ten US printings in the 1960s and today can be found in over ninety reissues worldwide.

On September 30, a standing-room-only crowd crammed into Birdland for the annual Gretsch Drum Night (the 1960 show was released on vinyl in 1963). Eric sat in with an Elvin Jones Septet comprised of the classic Coltrane quartet minus the tenor man but with Charles Davis on baritone, trumpeter Lee Morgan, and trombonist Frank Rehak. They dueled that night with a Philly Joe Jones quintet including Sun Ra's tenorist John Gilmore and future Dolphy collaborator Andrew Hill on piano.

One can imagine the lift such gatherings brought to Dolphy's spirits, taking the stage and socializing with friends and collaborators. These sounds, names, and faces were all part of his growing New York musical community. His professional life following the *Conversations / Iron Man* sessions was slow to revive, and with no future recording plans with FM and a lack of gigs for his own group, things weren't adding up. Dreams of Paris had taken hold, and yet he would miss casual times like Gretsch Drum Night.

October proved slow; Dolphy kept busy by practicing, composing, and learning more about progressive jazz musicians planning moves to Europe. Unbeknown to him, a Blue Note offer for what became *Out To Lunch!* was soon to fall into his lap.

The pitched battles of the Civil Rights Movement took many forms. On October 27, Dolphy participated in a Five Spot benefit for CORE (Congress Of Racial Equality), one of the groups behind the March On Washington. He appeared with Hutcherson, Lasha, Booker Ervin, Bill Evans, Ron Carter, Paul Bley, Zoot Sims, and bassist Henry Grimes, among many others, in a concert MCed by Alan Grant and Ira Gitler. The previous week at the club, Don Heckman and Billy Taylor hosted a similar CORE benefit with an equally impressive line-up. The freedom exhibited by the new thing engaged meaningfully with the protest and hope lifting the movement. But instrumental avant-garde jazz as direct, popular protest music took a backseat in this regard to what was developing as soul music, where Sam Cooke, Ray Charles, Aretha Franklin, and Solomon Burke were the Black singers pushing forward; and in folk music, after Bob Dylan released 'Blowin' In The Wind.' Cooke's 'A Change Is Gonna Come' came out in early 1964; James Brown's Black consciousness funk and pop culture resonating with Stokely Carmichael's 'Black Power' chant was just around the corner.

In the second week in November—a year to the month after the Ree Dragonette collaboration—Eric played the Village Art Center in conjunction with an exhibition of paintings by Nora Jaffe, who had just enjoyed a Museum Of Modern Art show of her work curated by Peter Selz. The musician's already eclectic, multi-pronged aesthetic as an avant-garde jazz rebel had spread further into crossover collaborations with poetry, painting, and multimedia happenings. His sound and charisma of aesthetic deviance had become part of an edgy underground soundtrack—one that included Ornette, Coltrane, and Sun Ra—playing to hip crowds in galleries, cafes, bookstores, and film screenings. His small yet growing audience knew not to expect him on prime-time television, standard jazz festival programs, or in regular radio rotation.

Immediately after the November 11 Village Art Center gig, Dolphy rejoined Coltrane's group at Philadelphia's Showboat for what may have been the remainder of that week, the quartet's first stateside engagement since returning from a recent European tour. Then, on November 29 at New York's Hunter College, Orchestra USA welcomed guest soloist Gerry Mulligan on baritone sax in a program of works by Lewis, McFarland, and Yugoslavian composer Miljenko Prohaska, director of the Zagreb Radio orchestra, with his 'Concerto No 2 For Orchestra' and 'Intima.' *DownBeat* editor Gene Lees, echoing other reviewers, noted Eric's defining role in the program, reporting that the orchestra's performance 'was neither clean nor particularly sensitive' but that 'Eric Dolphy's presence in the woodwind section, however, was a distinct asset. He added a quality of moaning bite to the section work and played some distinctly lovely flute solo passages.'[6]

Facing another cold winter at the end of his third year in New York, Dolphy fronted a band at the Five Spot for a single night in December. Five and half years previously, he had left Los Angeles with Chico Hamilton, ultimately finding his new home; now he was looking to leave New York. Paris moved to the forefront of Eric's thoughts as he heard that Leo Wright abandoned the Dizzy Gillespie

Quintet to remain in Europe, first for gigs in Scandinavia and Germany. Word had also reached him of George Russell's impending relocation to Sweden in January, to escape the racism and lack of work in the USA. Dexter Gordon's recently released and aptly titled *Our Man In Paris* had been recorded the previous April in the French capital, with Bud Powell, Kenny Clarke, and French bassist Pierre Michelot. But as 1963 came to an end, Dolphy's near-term calendar captured his attention, primarily the final steps in preparing his masterwork, *Out To Lunch!* And rejoining Mingus meant readying for a spring tour that would be his ticket across the Atlantic, to Joyce and a new life.

From the CORE benefit to art gallery improv, Orchestra USA to blowing with Coltrane, Eric welcomed 1964 with two separate New Year's Eve performances. Lincoln Center's Philharmonic Hall hosted a star-studded line-up of the Coltrane Quintet, Cecil Taylor's Jazz Unit (Jimmy Lyons, Albert Ayler, Henry Grimes, and Sonny Murray), and Art Blakey's Jazz Messengers (Hubbard, Curtis Fuller, Shorter, Cedar Walton, Reggie Workman, and vocalist Wellington Blakey), in that order. 'Dolphy also played a very wild alto solo—in fact, I think it was probably the most completely satisfying effort of his I've ever heard. He sounded so much better than he has on recent recordings,' wrote Amiri Baraka (as LeRoi Jones) in his *DownBeat* review, likely referring to the group's rendition of 'Impressions.'[7] Too bad, then, that the concert was recorded for commercial release without ever seeing the light of day. Their set was rounded out with 'My Favorite Things' and 'Alabama,' the latter being Coltrane's response to the Birmingham church bombing—a tune in which he musically mirrored the speech intonation and rhythm of Dr. Martin Luther King's 'Eulogy For The Martyred Children,' delivered at the funeral service on September 18.

Baraka knew Eric's cousin Lorenzo Thomas from the Umbra Poets Workshop gatherings and had just published *Blues People*, subtitled *Negro Music In White America*. In his discussion of 'the modern scene,' he argues that in the mid-1940s, beboppers had taken their jazz 'outside the mainstream of American culture' in order to make the music speak once again with an '*antiassimilationist* sound.' He notes that 'jazz fan magazines like *Downbeat*' were so guilty of reactionary criticism of bebop that 'they have had to re-review classic bebop records by Charlie Parker, Thelonious Monk, etc., and give them wild acclaim because their first reviews were so wrong-headed.' He then implores his readers to understand how jazz in the early 1960s again needed a 'valid separation from, and anarchic disregard of, Western popular forms,' and how a new generation of Black musician was now 're-emphasizing the most expressive qualities of Afro-American musical tradition while also producing an American music which has complete access to the invaluable emotional history of Western art.' Cecil Taylor and Ornette are identified as 'the most important of these recent innovators,' along with Coltrane and Rollins.[8]

Baraka's positive reception of Dolphy's oeuvre and New Year's Eve soloing brought the musician into this vanguard of 'anarchic disregard,' an argument about which Geri Allen would note:

> The major point Baraka seems to be postulating is that the reasons white critics seemed to miss the boat (by attaching their cultural value judgments or attaching European-based aesthetic systems to Black American music) in their criticism of Black American music was because of a lack of understanding of the ethnology that this music is spawned from. As a result of artistic nonconformity and originality, these pioneers, including Eric Dolphy, were being grossly misunderstood, and until very recently there has been very little truly serious documentation on their lives and works.[9]

Coltrane's ensemble opened the show that final evening of 1963, allowing Dolphy plenty of time to slip away to perform at another New Year's Eve event—a jazz marathon at 20 Spruce Street. According to *DownBeat*, 'Ndugu Ngoma presented a music Marathon . . . Louis Brown's group with pianist Larry Willis 9:30pm–1:30am, Randy Weston's Quintet played until 5:30am; The Nadi Qamar Ensemble with reed man Eric Dolphy and dancers Ilau and Ayinka performed from 6 to 7am.'[10]

Had he lived, Dolphy arguably could have further collaborated with Qamar and musicians like him, steeped in jazz yet searching for more technique and inspiration from the music of Africa, India, and other global sources. Born Spaulding Givens in 1917, Qamar recorded a bass/piano duo with Mingus in Hollywood in April 1951, as released on a Debut Records album supervised by Richard Bock, *Strings And Keys*. Two years later, after Qamar and Mingus relocated to New York, Max Roach joined them as a trio for another set of standards released only many years later on an Original Jazz Classics compilation featuring the reissued duet work, *The Charles Mingus Duo & Trio, With Spaulding Givens & Max Roach: Debut Rarities, Volume*

2. Taking an ethnomusicological turn toward sub-Saharan African music, Qamar developed the Mama-Likembi, an instrument consisting of multiple lamellophones (thumb pianos), for which he further developed tunings and a notational system.* In the 1970s, Qamar recorded two albums on the Folkway Records label featuring music for the Mama-Likembi, *The Nuru Taa African Musical Idiom Played By Nadi Qamar On The Mama Likembi* (1975) and *Likembi Song Book* (1979). He died of COVID-19 in 2020 at the age of 103.

1964

In early 1964, Orchestra USA extended its season to four monthly performances, January through April, conducted by Schuller, the first held on January 3 at the Brooklyn Academy Of Music in an exhausting program of Stravinsky, Mozart, Ives, Schubert, Webern, Dvorak, Henze, Milhaud, and Lewis. On the same program was Schuller's *Journey Into Jazz*, with Nat Hentoff's narrative, as premiered at the summer 1962 Washington DC International Jazz Festival (with Dolphy onstage). In addition to his later work as a major jazz critic for the *Village Voice* and the *International Herald Tribune*, Orchestra USA trombonist and bass trumpet player Michael Zwerin was also the president of the Capital Steel Corporation. At nineteen, he left his gig with Miles Davis's *Birth Of The Cool* ensemble to attend college. He chronicled some of Orchestra USA's internal dramas, noting Lewis's consternation with Dolphy's unpredictable style and his favoritism toward Phil Woods as the go-to alto soloist. Zwerin and Dolphy were catalysts in forming the Sextet Of Orchestra USA, which later that month recorded an album of Kurt Weill compositions featuring several admirable Dolphy solos.

Forty years after Dolphy's death, Zwerin wrote about the jazz icon in the *New York Times*, dubbing him the 'undisciplined genius' in an article reporting on the 2004 Sant'Anna Arresi Jazz Festival in Sardinia, Italy, being dedicated to Eric's memory. 'His raw textures, belligerent intonation and threatening degree of dissonance adhered to some un-catalogued system of sound,' he wrote, continuing, 'tonality is a natural force, like gravity, and Dolphy had more than one center.' Zwerin observed as Orchestra USA's professional musicians watched and listened to Dolphy play, stating that they 'were afraid that they were going to have to learn

---

* In Africa, similar instruments are known by various names in different cultures and languages: *likembe* in the Congo, but elsewhere *mbira*, *sanza*, *kadongo*, and *akogo*.

to play like that. . . . Although he played the written parts with concentration and professional discipline, his "incredible cries" were not really with the program,' he noted, adding that, during rehearsal, Lewis 'stopped the orchestra in the middle of a Dolphy improvisation to ask him to play "closer to the melody" This was somebody in the process of changing our ears. Arguably, we should have been trying to play closer to his melody.' Thick-skinned and familiar with criticism, Eric blew off the tension and adjusted accordingly. But Zwerin could see how he really felt about being replaced on orchestral flute by a ringer at show time: 'When, at the last minute, a classical flutist was engaged to play the concert, Dolphy turned up his collar and said, I feel a draft.'[11]

The sextet recorded *Mack The Knife And Other Berlin Theater Songs Of Kurt Weill* a week after the orchestra's Brooklyn concert. Eric plays only on side A, featuring tunes taken from the Weill/Brecht opera *The Rise And Fall Of The City Of Mahagonny*: a solid bass clarinet solo on 'Alabama Song,' a scored flute doubling with Nick Travis's trumpet on 'Havana,' and an expressionistic, fiery alto solo, channeling Parker, on 'As You Make Your Bed.' Zwerin (bass trumpet), John Lewis, Jimmy Raney, Connie Kay, and Eric's trusted friend Richard Davis rounded out the sextet. With inevitable connections drawn between 'Alabama Song' and the Birmingham terrorist murders the previous fall, Zwerin asked Dolphy to express himself along those lines, stating that 'the harmonic changes in Eric's part are a variation. By keeping to these changes, Eric automatically played what musicians call "outside."' The bass clarinet's strained, thin, upper register sound—'particularly as Eric uses it in his fantastic choruses in Alabama Song—reflects the suffering and hopelessness of not only the time and place of Weill's Berlin but really of anytime, anywhere.'[12] Tragically, neither Dolphy nor Travis would live to complete the album, with Jerome Richardson and Thad Jones replacing them in a follow-up session later that year.

Dolphy rejoined Coltrane and company for a Half Note engagement from January 17 until the end of the month. He was offered his own Sunday afternoon Five Spot gig, likely on January 26—one show in a brief series featuring Jackie McLean, Roy Haynes, and pianist Larry Willis's trio. That month, the venue was hosting a Mingus Workshop residency, and Booker Ervin had just left the group. In addition to Coleman Hawkins, Mingus also called Sonny Rollins to sit in; according to him, 'Eric Dolphy was giving him [Mingus] some kind of trouble, so he brought me down to the Five Spot on Eighth Street to play with Eric . . . in

Mingus's mind it was something like, Man, I've got Sonny here, so you'd better be cool.'[13]

This was around the time when Eric would have digested *DownBeat*'s review of last summer's *Conversations*, which reluctantly praised Dolphy's playing while also making disparaging comments, as in this opening line: 'Dolphy's style is exciting and unique, yet it must be kept in mind that his greatest assets stem from the *manner* of his playing, not from the originality of its musical content.' Veiled dislike mixed with ambiguous approval throughout the review, with positive qualities quickly qualified in condescending quips. 'Dolphy has been identified with the "new thing," and this seems to be in error. Dolphy is the old thing but stated with the hollering pugnacity of the newer school,' the reviewer continued, focusing on alleged aesthetic and stylistic contradictions, 'lamentable exceptions,' and 'old cliches,' before concluding, 'Dolphy will continue to squawk his way to higher levels.'[14] Ironically, the three-and-a-half-star review applauded the Dolphy/Davis duets, which transcend jazz and point to Dolphy's universalist desire to play, arrange, and compose without boundaries, singling out for praise the chamber music–like 'Alone Together' on an album full of great, straight-up, barn-burning jazz.

LEONARD BERNSTEIN YOUNG PEOPLE'S CONCERT

Joyce and Paris grew to dominate Eric's hopes and dreams. He had to escape to survive, cross an ocean to reunite with his love, and visit European capitals to find broader acceptance from paying audiences, where any bad press would be in a foreign language he could more easily ignore. It was not just the Blue Note recording session in late February and the pending Workshop projects that uplifted Dolphy in his final months in New York. Leonard Bernstein had arranged for Schuller and Dolphy to take the Young People's Concert stage with four other 'very distinguished young stars of the jazz world' (as Bernstein described them): Don Ellis, Benny Golson, Richard Davis, and drummer Joseph Cocuzzo. They joined members of the New York Symphony Orchestra for a rousing version of Schuller and Hentoff's *Journey Into Jazz*. The sometimes-surreal event was best described by Simosko and Tepperman:

> On Saturday, 8 February 1964, at noon, the Leonard Bernstein Young People's Concert misleadingly titled 'Jazz In The Concert Hall' involved

> the videotaping of *Journey Into Jazz*... shown on television the following March 11th... the names of both Dolphy and Schuller were misspelled (as 'Dolfy' and 'Schuler') in the accompanying film guide, and the erroneous impression that Aaron Copland's 'Concerto For Piano And Orchestra' and Larry Austin's 'Improvisation For Orchestra And Jazz Soloists' had a great deal to do with jazz is also perpetuated.[15]

Dolphy's presence on screen is minimal, as striking as he is when he stands to blow his horn following short solos by Ellis and Golson. His solo is intruded upon by Bernstein's recitation of Hentoff's narration: 'Jazz is people!' The camera pans to the right of Dolphy to reveal a few members of the orchestra's brass section in the background as Eric claws his way to intense abandon; Golson turns his head about with an ear-to-ear smile, glancing at Ellis, as several members of the otherwise stone-faced philharmonic are either visibly shaken, break out into laughter, or involuntary twitch.

'Hey! All this music is us!' the maestro continues, Dolphy's saxophone filling the hall. Ellis and Golson stand to join Eric in three-horn polyphony as the camera cuts to junior audience members: a young girl, her furrowed brow showing concern, and a few other kids in succession watching, listening to what was certainly considered fun cacophony. On cue, the camera catches the three soloists cutting out and taking their seats.

'Late that night, when Peter Parker returned home,' Bernstein intones from Hentoff's script, 'he made a new sign and put it on his door. It said *Music Is Being Made. Come On In*.' With that, the three zealous soloists return for Schuller's tutti orchestra finale.

Two weeks after filming with Bernstein, Dolphy joined Hubbard as invitees to the Night Of Jazz In The Abstract, hosted by the Modern Jazz Musical Art Society of Community College, Brooklyn, and held at the Klitgord Center on the evening of Tuesday, February 20. This came during a time he was still sitting in on Mingus Workshop gigs at the Five Spot, where the group had taken over in late January following Monk's seven-month run. It is not known what, or with whom, Eric and Freddie played that night in Brooklyn. What *is* known is that Eric's ever-worsening diabetes had led to symptoms severely impacting his professional career, as he couldn't always play his horn due to slow-healing mouth infections or oral thrush. Ken McIntyre and Jerome Richardson subbed for him at the club.

Downtime gave Dolphy plenty of opportunity to do two things: work on material for *Out To Lunch!*, and read *DownBeat*'s lethargic review of *Eric Dolphy At The Five Spot, Volume 2*, in which Harvey Pekar complained that there were only two numbers ('one on each side') and suggested Eric's bass clarinet solo on 'Aggression' suffered from a lack of 'melodic substance' and of 'running his fingers up and down the horn with no purpose,' adding that his flute tone on 'Like Somebody In Love' 'lacks body,' and is 'thin and piping.'[16] Dolphy was dismissed as the weak link, the floundering soloist, and the least musical of the quintet. Otherwise, the review gave kudos to the 'memorable' and 'creative jazzman' Little (without mentioning the young trumpeter's tragic death), praising the 'brilliant' and 'outstanding' Mal Waldron, pointing to Davis as the 'most imaginative and technically adroit of the excellent bassists to emerge recently,' and applauding Blackwell, who 'excels' and 'keeps up an exciting dialog with the soloists.' A threatening Mingus responded to Pekar's separate review of his blues singing by penning a response to the magazine that, 'no one could sing my blues but me . . . just as no one could holler for you [Pekar] if I decide to punch you in your mouth. So don't come near me ever in this life.'

LEONARD FEATHER'S EARLY 1964 INTERVIEW

In an unpublished, undated interview with Leonard Feather, completed sometime in early 1964, Eric defended his playing while answering the retired critic's fairly obtuse questions.* Excerpts appear in some issues of the *Eric Dolphy Memorial Album*, as is the case with that 1967 title from Fontana's 'Leonard Feather Presents' series (not to be confused with Prestige's *Eric Dolphy/Booker Little Memorial Album*, recorded live at the Five Spot). The aim of the interview was to provide readers insight into Dolphy's methods and some type of context for 'free' playing.

Feather asks what limitations exist, if not harmonic, and how Dolphy's approach might amount to something other than an arbitrary process. He admits to difficulty in understanding how solo material might derive from sources other than chords and scales. Of all the musical elements informing improvisation, pitch is just one, and the idea of timbre, bird song textures, noise, spontaneous

* The quoted interview excerpts here are taken directly from Alan Saul's transcription of an audio recording.

ensemble interaction, and subjective ideas of phrasing don't seem to be on Feather's radar. Eric, attempting to wing a discussion of complex improvisational strategies concerning pitch choice, replies, 'You can play every note that you like. Of course, you only can play what you can hear, and quite naturally ... more or less I guess what I hear is not to your hearing, to what you're hearing. So quite naturally, I hear more notes on the same thing that's been said before.' This leads to the musician providing examples of how he developed an ear toward hearing notes outside of the chord, scale, or key typically found in tonal structures implied by chord progressions, and how he developed an intuition for phrasing melodic gestures. He gives the example of playing flatted ninths against a standard seventh chord; of playing within a mode yet also playing notes that are not in the mode; and of 'running' the chords (arpeggiating those chordal notes) while including other pitches. Dolphy explains how he developed the ability to hear more notes not in the chord, but never played to simply show off a particular technique. Regarding how critics have responded to his note selection, Dolphy states, 'A lot of people say they're wrong [his pitch choices]. Well, I can't say they're right, and I can't say they're wrong. To my hearing, they're exactly correct. For my hearing I'm right, and ... it opens up a whole different kind of hearing.'

Asked if he thinks bebop players such as Parker and Dizzy 'lack freedom, or sound old-fashioned' to his ears, Dolphy replies:

> No, it's a funny thing ... I'll even go farther than that. ... I played at a festival in Washington DC, and I got a chance to hear the Eureka Jazz Band [Dixieland, or traditional jazz] ... you just hear the band and you hear the lead trumpet player's playing the melody, and probably more or less you hear the other sounds. ... I stood right in the midst of them, and I couldn't see much difference between what I was doing to what they were doing, and the fact that they ... were more tonal, of course, but they had a lot of freedom to what they were playing ... I think they were the first freedom players.

Feather then questions the Coltrane/Dolphy axis of extended solos over minimal harmonic change. One of the interview's more telling lines of discussion occurs as the musician attempts to connect the dots between this musical challenge, melodic improvisation, and performative aspects of traditional and non-Western music:

> You see, that is another complexity in itself of playing on one or two changes. It's a challenge . . . where a creative musician, if he is creative enough, is to create on that limited amount... and it gives him the chance to unfold a lot more. . . . Not speaking about Mr. Coltrane, but speaking about music in general, of all types of forms, like in Indian music... they only have usually one [extended tonal center]... they call it a raga, or scale, and they'll play for twenty minutes. . . . I've heard it said that Bartok and Kodaly collected many folk themes on [Hungarian and Romanian folk music]... I've heard records by them... this particular thing goes over and over, and to the listener that doesn't pay attention close to the notes, the typical sound will get monotonous. But to the person that listens to the actual notes and the creation that's going on and the building within the players and within themselves, they'll notice that something is actually happening. So actually, I think that all this in a way has a connection with the artist over here, and everywhere; it's not a question of anybody trying to outdo them and stuff, it's just the fact that they're just going through the same development. And out of this I'm sure will come something else, it just has to go ahead.

In politely arguing for the Black community's foregrounding as a primary cultural source for the new thing, Eric's responses provided plenty for the jazz world to think about. Feather never published the interview in full. It is not irrelevant that one would soon see Amiri Baraka, hired by *DownBeat* that year, calling out the magazine and the jazz industry for misreading innovation rising from the marginalized edges of Black music in the early 1960s. Baraka was not alone in problematizing the discursive arena in which white jazz critics told Black musicians what they should play, rigidly defining what was acceptable to jazz while disparaging innovation.

Geri Allen completed a master's thesis on Eric Dolphy, emphasizing this moment in time when iconoclastic, original African American jazz voices were being policed by a jazz industry dominated by white commentators, label owners, and industry insiders. This increasingly 'abstract' modern art form was, in the eyes of a conservative core, drawing away from the mainstream jazz power structure, which was simultaneously losing its standing to rock'n'roll, soul, and R&B, and to social and technological change.

In late February, Eric ignored the torpedoes as he led his ensemble into the RVG studio to record what many contemporary jazz historians consider one of the most inventive, artistically successful jazz records to emerge from the early 1960s avant-garde scene. Preparations for *Out To Lunch!*—the compositions, arrangements, and rehearsals—flowed through difficult times including Eric's eroding health. Yet the optimism, humor, beauty, and artistic complexity of the now-famous album transcend such struggles, as well as the violent reactions to the Civil Rights Movement dividing the country, and the desperation Eric faced in his diminishing ability to make a living in the USA. He did not compromise his vision, despite these many challenges. Still under contract with FM, he recorded *Out To Lunch!* knowing that in six weeks he would be leaving the United States for at least a year.

11 *OUT TO LUNCH!*, THE MINGUS TOUR OF EUROPE

FEBRUARY–APRIL 1964

There is always something new to hear in *Out To Lunch!* Dolphy's pinnacle work simultaneously points to a reimagined Afro-descendant lineage, a neo-African past seen through the progressive glasses of early 1960s modernism and Civil Rights–era awareness. In these tracks, a universalist avant-garde laced with submerged grooves is punctuated with Bartokian swing, squared by motoric pulsations, a funky modernist soundscape propelled by communal improvisation. The album's brittle sheen is balanced by warm timbres, its structured regularity vexed by asymmetry and guttural convulsions straight out of early blues and twentieth-century chamber music. *Out To Lunch!* is folk music from the future filtered by African American sensibilities found in good-time music, in the non-pitch-derived palette of human sounds, in profound group expression. The improvisations throughout the album often seem to grow from compositional themes, and rather than being a free-for-all jam, Dolphy's atmospheric tunes retain a magical spell over the entire session's proceedings.

Of drummer Tony Williams, Dolphy said he 'doesn't play time, he plays pulse,' preemptively dismissing concerns that the drummer doesn't swing much on these tracks. Williams was barely eighteen when on Tuesday, February 25, he walked into Rudy Van Gelder's studio with Eric, Richard Davis, Bobby Hutcherson, and Freddie Hubbard to make the record. The Reid Miles–designed album cover features a seven-handed clock of which the three short hands and four long hands point to any number of possible times. 'Will Be Back' reads the sign. But at which time: 2:15, 5:51, 8:36, or whenever? Damn right Williams doesn't play time. But he played with Sam Rivers at thirteen, with Jackie McLean at sixteen, and joined Miles Davis's Second Great Quintet at seventeen in the late spring of 1963, destined to a career that helped propel jazz to new heights. As one of jazz's greatest drummers, the young man's wealth of skills included listening to his bandmates in real time, driving ahead with 360-degree vision, fitting his intense color palette, sensitive polyrhythmic pulses and beats into musical landscapes as they unfolded. Before the end of the 1960s, the youthful virtuoso had helped spawn the fusion genre with his trio Tony Williams Lifetime, joined by British guitar virtuoso John McLaughlin and organist Larry Young (both of whom also appear on Miles Davis's *In A Silent Way* and *Bitches Brew*).

Out To Lunch! inimitably defines the crossroads of the era: the transition from what might be possible with the new thing, to a creative music inspired by compositional structures lending themselves to both scored ideas and free-wheeling improvisation. Eric notated some of his synthetic scales beneath the staves of some parts as an improvisational resource. Always present in the rich chromatic palette is humor and the aura of a naturally unfolding free-jazz pathos within compositional frameworks. In this elegant cauldron, listeners find both playful wit and intellectual vigor, studied exactitude and marvelous cacophony.

'Hat And Beard' starts side A. Eric clarified that when composing the tune in response to Dragonette's poem 'Like Pharoa's Eye, Like Onyx Stone' for the *Reflections And Entrances* concert in November 1962, he was thinking about Monk, stating, 'He's so musical no matter what he's doing, even if he's just walking around. It opens in 5/4, but once the whole group is in, the basic count is really 9/4.'[1] The opening tag's sting introduces a thematic descending bass line, snappy ride cymbal, and a set of horn stabs accented with vibes followed by the bass clarinet's unison with Davis's ostinato. Williams's percussive strikes of crisp snare and chime-like cymbal bell strokes grace the bass's hypnotic repetition, Eric harmonizing the pattern. Hutcherson smoothly doubles Davis as Dolphy drops out in preparation for his and Hubbard's new 9/4 phrase, repeated four times before returning to the descending theme, now with vibe voicings switching about.

The arrangement leads not just to a spectacular bass clarinet solo, but also to an *Out To Lunch!* hallmark, the rhythm section's clever circus of intuitive accompaniment. The track represents one of Dolphy's plateau performances on the instrument. Williams thrashes about freely, accenting, side-stepping, and responding to Dolphy's multipronged outbursts. These three players independently coalesce for Hubbard, the mood shifting to a focused study, his trumpet quickening in rapid-fire discharges. 'Hat And Beard' gets downright spacey on Hutcherson's watch, a floating world bound by the thinnest of sonic threads, stitched with colorful ebbs and flows from bass and drums. The 9/4 material's reprise smacks listeners, and the descending bassline disappears into the sunset, or is it the fog? In the studio that day, six takes of this number followed four takes of 'Gazzeloni,' all taking up an entire tape reel—luxurious studio time that Prestige would never have paid for. James Newton later shared that Eric had worked up alternative arrangements for 'Hat And Beard' and 'Gazzelloni.'

Lyrical feelings suffuse the album, and in addition to everything else that can be said, *Out To Lunch!* is a melodic powerhouse. 'Something Sweet, Something Tender' starts as a dark yet inviting bass/bass clarinet duet, and then a beautiful counterpoint with Hubbard unfolds with Williams' minimal snare and cymbals. Dolphy's solo is a masterful weaving of post-bop figures exploring every nook and cranny of the harmonic landscape, hurriedly visiting the remotest possibilities of an otherwise languid ballad, which ultimately leads to an impeccable unison coda with Davis. There is a distinct compositional vision found in this arrangement, from the finely wrought intro, the tune itself, the contrasting disposition of his singular solo (Hubbard does not solo), and the daringly simple yet touching outro. Dolphy chose the number's second take, commenting, 'I think the title explains the tune. The opening bars, with Richard bowing under me, set up the whole piece. The group got just the lyrical feeling that I wanted, and, taking it out, Richard and I really got together in the unison duet.'[2]

Side A ends with a tribute to Italian flutist Severino Gazzelloni, an orchestral and chamber musician specializing in avant-garde repertoire, who for thirty years was the principal flutist for Italian state radio's (RAI) National Symphony Orchestra. Luciano Berio composed for him his 1958 work for solo flute, 'Sequenza I,' from the set of challenging concert pieces the Italian modernist wrote for solo and small chamber settings. Ernst Krenek, Stravinsky, and Pierre Boulez all wrote for Gazzelloni, who was also close friends with Italian film composer Nino Rota. Dolphy knew his recordings well.* Less than two months after the *Out To Lunch!*

---

* In 1962, Time Records released the album *Severino Gazzelloni & Aloys Kontarsky: Music For Solo Flute / Music For Flute And Piano*. Here, Kontarsky accompanies the flute virtuoso on two works, Niccolò Castiglioni's 'Gymel' and Bruno Maderna's 'Honeyrêves.' The rest of the album is comprised of solo flute works: the premiere recording of Berio's 'Sequenza,' Franco Evangelisti's 'Proporzioni,' and 'Somaksah' by Japanese composer Yoritsune Matsudaira.

sessions he would meet Gazzelloni for an April lesson in Milan during the Mingus sextet tour, where it is thought that Eric was able to share a tape of 'Gazzelloni.' Dolphy described the tune: 'Everybody holds to the construction for the first thirteen bars, then—freedom.'

The 'construction' is an angular, up-tempo head foregrounding flute and near-unison vibes, a leaping, craggy contour followed by calm, then repeated with Hubbard accenting the line. The tune runs for only a half-minute of the seven-and-a-half-minute track. What follows finds each musician steering their own way. Williams takes liberties with percussive melodies, creative patterning, and colorful kit playing. Hutcherson's picturesque clouds of vibe resonances float behind Dolphy's aggressive flute explorations and emerge as a real counterpoint. Davis sets a strong pulse to which Williams is tethered at times. It's a sonic environment in which Dolphy visits overblowing, harmonics, multiphonics, trills and tremolos, and otherwise ornaments strong hard-bop references with timbral spice. Hubbard takes the spotlight with trumpet flurries as Williams and Hutcherson communicate rapid-fire exchanges. Hutcherson's inventiveness propels the track, lighting his way through the dark with William's frenetic improvisations: vibes and drums as played by these two make for a unique *Out To Lunch!* stamp.

With Davis's fine solo ending, we see that six minutes have flown by; following the head's return, the coda freely deflates as they simply allow 'Gazzelloni' to gradually run out of gas. But what a run, as James Newton comments: 'Some of Eric's [flute] solos . . . were harder than Berio's "Sequenza," the most challenging music in the classical repertoire of that timeframe. The transcriptions of Eric's solo demanded so much more technically than the Berio.'[3] Peter Guidi has suggested that 'Gazzelloni [himself] in turn was impressed by the adventurous rhythmic innovation used by Dolphy in his improvisations.'[4] In the mid-1980s, contemporary concert flute virtuoso Robert Dick would begin his influential album *The Other Flute* (on Schuller's GM Recordings) with his own version of 'Gazzelloni,' noting that the piece is 'a vehicle for improvisation composed by the great Eric Dolphy' and citing Dolphy's own liner note remark, 'Then—freedom.'[5]

The roughly twenty-two minutes of music on side A is pure gold. It's hard to imagine what more could be in store on side B until one realizes that Eric has yet to touch his alto saxophone. The title tune, 'Out To Lunch,' is a celebratory processional down Main Street, heralding the arrival of an avant-garde circus, with its march-like snare intro and on-beat vibe riff. With this cathartic tune Dolphy has constructed and climbed his own free jazz mountain and is now holding forth with a crack team that collectively gets it: 'In the improvised sections,' the composer continued, 'the rhythms overlap. The bass follows no bar line at all. … Even though the rhythm section breaks the time up, there's a basic pulse coming from inside the tune. That's the pulse the musicians have to play.'[6]

Speaking of time, at over twelve minutes, this piece really establishes the album's open atmosphere, one of free improvisation, shown in the delicate liberties Hutcherson takes in his solo, with its contrasts of repetition and complex webs of singular tones, harmonies, and polyrhythms. Davis's 'outside' solo manages to bring the number down into the soul. Individually exposed voices of a spaced-out trading sequence between alto and trumpet feature Williams's scholarly kit briefly taking the spotlight before the chart's reprise: the procession disappears down the street. After three takes, Van Gelder had to change out the reel, and the group ran the number twice again on reel three, Dolphy settling for the fifth and final take. One can dream of a future Blue Note release of the complete session's alternate takes.

The title of 'Straight Up And Down' is a not-so-inside joke because the tune is an obstacle course of pratfalls, leaps, out-of-time fragments, and slapstick intervals, all lovingly accented by Davis and Williams. 'This one reminds me of a drunk walking, straight up and down I call it,' Dolphy explained. The head's repeat takes us to the minute mark: it's as thorny a tune as Dolphy ever composed and remains one of his weightiest. In it, he shares his alto's near scathing yet ballad-like embrace of rebranded human speech and stream-of-consciousness jazz history: blues, R&B, Bird, and lots of space for extended technique with veins both humoresque and braggadocio. Hubbard's solo rings true in conjuring the spirits of the session. The trumpeter's slight quotation from 'Green Dolphin Street' (a number on which he played on *Outward Bound* four years previously) signals his baton pass to Hutcherson's graceful solo, full of pointillistic flair and fast, glassy scalar runs. The vibist grabs another mallet before the sonics momentarily fade out. It's a cue for the end, and a brazen bang brings back a truncated tag ending of the unique theme. The band muscled its way through four takes of 'Straight Up And Down,' the last piece recorded that day. The music dies out, closing forever the recorded life of Dolphy as a session leader for a studio album project.

Released within weeks of Eric's death, *Out To Lunch!* is a true American masterpiece. Some of what he had to say about 'Straight Up And Down' applies to the whole album and its collaborative nature: 'It gasses me that everyone was so free. I wanted a free date to begin with.' Then, emphasizing Williams and Davis, he added, 'All rhythm sections are different, but this one was really open, that is, they can play different kinds of ways, like Tony does here, different ways, but you can still count in.' The recording secured a place for jazz's avant-garde, and Blue Note reprinted the album fifteen times during the 1960s and 70s. Today, there exists at least 104 reissued versions worldwide. Dolphy proved that like-minded musicians could come together in the studio, or onstage, and produce inventive music with only a modicum of structure such as written heads, indications/cues for entrances and exits, and perhaps a notion of character and atmosphere. Defining 'jazz' had become increasingly difficult. The artists who began communicating on this level throughout the 1960s redefined the label as they opened up to world music, the European avant-garde, rock, and technological change.

Some of the album's new landscape of collective virtuosity, structured improvisation, and compositional flair can be placed in relation to a type of new music, à la third stream. *Out To Lunch!* helped launch a jazz parallel to certain chamber music emerging from the classical avant-garde, where indeterminate elements and outcomes, among other creative strategies, had been gaining attention from the recent works of Cage and others. Of course, avant-garde jazz never needed approval from, or comparison to, contemporary concert music for validation. Yet here Dolphy's vision and hybrid accomplishments in crossovers of jazz and classical certainly taunt today's audiences with what might have been had he lived: one can imagine his future *Out To Lunch!* creative palettes conjoining with experimental concert music. Sadly embedded in the album's liner notes, however, was Eric's tragic message to the world: 'I'm on my way to Europe to live for a while. Why? Because I can get more work there playing my own music, and because if you try to do anything different in this country, people put you down for it.'

AFTER *LUNCH*

At some point following their introduction through Gunther Schuller in 1962, a young music student named Bob James befriended Eric in New York. Much later a leading proponent of smooth jazz fusion, the composer/pianist was at this time heading a unique trio that had won an April 1962 University Of Notre Dame collegiate music competition judged by Quincy Jones, first prize being a Village Vanguard gig and a Mercury Records contract. Soon that year, James hooked up with Schuller for several third stream programs, performing with Dolphy at one such concert in Chicago. With fellow University Of Michigan students Ron Brooks on bass and Bob Pozar on drums, the Bob James Trio cut their eclectic *Bold Conceptions*, an amalgam of standards and experimentalism released in 1963—the year James received his master's degree. He then worked in Maynard Ferguson's band, following in the steps of Jaki Byard, and gigged regularly with Sarah Vaughn, in the steps of Richard Davis.

James was invited back to Ann Arbor for the 1964 ONCE Festival Of New Music, an annual event started in 1960 by the ONCE Group, a collective of independent avant-garde composers loosely connected to the university including Robert Ashley, Gordon Mumma, Roger Reynolds, and others soon to form important roles in the experimental avant-garde. Support for the Festivals came from the Dramatic Arts Center, a community organization. (Mumma relates that all attempts to enlist support from the University of Michigan 'met with resistance and even animosity.'[7])

Eric agreed to perform with the trio on all three of his instruments for James's 'A Personal Statement,' augmented by countertenor David Schwartz singing James's original, socially conscious text denouncing racism and segregation. When in April 1964 Dolphy handed over several boxes of personal items for Hale Smith to watch over during his final European tour, the title 'Jim Crow' was written on the tape box housing Eric's copy of James's piece. Following Smith's transfer of Dolphy's belongings to James Newton (and ultimately to the Library Of Congress), that erroneous title naturally made its way onto the 1987 Blue Note release *Other Aspects*, along with the belief that it was Dolphy's composition.

For the festival, Eric composed 'Strength And Unity,' a piece in 5/4 scored for brass with eight additional French horns and alto sax solo, to be performed by the ONCE Chamber Ensemble, directed by Louis Stout. The March 1 performance was held in Ann Arbor's VFW Hall's basement ballroom, with Dolphy's new piece starting the program. As Ralf Dietrich recalled, 'There was neither time nor money for more than one rehearsal. The piece featured frontman Dolphy intensely high above the other players for the duration of the piece—about ten minutes,' and was followed by 'a couple of improvisations that the four men most likely had agreed on in the Falcon Bar the night before while rehearsing 'on the job.'[8]

That basement concert closed with James's 'A Personal Statement,' which the quintet recorded the following day at the college town's WUOM radio station studios. The tape was later rescued from a station garbage bin by ONCE Festival staff and was ultimately the source for the Blue Note release. James created in his piece plenty of space for Dolphy to improvise on all three instruments. His alto sax tone first emerges from the pedal-point-like sustained pitch of the countertenor Schwartz, under which had been heard sporadic percussion clusters and gestures. The descending sax line is improvised yet settles on the pitch Schwartz then grabs for his next stanza of long, sustained syllables. Sparse, dissonant exchanges of isolated timbres transition to more terse material, only to be broken up by a brief melodic statement by Dolphy. This late-1950s academic modernism is an experimental step further away from Schuller's third stream, as bassist Brooks sides with Eric's jazzy lines contrasting the rigidity of James's piano and the vocal line's abstract remoteness. Colors wash over the piece as Dolphy's spirited flourishes are matched by cymbal rolls and crashes, a bright transition at 5:20 to the first proper appearance of an embedded jazz number signaled by a jaunty bass ostinato marked by Eric's smorzando accents. And it is a tune, with Schwartz briefly entering with the light melody and the James trio emerging for choruses.

After several minutes, Dolphy brings on an adventuresome yet unusually relaxed solo. Nine minutes into the fifteen-plus minute work, an aggressively scored passage for Schwartz's re-entry into the fray is characterized by nervous rhythmic reiterations in tandem with Eric's alto. Before the twelve-minute mark, the piece gradually descends into the murky waters of the piano's lowest notes. What emerges is a foreboding *chalumeau*-register bass clarinet, dark smears of a droning low voice and wild woodblock flurries punctuating James's stabbing low pitches. Brooks is in there somewhere, adding to the shadowy mud. The tutti madness grows in a bright crescendo, climaxing with the arrival of loud, super-refined, asymmetric rhythmic attacks using sharp, newly fashioned timbres. It's a very brief transition to the remaining minute and a half of the piece, a reprise of the long, sustained reflections of the countertenor. Dolphy has switched to flute and enters with key clicks and breathy pointillistic lines blending with the undergrowth supporting the voice. The purely tonal ending of this formally uneven composition is marked by a codetta of surprisingly relaxed piano chords supporting a brief flute solo.

It remains a curious mystery that on March 29, *Boston Globe* columnist Harvey Siders wrote of the 'atonality and rhythmic freedom of Bob James's and Eric Dolphy's "Improvisations,"' in his article titled 'Why All This Jazz About Third Stream.'[9] Siders cites the two and their collaboration as examples of 'well-trained jazz musicians writing and playing in the extended forms of their classical counterparts,' an enigmatic mention of them in relation to a piece entitled 'Improvisations,' seemingly unrelated to either 'A Personal Statement' or the ONCE Festival, suggesting the two had collaborated in an otherwise undocumented public performance.

WITH MINGUS AT CORNELL UNIVERSITY AND TOWN HALL

At a time during which he sat in on several Half Note sets with Coltrane a full year after leaving the group, Dolphy's well-documented March activities with Mingus intensified. The Workshop played extensively in the weeks prior to the European tour in April, with several important recordings emerging from those performances. Early March was also a period when Eric suffered from a slow-to-heal case of oral thrush mouth infection brought on by undiagnosed diabetes: Ben Webster, then tenor man Clifford Jordan, filling in for him at the Five Spot residency as needed. Joining Byard and Richmond was the historically underrated trumpeter Johnny Coles as a replacement for Tommy Turrentine, with Jordan eventually tapped for the sextet's tour. One of Mingus's most celebrated ensembles was slowly sculpted into a sextet, playing pieces that would help form Mingus's tour set lists.

The March 18 Cornell University concert presented new material such as the complex suite 'Meditations' (variously titled 'Meditations For A Pair Of Wire Cutters,' 'Meditations On Integration,' and 'Praying With Eric'), long thought to have premiered as a complete work at the NAACP benefit concert at Town Hall on April 4. 'Meditations' is often singled out as one of Mingus's most creative, demanding works, juggling themes and near-free sections, and one that picks up steam throughout its iterations in live performances. The compositional tour de force features Dolphy's flute and bass clarinet and is featured throughout the tour.

The Cornell concert recording was released on Blue Note only in 2007

(*Charles Mingus Sextet with Eric Dolphy: Cornell 1964*). According to Alan Saul, 'David Ackerman obtained the tape from the Cornell University radio station, where he worked, and called Mingus and visited his apartment to give him the tape.' The recording then languished among Mingus's possessions for forty years. The group's Wednesday evening appearance at Cornell's Bailey Hall marked the school's Festival Of Contemporary Arts' first inclusion of jazz. The audience had no idea that the recently coalesced musicians taking the stage were to be one of Mingus's great sextets premiering a classic program in the making, the European tour ultimately producing a treasure of live recordings documenting Dolphy's final performances with Mingus.

Consecutive solo performances open the Cornell concert, Byard with his compendium homage to Tatum and Waller, 'ATFW' (an opening spot Byard kept throughout the European dates), and Mingus's bass rendition of Strayhorn's 'Sophisticated Lady.' The sprawling 'Fables Of Faubus' would be worked up over the coming weeks, growing to a near-thirty-eight-minute epic at Wuppertal Town Hall in Germany. Here, the band is super tight and aggressive in its musical flogging of the Arkansas governor, the evening's first tutti number. Coles plays sweetly, cleanly, and with a coolness, capable of understatement yet piercing through the mix with biting expressivity. The rumblings of 'Fables Of Faubus' are seldom without Eric's bass clarinet champing at the bit, and he is wedded like iron to Jordan's sax riffs, pumped out with the rest of the band in support of Cole's inspiring solo. With Byard's scholarly yet streetwise work carrying the tune to the ten-minute mark, Jordan takes the spotlight with an encyclopedic range of ideas before passing things over to Mingus's long solo narrative. This subdued low register gives way to a frantic Dolphy, whose bass clarinet soon takes its place within the quietude of a reflective low-end monologue, spiced with hectic runs, and with Mingus's scrapings, others markedly distant in the mix due to Eric's proximity to the mic. What follows is a cadenza from the depths of Dolphy's musical wisdom, aided by Richmond and Mingus trading fours behind the master musician. This is the closest, most in-your-face recording of Eric during a live performance; one gets to hear a lot of the timbral nuances and harmonic richness of his instrument because he's playing right into the mic.

Dolphy stays on bass clarinet, accompanying Coles's tastefully muted lines, for the loping, throwback ballad 'Orange Was The Color Of Her Dress, Then Blue Silk,' which Mingus recorded the previous fall as a very different piano solo. The wistful tune, premiered here in its full compositional form and sextet arrangement, is periodically touched by scored wind cadences, with Eric's prominent bass clarinet again close to the mic. The transition from Jordan's safe and solid work to Dolphy's romp is yet another spot where Mingus steps in to 'converse,' literally shouting encouragement as Eric flies up into a very pinched yet expressive set of clarino register notes, the instrument's highest range. There are unwanted intonation problems in his playing to follow, emerging from the softly sculpted closing section in counterpoint with Jordan. 'Orange Was The Color' also played a regular role in the April tour as a Dolphy showcase.

Billy Strayhorn's 'Take The A Train' further reveals the Workshop's wide range of talent, with Coles and Byard's solos shining brightly. What is also effective here is that Dolphy solos last, still on bass clarinet, after the entire band has spent twelve minutes playing relatively old-school (on European stages, he would play the head on alto and switch to bass clarinet for his solo). There's a heavy Parker-esque presence until others fade out for Eric's unaccompanied cadenza, a framing of his pyrotechnics as the band slowly returns, like a sonic firetruck arriving to extinguish the musical fires onstage. No one in the Ithaca crowd had heard anything like this.

The lyricism of 'Meditations' has a Debussy-like flair full of Impressionistic mystery and colorful introspection. Poor mic placement muffles some of Byard's brilliance but not the material's scope, and one quickly hears Mingus's direction in classically infused music—an avenue for Dolphy's flute to add a refined, tonal air to the harmonically rich lines Mingus weaves starting with their sinewy doubling of the tune. Mingus bows upper bass registers like the cello he played as a Watts adolescent. Scraping chordal jabs of dissonant winds, direct-cut double time measures, and scored textures set off the exposed solos. An extended pseudo-classical section by Byard is effective, particularly when Eric's flute sings a brief melody, then in trio with Mingus's 'cello,' an otherworldliness jazz rarely offered. Mingus could hardly wait for Eric to switch to the bass clarinet still slung around his neck (in later recordings, he makes the change in ten seconds) and to create another outrageous solo above scored sections of the arrangement's swirling musical landscape full of Byard's massive piano chords. Twenty-five minutes into the thirty-one-minute performance, a newly configured tune and curving cadences bring around the theme. A reprise of the opening textures brings Eric back to the flute, partly leading a slow decompression from this epic saga: his intonation freely floats about, easing in and out of quarter-tone pitches, matching high register arco bass in the coda's dreamy mists.

'So Long Eric' was retitled after Mingus learned of Dolphy's plans to quit the band following the European tour. Here, the tentative opening is way under tempo from the Town Hall performance recorded seventeen days later (it would speed up further in Europe). The number was not originally 'about' Eric at all, and Dolphy does not even solo on it, giving evidence of the work's origins in other contexts, namely Mingus's celebration of the blues.

Following a cornball rendition of 'When Irish Eyes Are Smiling' (the concert followed St. Patrick's Day) with Dolphy on a squirrely, low bass clarinet, Mingus closed the concert with a fast-paced 'Jitterbug Waltz,' the joyous Fats Waller tune featured on *Conversations*. In the next evening's *Ithaca Journal*, reviewer John Huggler, after describing the other members of the band in positive terms, wrote, 'There are really only two words which can attempt to describe Eric Dolphy—simply put, Eric Dolphy.'

FINAL SPRING

Point Of Departure was the fourth Blue Note record in less than two years for pianist and composer Andrew Hill. The March 21 session brought in the exceptional rhythm section from *Out To Lunch!*, Richard Davis and Tony Williams, along with Dolphy, Kenny Dorham and Joe Henderson, the latter who had recorded four Blue Note records in the past year, three with Dorham. The superlative band often challenged Hill as both a soloist and composer. Most of the arrangements were put together with care, though a few are overly busy or self-consciously abstract, threatening to muffle ensemble color and nuances.

Nat Hentoff accurately described Eric's solo on 'Refuge' as 'slashingly, viscerally exciting as well as technical formidable,' and the Monkish charm of 'New Monastery' provokes keen alto sax exorcisms: his work on the alternate take is his best soloing from the session. The wickedly disjunct head of 'Spectrum' is a curious amalgam of richly harmonized horn motifs, an attractive composition that leads too quickly to a middle-of-the-road piano solo. Hill's repetitive comping is too far up in the mix, overpowering Eric's incisive bass clarinet solo. The unbalanced tune then gives way to a semi-free group jam still dogged by incessant keyboard tolling, clouding otherwise inventive play from the group.

'Flight 19' nearly suffers the same fate as 'Spectrum,' as the musicians bring great vibrancy to the 'flight,' while a near-meandering piano sits way up in the mix, but the tune comes around to free exchanges now mediated by Hill rather than dominated by him, and it is this less-structured passage that arguably saves the track. Along with Dorham's admirable work, Dolphy's bass clarinet solo on 'Dedication' earns kudos on an otherwise unsuccessful chart.

A sideman to the end of his US career, Dolphy is here on his second Blue Note recording courtesy of FM Records. Hill went on to an under-the-radar yet productive career as session leader with Blue Note and a handful of other labels, releasing over thirty discs—a significant number, considering the narrow attention paid to him as either composer or pianist. He poignantly commented on Dolphy's humanity, admirable outlook, and value as a collaborator:

> Eric was so important because while people are becoming individuals, he'd already developed his individuality. He's another one, like Kenny [Dorham], who maybe didn't get all the attention he deserved because he was such a sweet, beautiful person. People tend to take kindness for weakness because they don't know that an artist—a real artist—can afford to be kind because he can't be bothered with petty thoughts.[10]

THE WORKSHOP AT TOWN HALL

Eric passed away before Mingus released the Town Hall concert recording on his Jazz Workshop label, which included 'So Long Eric' and 'Meditations,' the latter here post-titled 'Praying With Eric.'* Mingus shuffled some of the titles from the Cornell gig and added two numbers on which Eric plays alto: the medley 'Parkeriana' and, from Mingus's *All Night Long* film score, 'Peggy's Blue Skylight.' Between this show and the Cornell set list, the European tour's tune pool was established. In his original album notes, Mingus dedicated the record to the NAACP coordinator who had helped organize the benefit, Mrs. Dupree White. At the time, there had been news of impending federal legislation, soon known as the Civil Rights Act, which President Johnson signed into law that July, authorizing

---

* Confusion later surrounded reissues of *Town Hall Concert, 1964, Vol. I*, with the material somehow being misidentified as stemming from a Carnegie Hall concert. Further misunderstandings arose from the United Artist Jazz album *Town Hall Concert*, recorded on October 12, 1962—the same title given to the reissue of this album by Fantasy Records.

the federal government to combat racial discrimination in employment, voting, and the use of public facilities. The album was further dedicated to 'Eric Dolphy, who knew their destiny's journey and told no one or discussed their condition other than with their doctors'—an uneasy statement, pointing perhaps to an underlying guilt he felt for Eric's tragic end. 'They performed their duties to give you and me this music and moments to brave our destinies,' Mingus added, before promising that the money owed to Eric from this album would be paid to his 'living family.'

Included with the Jazz Workshop release was an untitled poem by the bassist who was soon to lose one of his closest friends:

When I am alone and lonesome
At least there is a memory
Of someone to offset my woes
But I am lonely here
And this is a bottom too real
To be alive
Lonely is not living
Alive

The long blues number renamed 'So Long Eric' contains one of Dolphy's best alto solos, the power and integrity of which resides in an illuminated position among his greatest moments—a fitting emblem of his final live US recording. 'Meditations For A Pair Of Wire Cutters' (otherwise 'Meditations') received the new title 'Praying With Eric' following Dolphy's death. As heard on the recording, Mingus unpacked the title for the Town Hall audience that evening:

> Eric Dolphy explained to me that there was something similar to the concentration camps once in Germany now down South. And the only difference between the electric barbed wire is that they don't have gas chambers and hot stoves to cook us yet. So, I wrote a piece called 'Meditations' as to how to get some wire cutters before someone else gets some guns to us.

On April 6 at Webster Hall Studios, Eric read through parts for Verve's follow-up to the previous September's *The Individualism Of Gil Evans* session, playing on 'Las Vegas Tango' and 'Hotel Me' but taking no solos. He was seeing friends and music collaborators for what would be the last time: Garvin Bushell, Ron Carter, Paul Chambers, Elvin Jones, Steve Lacy, Jimmy Cleveland, and others. Johnny Coles was there too; in four days, they would be playing Amsterdam's Concertgebouw together. Alan Saul shares that in early April, likely following the Verve date, Hale Smith hosted a recording session for a septet featuring Eric that produced a 45rpm recording; according to Smith, 'This was Dolphy's last studio session in the US. There were two compositions played, a ballad and a 12/8 thing.'*

Dolphy's impending departure for Europe echoed his last days in 1958 Los Angeles before joining Chico Hamilton on a trajectory of hope and optimism. Now, six years later, his frustrations with the lack of opportunity and critical hostility were countered by dreams of marrying Joyce and career success across the Atlantic. He was eager for new collaborations, new compositions, new venues. He had embryonic designs for a worldwide tour and to lure Albert Ayler, Cecil Taylor, and other musicians to Paris.

Dolphy packed his things and gave up the South Street apartment, his home for nearly four years, his personal belongings worth keeping fitting into a few boxes that Hale and Juanita Smith agreed to store at their home. That February, The Beatles played *The Ed Sullivan Show* to seventy-three million Americans, one of their biggest fans being the Smiths' daughter, Robin. Eric brought her a set of Beatles cards on one of his last visits. In the waning days of stateside life, he drove his VW Beetle to meet Juanita at the United Nations, where she worked, and where she secured a pass for him to enter the parking structure to drop off his boxes. He handed over a Wollensak tape recorder, books, unreleased tape recordings, sheet music, and manuscripts of current compositions. It all remained in Smith's studio for twenty-two years, until James Newton was entrusted with the collection. Eric went with Coltrane the next day to bid farewell to Hale at his job at the E.B. Marks publishing company, though Hale was not there. None of them knew they would never see each other again. As Juanita shared, 'Then he went to the airport. Eric called from the airport, but we weren't home either. My oldest son spoke to him. He was the last one to speak to him, and before he hung up,

* The other musicians were Seldon Powell (baritone), Joe Newman (trumpet), Melba Liston (trombone), Major Holley (bass), Earl Williams (drums), and Hale Smith (piano).

Eric told him, Put Mitzi on the phone. That was the dog. So Eric said goodbye to the dog.'[11]

MINGUS EUROPEAN TOUR

The Charles Mingus Jazz Workshop tour, produced by George Wein's Festival Productions, was a nice ticket to Europe: Amsterdam, Oslo, Stockholm, Copenhagen, Bremen, Paris, Liege, Marseille, Lyon, Biel-Bienne, Bologna, and Wuppertal. To Eric, the cities clicked off like a continental countdown to a new life—a cozy Parisian apartment, steady employment, appreciative audiences, and ultimately marriage. Brian Priestly states that the tour included stops in Zurich, Frankfurt, and Hamburg, resulting in seventeen performances in sixteen cities in eighteen days, though no known accounts or recordings exist of those three performances. To European fans of contemporary jazz, American players were cultural heroes, and this was Eric's fourth visit in less than four years. Eric knew what to expect, though it had been over two years since he faced such a demanding tour schedule. Although Mingus's angry confrontations with stage personnel, audiences, and hotel workers made for a sometimes chaotic tour, Dolphy later told Nathan Davis that he couldn't believe the positive response to his club appearances, adding that playing in Europe was 'the greatest success I had ever had.'[12]

The core concert set of up to six compositions per show drew from the Cornell and Town Hall programs, with four works played regularly: 'Meditations,' (flute, bass clarinet), 'Fables Of Faubus' (bass clarinet), 'So Long Eric' (alto), and 'Parkerania' (alto), sometimes titled 'Dedicated To A Genius.' The group often opened and closed the long 'Parkeriana' medley with Dizzy Gillespie's 'Ow!,' sandwiching in an amalgam of Parker references and quotes from Gershwin's 'They Can't Take That Away From Me' and 'If I Should Lose You' by Robin and Rainger. Each long tune was a suite-like structure of at least twenty minutes, telescoping in and out of hard and post-bop, blues, swing, old-time jazz, and gospel—medley-like numbers with highly segmented musical arrangements of rehearsed and cued passages, out-of-tempo sections, and long solos. Byard's unaccompanied 'ATFWUS,' with its encyclopedic stride references, started most shows, followed by Mingus taking the stage for 'Sophisticated Lady.' Added some nights were 'Orange Was The Color' (bass clarinet) and 'Peggy's Blue Skylight' (alto). Providing variety were the occasional 'Take The A Train' (alto, bass clarinet) and the Mingus/Dolphy bass/flute duets 'I Can't Get Started' at Wuppertal and 'These Foolish Things' at Stuttgart. Many of these tunes were reworked for certain shows, with solo assignments shifted, structures extended or truncated, and durations altered.*

AMSTERDAM

The April 10 Concertgebouw recordings are awkwardly unbalanced yet reveal great music performed by recently coalesced musicians sounding as if they'd been playing together for months rather than weeks. A mic seems to point to Richmond's hi-hat: when Dolphy takes his solo on 'Parkerania,' one can hear his exact synchrony with the pulse, and when he leaves it for off-kilter phrasing and leaping gestures. On 'So Long Eric' (the tempo of which is faster than the widely known Town Hall recording), Dolphy unwinds what may be one of his career's most demanding alto solos. Augmenting his mastery of blues, bebop, and post-bop is a renewed dedication to increasingly abstract sound palettes and an unbridled romp through the instrument's capabilities. During the altoist's cadenza, Mingus mumbles an encouraging 'Go ahead.' It's Dolphy's marathon to run, and he sprints the entire way.

After 'So Long Eric's' nearly half-hour workout of breakneck music, Mingus speaks to the audience, sharing that the tune has had many titles. Tonight it is 'Don't Stay Over Here Too Long Eric.' One hears Mingus's biting sarcasm as he announces that Dolphy is 'leaving the band because America is so beautiful and free. He's going to stay over here for a while.' Lamenting what was to be a temporary parting with his group's key horn player as well as a close friend, the acerbic bandleader conveys, as he was often able, a larger truth by invoking by inversion an 'ugly' America and its marginalization of artists. No doubt tinged with unspoken reference to the United States' increasingly violent racial politics

* The first commercially available Mingus tour recordings were released well over a decade later. Italy's illicit bootleg label Unique Jazz released *Mingus Sextet Live In Europe* in the late 1970s, including Bremen performances of 'Meditations,' 'ATFWUSA,' and 'Sophisticated Lady'; and the double-LP set *Mingus In Stuttgart April 28, 1964 Concert*. Among other releases from this tour, the German label Enja followed suit with official issues of the Wuppertal concert authorized by Mrs. Susan Graham Mingus and Jazz Workshop Inc, *Mingus In Europe Vol. I* (1979) and *Vol. II* (1981). The Simosko and Tepperman discographic research of the tour references television and radio broadcasts from Liege, Marseille, and Bologna with, at the time, no known available recordings. The Liege performance has since been released on video.

surrounding the Civil Rights Movement, Mingus's message to the audience further branded Dolphy's move as an escape of sorts, from both the hypocrisy of racism and from his struggles with the limits placed on innovation by the jazz world.

Smoothly turning from such succinct rhetorical flourishes, the transition from the near-abstract abandon of 'So Long Eric' to the poetically playful ballad 'Orange Was The Color Of Her Dress, Then Blue Silk' reminds us why the Mingus Workshop was such a crowd pleaser. The Amsterdam recording's mic placement now sonically embraces the lyrical arrangement's rich bass clarinet part. Coles takes a beautiful flight shaded with half-fingered cracked notes reminiscent of Miles, followed by Mingus flailing a bit on his solo. Eric's solo is a screaming old-school celebration, playing to the changes with willful dispatches of blues luster and bubbling fury. He leaps to new levels of high and low register, playing multiple lines simultaneously. 'Sophisticated Lady' lays on the sentiment, giving the audience a chance to breathe before 'Meditation For A Pair Of Wire Cutters,' with Dolphy starting on flute only to quickly shift to bass clarinet. Here he unpacks his suitcase of devices, including lip smacks, rich multiphonics, split tones, and heavily accented attacks, all leading to a unique cadenza. It's a three-and-a-half-minute long exorcism, wildly applauded as Coles takes over. The tune ends with a trio of piano, cello-register bowed bass, and flute, an eerie coda of sorrow and forsakenness speaking to America's racial divide.

Dolphy's rich bass clarinet is notable during the 'Fables Of Faubus' intro, the epic suite taking the Dutch audience on a rollercoaster ride of styles and attitude. Emerging from Mingus's solo are Dolphy's fireworks, leading to a cadenza with Byard's massive forearm chords and Mingus's lowest drone.* After the concert, Mingus and Dolphy were interviewed by Michiel de Ruyter for his radio program 'Radio Jazzmagazine,' the Dutchman following up on Mingus's stage comments about Dolphy leaving the group. With a bit of reluctance, Eric confirmed his plans to stay in Europe following the tour, adding that he'll live in Paris. In less than two months, de Ruyter would co-produce one of Dolphy's final recordings, at Hilversum.

---

* In 1985, Ulysse Musique (with the approval of Sue Mingus) issued the double-LP *Concertgebouw Amsterdam*. Inopportune editing mars several takes, and some of Dolphy's soloing is badly affected. In 2009, Jazz Collectors label released the less-edited two-CD set *Charles Mingus/Eric Dolphy Sextet: Complete Live In Amsterdam* with more tracks. The concert was also broadcast to a television audience.

FROM OSLO TO LIEGE

This six-man jazz circus traveled to Oslo's Aula University on April 12, adding 'Take The A Train' and 'Parkerania' to the set list.* Before their next show on April 13, the Workshop took the stage of an empty Koncerthuset in Stockholm to film rehearsals of 'So Long Eric' and 'Meditations.' This was the same venue Eric played with the Coltrane Quintet on November 23, 1961. Its grandiose construction was completed in 1926 to host the Nobel Prize ceremony; the Workshop's members were filmed with their backs to the plush interior, designed for the Royal Stockholm Philharmonic Orchestra.† That evening, they played 'Orange Was The Color,' 'Peggy's Blue Skylight,' 'When Irish Eyes Are Smiling,' and 'Fables Of Faubus,' the latter making it onto a 1991 bootleg from the French label Royal Jazz *Charles Mingus Sextet Live In Stockholm 1964*, originally mislabeled as having been recorded in Oslo.‡ The audience sitting in the Large Hall Of Copenhagen's Odd Fellow Palace the following night of April 14 was regaled by two long sets featuring 'Meditations' and 'Fables Of Faubus.'§

Traveling on Wednesday to the German city of Bremen, the Workshop did their thing on April 16 in what was then known as Radio Bremen Sendesaal (Studio F), an acoustically cutting-edge 'room-within-a-room' performance and recording hall in the Bremen-Schwachhausen. The venue's ceilings and walls are supported by over 650 industrial springs mounted on the building's outer shell, isolating it from external noise. Of note in the radio broadcast performance are Eric's no-holds-barred alto solos on 'Parkeriana,' and 'So Long Eric,' its diamond-

---

* In 1989, the Italian label Jazz Up released *Charles Mingus Featuring Eric Dolphy—Live In Oslo 1964*, revealing an ensemble in top form with consistently hot blowing. Norwegian Broadcasting Corporation television video found its way to the Shenachie label's VHS title *Charles Mingus Sextet* (1993) and later the Impro-Jazz DVD *Eric Dolphy In Europe 1961–1964* (2006) and the 2007 Jazz Icons DVD series title *Charles Mingus Live In '64*, a collection of excerpts from three concerts: Oslo, Stockholm (rehearsal only), and Liege (television studio broadcast).

† The rehearsal appears with 1960 Antibes Festival footage on the 2007 Impro-Jazz DVD *Eric Dolphy With The Charles Mingus Sextet: Stockholm,1964; Antibes, 1960, Featuring Bud Powell.*

‡ In 1992, the Italian label Bandstand issued the authorized CD *Charles Mingus Meditations On Integration*, which includes three tracks from the Stockholm concert: 'Peggy's Blue Skylight,' 'Fables Of Faubus,' and 'Orange Was The Color.'

§ Several tracks are heard on the Italian bootleg album *Charles Mingus: Astral Weeks* (Moon Records, 1990). Other titles from that performance trickled out on various unofficial releases in Europe. The Hi Hat label's unofficial release *Charles Mingus Sextet: Copenhagen, 1964* (2017), for example, is a remastered double-CD bootleg featuring both sets.

like passages hewn with exhortations, humor, and a gusto for the unpredictable taking even bandmates by surprise.* The ensemble is in full control of Mingus's large, complex suites, transcending the mere satisfaction of form.

These are great performances, and among the best is Coles's sublime solo on 'Meditations On Segregation,' from the tour's last complete concert featuring the trumpeter. On the road in Europe for only one week, Coles collapsed with a ruptured stomach ulcer after leaving the stage in pain near the end of 'So Long Eric,' the evening's opening number at Paris's Salle Wagram on Friday, April 17.† One does not hear Coles's horn in the head arrangement's final statements of that tune. According to other Workshop members, after seeing Coles being attended to, Dolphy exhorted the band to continue with 'Parkerania' and play through the complete concert program. Though potentially life-threatening, Coles's condition was no surprise to him, as he had undergone recent stomach surgery in the USA and apparently ignored doctors' orders not to tour with Mingus that spring. French surgeons at the American hospital in Neuilly saved his life and cared for him for three weeks.

The Workshop's concert at the Theatre des Champs-Elysees on Saturday, April 18, was prepped with rehearsals of new arrangements, last-minute adjustments explaining the late start time of 12:10am Sunday morning, and the subsequent dating of the concert by some sources to the April 19.‡ The hospitalized trumpeter's instrument sat onstage, upright on a chair. Dolphy's solos from this show exhaust superlatives, particularly his bass clarinet work on 'Fables Of Faubus.'

That Sunday morning, the group missed their scheduled train to Belgium, leading to the cancelation of their main concert performance at Liège's Palais Des Congrès. Despite their late arrival, the quintet managed to perform a set for the Belgian TV show *Jazz pour tous*, produced by bassist Benoit Quersin for the RTB.§

---

* The 2010 Jazz Lips bootleg of this performance reveals mediocre microphone placement, with a booming bass, backing horns too far behind, some drum distortion, and Byard too low in the mix.

† Recordings from that Friday concert were partially released in 1996 as the Mingus album *Revenge*; a complete version followed on Domino Records in 2015 as *The Salle Wagram Concert*.

‡ The French label America Records released the live recordings as *The Great Concert Of Charles Mingus* in 1970—a three-LP set featuring the performance and selected to win that country's Grand Prix Du Academie Charles Cros and *Melody Maker*'s 'Album Of The Year' award. The stateside Prestige release came two years later. 'So Long Eric' (actually recorded at the Salle Wagram performance) is mistitled as 'Goodbye Porkpie Hat' on many issues.

§ A newly colorized version can be found on YouTube.

A small, drab television studio, equipment pushed aside, hosted the hot group, capturing Dolphy's unusual solo on 'Peggy's Blue Skylight' and his extensive bass clarinet forays on 'Meditations.' Here, Eric's phrases of intelligible yet incomplete sentences are arranged into ever new juxtapositions, inventing new life forms that seem to breathe and chatter, channeling both avian and animal spirits.

MARSEILLE, LYON, BIEL-BIENNE/BOLOGNA, WUPPERTAL, AND STUTTGART

The group traveled to Marseille on April 20 for a television broadcast that night, presenting 'So Long Eric,' 'Meditations,' and 'Parkeriana.' Alan Saul states that they played in Lyon the next evening, before relaxing and traveling on April 22 (Mingus's birthday) on their way to Biel-Bienne, Switzerland, for a Wednesday tour date. This seems more likely than what Priestly suggests, his nearly impossible schedule listing four engagements (Biel-Bienne, Zurich, Frankfurt, and Hamburg) in the forty-eight hours before the group reached Italy. In any case, there are no available recordings from Zurich, Frankfurt, or Hamburg, and neither Saul nor Simosko and Tepperman mention those cities. During the sextet's travel from Belgium to Marseille, Dutch radio producer Michiel de Ruyter broadcasted his Dolphy interview, recorded following the first Amsterdam concert.

After confirming that Eric was planning to stay in Europe following the Mingus tour, de Ruyter suggested he would 'like to be in a group where you are as free as possible.' Dolphy's reply emphasized his eclectic passions—both free and traditional forms of jazz, third stream, classical, and playing with talented musicians:

> Yes, I would like to, for a while. Listen, the thing is, I enjoy playing all kinds of ways . . . that develops you because music regardless of what it is, what label we put on . . . basically it's creative. Because when you think about it, when you hear music after it's over, it's gone in the air, you can never capture it again, so it's pure creation. When you listen to Beethoven, Brahms, or you listen to Mingus or Coltrane or Stravinsky, Ravel or Duke Ellington or Sonny Rollins, Roland Kirk . . . Oscar Peterson, Ella Fitzgerald . . . I'll tell you, I played, and Gunther Schuller arranged it, a piece for Orchestra USA and Leonard Bernstein liked us. He wanted to do it with the [New York] Philharmonic. . . . Those great musicians, it's great to play with them. Every musician that has his contribution is a great musician whether he has a name or not.

The tour plane descended into Bologna on April 24, and during a forty-eight-hour Italian sojourn, Eric managed to break away from the crowd to visit the great flutist Gazzelloni for a lesson that likely occurred in Milan (a four-hour round trip) the next day. There is no record of a performance in Milan, but Mingus purchased an ill-fated bass there before the tour's next stop in Wuppertal on Sunday, April 26.* Eric shared with the flutist a tape of his composition 'Gazzelloni' from *Out To Lunch!* We can imagine the cutting-edge Italian master of avant-garde concert flute listening to Eric's homage while discussing Varèse, Berio, and perhaps future third stream dreams. No doubt Dolphy shared his experience of performing 'Density 21.5' and his impressions of Gazzelloni's recordings of modernist flute solos and those with pianist Aloys Kontarsky.

With Wuppertal and Stuttgart awaiting the sextet during the last few days of April, German press reports of Mingus's confrontational violence and accusations of Nazism irked the locals, with articles from daily newspapers detailing offensive outbursts from the tour's dangerous, carnivalesque procession. Additionally, with Eric's impending exit the Mingus/Dolphy relationship became tense and a source of group friction. Before they parted ways, never to see each other again, Eric openly mocked Mingus for telephoning Collette in hopes of hiring him as a replacement for the Workshop's upcoming West Coast gigs, simply because the wages would be too low for his former mentor. However, Collette did join Mingus's eleven-piece band that September at the Monterey Jazz Festival.

Many of the tour's concerts started up to an hour late, with various anecdotes of Mingus being restrained by police at different locales, his aggressive behavior in Biel-Bienne including kicking a tape deck into pieces and ordering another tape to be confiscated. Somewhere in Germany (Hamburg, Wuppertal, or Stuttgart), the bassist brandished a knife after kicking in doors at the venue and destroyed a mic and a telephone. He later claimed:

> We couldn't eat or drink or nothing. In the hotels our rooms weren't

---

* The Wuppertal Town Hall concert (Historische Stadhalle) produced an official album release authorized by Sue Mingus and Jazz Workshop Inc. in 1984. The performances appear on the Enja label's *Mingus In Europe, Vol. I* (1979) & *Vol. II* (1984). On the first volume's 'I Can't Get Started,' a flute/bass duet mistitled in some releases as 'Starting' is erroneously attributed to Eric; 'Peggy's Blue Skylight' is mistitled on the second volume as 'Charlemagne' and erroneously attributed to Jordan. 'Orange Was The Color' is the only other track on *Vol. II* to feature Dolphy.

> cleaned. George Wein, who was booking us there, was Jewish; he spoke the language.... When he got downstairs, everybody stood to attention, the elevator operator, the desk clerk!... After that, as soon as it happened, they put swastikas on Eric's door.[13]

Outweighing the controversies as the group continued to Germany were the powerful musical performances at Wuppertal and Stuttgart. A freely adapted 'I Can't Get Started' made for a fanciful flute/bass duet at Wuppertal, made available twenty years later on *Mingus In Europe, Volume 1* (Enja, 1984)—a disc that includes a thirty-seven-minute rendition of 'Fables Of Faubus.' Mingus announces here that he had yet to use the bass he had onstage, the instrument just acquired in Milan. Dolphy's lucid bass clarinet work on the latter track includes his part in an extensive, audience-pleasing Mingus/Dolphy conversation. The remainder of that program can be found on that label's second volume (neither of which was released on vinyl in the USA).

Listeners had to wait only a decade to hear *Charles Mingus Live In Stuttgart!*, an unofficial bootleg release from the Italian label Unique Jazz. That concert performance—Eric's last known gig with Mingus—was broadcast live on local television and radio from the Mozart-Saal/Liederhalle. In particular, Dolphy's epic bass clarinet solo on "Fables of Faubus," and his conversational outpouring with Mingus captured on that recording, mark the end of their musical lives together, and what showboating may have characterized these exchanges in the past are here fully overshadowed by the poignant historicity of their personal and artistic parting of ways.

'One of the last times I saw him was at a party in Europe,' the bassist recalled. 'When I got there, the room was full of people talking and drinking. In a corner, listening to a Charlie Parker record, there was Eric practicing along with the record. He had music on his mind all the time.'[14] Years later, Mingus shared that toward the end of this final tour, Eric 'talked about God—that seemed to be his only subject... he and John Coltrane were eating honey, I think it was a vegetarian diet, and trying to find the Lord.'

In an interview with *DownBeat*'s German correspondent Joachim Berendt, completed toward the tour's close, Eric echoed the words of many African American artists who left the USA for Europe: 'I'd like to stay in Europe.... There is no race trouble. I'll live in Paris.'[15]

Berendt was the TV producer who in August 1961 had booted Eric from his headlining spot on *Jazz, Heard And Seen* out of concern for ratings. Such undignified bumps in the road were now irrelevant to Dolphy on his final departure from Mingus's group, as he escaped to the promise of springtime Paris, marriage, and music played his way.

12 PARIS, LAST RECORDINGS, DEATH IN BERLIN, AFTERMATH

MAY–JULY 1964

On a short residential block at the northern edge of Paris's trendy Montmartre, an old Army friend's small apartment on quaint Rue de la Fontaine-du-But provided a haven to the soon-to-be thirty-six-year-old Eric Dolphy. He eased into a new life's routine of practicing, visiting Joyce, and composing a string quartet for their wedding, titled 'Love Suite.' He had started the piece in New York, sharing it with Richard Davis, and, during his last days there, decided to leave behind other original pieces such as an untitled solo bass clarinet work and two works for jazz ensemble, 'Song F.T.R.H.' and 'On The Rocks.' Joyce had been affiliated with the Royal Danish Ballet and was studying dance in Paris. 'We were going to get married in Europe,' she states in the film *Last Date*, explaining that their plans were for a July ceremony before learning of a two-month waiting period for foreigners to receive official approval. To accommodate her, Eric began arrangements to rent a larger flat in his apartment building.

Throughout May, the couple went museum-hopping, saw the sights, and rubbed elbows with fellow American musicians. Eric got busy creating a network of new friends and professional contacts, socializing, and familiarizing himself with Paris's many jazz clubs: the Blues Bar, Caveau de la Huchette, La Calavados, Cameleon, Kentucky Club, The Living Room, Riverboat, and the Slow Club among others. Johnny Griffin, Art Taylor, and Jean-Luc Ponty had just replaced Toshiko and Charlie Mariano at the Blue Note; Memphis Slim held forth at Trois Mailletz until June, when he switched to the Mars Room. Erroll Parker, Kansas Fields, and Roland Haynes were at the Ladybird until Sonny Grey arrived in June and soon joined in sessions with what would prove to be Dolphy's last group.

On May 18, Eric paid a visit to the Mantes-la-Ville Selmer factory northeast of central Paris, ordering a new bass clarinet that he picked up the second week of June. He had been a sponsored Selmer artist for some time, with French advertisements featuring a photo of him blowing on alto with the caption, 'Eric Dolphy plays on Selmer.'*

Within weeks of arriving in Paris, Dolphy was sitting in with a piano-less quartet led by trumpeter Donald Byrd at Madame Ricard's Latin Quarter club and restaurant Le Chat Qui P*êche*, a few blocks from the Notre Dame Cathedral. A quick Paris Metro train from the Porte de Clignancourt station in Dolphy's new neighborhood delivered him to the St. Michel stop around the corner from the club. Tenor player Nathan Davis, bassist Luigi Tristardi, and drummer Jacques Tulow rounded out the group. Byrd was enjoying the recent release of *A New Perspective*, his tenth Blue Note album as leader/co-leader in less than five years.

American jazz artists were in high demand, as Davis later shared: 'Very few people had heard of Nathan Davis. But on a Tuesday night I'd have four or five people deep, three or four blocks long to get in to hear me with a French rhythm section.'[1] Davis had been playing with drummer Kenny Clarke's band in Paris before taking part in the two-week Chat Qui Pêche engagement, and at Dolphy's request he was soon asked by Byrd to participate in more projects.† Davis recalled that Dolphy was sharing *Out To Lunch!* material and coaching players on soloing over the freer pieces and thornier altered harmonies, and how to produce and employ multiphonics and other extended techniques.[2] Davis had 'never been in a band that practiced as much as we practiced; we had daily rehearsals and played every night from 10pm till 4am. When we would finish playing, we would go to the Living Room to hear Aaron Bridges and Art Simmons, who were Tatum-esque pianists. [Dolphy would] say, Listen to Art Tatum—the first thing you need to do every day is listen to him.'

After several group performances toward the end of May, Madame Ricard (the 'Grand Old Lady Of French Jazz') made Eric the group's co-leader, their playlist growing to include his standard tour repertoire. Eric also established a working

---

* Alan Saul later discovered that, by 1961, Eric had insurance coverage for 'a Selmer alto, a Buffet soprano [B-flat] clarinet, a Selmer bass clarinet, a Buffet bass clarinet, a Powell flute, the Wurlitzer, and a piccolo.'

† Simosko and Tepperman state that the Chat Qui Pêche engagement was Nathan Davis's gig, but *DownBeat* announcements identify the residency as Byrd and Dolphy's.

relationship with pianist Kenny Drew, who had moved to Paris in 1961 and was now gigging with bassist Guy Pedersen and drummer Daniel Humair—the latter of whom Dolphy had played with at the Club-Saint Germaine at the end of his solo European tour in September 1961. On May 28, this quartet played 'Les,' 'Serene,' and Monk's 'Epistrophy' for a live ORTF national radio broadcast.

The need to link up with accomplished American performers such as Drew was matched by a reliance on good European rhythm sections. Eric expressed a serious desire to lure Woody Shaw, Richard Davis, and Billy Higgins to professional lives in Paris. As he settled into what was proving to be a more comfortable expat professional life, his words from four years earlier, captured in the *Jazz Review* cover story that introduced him to New York audiences, once again framed his renewed life: 'I feel very happy to be a part of music. . . . It is really wonderful to feel I can make my living as a musician now because I never wanted to do anything else.'[3]

FIVE DAYS IN HOLLAND

Amid this brew of activities, the jazz man flew to Holland, where club owner Paul Karting had booked a busy itinerary in Amsterdam and other Dutch locales. Dolphy's final tour started with a May 29 afternoon rehearsal at the home of pianist Misha Mengelberg. Eric showed up with his driver (Ruby Kamerbeek) and Karting in tow and was soon joined by bassist Jacques Schols and drummer Han Bennink. Dolphy had heard the Mengelberg trio on a recording shared by Karting and agreed to play with them. The quartet performed that evening at the Modern Music Club in Bergen, near the North Sea coast, forty miles from Amsterdam.

The next afternoon, the quartet regrouped at the restaurant of Amsterdam's Port van Cleve hotel for a rehearsal with Boy Edgar's Big Band, in preparation for a midnight concert at the Concertgebouw. As other fellow musicians have noted regarding Dolphy's deteriorating diet, Bennink recalled Eric drinking tea mixed with equal parts honey.[4] Following the afternoon rehearsal, the quartet played at De Heuvel, a Rotterdam club Karting managed, another eighty-mile roundtrip. As Karting shares[5]:

> Dinner in a small Amsterdam restaurant, the Cave. Eric was very enthusiastic about their Hungarian Goulash. 'I never had eaten so delicious as this,' Dolphy told us. Then to . . . Rotterdam . . . [playing first was] the

> Rotterdam Leo Meyer quintet, then Eric with the trio, we could arrive at [8:45pm]. The concert was sixty-five minutes.

Karting described the club, and the SRO audience exceeding fire code limits: 'I think there were four hundred people. But the music was so hot, there was an atmosphere like in a commune. Everybody was chained to the things that happened on stage. It was a swirling unit, audience and music.' In attendance were a few members of the Rotterdam Philharmonic, including oboist Gijs de Graaf, who Karting described as being 'very interested to do new things with Eric and several friends from the Rotterdam Philharmonic.'

Such a scenario of world-class orchestral musicians rallying behind a planned collaboration with Dolphy marks the jazz musician's ascendance within his universalist aesthetic. As with other speculative questions regarding what Eric would have done had he lived, one cannot rule out high-level projects with great world orchestras.

It was in this spirit that Dolphy asked Mengelberg about John Cage and other composers the pianist had met at the Darmstadt International Summer Courses for New Music. The open-minded Mengelberg, who counted Cage as an influence along with Monk and Duke Ellington, held his own growing position in the crossover world of contemporary avant-garde concert music and jazz by winning the 1961 Gaudeamus International Composition award. By the time Dolphy arrived for the tour, Mengelberg was in his sixth and final year of formal study at the Royal Conservatory at the Hague and had become associated with the Fluxus movement. Yet, as Dolphy's recording with the trio came to be known as the 'Last Date,' it was Mengelberg's first date—his debut recording. Bennink later acknowledged that Eric's conversation during the Dutch tour was dominated by a discussion of music with Mengelberg, the pianist, for instance, suggesting the group tackle compositions by American jazz pianist Herbie Nichols and Monk.

The quartet left De Heuvel at 11:30 and drove back to Amsterdam. Karting described the rest of the evening:

> Arrived about [12:30am]. In Amsterdam the night concert started with Boy's Big Band till [12:45], then intermission. After the intermission the Eric Dolphy quartet played some compositions by Eric, and the quartet played three compositions with big band. The first big-band arrangement

> was '245' then an arrangement by Boy Edgar, 'Blues Minor' with Eric on alto sax, with the quartet and Boy's Big Band, and closing with the second big band arrangement of Eric Dolphy, 'G.W.' by the quartet and the big band. After the two big band pieces, which were European premieres, the quartet started to play without the big band.

Following the concert, the group visited an unidentified American journalist working for *Time* magazine and talked about 'everything that was interesting. At five o'clock in the morning, we went to the Museum hotel ... and had four hours to sleep. That evening Eric had to play in Tilburg.'

The Tilburg–Eindhoven–Hilversum–Amsterdam itinerary covered at least two hundred miles between Sunday and Tuesday. Dolphy's group played Tilburg under the auspices of the Two Beat And Modern Jazz Society, taking up all of Sunday, May 31. The town is only twenty miles from Eindhoven, closer to the Belgian border, where they then played a Monday evening gig at the Café de Kroon. Han Bennink eventually released an illicit tape of 'Epistrophy' from this concert on the Instant Composers Pool collective's label.*

The next evening at Hilversum, an hour southeast of Amsterdam, the quartet played a set at VARA Studio 5 for the *Jazz Magazine* radio program produced by Aad Bos, Kees Schoonenberg, and Michiel de Ruyter, the latter having interviewed Eric on the first night of the Mingus tour in April. The recording quality is rich and balanced. Following Bos's introductions, the group played Monk's 'Epistrophy,' with Eric's bass clarinet calling out an exclamatory intro. Mengelberg and crew provide a minimal backing for Dolphy's cavalcade of blistering riffs, curious sequences, overblown split tones, harmonics, and his patented phraseology of truncation, varied repetition, and multidirectional excursions. (It was this exposure to bass clarinet that Bennink soon acquired the instrument for himself.) A certain plodding stiffness sets in with the rhythm section underneath Mengelberg's effective, pianistic solo. Before the tune's final iteration, Dolphy returns to the spotlight with a brief yet intense study in low register gestures gradually blooming with ascents to high register hits and the theme's restatement, though the rhythm section meanders a bit, and some energy leaks from the room.

---

* Domino Records' 2010 album *The Complete Last Recordings In Hilversum & Paris, 1964* includes this Eindhoven 'Epistrophy' as a bonus track, erroneously providing the source as a 'live broadcast.'

As Mengelberg mischievously states, he wrote the long, clever line for 'Hypochristmastreefuzz' with no breath points as a challenge to Eric's bass clarinet (the title refers to the mess under the Christmas tree after opening presents). Again, Eric is in top form on this up-tempo, quirky tune, quickly accessing his compendium of edgy ideas, stringing together unpredictable phrases and unique sounds, and displaying his penchant for free exploration. Schols struggles to start his bowed bass in duet with Eric's flute on the intro to 'You Don't Know What Love Is,' but none of this fazes Dolphy as he produces a wonderful solo, the beautiful recording capturing his split tones, flutter tongue, and harmonics. 'South Street Exit' finds Dolphy widening his flute playing to approach his reed instruments' expressive idiosyncrasies, while 'Mandrake' continues in its usual pairing with 'South Street Exit,' before the program closes with a rousing 'Miss Ann.'*

According to Karting, before Dolphy flew back to Paris on the morning of Wednesday, June 3, the two of them laid plans for the coming October 'to do a classical piece ... with members of the Rotterdam Philharmonic. Eric told me he wanted to do several orchestral pieces ... with two different groups. The first group has eight horns (French horns and/or mellophoniums), two baritone horns, tuba, and the quartet.† The second group has an oboe, flute, two horns, clarinet, bassoon, and the quartet.' Employed in concert band settings, mellophoniums (or mellophones) have a range similar to the French horn and feature straight-facing bells. These orchestrations would have been categorically linked to Dolphy's previous work with *Africa/Brass*, his charts performed at the University Of Illinois, and the arrangements he made for larger groups back in his Los Angeles days.

During this busy schedule's heady mix of travel and gigging, Eric purchased wedding rings from a Rotterdam jeweler named Charles Gelauff, who had played trumpet with Coleman Hawkins in the mid-1930s. On June 21, he sent this note to Karting, posthumously delivered:

---

* The 1964 album featuring the Hilversum broadcast, *Last Date*, released by the Dutch label Fontana, replaced the proper title 'Mandrake' with that of the original Dragonette poem, 'The Madrig Speaks, The Panther Walks'—a curious error duplicated in the Limelight label's US release the following year, and in some subsequent reissues.

† Likely his piece penned for the ONCE festival, 'Strength And Unity,' and 'Red Planet,' as arranged by Dolphy for the Illinois concert.

Dear Paul,

Thanks for the very successful trip in Holland. I enjoyed it and would like you and everyone to know about it. If you could write me and let me know the possible dates that would be open so we could plan on something in Holland. About the news in Paris, well Sonny Stitt is at the Blue Note and Sonny Criss is at the Blues Bar, Art Simmons is still at the Living Room. Donald Byrd and myself finished up this week [at Le Chat Qui *Pêche*]. Give my best to Rubie and his movie star wife. Also to Jack and Misha, and if you can let me know what Han Bennink is doing the rest of the summer and how I can get in touch with him.

Take care and the best always, yours truly,

Eric Dolphy

Bennink also tearfully received a card from Eric after his death, asking him to join in a Copenhagen residency to have included Bobby Hutcherson.

LAST WEEKS AND LAST RECORDINGS

By the mid-1990s, it was established that recordings Eric made in Paris subsequent to his Holland sessions constituted his true 'last dates.' Upon returning to the City Of Light, he stepped right back into ensembles that formed a vortex around his Le Chat Qui Pêche connections. Byrd replaced Dexter Gordon at the Blue Note on the first of the month and joined the septet Eric was putting together, with a playlist including 'Springtime,' '245,' 'G.W.,' 'Serene,' 'Ode To Charlie Parker,' and 'Les.' This group recorded at Le Chat for the ORTF program *Jazz aux Champs Elysees*, produced by pianist Jacques Diéval and broadcasted on June 11: Byrd, Davis, and Diéval were joined by Jacque Hess on bass, Franco Manzecchi on drums, and Billy Brooks on congas. Eric then rehearsed and recorded with a larger group right up to his departure for Berlin on Saturday, June 27.

Making music dominated Eric's life, and in addition to these activities during his final weeks in Paris, he sat in on performances and recordings with Sonny Grey's big band, Jacques Diéval's All-Stars, and, according to Nathan Davis, led various ensembles that he called together to play his original works, and Byard's 'Ode To Charlie Parker.' A recording of 'Naima' proved to be Eric's final goodbye to Coltrane. As Geri Allen suggests through interviews with Davis, more recordings produced by Diéval were made over roughly a two-week period: 'Sonny Gray, the trumpeter who was also in Paris during this period, participated in these sessions… the only member of the unit then performing at Le Chat Qui Pêche who didn't participate in this recording was Jacque Tulow on drums.'*

The promise of opportunity fueled Eric's plans. On his mind were Richard Davis, Billy Higgins, and Woody Shaw; he told Nathan Davis that he would bring them over to Paris to play and record when he returned from Berlin.[6] Other names on Dolphy's list of future collaborations included Cecil Taylor and Albert Ayler, the latter recording with bassist Gary Peacock and Sonny Murray on percussion that June 14 at New York's Cellar Cafe for what became the *Prophecy* album. Regarding Taylor, with whom there is no evidence of Dolphy having played, there is this account from Jeanne Phillips:

> Even a musician as great as Eric Dolphy looked forward to the time he could play with Cecil. Eric had all of Cecil's records . . . and he used to say, 'I think I'm learning how to play with Cecil.' . . . Before Eric went to Europe… he dreamed he was on the bandstand with Cecil… and he was waiting for his turn to play. He kept saying to himself, 'At last, I'm going to play with Cecil.' And before he could play, he fell down dead on the bandstand. This was the last time I talked to him before he went to Europe, and the next thing I heard, Eric had died.[7]

No one knows the details of what Joyce later described as club bookings that stretched into the next year and a 'world' tour that would take Eric to Australia and Japan. Sadie later shared that Eric already had a contract to play in Japan. Other rumors of upcoming projects included a headline gig at London's Ronnie Scott's with George Russell's sextet, to be filmed for television broadcast. However, in the face of these visions for a newly energized career, home, and family, a dark reality

---

* Subsequent releases of these recordings include: *The Complete Last Recordings In Hilversum & Paris, 1964* (Domino, and also released on Norma Records, Japan), re-issued and remastered by Hi-Hat as *Eric Dolphy Septet With Donald Byrd: Paris '64* (2018). The Italian label Jazzway released select live tracks as *Eric Dolphy: Naima* (1987); select tracks were released on a 1988 LP by West Wind entitled *Unrealized Tapes*.

had settled in. A friend of Dolphy biographer Thierry Bruneau remembered finding Eric one night sitting on a Paris bench and in terrible shape. The fellow recognized him as a musician from a club performance and asked if he was all right. Eric responded that he needed to eat something sweet, and the two drove around looking for a store or café where he could indulge.

Joyce vividly recalled seeing Eric play for the last time during his final week in Paris and related how uneasy he seemed onstage, though playing well and 'blowing his guts out.' The night before, she had visited his apartment and saw that he was not looking good, with dark circles under his eyes. Most disturbing were Eric's accounts of hallucinations, as he asked her if she had seen the naked people swimming in the pond's blue water under the sky that was so blue, and the sun that had been so bright and shining.*

On what must have been the morning of Friday, June 26, Joyce reported his unhealthy appearance and strange behavior to her dance troupe's physician. The doctor reassured her that he would pay a visit the next day, but that was the morning Eric left for Berlin. His body was slowly shutting down. With insufficient insulin over such a long period of time, his blood glucose levels had been severely compromising biochemical processes providing energy to his heart, brain, and muscles. It was impossible for Eric not to have been suffering regular symptoms for many weeks, if not months: exhaustion, disrupted hunger patterns, joint and muscle pain, confusion, and slow-to-heal infections.

In *DownBeat*'s early June issue, Leonard Feather reviewed the Schuller/Bernstein *Jazz In The Concert Hall* film broadcast from earlier in the year, featuring the Schuller/Hentoff piece *Journey Into Jazz.* In surveying informal responses to the film from friends and acquaintances, the writer stated:

> Perhaps the most significant comments came from Miles Davis. Of Eric Dolphy, whose alto was a prominent feature, he said, 'Dolphy is ridiculous. I never liked his saxophone. He used to copy Bird, then changed styles just to be different.'[8]

---

* Dutch radio host Michiel de Ruyter later commented that Dolphy was four days behind schedule in getting to Berlin due to ill health and that Leo Wright was subbing for him. This was not confirmed by Karl Berger. In the liner notes to *Last Date*, Wright told de Ruyter that he had 'reached the hospital at ten past seven in the evening, just ten minutes after Eric died.'

Feather unwittingly leaned heavily on Dolphy the month of his death. In the June 18 issue of *DownBeat,* he began his 'blindfold test' segment with Miles by misidentifying the title of Eric's *Far Cry* track 'Miss Ann' as 'Mary Ann.'[9]

> DAVIS: That's got to be Eric Dolphy—nobody else could sound that bad! The next time I see him I'm going to step on his foot. You print that. I think he's ridiculous. He's a sad s***.
> FEATHER: *DownBeat* won't print those words.
> DAVIS: Just put he's a sad shhhhhhhhh, that's all!

DEATH IN BERLIN

A decade earlier, in 1954, a nineteen-year-old Karl Hans Berger had become the house pianist at the newly founded Heidelberg jazz club Cave 54. A philosophy student throughout the 1950s, he had established a music career with his wife, the vocalist Ingrid Sertso. A Heidelberg friend had launched a small network of jazz clubs called Tangente, including one in Berlin that the couple helped open in the spring of 1964. In 1972, Berger and Sertso would help found the Creative Music Studio (CMS) in Woodstock, New York, in partnership with Ornette Coleman.

Berger's connection to Dolphy dates to the Antibes Festival in July of 1960, where he played with the ensemble of Vienna-born saxophonist Hans Koller, the first European jazz musician to receive a five-star recording review in *DownBeat.* The group took the stage immediately before the Mingus Workshop that day, and backstage introductions were made all around. Four years after that meeting, the couple played Le Chat Qui Pêche and again ran into Dolphy. The Tangente club owner had asked Berger to bring a known, American jazz name to headline for the new club's 'Jazz Galerie' night, backed by the Berger-led house band with Hans Rettenbacher on bass and Klaus Hagl on drums. Berger naturally invited Dolphy for a weekend engagement in late June. During their conversation, the couple listened to him lament Miles's harsh words. Dolphy said,' I don't know why Miles put me down like that. I really like him.'

Back in Germany on the afternoon of Saturday, June 27, the couple drove to West Berlin's Tempelhof Airport, picked up Eric, and returned to the hotel where they were all staying.[10] Fifty-eight years later, the two recalled Dolphy appearing physically uncomfortable and sweating profusely. At the Xantener Eck Hotel, a three-star pension hotel at Xantenerstrasse and Brandenbergstrasse, Eric ordered sweets for dinner: ice cream, Coca-Cola, and juice. The three then departed for the engagement's opening night, where attendance turned out to be less than expected, despite the city being crowded with convention goers and summer tourists. Dolphy carried three-ring binders with his arrangements and presented the musicians with parts.

The gig started off as best it could, and Berger recalled playing '245' among other tunes as the quartet made it through the opening set to intermission. But with an already ill Dolphy starting to show signs of confusion, they cut the evening short and returned to the hotel. The next morning, Berger and Sertso called a doctor from Eric's room, against his wishes, the pianist recalling Dolphy's desire to avoid such troubles and to simply play as scheduled that evening. Making a Sunday house call, the doctor quickly concluded that Eric was suffering from exhaustion and prescribed pills after being assured that Dolphy was not a drug addict. The doctor suggested that they call again on Monday and provided what was likely a sedative to calm his new patient. Dolphy instructed them to not cancel that evening's gig and then rested and slept most of the day.

Naturally, over half a century later, those involved with events that Sunday have varied recollections. Tangente employee Hartmut Topf, self-identified as the venue's tour manager, claimed he was assigned to fetch Eric that morning from the Xantener Eck for a sound check, and that he found Dolphy in a terrible state, wearing a red T-shirt, sweating and eating ice cream, with a bowl of ice water by his bed.[11] Topf's friend Hans Häuschler attended that evening's performance and claimed to have witnessed Topf arrive at the club in a taxi with Dolphy, who tiredly emerged and walked uneasily through the front door.

Today, Berger and Sertso do not recall Topf, or any club employee, arriving at their hotel that day for the purpose of transporting Eric to the Tangente, stating rather that the three of them drove to the club together. There waited an audience even smaller than Saturday's. But Häuschler noticed that, following a delay in the show's start, someone walked onstage only to disappear. He then heard from Topf that something was wrong, and the two discussed the likelihood of Dolphy being on drugs, perhaps too high on hashish. Topf recalled Eric then appearing onstage and flopping into a chair, standing up and staggering back and forth with a towel, perhaps fanning himself and attempting to play only to give up. In Häuschler's account, Eric dropped his instrument to the stage floor and collapsed, at which point a few audience members began leaving the club. Topf went backstage to investigate, returning to Häuschler to share that Dolphy was being taken to the hospital.

Sertso remembered things differently. 'He played the first song with us. Then he said, Excuse me, I have to go into the dressing room. He didn't return to the stage.' She remembered conferring with Berger after another few songs—'We have to look where Eric is'—and, upon venturing backstage, found Eric on the floor asking for help. 'We immediately brought him to the hospital.'

Berger recalled yet a third version: Dolphy never made it onstage that evening, having collapsed backstage before appearing for the audience. Neither of the performers recalled him dropping his instrument or collapsing onstage. Regardless, the show was abruptly canceled, and they drove Eric to the Achenbach Hospital, where staff took him in on a stretcher. The following day, Berger spoke by telephone with a hospital doctor who stated that Eric had become comatose; he had passed out from the highest blood glucose levels they had ever seen and remained unconscious in a diabetic coma. Berger recalled the doctor warning that 'it was way beyond saving him.' He telephoned Sadie with that news, recalling how she was shocked to hear of any such health problem, stating that Eric had never complained of any health issue. He then called Joyce, who later spoke with the doctor while Eric was still comatose. One of Berger's next phone calls was to multi-instrumentalist Leo Wright, then playing in a Berlin radio big band, to book him as a replacement for Monday evening's show.

Eric Dolphy Jr. died of a general circulatory collapse around 7pm that Monday, June 29, 1964. The direct cause was likely insulin shock from an injection administered by a doctor trying to bring him out of the coma in a last-chance effort to prevent brain damage and save his life. This is the explanation Hale Smith was given by Sadie.[12] The official autopsy completed by the US government foreign office on October 20 presents his cause of death as 'severe disturbance of the metabolism (diabetic coma).' The American Foreign Service's 'Report Of The Death Of An American Citizen' states the place of death not as Achenbach but rather the Wilmersdorf City Hospital on Lietzenburgerstrasse, suggesting that Eric was transferred before becoming comatose. Regardless, the very next day, Eric Sr. and Sadie were notified by US embassy telegram of their only child's death. Later, Sadie shared with *DownBeat* that Eric had no record of heart disease, or of diabetes, 'because he never complained about anything.' She attributed his death to 'his constant drive.'[13] She and Eric Sr. had not seen him since his trip to Southern California for the Ojai Festival over two years earlier.

The Smiths were in Cleveland celebrating Hale's thirty-ninth birthday on June 29 and soon received the news through Eric's network of close friends and family.[14] Soon after Berger and Sertso had been informed of his passing, a young African American couple they had never seen showed up at the club, asking for Eric's instruments. They declined and locked his alto, flute, and bass clarinet in a back room, eventually delivering all his belongings to the US embassy, which the couple reported to Joyce by telephone. Joyce's brother was a US serviceman, perhaps even stationed in Germany; he retrieved the jazz musician's body for transport back home to Los Angeles. That week, one Berlin newspaper storyline was headlined 'A Bright Star Extinguished'; another newspaper article related that 'a shadow of mourning lay over the jazz evening in the Gallery Tangente. A number of Berlin jazz fans and well-known musicians had come together to commemorate the colored American Eric Dolphy, who had died on Monday in Berlin.'[15]

Eric Dolphy Jr. was laid to rest in Los Angeles nineteen days following his thirty-sixth birthday, on July 9, at Angelus Rosedale cemetery. His gravesite is slightly over a mile from his childhood home, as a bird might fly. The *California Eagle*'s Howard Morehead commented:

> Musician friends of the late Eric Dolphy were drug by the way fellow jazzman, Charlie Mingus, acted during Eric's burial. They say that he threw himself on the grave and really boo-hooed. They all concur that he's never been that tight with anyone.... Eric and I went to City College together and one night not long after the late great Charlie Parker died, we sat up all night listening to some tapes of Bird.[16]

As Santoro relates in his Mingus biography, during the burial service Mingus stood at the graveside and shouted, 'I'm sorry, Eric.' The day before, his wife Judy bore his son, whom they named Eric Dolphy Mingus. 'Mingus broke down. Only Dannie Richmond rivaled Dolphy's musical and personal link with him. Only Buddy Collette and Britt Woodman went as far back. Jaki Byard felt there was something unresolved between the two.'[17] Priestly adds, 'That his friend and colleague... should die in mysterious circumstances, and in Berlin, seems to have burst the dam of Mingus's emotions.'[18]

The bassist had taken his post-tour Workshop to a residency at the Five Spot, starting in early June. One evening at the club that September, following Eric's passing, Mingus abruptly stopped playing after having started 'Meditations,' and, following a bit of silence, lunged forward, kicking over a table in the front row of the small club. He loudly accused the woman sitting there of sexually pursuing him. The woman, and a man at the bar, responded with their own shouts. According to an audience member, Mingus left the stage with his bass in hand:

> As he walked past the tables to the rear of the Five Spot the two voices still criticized and ridiculed him. He reached the door to the kitchen, paused, and then suddenly dropped his bass to the floor. As it cracked and broke, Mingus stormed through the doors.[19]

It was the bass he had purchased in Milan for $2,200 (roughly $20,000 today). He gave pieces of the instrument to his son to paint on. For over a year, Mingus refused to discuss Dolphy's passing with jazz writers. In belatedly published letters he sent to various journalists, he commented:

> I just kinda feel like if I just believed a little more inside myself, and not the outside, I'd see Eric Dolphy somewhere way back in my mind's eye of conversation unfinished ... This time I'd just end my thoughts out there with him, and everyone I know in jazz circles would be much happier without us both ...

In the meantime, contradictory, inaccurate accounts of Eric's death quickly circulated. Perhaps the most widespread was that emergency room doctors had assumed he was a drug addict and simply allowed him to die, or that they treated an assumed drug addict with the wrong medication. Many go so far as to echo Mingus's complaint: 'I believe Eric was murdered. So does New York doctor Finkelstein, who checked Eric just before we left for Europe. He was operated on for a tumor on the forehead. This would not have been done if Eric had been diabetic.'[20]

Mingus was justified in his suspicions regarding Dolphy's—or any African American's—health care in the USA. Eric had cleared a physical examination in New York before the European tour's departure and had undergone surgery to remove the cyst on his forehead. He passed professional medical exams and a surgical procedure without word of advanced diabetes.

On July 30, before announcing Eric's passing, *DownBeat* printed a review of *Eric Dolphy in Europe, Vol 1.* Though the album received only three and a half stars, Bill Mathieu offered some late praise:

> One thing is made clear by this album: Dolphy's playing has changed remarkably in the last three years—and for the better. His recent FM release, *Conversations*, is testimony to his advancing ideas and his increasing capability…
>
> The not-quite-making-it articulation adds to the sense-searching implicit in all Dolphy's work. It takes courage to play right on the edge of—or over —one's technical capacity. … I see Dolphy rather as a synthesizer of the past, possibly the best one there is. He stands at the fork of Charlie Parker's Road. His playing does not have the same evolved concept of freedom (especially in respect to tonality) that belongs to Archie Shepp, Ornette Coleman, and Cecil Taylor, though I suspect he will go in that direction.

1964 MEMORIALS

In Paris that summer, Ted Curson put together a group and entered a studio there on August 1 to record the Fontana label album *Tears for Dolphy*, for which he penned the title track. 'Jazzmen Swell Roster For "Eric Dolphy" Concert,' read an August 13 *Los Angeles Sentinel* storyline, accompanied by a photo of Buddy Collette. The tribute coming from his deep circle of friends welcomed the public and was held two miles from the Dolphy home at the Basin Street West Club, at Western and Pico Boulevard, with admission by donation. Performers came from all over Southern California: Gerald Wilson's band featuring Harold Land, Teddy Edwards, and Lester Robinson; the Buddy Collette Quintet; the Hampton Hawes Trio; the Curtis Amy Sextet; the Onzy Matthews Big Band. Eric's friend since childhood, Vi Redd, played too, as did Red Callendar, Ernie Freeman, Roy Ayers, John Henderson, Gene McDaniels, Al McKibbon, and Jack Wilson.

The previous week, local Black newspapers published announcements, one of which informed readers that the concert was 'being handled by his colleagues, Gerald Wilson and Buddy Collette,' and would run continuously from 5 to 10pm;

'all proceeds will be turned over to Mrs. Eric Dolphy Sr. to help in defraying the costs incurred as a result of her son's sudden death.'[21]

On the day of the concert, John Coltrane was in the middle of a long engagement at San Francisco's Jazz Workshop. Eric's flute and bass clarinet were bequeathed by Eric Sr. and Sadie to Coltrane, who played the flute on one of his last recordings. It is said that Sadie had been having nightmares of her late son playing those instruments and had wanted Coltrane to have them.[22] Trane was in mourning over the loss of his musical brother of a decade, keeping busy with a club schedule, allowing his performances to aid and channel his grief. He canceled recording sessions in the months following Eric's passing while focusing on special material to be recorded that December: *A Love Supreme*. In light of Coltrane's spiritual and artistic journey with Dolphy, one can imagine this timeless disc's inspiration partly emerging from reckoning with the loss of his musical and spiritual comrade. He said of Eric's passing, 'Whatever I'd say would be an understatement. I can only say my life was made much better by knowing him. He was one of the greatest people I've ever known, as a man, a friend, and a musician.' While on the road thereafter, Coltrane traveled with Eric's photo, taping it to his hotel room's wall.[23]

In August of 1965, Coltrane telephoned the Dolphys to ask about their safety during the Watts uprising. By that time, he had completed the *Transition* album recordings, marking the telling continuation of the spirituality expressed in *A Love Supreme* and following a trajectory toward the free jazz found in his live sets and on *Ascension*, *Om*, and *Interstellar Space*.

DownBeat's August 13 issue featured a formal death announcement. The magazine—an ogre to this musician, one that both lifted and tormented the man's professional life—was on this occasion judicious, referring to the deceased as 'one of the most significant and accomplished musicians associated with the new wave of jazz freedom,' adding that he 'rapidly established himself as a leading voice in the jazz avant-garde.' This short article, titled 'Reed Man Eric Dolphy Dies In Berlin,' announced that 'the news, spreading quickly through the jazz world by word of mouth, was met with a shocked disbelief that was almost anger.'

Nat Hentoff wrote poignantly in the magazine's follow-up issue:

> What he was capable of is still alive on records and in memories. Like Booker Little, he died much, much too young. There is never any right

> age to die, but Eric went far too soon. There was so much more to come, so much more he was reaching for and would have eventually found, only then to go on to search more deeply into himself and into the world around him. At least, while he was alive, Eric was fully alive in his music by contrast to those of us who mostly just exist and whose reactions are mostly veiled—to ourselves as well as to others.[24]

Eric Sr. and Sadie drove across the continent that October to collect Eric's things, visiting with New York family. Don Heckman, a young, supportive voice for Eric in jazz criticism, wrote a notable early October *DownBeat* cover story, 'The Woodwinds Of Change,' in which he 'analyzes the innovations in jazz expression brought about by such men as John Coltrane, Eric Dolphy, Roland Kirk, and Steve Lacy.' The cover was dominated by a dramatic Herb Snitzer photo of Dolphy on bass clarinet and Coltrane on soprano sax, blowing hard at the Village Gate. In the original photo's uncropped foreground were Reggie Workman and Jimmy Garrison. The article contained a dedicated sidebar, 'The Value Of Eric Dolphy,' thoughtfully summarizing the historical importance of Eric's bass clarinet playing and how, as a non-reed instrument, the flute was approached by the innovative musician in an entirely different manner from other jazz musicians. 'That he came as far as he did toward this goal while performing brilliantly on two other instruments only serves to underline the great void his death has left.'[25]

Several more notable testimonials appeared before the end of 1964. Dolphy was elected to the *DownBeat* Reader's Poll Hall Of Fame, and Fontana Records produced an album titled *The Winners Of DownBeat's Readers Poll, 1964*, with a cover image of Eric playing alto sax. His featured track on that disc is the soaring, searing alto solo on 'Bemoanable Lady,' from Mingus's strange *Pre-Bird*.

In December, Cambridge Records released *Dedicated To Eric Dolphy*, a touching album spearheaded by vibist/composer Harold Faberman and featuring Jerome Richardson, Richard Davis, Mel Lewis, George Duvivier, Jim Hall, and others performing works by Faberman, John Lewis, William Smith, and Schuller. Leonard Feather, who held Dolphy up to ridicule in his *DownBeat* blindfold tests, wrote the album's liner notes; following introductory paragraphs of predictable accolades, he wrote that Dolphy 'fell far short of his ultimate objective. . . . His technique still trailed behind his restless ideas; some of the exotic tonal effects in which he indulged seemed less like innovation than grotesque sound for its own sake.'[26]

There remains still today the matter of unreleased recordings made by several groups Eric had been playing with in mid-June. He recorded twice on Blue Note with the permission of FM Records in early 1964, and it is unknown what capacity either label would have had in dealing with Eric's future recordings. Byrd, a Blue Note artist featured on the Paris recordings, convinced his label to negotiate for these tapes with pianist and session producer Jacque Diéval. According to Geri Allen, writing in 1983:

> A futile attempt to retrieve these tapes was recently made by Frank Wolff of Blue Note Records . . . who was interested in securing these tapes for possible marketing. The tapes were found in the possession of the State of France and the only avenue to secure these, the last documented recordings of Dolphy's works, was through Jacque Diéval who had the power to release these tapes. Diéval, however, is said to have asked Wolff to include some of his recent trio recordings as a part of the package, and he would then sell the Dolphy tapes as well. Blue Note Records was only interested in the Dolphy recordings, so they were forced to abandon these urgently needed historical documents.[27]

After Blue Note rejected the Frenchman's self-interested offer, Byrd turned unsuccessfully to an equally nonplussed Columbia Records. Following the pianist's death in 2012, control of the tapes likely fell to the French government.

AFTER DOLPHY

It is perfectly human to deny the news of a loved one's death, or that of a friend, or cultural hero as Dolphy was to so many. Amiri Baraka recalled spending time in solitary confinement following the Newark riots of 1967, sitting in his jail cell, whistling every Coltrane tune he could think of, only to be told of the musician's death at the end of the day. 'But I knew even then that that was impossible.'[28] Many felt similarly about the news of Eric Dolphy's passing: that it was impossible. Coltrane's funeral service opened with the Albert Ayler Quartet and came to an end with the Ornette Coleman Quartet. Dolphy's spirit had company that afternoon, as he and Coltrane listened to their friends play with such passionate, hard-earned freedom. Coltrane, who died of liver cancer three years after Eric's passing, moved into radical new territory during live performances and on many tracks from the sixteen albums he recorded before leaving the world. He modified his solo style, formal structures, and range of collaborators, openly expressing his spiritual quest and religiosity. 'Selflessness,' a wide-open jam featuring Pharoah Sanders and Alice Coltrane, among others, was recorded in October of 1965, but like many other Coltrane recordings from after 1964, it was not released for years.

If Dolphy had lived longer, he might have been motivated to make a return visit to New York in October 1964 to collaborate in Bill Dixon's groundbreaking series of concerts, *The October Revolution In Jazz*, and in one of its treasured outgrowths, the Jazz Composers' Guild, dominated by some of the best free-jazz minds the city had to offer. Though invited, Ornette quietly declined and later returned to his place on club stages, bringing a trio into the Village Vanguard that January. Roswell Rudd, Archie Shepp, Cecil Taylor, Burton Greene, Sun Ra, and Carla and Paul Bley—to name just a few participants in a newly reinvigorated progressive jazz scene—continued spreading their sounds, sharing their music in clubs and festivals as the name Eric Dolphy slowly entered history. It is easy to imagine him making records for ESP-Disk, Bernard Stollman's quixotic label, which issued a series of free jazz releases throughout the 1960s, the first being Ayler's *Spiritual Unity*, recorded in the weeks following Dolphy's death. By the start of 1965, a host of progressive and free-jazz players had helped create a larger avant-garde wave that flowed in multiple directions and still exists today.

Writing about 1960s avant-garde jazz, George E. Lewis captured the depth of free jazz movement influences found in groups such as Chicago's AACM (Association For The Advancement Of Creative Musicians), of which he was a member—a collective that, by 1963–64, had begun incorporating unusual instruments, timbral experimentation, and new creative concepts into their compositions and collective improvisations.* The model of artists cooperatively managing their own music—without the intervention of club owners, critics, or record executives—as exemplified by the AACM and Jazz Composers' Guild, spread to other collectives like St. Louis's Black Artists Guild.

Reeds player and composer Roscoe Mitchell is but just one example of the successful, radicalized jazz musician of his generation, uncompromising in his

---

* The AACM's members included many other progressive jazz legends: Muhal Richard Abrams, Fred Anderson, Renee Baker, Jack DeJohnette, Fred Hopkins, Steve McCall, Wadada Leo Smith, Ann E. Ward, and Rita Warford, and Famoudou Don Moye, to name only a few.

embrace of all instrumental sound, advanced methods of solo and collective improvisation, and his bonding of music's meaning to the self and community. Mitchell, along with fellow multi-instrumentalists Lester Bowie, Malachi Favors, Joseph Jarman, and Phillip Wilson, formed the Art Ensemble Of Chicago, which toured Europe in 1968. A few of the many other jazz artists emerging from this milieu of the 1960s avant-garde include Anthony Braxton and Henry Threadgill.

Subsequent generations have had to make do with memories of Dolphy and documents of his work: recordings, film and video, photographs, and the published words by and about him. Few jazz musicians have overtly copied the Dolphy style as part of their own manner of improvising, particularly the leaps, bird calls, and specific signature riffs and passages that mark his output. No one capable of imitating his virtuosity and extending their own improvisational freedom would have simply copied his licks, so to speak. Rather, a larger, more important influence flows in the freedom that countless players recognized in his music—and who, instead of mimicking the master, took license and inspiration to imbue their own vocabularies with new palettes of sound, techniques, references, and a revitalized sense of discovery.

Multifaceted musicians producing cross-over works using jazz, improvisation, global traditions, and contemporary classical music never disappeared, and they are too numerous to outline even briefly. Many years after Dolphy's death, Gunther Schuller reflected on the impact Eric had had on the nascent third stream scene, pushing jazz and classical music 'to cross-fertilize in significant ways, technically, conceptually and stylistically, a process that has continued so that we have now reached the point where the borderline between what used to be called jazz and what used to be called classical music is so blurred and so overlapping it defies labeling.'[29] Jazz musicians and contemporary classical composers have since gone wherever they wished in search of stylistic fusions and inspiration.

Perhaps freedom itself, and the truths that only freedom and music can bring, have remained Eric Dolphy's most important gift.

ACKNOWLEDGMENTS

This book could not have been written without the love, encouragement, and patience of my wife Nanci. Two talented friends who provided essential editorial assistance and to whom I am indebted are Carter Scholz and Jeff Schwartz. Jawbone Press editor Tom Seabrook further shaped and greatly improved the book with his diligence and thoughtful suggestions. A sabbatical granted by California State University, Dominguez Hills, proved extremely helpful in the preparation of this project.

For many years, the earliest hints of this book sat in the form of a bare-bones skeleton I called the 'Dolphy Diary,' a side project of mine drawing together facts, references, discographic detail, and timelines of this great artist's life. In conversations over those years, many musicians from the jazz and improvisation communities I have participated in have offered their insight and passion regarding Eric Dolphy's recordings, development, and impact. Thanks for sharing.

WORKS CITED

BOOKS

George Reid Andrews, *Afro-Latin America, 1800–2000* (Oxford University, 2004)

Amiri Baraka (as Leroi Jones), *Blues People: Negro Music In White America* (Quill/William Morrow, 1999)

Cora Bryant et al, *Central Avenue Sounds: Jazz In Los Angeles* (University Of California, 1998)

Nick Catalano, *Clifford Brown: The Life And Art Of The Legendary Jazz Trumpeter* (Oxford University, 2001)

Bill Cole, *John Coltrane* (Da Capo, 2001)

Ted Gioia, *West Coast Jazz: Modern Jazz In California, 1945–1960* (University Of California, 1998)

Raymond Horricks, *The Importance Of Being Eric Dolphy (Jazz Avant-Garde Series)* (DJ Costello, 1989)

Steven L. Isoardi, *The Dark Tree: Jazz And The Community Arts In Los Angeles* (University Of California, 2006)

Ekkeherd Jost, *Free Jazz* (Da Capo, 1981)

Robin D.G. Kelley, *Thelonious Monk: The Life And Times Of An American Original* (Free Press, 2009)

Richard Koloda, *Holy Ghost: The Life & Death Of Free Jazz Pioneer Albert Ayler* (Jawbone, 2022)

Richard Kostelanetz, *The Theater Of Mixed Means: An Introduction To Happenings, Kinetic Environments, And Other Mixed-Means Performances* (Dial, 1968)

Aiden Levy, *Saxophone Colossus: The Life And Music Of Sonny Rollins* (Hachette Book Group, 2022)

George E. Lewis, *A Power Stronger Than Itself: The Aacm And American Experimental Music* (University Of Chicago, 2008)

John Litweiler, *Ornette Coleman: A Harmolodic Life* (William Morrow & Co., 1992)

Olivier Messiaen, John Satterfield (trans), *The Technique Of My Musical Language* (Alphonse Leduc, Editions Musicale, 1944)

Barry Miles, *Zappa: A Biography* (Grove, 2004)

Ingrid Monson, *Saying Something: Jazz Improvisation And Interaction* (University Of Chicago, 1996)

Gordon Mumma, *Cybersonic Arts: Adventures In American New Music* (University Of Illinois, 2015)

Eric Porter, *What Is This Thing Called Jazz? African American Musicians And Artists, Critics, And Activists* (University Of California, 2002)

Lewis Porter, *John Coltrane: His Life And Music* (University Of Michigan, 1999)

Roy Porter and David Keller, *There And Back: The Roy Porter Story* (Bayou, 1991)

Brian Priestly, *Mingus: A Critical Biography* (Da Capo, 1983)

Ben Ratliff, *Coltrane: The Story Of A Sound* (Picador, 2008)

Uwe Reichardt, *Like A Human Voice: The Eric Dolphy Discography (Jazz Index Reference Series no. 2)* (Norbert Ruecker, 1986)

Gene Santoro, *Myself When I Am Real: The Life And Music Of Charles Mingus* (Oxford University, 2000)

Vladimir Simosko and Barry Tepperman, *Eric Dolphy: A Musical Biography And Discography (Revised Edition)* (Da Capo, 1996)

Herb Snitzer, *Glorious Days And Nights: A Jazz Memoir* (University Press Of Mississippi, 2011)

John F. Szewd, *Space Is The Place: The Lives And Times Of Sun Ra* (Pantheon Books, 1997)

Horace Tapscott, Steven Isoardi (ed), *Songs Of The Unsung: The Musical And Social Journey Of Horace Tapscott* (Duke University, 2001)

Lorenzo Thomas and Aldon Nielsen, *Don't Deny My Name: Words And Music And The Black Intellectual Tradition* (University Of Michigan, 2008)

David Toop, *Into The Maelstrom: Music, Improvisation And The Dream Of Freedom: Before 1970* (Bloomsbury Academic, 2016)

Peter Vacher, *Swingin' On Central Avenue: African American Jazz In Los Angeles* (Rowman & Littlefield, 2015)

Val Wilmer, *As Serious As Your Life: Black Music And The Free Jazz Revolution, 1957–1977* (Serpent's Tail Classics, 2018)

Mike Zwerin, *Close Enough For Jazz* (Quartet, 1983)

CHAPTERS, JOURNALS, THESES

Geri Allen, *Eric Dolphy: A Musical Analysis Of Three Pieces With A Brief Biography*, master's thesis in ethnomusicology, University Of Pittsburgh, 1983; cited in *Jazz & Culture* vol. 3 no. 2 (University Of Illinois, fall/winter 2020)

Paul Austerlitz, 'Jazz Consciousness,' in Lewis R. Gordon and Jane Anna Gordon (eds), *A Companion To African American Studies* (Blackwell, 2006)

Ralf Dietrich, 'Bob James And Eric Dolphy: ONCE In A Lifetime,' *Semja Update: Southeastern Michigan Jazz Association newsletter*, December 1999

Jacqueline Cogdell Djedje, 'California Black Gospel Music Traditions,' in Jacqueline Cogdell Djedje and Eddie S. Meadows (eds), *California Soul: Music Of African Americans In The West* (University of California, 1998)

Yoko Suzuki, 'Invisible Woman: Vi Redd's Contributions As A Jazz Saxophonist,' *American Music Review* vol. XLII no. 2, spring 2013

LINER NOTES

George Avakian, liner notes to *The Sextet Of Orchestra USA* (RCA, 1965)

Sara Cassey, liner notes to *Just Jazz!* (Audio Fidelity, 1965)

Robert Dick, liner notes to *The Other Flute* (GM Recordings, 1986)

Ron Eyre, liner notes to *Outward Bound* (Prestige, 1960)

Leonard Feather, liner notes to *Dedicated To Eric Dolphy* (Cambridge Records, 1964)

Ira Gitler, liner notes to *The Great Concert Of Eric Dolphy* (Prestige, 1974)

Joe Goldberg, liner notes to *Out There!* (Prestige, 1960)

Uri Hampton, liner notes to *Charles Mingus/Eric Dolphy Sextet: The Complete Bremen Concert* (Jazz Lips, 2010)

Nat Hentoff, liner notes to *Charles Mingus Presents Charles Mingus* (Candid, 1961)

Nat Hentoff, liner notes to *Images* (Prestige, 1975)

Nat Hentoff, liner notes to *Last Date* (Limelight, 1979)

Nat Hentoff, liner notes to *Point Of Departure* (Blue Note, 1964)

Nat Hentoff, liner notes to *Screamin' The Blues* (Prestige, 1961)

Morton James, liner notes to *Eric Dolphy In Europe* (Essential Jazz Classics, 2019)

Ashley Kahn, liner notes to *John Coltrane With Eric Dolphy: Evenings At The Village Gate* (Impulse!, 2023)

Bill Kirchner, 'The Sessions,' liner notes to *Eric Dolphy: The Complete Prestige Recordings* (Prestige, 1995)

John Kruth, liner notes to *Eric Dolphy: Musical Prophet* (Resonance Records, 2019)

Ken McIntyre, liner notes to *Eric Dolphy: Fire Waltz* (Prestige, 1978)

James Newton, 'From The Field Holler To Outer Space,' liner notes to *Eric Dolphy: Musical Prophet* (Resonance Records, 2019)

James Newton, liner notes to *Eric Dolphy: Other Aspects* (Blue Note, 1987)

Robert Palmer, liner notes to *Ornette Coleman: Beauty Is A Rare Thing* (Atlantic/Rhino, 1993)

Robert Palmer, liner notes to *Mingus at Antibes* (Atlantic, 1976)

Molly Sants, liner notes to *Eric Dolphy: Out There + Looking Ahead* (American Jazz Classics, 2011)

Phil Schaap, liner notes to *Eric Dolphy: Dash One* (Prestige, 1982)

Gunther Schuller, liner notes to *Vintage Dolphy* (GM Recordings, 1986)

Vladimir Simosko, liner notes to *Eric Dolphy: The Illinois University Concert* (Blue Note, 1999)

A.B. Spellman, liner notes to *Out To Lunch!* (Blue Note, 1964)
Simon Spillett, liner notes to *So Many Things: The European Tour 1961, The John Coltrane Quintet Featuring Eric Dolphy* (Acrobat, 2015)
Zan Stewart, 'Out There: The Angelic Passion Of Eric Dolphy,' liner notes to *Eric Dolphy: The Complete Prestige Recordings* (Prestige, 1995)
David Wild, liner notes to *Coltrane: The Complete 1961 Village Vanguard Recordings* (Impulse!, 1997)
Martin Williams, liner notes to *Ezz-thetics* (Riverside, 1961)
Martin Williams, liner notes to *Vintage Dolphy* (GM Recordings, 1986)
Patricia Willard, liner notes to *Black California* (Savoy/Arista, 1976)
Reggie Workman, liner notes to *John Coltrane With Eric Dolphy: Evenings At The Village Gate* (Impulse!, 2023)
——, liner notes to *Eric Dolphy/Booker Little Quintet At The Five Spot: Complete Edition* (Essential Jazz Classics, 2012)
——, liner notes to *Gongs East* (Warner Bros, 1959)
——, liner notes to *Iron Man* (Douglas International, 1968)

FILMS/DVDS

Hans Hylkema (director), *De Laatste Sessie* (*The Last Date*) (Blowpipe/Moskwood Media, 1991)
Tom Surgal (director), *Fire Music: A History Of The Free Jazz Revolution* (2021)
Eric Dolphy In Europe: 1961–1964 (Impro-Jazz DVD, 2006)
Charles Mingus Live In '64 (Realin' In The Years Productions/Naxos DVD, 2007)

PERIODICALS

Phyl Garland, 'The Many "Bags" Of Oliver Nelson,' *Ebony*, November 1968
Geoffrey Himes, 'Eric Dolphy: It's All Out There Now,' *Jazz Times*, June 18, 2020
Bobby Hutcherson, 'Bobby Hutcherson On Eric Dolphy' *Stop Smiling* issue 34, 2008
Graham Lock, 'The Man Who Never Wasn't,' *The Wire* no. 22, December 1985: 16–17
Marc Meyers, 'George Wein On The Rebel Festival,' *Jazzwax*, July 2010
Mitch Meyers, 'Spirits, Ghosts, Witches, And Devils: The Life And Death Of Albert Ayler,' *Magnet*, October/November 2004
M.H. Miller, 'The Man Who Brian Eno Called "The Daddy Of Us All,"' *New York Times Style Magazine*, July 22, 2020
Bill Shoemaker, 'Gunther Schuller: Third Stream From The Source,' *Jazz Times*, March 12, 2021
Kirk Silsbee, 'Don Cherry Interview,' *Cadence* no. 29 (4), April 2003: 5–11
Martin Williams, 'Introducing Eric Dolphy,' *The Jazz Review* vol. 3 no. 5, June 1960: 16-17
——, *The Wire* issue 2, winter 1982–83
——, *The Wire* issue 3, spring 1983

DOWNBEAT

Amiri Baraka (Leroi Jones), 'Caught In The Act,' *DownBeat* vol. 31 no. 2, January 16, 1964
Bill Coss, 'Cecil Taylor's Struggle For Existence: Portrait Of The Artist As A Coiled Spring,' *DownBeat* vol. 28 no. 22, October 26, 1961: 21
Bill Coss, 'Caught In The Act: A Report Of A Most Remarkable Event,' *DownBeat* vol. 29 no. 30, December 6, 1962: 40
Bill Coss, review of 'Reflections And Entrances,' *DownBeat* vol. 30 no. 2, January 17, 1963: 42–43
Bill Coss, 'John Lewis And The Orchestra,' *DownBeat* vol. 30 no. 4, February 14, 1963: 20
Bill Coss, 'Caught In The Act,' *DownBeat* vol. 30 no. 4, February 14, 1963: 38
Don DeMichael, review of *Outward Bound*, *DownBeat* vol. 27 no. 18, September 1, 1960: 35–36
Don DeMichael, review of Oliver Nelson, *DownBeat* vol. 29 no. 7, March 29, 1962: 32
Don DeMichael, 'John Coltrane And Eric Dolphy Answer The Jazz Critics,' *DownBeat* vol. 29 no. 8, April 12, 1962: 20–23
Don DeMichael, review of *Far Cry*, *DownBeat* vol. 29 no. 29, November 22, 1962: 30
Leonard Feather, 'Blindfold Test,' *DownBeat* vol. 28 no. 6, March 16, 1961: 33
Leonard Feather, 'Blindfold Test,' *DownBeat* vol. 29 no. 13, June 21, 1962: 35
Leonard Feather, 'Blindfold Test,' *DownBeat* vol. 30 no.23, August 15, 1963: 35
Leonard Feather, 'Blindfold Test,' *DownBeat* vol. 31 no. 12, May 21, 1964: 32

Leonard Feather, 'Blindfold Test,' *DownBeat* vol. 31 no. 14, June 18, 1964: 31
Leonard Feather, 'Feather's Nest,' *DownBeat* vol. 31 no. 13, June 4, 1964: 37
Ira Gitler, review of *Charles Mingus Presents Charles Mingus*, *DownBeat* vol. 28 no. 7, March 30, 1961: 38
Ira Gitler, review of Cal Tjader's *Latin Bag*, *DownBeat vol.* 29 no. 4, February 15, 1962: 34
Ira Gitler, review of *Coltrane: 'Live' At The Village Vanguard*, *DownBeat* vol. 29 no. 9, April 26, 1962: 29
Ira Gitler, review of Booker Little's *Out Front*, *DownBeat* vol. 29 no. 5, March 15, 1962: 34
Don Heckman, 'Ken Mcintyre, A Musician's Philosophy,' *DownBeat* vol. 30 no. 29, November 7, 1963: 18-19
Don Heckman, 'The Woodwinds Of Change,' *DownBeat* vol. 31 no. 27, October 8, 1964: 8
Nat Hentoff, 'Second Chorus,' *DownBeat* vol. 31 no. 24, August 27, 1964
Gene Lees, 'View Of The Third Stream,' *DownBeat* vol. 31 no. 4, February 13, 1964: 16–17
Phillip Lutz, 'Eric Dolphy: The "Prophet" Of Freedom,' *DownBeat*, December 17, 2018
B.M., review of *Conversations*, *DownBeat* vol. 31 no. 2, January 16, 1964: 26
Harvey Pekar, review of *Eric Dolphy At The Five Spot, Volume I*, *DownBeat* vol. 29 no. 22, August 16, 1962: 24–25
Harvey Pekar, review of *Eric Dolphy At The Five Spot, Volume II*, *DownBeat* vol. 31 no. 4, February 13, 1964: 24
John Tynan, 'Take 5,' *DownBeat* vol. 28 no. 24, November 23, 1961: 40
John Tynan, review of *Free Jazz*, *DownBeat* vol. 29 no. 2, January 18, 1962
John Tynan, 'Chico's Changed,' *DownBeat* vol. 30 no. 8, March 28, 1963: 18–19
John Tynan, review of *Pre-Bird*, *DownBeat* vol. 28 no. 26, December 21, 1961
Pete Welding, review of Max Roach's *Percussion Bitter Sweet*, *DownBeat* vol. 29 no. 1, January 4, 1962: 30
Pete Welding, review of Ron Carter's *Where?*, *DownBeat* vol. 29 no. 19, September 27, 1962: 27
Pete Welding, review of *Jazz Abstractions*, *DownBeat* vol. 29 no. 30, December 6, 1962: 34
Pete Welding, review of *John Coltrane 'Live' At The Village Vanguard*, *DownBeat* vol. 29 no. 9, April 26, 1962: 29
Martin Williams, review of *Jazz Abstractions*, *DownBeat* vol. 29 no. 10, May 10, 1962: 33–34
Martin Williams, review of Sonny Rollins/John Lewis Concert at the YM-YHCA, *DownBeat* vol. 29 no. 14, July 5, 1962: 38
J.S.W., review of *Caribé*, *DownBeat* vol. 28 no. 11, May 25, 1961: 34
——, 'Caught In The Act,' *DownBeat* vol. 30 no. 11, May 9, 1963: 34
——, 'Caught In The Act,' *DownBeat* vol. 30 no. 27, October 10, 1963: 47
——, 'Caught In The Act,' *DownBeat* vol. 31 no. 9, April 9, 1964: 43
——, 'Chords And Discords,' *DownBeat* vol. 29 no. 11, May 24, 1962: 8
——, 'Chords And Discords,' *DownBeat* vol. 30 no. 10, April 25, 1963: 9–10
——, 'Reed Man Eric Dolphy Dies In Berlin,' *DownBeat* vol. 31 no. 23, August 13, 1964: 8
——, 'Strictly Ad Lib,' *DownBeat* vol. 30 no. 11, May 9, 1963: 6
——, 'Strictly Ad Lib,' *DownBeat* vol. 29 no. 8, April 12, 1962: 11
——, 'Strictly Ad Lib: Chicago,' *DownBeat* vol. 30 no. 4, February 14, 1963: 47
——, 'Strictly Ad Lib: Cincinnati,' *DownBeat* vol. 30 no. 7, March 14, 1963: 46
——, 'Strictly Ad Lib,' *DownBeat* vol. 30 no. 17, August 1, 1963: 43
——, review of George Russell's *Ezz-Thetics*, *DownBeat* vol. 28 no. 23, November 9, 1961
——, advertisement for George Russell's *Lydian Chromatic Concept*, *DownBeat* vol. 29 no. 21, August 2, 1962: 4
——, letter to the editor, *DownBeat* vol. 28 no. 10, June 8, 1961: 8
——, Dolphy receives the New Star Alto award, *DownBeat* vol. 28 no. 17, August 3, 1961
——, review of John Coltrane Sextet at Monterrey Jazz Festival, *DownBeat* vol. 28 no. 23, November 9, 1961

CALIFORNIA EAGLE

C.E. Lloyd, 'City College News,' *California Eagle*, December 16, 1948: 7

C.E. Lloyd, 'Casing The Kids,' *California Eagle*, April 28, 1949: 7
Howard Morehead, 'Hollywood My Way,' *California Eagle*, July 23, 1964: 19
Phyllis Scott, 'Trail Blazers: Fay Allen,' *California Eagle*, April 10, 1947: 7
Bill Smallwood, *California Eagle*, September 8, 1960
Bill Smallwood, *California Eagle*, June 1, 1961
Bill Smallwood, 'Joyce Mordecai Visited Los Angeles,' *California Eagle*, August 16, 1962
——, 'LACC fraternities At The Pueblo Del Rio Clubhouse,' *California Eagle*, October 2, 1947
——, 'Blondy Smith And Crew Newest Act In Business,' *California Eagle*, September 9, 1948: 17
——, 'Porter Hired Don Fields As His Manager,' *California Eagle*, October 21, 1948: 16
——, 'Briefly Joining Trumpeter Nat Meeks's Be-Bop Orchestra,' *California Eagle*, November 4, 1948
——, 'Roy Porter And Band Are Fast Climbing Into The Local Spotlight,' *California Eagle*, January 27, 1949
——, 'Monte Easter's New Octet Known As Monte's Challengers,' *California Eagle*, February 3, 1949
——, 'Dolphy's Combo Visits Dorsey High,' *California Eagle*, March 3, 1949
——, 'Roy Porter And His Band Have Waxed Some New Numbers On Knockout Label,' *California Eagle*, September 1, 1949: 14
——, 'This Year's Affair One Of The Best,' *California Eagle*, June 9, 1955
——, advertisement placed by the Club Oasis, *California Eagle*, March 29, 1956: 10
——, 'Clever Comic In New Revue For Funsters,' *California Eagle*, February 18, 1957

LOS ANGELES SENTINEL

Florence Cadrez, 'Mostly 'Bout Musicians,' *Los Angeles Sentinel*, January 17, 1957: A17
Hunter Hancock, 'Huntin' With Hunter,' *Los Angeles Sentinel*, October 14, 1948: 19
Hazel L. Lamarre, 'APPLAUSE!: In the Theatre,' *Los Angeles Sentinel*, April 14, 1955: A10
Stanley Robertson, 'A Square In The Social Circle: Laments Of A Bleary Eyed Week-Ender,' *Los Angeles Sentinel*, November 9, 1950: C3
Stanley Robertson, 'A Square In The Social Circle: Orchids And Onions,' *Los Angeles Sentinel*, March 20, 1952: C4
Stanley Robertson, 'Three Jazz Musicians Face Narcotic Raps,' *Los Angeles Sentinel*, February 21, 1957: A1
Stanley Robertson, 'L.A. Confidential: Time To Say Goodbye,' *Los Angeles Sentinel*, November 29, 1990: A6
Stanley Robertson, 'New Abbey Lincoln Album Hits Pay Dirt,' *Los Angeles Sentinel*, August 17, 1961: C3
——, 'Woodlawn YW Lists Program During Yuletide,' *Los Angeles Sentinel*, December 25, 1947: 6
——, 'Roy Porter's New 17-Piece Band Is Top Local Outfit,' *Los Angeles Sentinel*, March 16, 1950: B2
——, 'Dillitanti Club Enjoys Outings,' *Los Angeles Sentinel*, August 30, 1951: C1
——, '"Way Out" Jazz Predicted For Ojai Musical Show,' *Los Angeles Sentinel*, April 26, 1962: C2
——, 'Jazzmen Swell Roster For "Eric Dolphy" Concert,' *Los Angeles Sentinel*, August 13, 1964: B5
——, 'A Tour Of Mainland China Is A Tour Of A Lifetime,' *Los Angeles Sentinel*, October 30, 1980
——, 'Eric Dolphy Remembered,' *Los Angeles Sentinel*, July 5, 1984: B9
——, 'Basin-West Blasts Again With Eric Dolphy Memorial,' *Los Angeles Sentinel*, August 6, 1984: B8
——, 'Phil Ranelin's *Who Is Eric Dolphy*... William Grant Still Community Arts Center,' *Los Angeles Sentinel*, March 17, 2005: B5

OTHER NEWSPAPER ARTICLES

John Bryan, 'Surprise Stars,' *San Francisco Examiner*, September 22, 1961: 10
Don Nelsen, *New York Daily News*, July 9, 1961: 123
William Ewald, 'Timex Jazz Show Was Death On Jazz,' United Press International, November 11, 1958
Don Heckman, 'Imagine The Melodies That Might Have Been,' *Los Angeles Times*, June 27, 2003: 181
William Grimes, 'Hale Smith, Who Broke Borders Of Classical And Jazz, Is Dead At 84,' *New York Times*, November 27, 2009

Harold L. Keith, 'Data 'Bout Discs,' *Pittsburgh Courier*, July 29, 1961: 29
E.B.R., 'Chico Hits It Right,' *Cincinnati Enquirer*, April 28, 1959
Ben Ratliff, 'Jazz Enigma Of The 60s Has An Encore,' *New York Times*, May 27, 2014
Harvey Siders, 'Why All This Jazz About Third Stream,' *Boston Globe*, March 29, 1964: 51
Art Smith, 'Jazz For The Masses? Not Hardly,' *Tampa Bay Tribune*, November 11, 1958: 89
Peter Watrous, '50 Years Of Jazz, In The Hands Of Gerald Wilson,' *New York Times*, October 20, 1988
Thomas Willis, 'Composer Gets Top Help In Musical Explication,' *Chicago Tribune*, October 20, 1963: 143
Russ Wilson, 'Charlie Mingus Is Sensitive, Dedicated Jazz Musician,' *Oakland Tribune*, December 11, 1960: 131
Russ Wilson, 'World Of Jazz: Charles Mingus Returns To Bay,' *Oakland Tribune*, December 16, 1960: 38
Mike Zwerin, 'Remembering Dolphy, "Undisciplined Genius,"' *New York Times*, October 6, 2004
——, 'Charles Mingus At The Showboat,' *Philadelphia Daily News*, October 12, 1960
——, 'Dance Unit to Appear,' *Los Angeles Examiner*, December 6, 1957
——, 'Mercury Records Line Up Featuring The Platters And Featuring Gerald Wilson,' *Evening Citizen News*, December 8, 1956: 17
——, 'Modern Jazz Musical Art Society Of Community College, Brooklyn,' *New York Daily News*, February 20, 1964
——, 'Nat Hentoff, Columnist, Critic, And Giant Of Jazz Writing, Dies At 91,' *Guardian*, January 8, 2017
——, 'Porter Band Plays Wichita Falls,' *Times Record News* (Wichita Falls), April 30, 1949: 10
——, review of *Screamin' The Blues*, *The Record* (Hackensack/Bergen), March 18, 1961
——, review of *Looking Ahead*, *Pittsburgh Courier*, December 12, 1960: 22
——, review of *Caribé*, *Pittsburgh Courier*, May 6, 1961: 29
——, 'Roy Porter Plays With Howard McGhee Group,' *Los Angeles Daily News*, June 4, 1945: 32

WEBSITES

Clifford Allen, 'Impressions Of Eric Dolphy,' *All About Jazz*, March 12, 2008
Jonathan Blumhoffer, 'Rethinking The Repertoire #19—Charles Ives' Orchestral Set No. 2,' *The Arts Fuse*, March 16, 2018
Coltrane Research Facebook Group
Eric Dolphy discography, compiled and maintained by Nobuaki Togashi, Kohji 'Shaolin' Matsubayashi, and Masayuki Hatta, jazzdisco.org
Monte Easter, Kansas City Jazz Homepage
Ethan Iverson, interview with James Newton, *Do The M@Th*, March 2017
Fred Jung, 'A Fireside Chat With Bobby Bradford,' *Jazz Weekly*, May 13, 2003
Thom Jurek, 'Bennie Maupin Biography,' *All Music*
John Kruth, 'Eric Dolphy Turns 80/God Bless The Child,' *Perfect Sound Forever*, August 2008
Susan Salluce, 'Howard "Boots" Mcghee: Legendary Long Boarder With A Legacy,' susansalluce.org, November 16, 2013
Alan Saul website, adale.org

MISCELLANY

Richard Davis, interview with Josephine Reed, 'Artworks,' NEA Jazz Masters Series
Tom Reney, 'Hampton Hawes And The Pardon From JFK,' New England Public Radio, July 14, 2015
Buddy Collette, interview with Steven Isoardi, UCLA Oral History/Central Avenue Sounds tape number V, side one, September 28, 1989
Bennie Maupin, interview with Greg Bendian, *Yale Oral History, Major Figures In American Music*, March 14, 2013
Ornette Coleman interview, *Yale Oral History, Major Figures In American Music*, December 19, 1985
Karl Berger and Ingrid Sertso, interview with Jonathon Grasse, unpublished, June 6, 2022
Guernsey's Jazz Auction, Lot 272 (Dolphy's alto), February 20, 2005
——, *The Report Of The Death Of An American Citizen*, issued by the American Foreign Service, US Mission Berlin, Germany, Consular Services, November 23, 1964
——, US Census, Panama Canal Zone, 1920
——, US Census, 1930, 1940, 1950
——, Costa Rica Registro Civil, 1823–1975

ENDNOTES

INTRODUCTION

1 Ted Gioia, *West Coast Jazz*
2 Ted Gioia, *West Coast Jazz*: 37–38
3 James Newton cited in Ben Ratliff, 'Jazz Enigma Of The 60s Has An Encore,' *New York Times*, May 27, 2014
4 James Newton, liner notes to *Other Aspects*
5 George E. Lewis, *A Power Stronger Than Itself*: 42

CHAPTER ONE

1 Raymond Horricks, *The Importance Of Being Eric Dolphy*
2 Vladimir Simosko and Barry Tepperman, *Eric Dolphy*: 37
3 Eric Dolphy, 'Music And People,' adale.org
4 Alan Saul interview
5 Alan Saul interview
6 Hans Hylkema (dir), *De Laatste Sessie*
7 Olivier Messiaen, *The Technique Of My Musical Language*: 34
8 Ethan Iverson interview with James Newton, DO THE M@TH
9 Martin Williams, 'Introducing Eric Dolphy,' *The Jazz Review* vol. 3 no. 5, June 1960: 16–17
10 Gene Santoro, *Myself When I Am Real*: 36
11 Horace Tapscott, *Songs Of The Unsung*: 35
12 Raymond Horricks, *The Importance Of Being Eric Dolphy*: 18, 29
13 Cora Bryant et al, *Central Avenue Sounds*: 150
14 Horace Tapscott, *Songs Of The Unsung*: 35
15 Vladimir Simosko and Barry Tepperman, *Eric Dolphy*: 30–31
16 Horace Tapscott, *Songs Of The Unsung*: 26
17 Brian Priestly, *Mingus*: 30
18 Brian Priestly, *Mingus*: 115
19 'Woodlawn YW Lists Program During Yuletide,' *Los Angeles Sentinel*, December 25, 1947
20 Collette interview with Steven Isoardi
21 James Newton, liner notes to *Other Aspects*
22 Robin D.G. Kelley, *Thelonious Monk*: 133
23 James Newton, liner notes to *Eric Dolphy: Musical Prophet* and *Other Aspects*

CHAPTER TWO

1 'Blondy Smith And Crew Newest Act In Business,' *California Eagle*, September 9, 1948: 17
2 Hunter Hancock, 'Huntin' with Hunter,' Los Angeles *Sentinel*, October 14, 1948: 19
3 Roy Porter, *There And Back*: 74–75
4 Roy Porter, *There And Back*: 75
5 Cora Bryant et al, *Central Avenue Sounds*: 151–152
6 C.E. Lloyd, 'City College News,' *California Eagle*, December 16, 1948: 7
7 'Briefly Joining Trumpeter Nat Meeks's Be-Bop Orchestra,' *California Eagle*, November 4, 1948
8 Peter Vacher, *Swingin' On Central Avenue*: 180
9 C.E. Lloyd, 'Casing The Kids,' *California Eagle*, April 28, 1949: 7
10 Roy Porter, *There And Back*: 82
11 Raymond Horricks, *The Importance Of Being Eric Dolphy*: 20
12 Cora Bryant et al, *Central Avenue Sounds*: 296–297
13 Tom Reney, 'Hampton Hawes And The Pardon From JFK,' New England Public Radio, July 14, 2015
14 Steven L. Isoardi, *The Dark Tree*: 34–35
15 Jung interview, and Steven L. Isoardi, *The Dark Tree*: 34
16 Martin Williams, 'Introducing Eric Dolphy,' *The Jazz Review*, vol 3 no. 5 June 1960: 16

17 John Kruth, liner notes to *Eric Dolphy: Musical Prophet*
18 Nick Catalano, *Clifford Brown*: 115
19 Kirk Silsbee, 'Don Cherry Interview,' *Cadence*, April 2003: 5–11
20 Gordon Mumma, *Cybersonic Arts*: 109
21 Bob Rosenbaum, 'An Interview With Harold Land,' October 28, 1984: 4
22 Raymond Horricks, *The Importance Of Being Eric Dolphy*: 23
23 Richard Kostelanetz, *The Theater Of Mixed Means*: 188
24 Ted Gioia, *West Coast Jazz*
25 Cora Bryant et al, *Central Avenue Sounds*: 339–340
26 Patricia Willard, liner notes to *Black California*
27 Michael Cuscuna, letter to Thierry Bruneau, adale.org
28 Steve Loza, *The Jazz Pilgrimage Of Gerald Wilson*: 50
29 Branch Corey, 'New Rock-Rollers Sound A Bit More Like Music,' Los Angeles *Evening Citizen*, December 5, 1956: 17
30 Joe Goldberg, liner notes to *Out There*
31 'Clever Comic In New Revue For Funsters,' *California Eagle*, February 18, 1957
32 Vladimir Simosko and Barry Tepperman, *Eric Dolphy*: 38
33 Steven L. Isoardi, *The Dark Tree*: 35
34 Steven L. Isoardi, *The Dark Tree*: 35
35 Vladimir Simosko and Barry Tepperman, *Eric Dolphy*: 39
36 Horace Tapscott, *Songs Of The Unsung*: 36
37 Vladimir Simosko and Barry Tepperman, *Eric Dolphy*: 39

CHAPTER THREE

1 John Kruth, 'Eric Dolphy Turns 80 / God Bless The Child,' *Perfect Sound Forever*, August 2008
2 Vladimir Simosko and Barry Tepperman, *Eric Dolphy*: 42
3 Vladimir Simosko and Barry Tepperman, *Eric Dolphy*: 13
4 Art Smith, 'Jazz For The Masses? Not Hardly,' *Tamba Bay Tribune*, November 16, 1958: 89
5 William Ewald, 'Timex Jazz Show Was Death On Jazz,' United Press International, November 11, 1958
6 Liner notes to *Gongs East*
7 Vladimir Simosko and Barry Tepperman, *Eric Dolphy*: 40–41
8 Adrian Levy, *Saxophone Colossus*: 330
9 Nat Hentoff, 'Second Chorus,' *DownBeat* vol. 31 no. 24, August 27, 1964
10 Martin Williams, 'Introducing Eric Dolphy,' *The Jazz Review*, vol 3 no. 5 June 1960: 16
11 Geoffrey Himes, 'Eric Dolphy: It's All Out There Now,' *Jazz Times*, June 18, 2020
12 William Grimes, 'Hale Smith, Who Broke Borders Of Classical And Jazz, Is Dead At 84,' *New York Times*, November 27, 2009
13 Phillip Lutz, 'Eric Dolphy: The Prophet Of Freedom,' *DownBeat*, December 17, 2018
14 Bill Kirchner, liner notes to *The Complete Prestige Recordings*
15 Ken McIntyre, liner notes to *Eric Dolphy: Fire Waltz*
16 Gene Santoro, *Myself When I Am Real*: 162
17 Vladimir Simosko and Barry Tepperman, *Eric Dolphy*: 43
18 James Newton interview with Geoffrey Himes
19 Brian Priestly, Mingus: 110
20 Eric Porter, *What Is This Thing Called Jazz?*: 116–117
21 Gene Santoro, *Myself When I Am Real*: 171
22 Cited in Paul Austerlitz, 'Jazz Consciousness': 219
23 Raymond Horricks, *The Importance Of Being Eric Dolphy*

CHAPTER FOUR

1 Don DeMicheal, *DownBeat* vol. 27 no. 18, September 1, 1960: 35
2 Phil Schaap, liner notes to *Eric Dolphy: Dash One*
3 Don DeMicheal, *DownBeat* vol. 27 no. 18, September 1, 1960: 35
4 James Newton, liner notes to *Eric Dolphy: Musical Prophet*
5 Vladimir Simosko and Barry Tepperman, *Eric Dolphy*: 45
6 Joe Goldberg, liner notes to *Out There*
7 *DownBeat* vol 28 issue 26, December 21, 1961
8 Nat Hentoff, liner notes to *Screamin' The Blues*
9 Vladimir Simosko and Barry Tepperman, *Eric Dolphy*: 46
10 Martin Williams, 'Introducing Eric Dolphy,' *Jazz Review* vol. 3 no. 5, June 1960: 16–17

11 Eric Dolphy Collection, Library Of Congress
12 Ken McIntyre, liner notes to *Fire Waltz*
13 Don Heckman, 'Ken McIntyre, A Musician's Philosophy,' *DownBeat* vol. 30 no. 29, November 7, 1963: 18–19
14 Marc Meyers, 'George Wein On The Rebel Festival,' *Jazz Wax*
15 Raymond Horricks, *The Importance Of Being Eric Dolphy*: 30
16 Alan Saul's transcription of the Feather/Dolphy interview
17 Robert Palmer, liner notes to *Mingus At Antibes*
18 Brian Priestly, *Mingus*: 113
19 Joe Goldberg, liner notes to *Out There*
20 Vladimir Simosko and Barry Tepperman, *Eric Dolphy*: 48
21 Bill Kirchner, liner notes to *The Complete Prestige Recordings*
22 Joe Goldberg, liner notes to *Out There*
23 Joe Goldberg, liner notes to *Out There*
24 Joe Goldberg, liner notes to *Out There*
25 Molly Sants, liner notes to *Eric Dolphy: Out There + Looking Ahead*

CHAPTER FIVE

1 *Last Date*
2 Val Wilmer, *As Serious As Your Life*: 89
3 Robert Palmer, liner notes to *Beauty Is A Rare Thing*
4 Raymond Horricks, *The Importance Of Being Eric Dolphy*: 26
5 Don DeMicheal, *DownBeat* vol 27 no 18, September 1, 1960: 35–36
6 Gene Santoro, *Myself When I Am Real*: 172
7 Bennie Maupin, interview with Greg Bendian, *Yale Oral History*
8 Ira Gitler, *DownBeat* vol. 28 no. 7, March 30, 1961: 38
9 Nat Hentoff, liner notes to *Charles Mingus Presents Charles Mingus*
10 Raymond Horricks, *The Importance Of Being Eric Dolphy*: 30
11 Vladimir Simosko and Barry Tepperman, *Eric Dolphy*: 52
12 Joe Goldberg, liner notes to *Out There*
13 Robert Levin, *Metronome* magazine, Spring 1961
14 Bill Kirchner, liner notes to *The Complete Prestige Recordings*: 28
15 Dolphy quote from Nat Hentoff, liner notes to *Far Cry*

CHAPTER SIX

1 Uwe Reichardt, *Like A Human Voice*: 23
2 Eric Dolphy, liner notes to *Caribé*
3 Vladimir Simosko and Barry Tepperman, *Eric Dolphy*: 54
4 Raymond Horricks, *The Importance Of Being Eric Dolphy*: 31
5 Raymond Horricks, *The Importance Of Being Eric Dolphy*: 31
6 *The Record* (Hackensack/Bergen, NJ) March 18, 1961
7 *Pittsburgh Courier*, December 12, 1960: 22
8 *Pittsburgh Courier*, May 6, 1961: 29
9 Mike Davenport, 'The Jazz Scene,' *Valley News*, April 1961
10 Leonard Feather, 'Blindfold Test,' *DownBeat* vol. 28 no. 6, March 16, 1961: 33
11 Ken McIntyre, liner notes to *Fire Waltz*
12 Robin D.G. Kelley, *Thelonious Monk*: 300
13 John Szwed, *Space Is The Place*: 190–191
14 John Szwed, *Space Is The Place*: 199
15 *DownBeat* vol. 28 no. 6 March 30, 1961: 73
16 Bill Kirchner, liner notes to *The Complete Prestige Recordings*: 29
17 Joe Goldberg, liner notes to *Straight Ahead*
18 Nat Hentoff, liner notes to *Images*
19 Martin Williams, liner notes to *Ezz-thetics*
20 *DownBeat* vol. 29 no. 21, August 2, 1962
21 Ethan Iverson interview with James Newton, DO THE M@TH
22 Harold L. Keith, 'Data 'Bout Discs,' *Pittsburgh Courier*, July 29, 1961: 29
23 *DownBeat* vol. 28 no. 23, November 9, 1961
24 Bill Smallwood, *California Eagle*, June 1, 1961
25 Vladimir Simosko and Barry Tepperman, *Eric Dolphy* Tepperman: 87
26 Pete Welding, *DownBeat* vol. 29 no. 19, September 27, 1962: 27
27 Pete Welding, *DownBeat* vol. 29 no. 19, September 27, 1962: 27
28 Gene Santoro, *Myself When I Am Real*: 110
29 Pete Welding, *DownBeat* vol. 29 no. 30, December 6, 1962: 34

CHAPTER SEVEN

1 'Combo Directory,' *DownBeat* vol. 28 no. 14, June 22, 1961: 19
2 James Newton, liner notes to *Eric Dolphy: Musical Prophet*
3 Cited in Zan Stewart, liner notes to *The Complete Prestige Recordings*: 17
4 Phil Schaap, liner notes to *Eric Dolphy: Dash One*
5 Richard David interview with Josephine Reed, 'Artworks,' NEA Jazz Master series
6 J.S.W., *DownBeat* vol. 28 no. 11, May 25, 1961: 34
7 Don Nelsen, *New York Daily News*, July 9, 1961: 123
8 Liner notes to *Musical Prophet*
9 Colin Fleming, 'Coda: An Eric Dolphy Solo Masterpiece: God Bless The Child,' *Jazz Times*, May 12, 2021
10 Michael Nastos, *All Music Guide*; Ben Ratliff, *New York Times*
11 Harvey Pekar, *DownBeat* vol. 29 no. 22, August 16, 1962: 24–25
12 *DownBeat* vol. 28 no. 17, August 3, 1961
13 Ira Gitler, *DownBeat* vol. 29 no. 5, March 15, 1962: 34
14 Bennie Maupin interview with Greg Bendian, *Yale Oral History*
15 John Litweiler, *Ornette Coleman*: 95–96
16 Ornette Coleman interview with Tim Page, *Yale Oral History*
17 Pete Welding, *DownBeat* vol. 29 no. 1, January 4, 1962: 30
18 Pete Welding, *DownBeat* vol. 29 no. 1, January 4, 1962: 30
19 Simon Spillett, liner notes to *So Many Things*
20 Reggie Workman, liner notes to *Evenings At The Village Gate*
21 Raymond Horricks, *The Importance Of Being Eric Dolphy*: 41
22 Stanley Robertson, 'New Abbey Lincoln Album Hits Pay Dirt,' *Los Angeles Sentinel*, August 17, 1961: C3
23 Vladimir Simosko and Barry Tepperman, *Eric Dolphy*: 115
24 John Bryan, 'Surprise Stars,' *San Francisco Examiner*, September 22, 1961: 10
25 See Ingrid Monson, *Saying Something*: 116–117
26 John Tynan, 'Take 5,' *DownBeat* vol. 28 no. 24, November 23, 1961: 40
27 Bill Coss, 'Cecil Taylor's Struggle For Existence: Portrait Of The Artist As A Coiled Spring,' *DownBeat* vol. 28 no. 22, October 26, 1961: 21
28 Ben Ratliff, *Coltrane*: 147–48
29 Amiri Baraka, *Blues People*: 146–47
30 H.P., *DownBeat* vol. 30 no. 24, August 29, 1963
31 *DownBeat* vol. 31 no. 12, May 21, 1964: 32

CHAPTER EIGHT

1 Eric Dolphy interview with Michiel de Ruyter, VARA, April 22, 1964
2 Bob Dawbar, *Melody Maker*, November 25: 1961: 8
3 Simon Spillett, liner notes to *So Many Things*
4 Simon Spillett, liner notes to *So Many Things*
5 Lewis Porter, *John Coltrane*: 194
6 *Oakland Tribune*, December 10, 1961
7 Pete Welding, *DownBeat* vol. 29 no. 2, January 18, 1962: 27
8 John Tynan, *DownBeat* vol. 29 no. 2, January 18, 1962: 27
9 Bill Cole, *John Coltrane*: 141
10 Lewis Porter, *John Coltrane*: 198
11 Barbara Gardner, 'Jazzman Of The Year'
12 Lewis Porter, *John Coltrane*: 193
13 Geri Allen, *Eric Dolphy*
14 Bill Cole, *John Coltrane*: 141
15 Bill Cole, *John Coltrane*: 144
16 Ekkehard Jost, *Free Jazz*: 29
17 Simon Spillett, liner notes to *So Many Things*
18 Ben Ratliff, *Coltrane*: 146
19 Ben Ratliff, *Coltrane*: 75–76
20 Ben Ratliff, *Coltrane*: 144–145
21 Ben Ratliff, *Coltrane*: 100
22 Ben Ratliff, *Coltrane*: 72
23 Bill Coss, 'Cecil Taylor's Struggle For Existence,' *DownBeat* vol. 28 no. 22, October 26, 1961: 21
24 Vladimir Simosko and Barry Tepperman, *Eric Dolphy*: 68
25 Sara Cassey, liner notes to *Just Jazz!*
26 Don DeMicheal, 'John Coltrane And Eric Dolphy Answer The Jazz Critics,' *DownBeat* vol. 29 no. 8, April 12, 1962: 20–23
27 Don DeMicheal, *DownBeat* vol. 29 no. 7, March 29, 1962: 32

28 Ira Gitler, *DownBeat* vol. 29 no. 9, April 26, 1962: 29
29 Pete Welding, *DownBeat* vol. 29 no. 9, April 26, 1962: 29
30 'DownBeat's Annual Combo Directory,' *DownBeat* vol. 29 no. 13, June 21, 1962: 19
31 Ben Ratliff, *Coltrane*: 143
32 George E. Lewis, *A Power Stronger Than Itself*: 47
33 Martin Williams, *DownBeat* vol. 29 no. 10, May 10, 1962: 33–34
34 Ethan Iverson, interview with Gunther Schuller (part 1), DO THE M@TH (with thanks to Duncan Heining for this source)
35 '"Way Out" Jazz Predicted For Ojai Musical Show,' *Los Angeles Sentinel*, April 26, 1962: C2
36 Martin Williams, *DownBeat* vol. 29 no.14, July 5, 1962: 38

CHAPTER NINE

1 'Strictly Ad Lib,' *DownBeat* vol. 29 no. 25, October 1962: 10
2 John Kruth, liner notes to *Musical Prophet*
3 Brian Priestly, *Mingus*: 139
4 Bill Coss, 'Caught In The Act: A Report Of A Most Remarkable Event,' *DownBeat* vol. 29 no. 30, December 6, 1962: 40
5 *Jazz News*, January 2, 1963
6 Thomas Willis, 'Composer Gets Top Help In Musical Explication,' *Chicago Tribune*, Saturday, October 20: 143
7 Pete Welding, *DownBeat* vol. 29 no. 31, December 20, 1962
8 Cited in Paul Austerlitz, *A Companion To African American Studies*: 220
9 Paul Austerlitz, *A Companion To African American Studies*: 219–220
10 Bill Coss, *DownBeat* vol. 30 no. 2, January 17, 1963: 42–43
11 Geri Allen, *Eric Dolphy*: 32
12 Don DeMicheal, *DownBeat* vol. 29 no. 29, November 22, 1962: 30
13 Mike Zwerin, *Close Enough For Jazz*
14 Richard Koloda, *Holy Ghost*
15 Ben Ratcliff, *Coltrane*: 95
16 Mitch Meyers, 'Spirits, Ghosts, Witches, And Devils: The Life And Death Of Albert Ayler,' *Magnet*, October/November 2004
17 *New York Daily News*, Sunday, March 3, 1963
18 Vladimir Simosko, liner notes to *The Illinois University Concert*
19 Ethan Iverson Interview with Gunther Schuller (Part 1), DO THE M@TH
20 Vladimir Simosko, liner notes to *The Illinois University Concert*
21 Don Heckman, 'Caught In The Act,' *DownBeat* vol. 30 no. 11, May 9, 1963: 34
22 Martin Williams, liner notes to *Vintage Dolphy*
23 Tynan, John, 'Chico's Changed,' *DownBeat* vol. 30 no. 8, March 28, 1963: 18–19
24 Albert Stinson, letter to the editor, *DownBeat* vol. 30 no. 10, April 25, 1963: 9–10
25 Martin Williams, liner notes, *Vintage Dolphy* (GM Recordings, 1986).
26 Martin Williams, liner notes, *Vintage Dolphy* (GM Recordings, 1986).
27 Bobby Hutcherson, 'Bobby Hutcherson On Eric Dolphy,' *Stop Smiling* issue 34, 2008
28 Robin D.G. Kelley, liner notes to *Musical Prophet*
29 'Ad Lib,' *DownBeat* vol. 30 no. 17, August 1, 1963: 43
30 Robin D.G. Kelley, liner notes to *Musical Prophet*
31 John Litweiler, *Ornette Coleman*: 108
32 Gunther Schuller, liner notes to *Vintage Dolphy*
33 Zan Stewart, liner notes to *The Complete Prestige Recordings*
34 Zan Stewart, liner notes to *The Complete Prestige Recordings*

CHAPTER TEN

1 Clifford Allen, 'Impressions Of Eric Dolphy,' *All About Jazz*, March 12, 2008
2 David Toop, *Into The Maelstrom*: 233
3 Liner notes to *Musical Prophet* and *Iron Man*
4 Liner notes to *Iron Man*
5 Leonard Feather, 'Blindfold Test,' *DownBeat* vol. 30 no. 23, August 15, 1963: 35
6 Gene Lees, *DownBeat* vol. 31 no. 4, February 13, 1964: 16–17
7 LeRoi Jones, 'Caught In The Act,' *DownBeat* vol. 31 no. 2, January 16, 1964
8 LeRoi Jones, *Blues People*: 181: 225
9 Geri Allen, *Eric Dolphy*: 23
10 'Strictly Ad Lib,' *DownBeat* vol. 31 no. 4, February 13, 1964: 10

11 Mike Zwerin, 'Remembering Dolphy, "Undisciplined Genius,"' *New York Times*, October 6, 2004
12 George Avakian, liner notes to *The Sextet Of Orchestra USA*
13 Aiden Levy, *Saxophone Colossus*: 422
14 B.M., *DownBeat* vol. 31 no. 2, January 16, 1964: 26
15 Vladimir Simosko and Barry Tepperman, *Eric Dolphy*: 78–80
16 Harvey Pekar, *DownBeat* vol. 31 no. 4, February 13, 1964: 24

CHAPTER ELEVEN

1 A.B. Spellman, liner notes to *Out To Lunch!*
2 A.B. Spellman, liner notes to *Out To Lunch!*
3 James Newton, liner notes, *Eric Dolphy: Other Aspects*. Blue Note, 1987.
4 Peter Guidi, *A Short History of the Jazz Flute*. www.peterguidi.com/history.html
5 Robert Dick, liner notes to *The Other Flute* (GM Recordings, 1986)
6 Eric Dolphy in A.B. Spellman liner notes, *Out to Lunch!*
7 Gordon Mumma, *Cybersonic Arts*: 24 (sincere gratitude to Carter Scholz for this source and for clarifying important aspects of the ONCE group)
8 Ralf Dietrich, 'Bob James And Eric Dolphy: ONCE In A Lifetime,' *SEMJA Update*, December 1999
9 Harvey Siders, *Boston Globe*, March 29, 1964: 51
10 Nat Hentoff, liner notes to *Point Of Departure*
11 Juanita Smith, liner notes to *Eric Dolphy: Musical Prophet*
12 *Last Date*
13 Brian Priestly, *Mingus*: 157
14 Nat Hentoff, liner notes to *Last Date*
15 'Reed Man Eric Dolphy Dies In Berlin,' *DownBeat* vol. 31 no. 23, August 13, 1964: 8

CHAPTER TWELVE

1 *Last Date*
2 Graham Lock, 'The Man Who Never Wasn't,' *The Wire* no. 22, December 1985: 16–17
3 Martin Williams, 'Introducing Eric Dolphy,' *Jazz Review* vol. 3 no. 5, June 1960: 16
4 Correspondence with the author, November 2023
5 Karting cited at Alan Saul's website, adale.org
6 Geri Allen, *Eric Dolphy*
7 A.B. Spellman, *Four Lives In The Bebop Business*
8 Leonard Feather, 'Feather's Nest,' *DownBeat* vol. 31 no. 13, June 4, 1964: 37
9 Leonard Feather, 'Blindfold Test,' *DownBeat* vol. 31 no. 14, June 18, 1964: 31
10 Unless otherwise noted, all accounts of Karl Berger and Ingrid Sertso are based on an interview with the author on June 6, 2022; Other remarks attributed to them are from the films *Last Date* and *Fire Music*
11 All references to Topf and Häuschler, and their comments, are from *Last Date*
12 Zan Stewart, liner notes to *The Complete Prestige Recordings*
13 'Reed Man Eric Dolphy Dies In Berlin,' *DownBeat* vol. 31 no. 23, August 13, 1964: 8
14 Geoffrey Himes, 'Eric Dolphy: It's All Out There Now,' updated June 18, 2020
15 German newspaper articles from stills featured in *Last Date*
16 Howard Morehead, 'Hollywood My Way,' *California Eagle*, July 23, 1964: 19
17 Gene Santoro, *Myself When I Am Real*: 230–231
18 Brian Priestly, *Mingus*: 159
19 Brian Priestly, *Mingus*: 160
20 Brian Priestly, *Mingus*: 160
21 'Basin-West Blasts Again With Eric Dolphy Memorial,' *Los Angeles Sentinel*, August 6, 1964: B8
22 Bill Cole, *John Coltrane*: 158
23 Ben Ratliff, *Ornette Coleman*: 68
24 Nat Hentoff, 'Second Chorus,' *DownBeat* vol. 31 no. 24, August 27, 1964
25 Don Heckman, 'The Woodwinds of Change,' *DownBeat* vol. 31 no. 27, October 8, 1964: 8
26 Leonard Feather, liner notes to *Dedicated To Eric Dolphy*
27 Geri Allen, *Eric Dolphy*
28 Amiri Baraka, liner notes to *The John Coltrane Anthology*: 32
29 Bill Shoemaker, 'Gunther Schuller: Third Stream From The Source,' *Jazz Times*

INDEX

ALSO AVAILABLE FROM JAWBONE PRESS

Who Killed Mister Moonlight? Bauhaus, Black Magick, And Benediction David J. Haskins

Lee, Myself & I: Inside The Very Special World Of Lee Hazlewood Wyndham Wallace

Complicated Game: Inside The Songs Of XTC Andy Partridge and Todd Bernhardt

Swans: Sacrifice And Transcendence: The Oral History Nick Soulsby

She Bop: The Definitive History Of Women In Popular Music Lucy O'Brien

Relax Baby Be Cool: The Artistry And Audacity Of Serge Gainsbourg Jeremy Allen

Seeing Sideways: A Memoir Of Music And Motherhood Kristin Hersh

It Ain't Retro: Daptone Records & The 21st-Century Soul Revolution Jessica Lipsky

Renegade Snares: The Resistance & Resilience Of Drum & Bass Ben Murphy and Carl Loben

Frank & Co: Conversations With Frank Zappa 1977–1993 Co de Kloet

This Band Has No Past: How Cheap Trick Became Cheap Trick Brian J. Kramp

Gary Moore: The Official Biography Harry Shapiro

Conform To Deform: The Weird & Wonderful World Of Some Bizzare Wesley Doyle

Holy Ghost: The Life & Death Of Free Jazz Pioneer Albert Ayler Richard Koloda

Happy Forever: My Musical Adventures With The Turtles, Frank Zappa, T. Rex, Flo & Eddie, And More Mark Volman with John Cody

Johnny Thunders: In Cold Blood—The Official Biography (Revised & Updated) Nina Antonia

Absolute Beginner: Memoirs Of The World's Best Least-Known Guitarist Kevin Armstrong

Turn It Up: My Time Making Hit Records In The Golden Age Of Rock Music Tom Werman

Revolutionary Spirit: A Post-Punk Exorcism Paul Simpson

Don't Dream It's Over: The Remarkable Life Of Neil Finn Jeff Apter

Chopping Wood: Thoughts & Stories Of A Legendary American Folksinger Pete Seeger with David Bernz

Through The Crack In The Wall: The Secret History Of Josef K Johnnie Johnstone

I Wouldn't Say It If It Wasn't True: A Memoir Of Life, Music, And The Dream Syndicate Steve Wynn

Forever Changes: The Authorized Biography Of Arthur Lee & Love John Einarson

Down On The Corner: Adventures In Busking & Street Music Cary Baker